A HISTORY OF
PRIVATE LIFE

Philippe Ariès and Georges Duby
General Editors

V · Riddles of Identity
in Modern Times

A HISTORY OF PRIVATE LIFE

V · Riddles of Identity in Modern Times

Antoine Prost and Gérard Vincent, Editors

Arthur Goldhammer, Translator

The Belknap Press of
Harvard University Press
CAMBRIDGE, MASSACHUSETTS
LONDON, ENGLAND

10 9 8 7 6 5 4 3 2

Originally published as Histoire de la vie Privée, vol. 5,
De la Première Guerre mondiale à nos jours, © Editions du
Seuil, 1987.

"The Italian Family: Paradoxes of Privacy" by Chiara
Saraceno was originally published as "La famiglia: i
paradossi della costruzione del privato," in *La Vita
Privata: Il Novecento*, © Gius, Laterza & Figli, 1988.

Parts of "The German Family between Private Life and
Politics" by Ingeborg Weber-Kellermann originally
appeared in *Die deutsche Familie*, © Suhrkamp Verlag,
1974, 1980, and *Die Familie*, © Insel Verlag, 1976.

Library of Congress Cataloging-in-Publication Data
(Revised for vol. 5)
A history of private life.

   Translation of: Histoire de la vie privée.
   Includes bibliographical references and indexes.
   Contents: v. 1. From pagan Rome to Byzantium /
Paul Veyne, editor—v. 5. Riddles of identity in modern
times / Antoine Prost and Gérard Vincent, editors;
Arthur Goldhammer, translator.
   1. Manners and customs. 2. Family—History.
3. Civilizations—History. 4. Europe—Social conditions.
I. Ariès, Philippe. II. Duby, Georges.
GT2400.H5713   1987   390'.009   86-18286

ISBN 0-674-39979-x (alk. paper) (cloth)
ISBN 0-674-40004-6 (paper)

Contents

A HISTORY OF
PRIVATE LIFE

Riddles of Identity
in Modern Times

A bourgeois family lived and received close friends and relatives in this private salon. The many photographs and postcards displayed were no business of mere acquaintances. Beyond the double doors, no doubt, was a more public salon for receiving guests.

1

Public and Private
Spheres in France

Antoine Prost

A less elaborate bourgeois interior in 1912, with an abundance of bibelots.

Introduction

PRIVATE life is not something given in nature from the beginning of time. It is a historical reality, which different societies have construed in different ways. The boundaries of private life are not laid down once and for all; the division of human activity between public and private spheres is subject to change. Private life makes sense only in relation to public life; its history is first of all the history of its definition. How did the distinction between public and private life evolve in France over the course of the twentieth century?

The question is important, particularly since it is not at all clear that the public-private distinction has the same meaning at different levels of society. There can be no doubt that for the bourgeoisie of the Belle Epoque "the wall of private life" separated two quite distinct domains. On one side of the protective barrier private life coincided more or less exactly with family life. Such matters as family fortunes, health, morals, and religion belonged to this private sphere. If parents were obliged to make discreet inquiries through a notary regarding a prospective marriage partner for one of their children, it was because they were just as careful to hide from public view information about a scoundrel of an uncle, a sister with tuberculosis, a dissolute brother, or the size of their own income. Jaurès, responding to a socialist deputy who reproached him because his daughter received communion, said: "My dear colleague, clearly you make your wife what you want her to be; I do not." With these words he indicated quite precisely where the boundary lay between his role as a public man and his private life.

This separation was enforced by a series of detailed prescriptions. Baroness Staffe, for example, mentions a number of such rules: "The less one pokes one's nose into other people's business, the more one merits the esteem and respect of one's neighbors . . . In a railway car or other public place, well-bred people never engage in conversation with strangers . . . Private matters are never discussed in the presence of others, not even with relatives or friends with whom one is traveling."[1] In upper-class homes there was a marked difference between the rooms designated for receiving guests and other parts of the house or apartment. Public rooms were for display, for whatever was deemed "presentable"; everything that should be shielded from indiscreet eyes was banished. The family proper had no place in the salon. When guests were being received, the children were not allowed to enter, Baroness Staffe tells us, and family photographs were considered out of place. But the public rooms were not open to just anybody. Every lady of good society had her "day" (and in Nevers in 1907 there were no fewer than 178 such days), but before paying a call on a prominent lady one had to be introduced.[2] The public rooms of the house thus constituted a transitional space between the public sphere and the strictly private.

In other strata of society the clear distinction maintained by the late-nineteenth-century bourgeoisie was not always apparent. Living conditions of peasants, workers, and the urban poor did not permit concealing from strangers a part of life that became, by virtue of its very concealment, "private." Let us walk, for instance, down a poor street in Naples with Jean-Paul Sartre: "The ground floor of every building contains a host of tiny rooms that open directly onto the street, and each of these tiny rooms contains a family . . . In these rooms people sleep, eat, and work at their trades. But . . . people are drawn into the street. They go outside for reasons of thrift, so that they won't have to light a lamp, or to enjoy the fresh air, and also, I suspect, out of fellow feeling, a desire to rub shoulders with everyone else. They drag tables and chairs out into the street or leave them on the threshold, half outside, half inside, and in this intermediate environment they perform the principal acts of their lives. Since there is no longer any outside or inside and the street is an extension of their living quarters, they fill it with their private smells and objects, as well as with their history . . . Outside is organically linked to inside . . . Yesterday I saw a mother and a father dining outdoors, while their baby slept in a crib next to the parents' bed and an older daughter did her homework at another table by the light of a kerosene lantern . . . If a woman falls ill and

Street in Naples, Italy.

This street in Croix-Rousse, residential today, once was noisy with looms, which the buildings, with their high ceilings and numerous large windows, were designed to accommodate. Here work and family life mingled.

stays in bed all day, it's open knowledge and everyone can look in on her."[3]

Clearly the meaning of private life for the poor of Naples was not the same as for the French bourgeoisie of the Belle Epoque. But perhaps the comparison is faulty: we are looking at two different cultural traditions, and the interpenetration of exterior and interior may well be a feature of Mediterranean culture that can also be found in the cities and towns of southern France. The fact remains that workers in Roubaix or the Croix-Rousse section of Lyons or the mining towns of northern France were no more able than villagers in Berri or Lorraine to protect their privacy from the scrutiny of neighbors; virtually everything that happened to them happened in public. In one sense, the possibility of having a private life was a class privilege limited to those who lived, often on private incomes, in relatively sumptuous splendor. Those who worked for a living inevitably experienced some intermingling of public and private life. In this respect, the twentieth century may be seen as a period during which the differentiation of public and private, at first limited to the bourgeoisie, slowly spread throughout the population. Thus, in one sense the history of private life is a history of democratization.

This democratization must not be viewed as automatic or conceived in simplistic terms. The private life available to workers or farmers in the late twentieth century was by no means the same as that enjoyed by the bourgeoisie of 1900. At the same time, what took shape outside this slowly constituted realm of privacy, and which for convenience I shall call the public sphere, was subject to new norms. The sharpened differentiation of public and private altered both private life and public life. Both were conducted in new ways and according to new rules. And, as new boundaries shifted and solidified, the substance of life also changed.

Clearly the history of private life, of the acquisition and organization of privacy, is a complex affair. The need to pay attention to social and cultural differences complicates the picture still further. It would be absurd to pretend that the findings presented in this book are in any sense exhaustive. It will be enough if we can identify major trends, raise important questions, and establish key distinctions.

In factories such as the Grenoble glovemaking shop depicted in the lower photograph the workplace was specialized and separate from private life. Nevertheless, home and work, both incorporated into the fabric of the city, remained fairly close together. Note the houses overlooking the scrap heap in the upper photograph (around 1920).

✍ Changing Workers and Workplaces

ONE of the greatest changes to occur in the twentieth century affected work. In broad terms, production moved from the private sphere into the public. The change took two forms. One was a differentiation and specialization of space: workplace ceased to coincide with living space. Hand in hand with spatial differentiation came a differentiation with respect to norms: the household ceased to be subject to rules pertaining to the work formerly performed in the domestic setting, while at the same time work, no longer subject to norms of a private order, came to be governed by collective contracts.

THE SPECIALIZATION OF SPACE

At the turn of the century it made a great deal of difference whether one worked at home or elsewhere. For a young girl the ideal was to stay home and not work. If obliged to work, it was best if she could do so at home—as a seamstress, for instance. Only girls at the bottom of the social hierarchy worked outside the home, in a factory or shop or as a servant in a private home.[1] In 1900 more than half, perhaps as many as two-thirds, of French workers worked at home. Today, by contrast, nearly all work outside the home. The transformation is stunning.

There were basically two different ways of working at home: one could work for oneself or for someone else. In between these two situations of course there was a range of compromises. But the striking fact remains that both forms of home-based work declined as the century progressed.

The number of workers employed at home is very diffi-

The Decline of Home Work

9

cult to ascertain. At the turn of the century several million people found themselves in this situation. Census figures from the period record what were called "isolated" workers, of whom there were some 1,502,000 in 1906. Of these, some were undoubtedly day laborers who actually worked outside the home for various employers, but most, male and female alike, worked in their own homes, primarily in the manufacture of textiles, clothing, shoes, and gloves but also in making eyeglasses, jewelry, and similar products on order from merchants. Sometimes the merchant delivered raw materials or semifinished products to the workers; in other cases the worker picked up new work when delivering finished pieces. Payment was by the piece.

The conditions of home work varied widely. Most home workers were paid very poorly, at rates far below those factory workers received. To eke out a miserable living they were obliged to work from dawn till well past dusk. Mémé Santerre and her family constitute an extreme case.[2] The Santerres were employed in the textile industry, where the putting-out system, under which home workers received raw materials from jobbers, survived until finally supplanted by factories after World War I. Family members worked as weavers only during the six winter months. In spring they took seasonal jobs on farms in Seine-Inférieure; they returned home in the fall and paid off their debts from the previous winter with what they had earned. Even domestic service paid better than weaving at home. The fact that the Santerres owned their own looms and were skilled weavers made no difference. They could not support themselves on what they earned by weaving, even though they subjected themselves to dreadful living and working conditions. After rising at four, the father and children went down to the basement to work at their looms; the mother prepared the frames, and the looms were kept humming until ten at night. They worked a roughly fifteen-hour day in a damp basement where it was often impossible to work without candlelight. Work was interrupted for a bowl of chicory with bread in the morning and for soup at noon and in the evening. On Sunday these fervent Catholics attended mass, then worked the rest of the day. Even on Catherine Santerre's wedding day, a festive occasion marked by a dinner of lamb chops, the family worked, a sign of the depth of their destitution.

Compared with such wretchedness, other home workers enjoyed better conditions. The glovemakers of Millau, for example, constituted a workers' aristocracy in the 1920s, a time when the Millau glove was a luxury item with which the mass-produced gloves of Grenoble could not compete. For the most part, however, home workers lived very poorly although they worked very hard. That is one reason why they gradually disappeared.

Many questions arise concerning the private lives of such workers. Where could Catherine Santerre have enjoyed privacy? On the hillside near her home where she spent a few fleeting moments with her beloved, whom she would later wed? In the bed in which she slept, done in by exhaustion? At her loom? Work was fully integrated into the private realm, although it would be more accurate to say that there was no distinction between living and working. Nevertheless, space was differentiated in the Santerre home: work was confined to the basement, while everyday chores were done on the ground floor. The family did not work in the same space in which they ate and slept. This was not typical. Usually work and domestic life coexisted in the same space. Léon Frapié in *La Maternelle* was ironic about the school-taught precept, "A

Seamstress working at home. Note the lamp, bottle and glass, and the remains of a meal.

The type of work done at home varied widely. Above is a fanmaker in a modest urban middle-class apartment, below a hairdresser and seamstress in a rural home. In both cases work would have been combined with the daily routine of family life.

place for everything and everything in its place." He describes a seamstress living in Paris's 20th arrondissement who had to clear the table in order to make room for herself to work and for her child to do homework.[3] Space was at such a premium in the typical nineteenth- or for that matter twentieth-century worker's apartment that it was impossible to set aside a special table or place for work.

Where work was done at home, the worker's home was to some degree inevitably open to strangers. The seamstress received clients; the weaver or glovemaker opened his doors to merchants or their agents. The family's combined work-place and living quarters sometimes became the scene of labor conflict. Jean Guéhenno recalls a dramatic occasion from his childhood. In Fougères his parents made shoes at home from lasts they purchased by the dozen. During a strike in the shoe industry at the turn of the century, Jean's father, his savings exhausted, could endure no longer and went out in search of lasts. Learning of this, the strikers burst into the Guéhenno home and accused the father of strikebreaking.[4] Thus even the most public of conflicts sometimes had a private setting. In one sense the person who worked at home ceased to have a home.

Home-based work did not disappear solely for economic reasons, although economic factors were no doubt decisive. Workers aspired to higher and more regular wages as well as to shorter working hours. When you worked in a factory, you knew when the day was over. The time not owed to the boss was completely your own, and that time increased steadily as the century progressed. The worker who worked outside the home could be truly at home during off hours. In this respect, the decline of home-based work reflects the growing insistence on the right to a private life.

Nevertheless, home-based work did not disappear entirely—far from it. The 1936 census counted some 351,000 home-based workers. Various factors contributed to the perpetuation of this group. During the Depression legislation tended to limit the access of foreign workers to the labor market, and it was easier for immigrants to do piecework at home than to obtain factory jobs. This arrangement served the interests of manufacturers determined to cut costs, and it also accorded well with the habits and traditions of numerous immigrants from Poland and central Europe. As a result, the number of home-based workers in the Parisian leather and fur industries increased. The Manouchians, an organization that played a notable role in the Resistance before being betrayed to the Gestapo, drew many of its recruits from this individualistic group of workers, many of whom were Jewish.

Today, home-based work is of negligible importance. It is ill-suited to the contemporary belief that the home is the bastion of privacy and free time is the worker's own, to do with as he or she pleases. Who would be willing to work at home for others, now that we are no longer willing to work at home even for ourselves?

The Self-Employed

More people are self-employed than are employed in their homes by others. The number of self-employed has also been decreasing, but the decline began later than that of the home-based employee. At the turn of the century the self-employed still accounted for more than half the population: 58 percent of farmers fell into this group, along with numerous artisans, merchants, and professionals. By contrast, in 1954 only a third of the working population was self-employed, and by 1982 it was only 16.7 percent. Self-employment has entered a period of sharp decline.

These figures give a rather confused image of an extremely important social transformation that has bestowed radically new meaning on the family. Among peasants, merchants, and artisans, the family is an independent production unit, an economic cell. The whole group has a part to play in running the family farm or business. Depending on age, strength, and skill, each family member plays a different role. On the farm the young and the elderly tend the cows, the boy of fourteen does the work of a hired hand, and the wife is in charge of the barn, the garden, and the chicken coop. Every available hand is needed when it comes to get in the hay or harvest the crop, particularly if storms threaten. In small businesses the wife usually keeps the books and, when not in school, the children help out in the store or shop and run errands.

Where the entire family is involved in earning a living, private life is not clearly distinguished from working life. The confusion is perhaps most evident when it comes to money: there is only one cashbox, and the grocer's son dips into it when he needs funds for a weekend's entertainment. Two budgets are merged: the money the farmer's wife spends on coffee, chocolate, or a scarf is money that may be needed to pay the rent or buy livestock. Limiting private expenditure is

Work and family merged into a single identity, as this distiller chose to have a family portrait photographed in his shop.

therefore the principal and often the only means of balancing the books of the farm or business and accumulating working capital. The success of the business is based on holding down household expenses.

In compensation the firm is private. If the family business succeeds, that success is recognized by the community. The family's place in the local hierarchy is measured by the amount of land and livestock it owns or by the number of workers it employs or by the recent repainting of its shop front. Being economic in nature, the private success is also public. Productive capital (business property, land, livestock, and so on) is therefore also wealth, which can be passed on by inheritance and divided up among heirs (sometimes in defiance of economic rationality). When the family business grows to the point where hired help is needed, the contradiction between private ownership and public economic function becomes apparent. Hired help may lose their jobs as the result of purely private events, such as the death of the business' owner.

An indispensable economic unit, this type of family plays a key role in the education of children and care of the elderly. On the farm or in the shop young people learn skills from relatives and friends; apprenticeship is a private family function. At the same time, aged parents unable to take care of themselves are provided with room and board by one of their children. This does not mean that the family is of the "patriarchal" type made familiar by an uncritical mythology.[5] In most parts of France other than the southwest, peasants live in nuclear families consisting of parents and children. The grandparents live nearby in a separate, usually smaller residence, and they maintain this independent household as long as they can. When this is no longer possible, particularly if the grandmother dies before the grandfather, the children will take in the surviving parent.

The Decline of the Family Business

The rise of wage labor stripped the family of its economic function. At the same time the decline of employment in the home went hand in hand with socialization of education and elderly care. Young people increasingly learn their trades in school, and a state-financed social security system has supplanted the family's role in care of the elderly.

Economic factors have been crucial in the decline of both self-employment and home-based work. Small farms and small businesses cannot produce and distribute widely used

consumer products at competitive prices. In France protec-
tionism and slow economic development for a long time
impeded the decline of the family business. Since World War
II, however, efforts to modernize the economy have accelerated that decline. There have been periodic outbursts by farmers and shopkeepers struggling for survival and demanding
the perpetuation of such advantages as fixed prices and tax
exemptions. The FNSEA (Fédération Nationale des Syndicats
d'Exploitants Agricoles, a farmer's group), the movement led
by Pierre Poujade (1953–1956), and Gérard Nicoud's CID-
UNATI (Comité d'Information et de Défense de l'Union Nationale des Artisans et Travailleurs Indépendants, an association of small businessmen and self-employed workers) all
produced impressive demonstrations of widespread opposition
to the government's modernizing policies. Nevertheless, the
inexorable laws of the market have scarcely been impeded by
sporadic social programs or legislative measures such as a 1973
bill to restrict the spread of discount retail outlets.

Social change has also been important. The decline of the
family business is not unrelated to the wide range of social
benefits now available to employees. In agriculture the effect
of this change can be measured by the fact that today the son
who works with his father on the family farm is often officially

A merchant at her cash drawer
in the 1950s. Behind her one
can imagine the door that
would have led to the family
quarters. Here, at this
crossroads between public and
private, neighbors gossiped
about one another's private
lives.

declared to be a farm laborer. In retail merchandising and the skilled trades the number of independent businesses has declined sharply. Owners of small business accounted for 12 percent of the work force in 1954, 10 percent in 1962, 9.6 percent in 1968, but only 7.8 percent in 1982. Two different phenomena are at work here: a slow decline in the number of small businesses and skilled tradesmen, and a change in the legal status of the small shop. Many small business owners have transformed their once privately held operations into limited partnerships or corporations, of which they then become salaried managers. In census figures they are therefore counted as management personnel rather than owners.

Severing the Family from the Business

The change from owner to manager is more than just a matter of vocabulary. Often it reflects a severing of the family from the firm. Business and private life become distinct and independent parts of life. The change has important consequences, and not just in the financial realm, where the family's private wealth and the firm's capital become clearly distinct. More generally we find an increased differentiation of time and space.

In earlier times two distinct types of activity were combined in family businesses and farms. A merchant might live with his wife and children in the back room of his shop, as bakers still do today in small French villages. Wealthier merchants might live in an apartment above the shop. Thus the back room served as both living space and storage area. Closets held merchandise along with the family's groceries and cooking utensils. The family ate in the same room where the shopkeeper did his books while the children did their homework; sometimes everyone slept there as well.

Lack of differentiation in space led to lack of differentiation in time. If customers found the doors of the shop closed, they did not hesitate to knock on the window of the back room where the family was eating, and someone would hasten to help them. Things began to change when the lady of the house, disturbed by a customer after closing time, ceased to accept the interruption as a matter of course and instead blurted out, "We'll never have any peace around here, that's for sure!" At that point living in one's place of business came to be seen as a kind of imprisonment in work. People began to insist on privacy, and, in order to protect that privacy from invasion by customers, it became necessary to find living quarters away from the place of business. Beds, armoires, and cook stoves began to vanish from the back rooms of shops all over France. Merchants rented apartments above street level or built homes in the suburbs. Henceforth they would have two addresses and, before long, two telephone lines, only one of which appeared in the phone directory. Anonymity was the price paid for peace and privacy.

To be sure, the transformation was neither universal nor total. It affected downtown businessman more than neighborhood shopkeepers and retailers of clothing, shoes, and appliances more than small bakers or grocers. In many villages the old living arrangements persist, but customers have been sensitized to the inadvisability of disturbing merchants outside normal working hours. Tradesmen, dependent on their workshops, sometimes need to work evenings and weekends and are therefore more reluctant than retailers to reside at a distance from their places of business. If they do live in a separate house, it is usually close by.

Nevertheless, the trend toward separate living quarters is unmistakable, as can be seen from a glance at the professions. Doctors, lawyers, and those quintessentially French professionals the *notaire* (notary) and the *huissier* (bailiff) are traditionally quite jealous of their status and independence, yet even here change is quite evident. Doctors have begun, for tax purposes, to declare their wives as receptionists. The women continue to answer the phone and open the door as before, but now their husbands pay them a salary (at least on paper) and they are registered with the social security authorities. In recent years professionals have begun to practice together as groups with corporate identities. By itself this might not require a change in the relation of professional to private life, but many doctors and lawyers no longer live next to their professional offices. It has become impossible to reach them outside of normal working hours, impossible to call the family physician at night. The doctor is not in; he has protected his privacy from his patients.

In sum, private life increasingly has been separated from working life. This new norm is so powerful that it tends to apply even in work situations where there is no real threat to privacy from the people with whom one does business. Among farmers, for example, there has been a significant move toward living quarters unconnected with the farm buildings proper. This can be traced back to the nineteenth century, when many farmers erected a wall between the common room and the barn. At best, though, in the farms of Normandy or the Beauce this meant that the family quarters would be built on one side of the barnyard, the barn, stables, and outbuildings on the other. The need to care for chickens and livestock meant that farmers, animals, and feed had to remain close together. Today these requirements no longer obtain. In prosperous regions many farmers have abandoned livestock breeding and, thus freed from the needs of the animals, have built modern homes at a good distance from barns and storage sheds. In the Beauce, for example, Ephraïm Grenadou built what he called a retirement house, which he moved into in 1965, long before his anticipated retirement.[6]

On the farm the need was not to protect the family's privacy, which was no more threatened in the old house than in the new one. It was rather to establish a clear distinction between work and private life. Today the very structure of private life is defined by its contrast with working life. A clear boundary divides two worlds that as recently as the turn of the century were still intermingled.

The Old-Fashioned Factory: A Semipermeable Wall

A symmetrical evolution resulted in a reorganization of the workplace, from which all nonproductive functions were eliminated. At the start of the twentieth century factory design was still quite haphazard. Work areas were adapted to the available space rather than laid out according to the demands of the production process. The factory was a hodgepodge of separate workshops. One of the best known, the Renault plant at Billancourt, was a maze of shops occupying some forty different buildings, not all connected.[7] Some were former homes turned into factory buildings, with huge rooms connected by narrow, winding staircases. Moving materials around these buildings required many hands, and for large numbers of jobs not requiring tremendous strength children were considered suitable. Parts and equipment flowed in complex patterns throughout the production area. It was not always clear where the plant began or ended. To go from one shop to another sometimes required crossing a street or courtyard that served other buildings. Nor was it easy to tell when workers were where they were supposed to be, because there were so many reasons for moving about the plant. Thus internal discipline was limited by the nature of the space available.

Some factories were even more confused in their organization than the Renault plant. Consider the Longwy Steel Mills, as described in property deeds dating back to the 1880s. Alongside blast furnaces and shops we find the manager's house, a dormitory for workers, a stable, a storage shed with hayloft, twelve barracks buildings, a bakery, and a canteen.[8] The steel company purchased much of the land put up for sale in its environs. Access routes, including railways (not all of the same gauge), were hemmed in by privately owned property. There was still no wall around the premises, and on cold winter nights tramps slept on the warm slag-heaps. In 1897 the management of the Neuves-Maisons mill called on the police to protect its access roads and railways.

It was not until relatively late that walls were built around plant perimeters, often in the wake of major strikes. These walls marked out boundaries that had not been necessary until they were challenged. At Le Creusot the factory walls were either constructed or rebuilt after the 1899 strikes. In Lorraine, following labor unrest at Pont-à-Mousson in 1905, "walls were built to protect the plant." By 1909 all major firms had adopted modern means of protection in case of strikes.[9] Workers were not the only people admitted through the gates, however. Writing in the 1920s, Georges Lamirand described how women with children used to bring meals to their husbands at the plant.[10]

Noon at a factory gate in Sologne. The factory yard is more or less open to the street.

Although the diversity of factory space resulted in part from the haphazard way in which factories had grown, there were other causes. Men and women were defined primarily in terms of their work. The notion that workers have lives outside work from which they derive a part of their identity is a modern one. At the turn of the century only the bourgeoisie, those who owned property or lived on private incomes, were fully entitled to a private life. The working classes were defined primarily in terms of work; their private lives were subject to the constraints of that work. Some workers lacked even homes of their own; they lived, ate, and slept at the places where they worked. In the Lyons region some textile firms were staffed exclusively by young peasant women who were housed in dormitories supervised by nuns.[11] Like the Catalonian textile colonies, these convent-factories organized the whole of life around work.

Most nineteenth-century hospitals were staffed by resident nurses and attendants, many of whom replaced the nuns who had previously filled the same roles. Their lives were harsh, almost cloistered. They could not go out without per-

Factory for manufacturing armor plate. The machinery is still belt-driven. This vast hangar with its chain hoists and overhead cranes was designed for the sole purpose of production.

mission, which was granted as a favor. Yet many hospital employees were married men and women who wished to lead a family life. Their confinement seemed unjustifiable, particularly since the only available lodging was in filthy dormitories that Dr. Bourneville stigmatized as breeding grounds for tuberculosis.[12] Gustave Mesureur, director of the Assistance Publique at the turn of the century, nevertheless refused to permit hospital staff to reside off the premises.

The right to reside elsewhere, tantamount to the right to a private life, was granted first to ranking male personnel, then to other male employees, next to married head nurses, and finally to other married nurses. Unmarried employees were supposed to fill all their needs at the hospital. The requirement that they reside on the premises remained in force until after World War II. Hospital dormitories developed a life of their own, akin to that found in boarding schools. Residents gathered in washrooms and kitchens. Still, there was no room for private life as such except outside the hospital, where nurses were rarely allowed to go, and in the solitude of the bedroom.

The time clock was used both to measure time and to control its use. The steady rhythm of the production process forced the worker to keep up.

The Specialization of the Workplace

Industrial buildings were redesigned along more rational lines over the course of the twentieth century, especially during the periods of reconstruction following the two world wars. The spread of Taylorism and scientific management played a role in this development. Mass production required continuous processing, often in vast, single-story structures. The new logic of production, reflected in the design of the Berliet plant at Vénissieux (1917), can be seen even more clearly in the Renault plant on Seguin Island (1930) and the Citroën plant on the quai de Javel (1933). No longer was the production process forced to conform to the limitations of a preexisting building. Now the building was designed to meet the requirements of the process. Work spaces became increasingly specialized. A factory was no longer a building in which things happened to be manufactured but a building designed for the manufacture of a particular product. Industrial architecture came into its own, creating new forms, particularly in the design of roofs.

Machinery was laid out in strict order, and each worker was assigned a specific place. Within the plant storage areas and materials-handling lanes were set apart from production areas. Management control over plant space and work time

The Renault plant in 1915 and in 1954. The island in the foreground, relatively untouched in 1915, became the site of a new factory in 1930. On the right bank the plant grounds, designed along modern lines in 1915 but with a few gaps remaining, has been filled in. Industrial space tends to be compact and continuous.

was increased. Time clocks were introduced; work was regulated by time-and-motion studies; wages were geared to output and productivity. Certain areas of the plant were designated off-limits without authorization. Ultimately this reorganization of the workplace took on a strong symbolic value, as in the Renault plant at Flins, where workers went on strike by "standing in the lane" while management looked on.[13]

Meanwhile, industrial zones began to be distinguished from the rest of the city. Access to factories was controlled by fences and gates. Guards were posted, and during strikes pickets marched in front of the main gate. Special gates were set aside for personnel, shipping, and receiving. Such specialization was impossible in the older style of plant. Instead of many separate buildings, new factories were constructed as a single unit. The mosaic of small workshops gave way to the compact modern plant.

Around the middle of the twentieth century a change occurred in the scale of industrial evolution. Modern urban

planning insisted that plants be confined to industrial zones. In older cities housing and workshops coexisted. Apartment buildings, warehouses, and shops shared the same courtyard. The shouts of children mingled with the hum of machinery, the whine of saws, and the pounding of hammers. But modern urban design, exemplified by the Athens Charter (1930), condemned such confusion. The criticism remained entirely theoretical, however, as long as the Depression continued to halt urban growth. After war demolished whole sections of European cities, however, theory became practice that continued during the subsequent period of rapid urban growth. Zoning policies enforced a rigid distinction between industrial and residential areas.

The first industrial zones were still fairly small, no more than a few acres in size. With economic growth, however, came an expansion of the horizon, with industrial or business zones of hundreds of acres now commonplace. Urban planners excluded all industrial construction from residential zones; only small stores were allowed. Thus modern planning en-

Parts are stored along the assembly line, this one at Renault. A great deal of space is required to store parts and machinery in the order in which they will be needed.

shrined as a principle and imposed on the entire population the old bourgeois predilection for residences away from industrial noise and squalor. Working-class residential neighborhoods sprang up next to older bourgeois residential neighborhoods. In older sections workshops closed and the space was converted to residential use. Gradually the urban fabric became increasingly uniform. The change can be seen in Paris in the 14th and 15th arrondissements and in the Les Brotteaux and Croix-Rousse sections of Lyons as well as in other cities.

The contrast between private life and work life is nowadays embedded in the very structure of modern cities and schedules. People no longer work where they live or live where they work. This principle applies not just to apartments and workshops but to whole neighborhoods. Every day huge populations migrate between home and workplace by automobile and mass transportation.

Nevertheless, the dichotomy is not absolute. Schools, post offices, hospitals, and retail stores are not located in industrial zones, even though they are the workplace of many employees. Zoning has led to such vast transformations that

Large companies soon separated work space from living quarters. The ideal was one home per family. This late-19th-century one belonged to the Saint-Eugène workers' housing complex.

The Alouettes housing area at Montceau-les-Mines (1867) shows how farmland was converted to both housing and production use.

nonproductive activities have begun to reappear even in industrial areas. More and more people (some 20 percent of all workers in 1983) eat lunch where they work. Cafeterias and restaurants are found in many factories. Employee organizations sponsor recreational activities. Conversely, some kinds of work have never left the private home. More and more people now work two jobs, one of which involves work at home.

Working Women

For generations the ideal for women had been to stay home and take care of the household. For a woman to work outside the home was a sign of extreme poverty and abjection. In what must be counted as one of the major evolutions of the twentieth century, housework is now considered to be a form of alienation, of subjugation to men, while working outside the home is a tangible sign of a woman's emancipation. In the 1970s most middle-class people cited equality of the sexes and the independence of women as justifications for women's work, while the working class generally cited economic reasons.

This undeniable change raises a number of questions. Why did it occur when it did and not sooner or later? The arguments used to justify female labor were just as valid a century ago as during the past two or three decades. Why did women have to wait until the middle of the twentieth century? And why did the change affect the urban middle class first, before spreading slowly and gradually to the rest of society?

One answer has to do with the fact that for many people home and workplace had coincided. As long as household chores and productive labor were performed in the household, the sexual division of labor was not perceived as involving inequality or subjugation. To be sure, certain customs indicated the subordination of women to men: in some rural households, for example, the wife served her husband and remained standing until he had finished eating. Nevertheless, household chores were not despised. Men and women watched each other do tiring work. Peasant and working-class women shouldered part of the burden of productive labor as well. A penny saved was a penny earned, and what was saved on household expenses could be invested in the family business. Men did their share of the household chores, chopping firewood, making utensils, and building furniture so as to avoid having to buy the equivalent in the marketplace.

When home and workplace became distinct places, how-

A vintner's home in Charente in the 1960s. The wife, standing, serves her husband and son. This kitchen apparently was also used for grooming, unless the mirror and brushes on the wall are mere decoration.

ever, marital equality ended and women became servants. The stereotype of the man who sits in his armchair and reads his paper while his wife works assumes that the husband is the one who "comes home from work," that is, who works outside the home. At the same time the household economy is "monetarized": economizing on expenditures becomes less important than bringing home a salary. Work for hire—man's work—takes on a new dignity, while the woman who stays home becomes her husband's domestic servant. No longer is the key fact that she works at home, but that she does so for someone else's benefit. The separation of home and workplace bestows a new significance on the sexual division of labor; it introduces into marriage a master-servant relationship characteristic of the bourgeoisie of an earlier period. This is intolerable, particularly since it has meanwhile become socially atypical to work in someone else's private space. In this century it has come to be seen as an emancipation for women to work because the nature of paid labor has changed so dramatically.

Women working in a brush factory in 1965. Not only is the work space specialized, so are the clothes the women are wearing.

THE SOCIALIZATION OF PAID LABOR

At the turn of the century working at home stood in opposition to working for others. Whatever form hired labor might take, it always involved working for someone else. Work was done not in a public space subject to collective norms but in the private domain of another person.

In this sense domestic service was the quintessential form of work for hire. Some 1,800,000 servants were employed in rural households in 1892; in 1906 some 960,000 individuals were employed as servants in bourgeois homes. In either case servants gave up any semblance of private life when they went to live in their masters' homes. Unlike day laborers and cleaning women, servants lived under the master's roof and shared the master's food, whether they ate in the kitchen or, in rural homes, at the family table. They had no privacy. Rural servants generally slept in the barn and carried their personal belongings in a pocket or rucksack. In town, maids often slept in a shed near the kitchen. Others had a room in the attic where they might keep toilet articles and a few trinkets. Homemakers' guidebooks recommended that the lady of the house regularly inspect all maids' rooms. In any case, maids had little free time to do anything in their rooms but sleep.

Relations among servants were subject to constant scrutiny by their masters. Vacations were as brief as they were infrequent, and mail was liable to be opened. If a maid met a soldier in a public park while taking the children for a walk, she risked losing her job if she invited him to call at the service entrance leading to the kitchen.

There is no better indicator of how difficult it was for servants to maintain a private life than the small number who married. In rural homes nearly all servants were single, and those who were married might as well have been single, for they lived apart from their spouses. In wealthy bourgeois and aristocratic households a chauffeur might marry a chambermaid and both retain their employment. If they wished to keep their jobs, however, they had better not have children, unless their employers had a porter's lodge available in the building or a gamekeeper's house on a country estate. Those who entered domestic service were expected not to reproduce, and the only private life they had was secret or marginal.

They did, however, share in the private lives of their

Domestic Servants

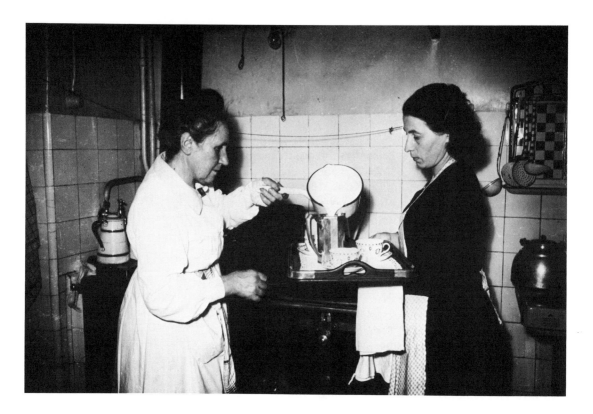

A cook and chambermaid, probably shown in the period between the two World Wars. The environment in which servants lived and worked contrasted sharply with that in which their masters lived.

masters. Involved in the most intimate aspects of the daily routine (waking up, going to bed, grooming, and dining), witness to those parts of life not governed by public or social convention, and often responsible for child care, servants knew more than anyone else about their masters' health problems, eccentricities, quarrels, and intrigues. Some masters confided in their servants, whose obligatory discretion made candor possible.

The master-servant relation had more in common with kinship than with the contractual relation between employer and employee. A servant was practically a relative, and poor relations—a spinster aunt, say—were practically servants. To be sure, the master-servant relation was hierarchical: one was superior, the other inferior. But family relations are also hierarchical, and the child who did not treat his parents as superiors was soon cut down to size. Servants were devoted to their masters and their masters' children, all the more so since they themselves were deprived of affection. In return, masters generally treated servants with benevolent familiarity,

The kitchen of a large upper-class household. The impressive array of cookware and the amount of vegetables to be peeled give some idea of the number of guests. Running such a household was like operating a small business, whose manager was the "mistress of the house."

attended to their needs, and took care of them when they were ill. Because servants were inferior, masters addressed them with the familiar *tu* (just as officers in the military used *tu* with enlisted men). Servants were discussed in the third person and referred to by their first names—Monsieur Jacques, Madame Louise—*monsieur* and *madame* being used even in referring to children. Last names were unnecessary, because what mattered was not the servant's family but the master's. Occasionally intimacy between masters and servants went even further. The number of illicit love affairs cannot be counted, but such things surely were not invented by the playwrights who satirized them on the stage.

The situation of rural servants was quite similar in most respects. They too lived in daily proximity to their masters and knew the family and its secrets. And occasionally the farmer's wife might have an illicit affair with the hired hand. The differences lie elsewhere. Most servants in bourgeois households were women who performed household chores, while most rural servants were men who worked on the farm.

A family of farm workers, 1949. While rural domestics lived in the shadow of the master, hired hands had homes and (large) families of their own. "Well-turned-out" children were everyone's pride and joy.

A worker (perhaps a farm worker) and his family at the entrance to their dwelling (around 1930). The door has no lock, and the clothing is shabby—yet the baby is king.

Farmhands were less directly involved in the private lives of their employers than were parlormaids and chambermaids. The laborer's term of employment was also shorter. A farmhand was usually hired for a year, and the expiration of that term was sometimes marked by a week's vacation, as Pierre-Jakez Hélias reports of Brittany in the 1920s.[14] By contrast, housemaids, even if their wages were annual, were hired for an indefinite period. On all but the largest farms hired hands were employed at that point in a farmer's life when his sons were still too young to do a man's work. When the boys reached age sixteen or seventeen, the hired man's services were no longer needed. But a bourgeois household without a servant was inconceivable, and while the number of servants employed was sometimes larger when there were young children about (requiring a wet nurse, nanny, or tutor), the very nature of the household routine required people to do housework, cook, wash dishes, and so on. Without at least a maid on tap, a family's social position was in jeopardy.

In both situations, the relation between master and servant was direct and personal. Whether on the farm or in the bourgeois home, servants reported to the master personally. The servant's duties did not end when his or her work was done, nor did the master fully discharge his obligation when he paid the servant's wage. Masters expected of servants not only work, whose content was never precisely defined, but assistance of various kinds as well as understanding, respect, and a pleasant demeanor. Ill-tempered and grouchy servants were not kept on. Conversely, servants were entitled to expect their masters not just to pay their wages but to display a degree of benevolence. Payot in his moral guide urges future maids not to stand for disrespect and not to remain in a home where they are taught nothing.[15] The mistress was supposed to educate the female servant and teach her how to keep house. The master-servant relation was not an impersonal labor contract; each party had to find the other suitable. At a time when marriages too were based on social proprieties, the master-servant relation had affinities with interfamilial relations; it belonged to the private sphere.

Workers Housed by Their Employers

In France at the turn of the century there was no statutory difference between domestic servants and other workers. Many working people lived in housing provided by their employers. Let us follow the census takers through a provincial town in 1911. We find a butcher's apprentice living under his employer's roof and bakery workers sleeping close to their oven. In the home of a chocolatemaker we find a dozen workers, mostly men; naturally they are employed in the manufacture of chocolate, but one of them is also a chauffeur. A dressmaker lives with her sister and a seamstress whom she employs and who probably also waits on the two sisters and cleans up after them.[16] It is impossible to draw a hard and fast distinction between a servant and a worker living in an employer's home.

It is just as difficult to distinguish between a domiciled employee and a nondomiciled one. Some factories provided quarters for at least some of their personnel, but these were relatively rare. More significant was the fact that employer-employee relations were in many respects identical to master-servant relations. Of course the size of the firm made a big difference from the worker's point of view. In smaller firms where the owner was personally accessible, workers were referred to by their first names as if they were servants of the master: Monsieur François, for example. A workman felt he could speak to the boss man to man. In larger firms (relatively rare in France, a country of small businesses), relations were less personalized and workers ceased to feel that they reported to a specific individual. Regardless of the size of the firm, owners treated their factories like their homes: they were private property, not public space. For a long time they refused to allow labor inspectors onto the premises and resented any such attempt as a violation of their privacy. The fact that the firm was often referred to as the "house" is significant.

Paternalism

Paternalism came naturally to this type of employer. It is a mistake to think of paternalistic behavior as a calculated pose. Admittedly paternalism served the interests of employers, but they would have gone bankrupt had they not concerned themselves with their own interests and it is pointless to criticize them for doing so. To contemporaries employers were either paternalistic or else harshly and cynically exploitative. The employer aware of the duties of his position saw himself as a "good father to his family." Was it not as families that prosperous French "houses" were managed? Assuming that the labor contract is a purely private affair, the only "good" employer is necessarily a paternalistic one.

In paternalistic firms the employer's whole family became

Employers drinking with their workers. Paternalism was not always rejected, not even when it was tinged with ideology. This photograph was taken during World War II; both employers wear the *francisque,* symbol of the Vichy government, on their lapels.

involved. The owner was expected to pay his workers in person, often making the rounds of the various departments. And his private life could not be totally private. In the provinces especially, he and his family lived at least in part in the public eye. To escape scrutiny one had to lead a double life, and one's private life came second. Employers were expected to appear with their wives to hand out school prizes, awards to workers, and so on. The wife was expected to devote her energies to charitable work and to supervise classes in home economics, dispensaries, and sewing circles. An employer's children also drew comment. Their escapades were remarked as they grew up, and their weddings were expected to be lavish occasions. The employer's family life was thus in part for show. His home occupied a prominent place on the factory grounds near the workshops and often enclosed by the same fence.

The conditions of employment included the worker's family. The behavior of his wife and children affected the way he was judged. When a child was born to an employee, the occasion often was marked by a gift or bonus, especially in businesses where the work force tended to remain stable. It was felt only natural that a firm should hire the children of its own workers; a miner who wished his son to be taken on had only to introduce him to the manager. In short, employer-employee relations were not unlike relations between rural landlords and sharecroppers, in that they embraced the totality of existence.

Today we reject such personalized relations of dependence and find it difficult to believe that people once willingly accepted them as self-evident and natural. Yet many workers felt gratitude toward their employers and looked upon them as benefactors. In the early years of the Third Republic an industrialist who brought prosperity to a canton was frequently elected *conseiller général* by his own workers; the choice was so obvious that no stuffing of the ballot box was necessary. Even after World War I iron miners in Lorraine contributed toward a bouquet of flowers to be delivered by a procession to their employer's residence.[17] On January 1, 1919, Renault workers presented founder Louis Renault with the Cross of the Legion of Honor and a gilt book containing 12,000 of their signatures.[18] While ancient traditions and management organizers may have played a part in such manifestations, the fact that they were not only planned but successfully carried out shows that many workers saw the firm as a sort of extended family presided over by the owner.

Not all workers were willing to enter into so unequal a relationship with their employer. Some, whether trained at school to show respect and gratitude or resigned to the status quo, were willing to be treated as what some employers referred to as "overgrown children," but by the end of the nineteenth century growing numbers of workers refused to accept this inferior status. Did not the schools of the Third Republic teach that all men are equal? To many workers the condescending benevolence of their employers seemed as intolerable as the condescension of aristocrats had seemed to the bourgeois of 1789. They wished to think of themselves as hired laborers, not indentured servants. The factory was not an extended family. It was a matter of dignity.

Because the labor contract brought the worker into the private domain of his employer, the inevitable conflicts of interest became personal confrontations. Strikes were seen as personal attacks on the employer. Did children or servants stage strikes? Striking workers, not content simply to state their demands, challenged the authority of the *père de l'usine,* the father of the factory. For this very reason early twentieth-century union leaders attached great importance to the strike:

The Severing of Personal Ties by Strikes

it served to educate, to mobilize, to train, and to create new opportunities.[19] A wage increase obtained by means of a strike was far more valuable than a wage increase willingly granted by an employer; the material benefit of the strike was accompanied by a moral benefit.

This employers could not tolerate. To them, a strike was an act of ingratitude, the sign of a bad attitude, an act of insubordination or even, as one employer put it, "mutiny."[20] After a wave of strikes in the time of the Popular Front (1936), one employer in the Côte-d'Or required any worker who wished to be rehired to sign the following letter: "Sir: We beg your forgiveness for our bad behavior toward you in going on strike and ask that we be rehired and allowed to redeem ourselves by our exemplary conduct in the future. Thanking you in advance, Monsieur Marchal, for your consideration. Yours truly . . ."[21]

It should be clear, therefore, why employers stubbornly refused to allow state authorities to intervene in strikes and why, in contrast, workers actively solicited such intervention. Employers viewed their businesses as an extension of their homes. Arbitration by a justice of the peace, envisioned by an 1892 law, would have placed them on a footing of equality with their workers. In their eyes such an idea was as senseless

Fiat workers on strike (Nanterre, 1936). The fence separates the street from the plant's property; the occupying workers have not torn it down. A difference remains between the street and the factory, but the street is empty, while the factory is full.

as allowing a judge to settle a dispute between a father and son. Arbitration would have made a public issue of a relationship that employers wished to keep strictly private. Conversely, workers demanded arbitration because they did not view strikes as a personal or family matter. Edmund Shorter and Charles Tilly argue that despite the unions' antistate rhetoric of the period, strikers had no compunctions about calling for state intervention. Between 1893 and 1908 some 22 percent of strikes went to arbitration. Of these, 48.3 percent were arbitrated at the behest of workers and 46.2 percent on the initiative of the justice of the peace. Virtually none went to arbitration at the request of the employer. The state justified intervention on the grounds that it was necessary to maintain law and order. During strikes the police were often summoned to protect an employer's private property, but the employer's intransigence often posed a threat to law and order in the streets. The state did not question the private character of the labor contract, but it did feel compelled to intervene to stem the public consequences of what was undeniably a private dispute. That intervention generally worked in favor of the workers, for the employer threatened with loss of police protection was generally forced to compromise.

World War I altered the situation, but only temporarily. In many plants for the duration of the war the labor contract ceased to be a purely private matter. The state had a paramount interest in maintaining war production; to that end it took youths out of the army and assigned them as industrial workers. These special workers were employed by the state, not by the plant owner, and in some cases they were subject to military authority. Strikes in key war industries could not be tolerated. Malvy, the interior minister, intervened in labor conflicts, and Albert Thomas, the minister of armaments, required factories under his jurisdiction to set up arbitration commissions and to allow election of shop delegates. In other words, the war made labor relations in certain sectors of the economy an affair of state. Labor issues that once had been private matters were now a question of national security.

For the same reason the war gave rise to the notion that the national wealth ought to be "returned to the nation." The 1921 platform of the CGT (Confédération Générale du Travail) used the term "nationalization," and the choice of this particular word, as opposed to collectivization, socialization, or "state-ization," was no accident. In this context the idea of abolishing private property stemmed not from an economic

Railway workers during the February 1920 strike wear armbands signifying that they are on the job against their will. Work rules negotiated in collective bargaining came first to nationalized service industries, then spread to the rest of the economy.

analysis of capitalism but from a new awareness, born of war, that certain types of labor are by nature public and in the national interest. Accordingly, the demand for nationalization was particularly powerful among railway workers, who had already proposed it just before the war. The size of railroad corporations had depersonalized employer-employee relations, and whatever services were to be rendered were owed to the worker's passengers rather than to his superiors. In February and May of 1920 there were major railroad strikes in France. The companies, ready for a test of strength, emerged victorious and fired 20,000 workers without provoking state intervention. Once all the troublemakers were dismissed, exploitation could resume as before. But conditions had changed. Nationalization, vigorously rejected in 1920, was accomplished without real resistance in 1937.[22]

The decisive change came at the time of the Popular Front. The plant occupations of June 1936 caused a furor among the bourgeoisie, for they seemed to fly in the face of private property. Factory owners feared a loss of social standing and power even more than higher wages and other costs. Forced to give in, they looked forward to taking revenge. Like those who lived through the occupations, historians have wondered about their meaning. Workers did not include expropriation among their demands, showed no interest in examining the books of occupied firms, and only rarely attempted to restart production without the help of management. It is tempting, therefore, to view the occupations as nothing more than the seizure of a useful bargaining chip in difficult negotiations. But this interpretation is not really satisfactory, for it suggests that one of the major conflicts in French social history was nothing more than a misunderstanding: factory owners feared a loss of property that the workers never threatened to inflict.

A more satisfactory explanation emerges if we view the status of the labor contract and of employer-employee relations as the central issue rather than ownership of the firm. Owners believed that because the firm was their property, the labor contract was purely private. But workers felt that, even though a firm might be privately owned, factories were public places where in a sense the workers were just as much at home as the owners. A workshop is not private in the same sense as a bedroom. Hence the labor contract, workers believed,

Plant Occupations during the Popular Front

When workers occupied factories, they enjoyed themselves in what was usually their workplace—a way of staking a collective claim to private property. The photograph shows a cookie factory in La Courneuve.

ought to be a public matter, and its contents ought to be determined not by personal negotiations between individual workers and their employers, which were impossible, but by negotiation between workers' unions and management. In this respect the major innovation was the introduction of collective bargaining. Although collective bargaining was legalized in 1920, it is interesting to note that it did not become widespread until after 1936.

The same argument explains why small employers felt particularly threatened by the Matignon accords, which, in 1936, ended the plant occupations. These accords were signed, on the side of business, by representatives of industry groups speaking for the owners of large firms in the mining, metal-lurgy, and machinery industries. Small businessmen accused these groups of selling them out. They forced France's prin-cipal business organization to change its name and bylaws to allow small business greater influence. They refused to nego-tiate with the CGT a second agreement that would have dealt with labor disputes and arbitration, because they felt that it would have interfered with their freedom to hire and fire as they saw fit. Large firms were ready for compromise, but small firms showed themselves intransigent. The explanation for this difference is simple. In large firms labor relations were anonymous and impersonal (though foremen and floor bosses continued to interact very directly with workers). In smaller firms, however, employer-employee relations remained highly personal, and workers still had much in common with servants. It was precisely this personalized relation to management that workers were now rejecting.

One anecdote brings this central issue of the day into sharp relief. It was told to me by Bénigno Caceres, who at the time worked for a small construction company in Toulouse. While he was enjoying the air outside his home one Sunday morning, his employer passed by. After greetings were exchanged, the boss said, "By the way, I left my car down the street. Would you be kind enough to wash it for me this morning?" To which Caceres responded: "Excuse me, sir, but that isn't covered by the collective bargaining agreement."

After 1936 labor became a matter of public policy. Collective bargaining was backed by compulsory conciliation and arbitration procedures. Wages were fixed by arbitrators. Within the firm, shop delegates served as public, collective spokesmen for workers whose problems with management might otherwise have remained personal matters. New legislation mandated a forty-hour week and paid vacations for all workers, who thus succeeded in staking their claim to privacy. In this respect private life as we know it today clearly dates from the period of the Popular Front. Since then it has been clear to everyone not only that every worker is entitled to a private existence but also that the workplace—factory, shop, or office—is not anyone's private domain but public space subject to impersonal norms.

The Vichy regime did not restore the full powers that employers had enjoyed before 1936. Circumstances forced the government to maintain wage controls and to allocate raw materials. Business organizations gained in power and exercised additional restraints on the management of individual firms. To be sure, the abolition of labor unions deprived workers of collective representation. But the so-called *charte du travail,* or labor charter, in attempting to reinstate private values as the foundation of all social relations, paradoxically relied upon a collective, public institution: the *comités sociaux d'entreprise,* or factory social committees. The aim was to abolish the distinction between employer and employee and promote harmony in the firm around charitable activities, in keeping with the paternalistic ideal of business as an extension of the family. Now, however, it was no longer possible to leave social assistance to the owner and his family and representatives. The charter assigned this task to the factory committees, which included representatives of blue- and white-collar workers and management. Though public in nature, these committees were supposed to promote respect for private values. Their very existence meant that the plant was no longer the owner's private domain.[23]

Now we can understand why the factory social committees were continued after the Liberation in the guise of *comités d'entreprise,* or factory committees. The latter admittedly differ from the former in two ways that radically alter their significance: employee representatives are elected, and only the unions may nominate candidates. Nevertheless, the actual responsibilities of the factory committees were not much broader than those of the social committees under Vichy. The possibility of a management role for the committes was excluded from the outset, but still they might have played a role in the organization of production. This did not happen. What is more, firms employing fewer than fifty workers are not required to have a committee. In businesses this small, labor relations are still highly personal in nature, and there seems to be no way to institutionalize the functions performed by the committees in larger firms.

Thus the Liberation marked yet another milestone in the transformation of labor relations to a less personalized system. The nationalizations carried out in the immediate postwar period, and, even more, the acceptance of those nationalizations by the general public, indicate the importance of this change.

1968: Self-Management

Still another stage was reached in 1968, a year that saw, in addition to much turmoil, calls for self-management and the passage of legislation governing union locals in industry. The aspiration of workers to manage themselves—which has become known as *autogestion,* or self-management—requires no comment. It is obviously based on the belief that a business is a collective enterprise, and its challenge is directed not so much at the ownership of property as at the power that goes along with ownership. Advocates of self-management call for an end to personal power in industry; in its stead they urge that power be exercised through work collectives. In many ways, therefore, self-management is the culmination of the evolution just described.

This *maison des syndicats* in the rue de la Grange-aux-Belles was the headquarters of the CGT in the early 1920s. Unions, legal since 1884, had established such headquarters, but their presence within the workplace was legally prohibited until 1945; their role was further expanded in 1968.

To understand the significance of the 1968 law on union locals, we must go back to the labor union legislation of 1884. The 1884 law did little more than recognize the right of workers to join together in work-related associations; it granted no specific rights to such organizations themselves. Furthermore, it authorized employers to band together in organizations as freely as workers and farmers. To be sure, labor unions were allowed to own such property as was necessary to discharge their functions and could appear as parties in court, but they had no status in business per se. The 1884 law did not authorize the unions to represent workers in negotiations with management. At best the unions were considered to be something like a proxy for their membership, but originally that is all they were. It was not unheard-of for employers to approve a wage increase in talks with a union but to insist that the increase applied only to union members on the grounds that nonunionized workers were in no way represented in the talks. Case law finally led to recognition of the union as the representative of all the workers, even in firms where union members constituted a minority of the work force. Collective bargaining led to even more sweeping industry-wide agreements, which applied to all firms in a particular branch of industry, even those in which the unions that were party to the agreements were not represented.

Recognition of the unions as the workers' representatives did not automatically give them a role to play within individual firms. Inside the factory, unions were illegal. The distribution of union newspapers, the collection of union dues, and the issuance of invitations to union meetings were all in violation of official industrial regulations. A worker could be summarily fired for such infractions. Thus, unions had the right to speak on behalf of workers, but their existence within the plant had to remain clandestine. As a result, delegates to the factory committees could not be selected by the unions. In 1945 the regulations were changed so that committee delegates could be nominated by the unions and then voted on by all employees. Their mandate stemmed from their election by the workers, not from the unions, whose position was precarious and whose representativity was subject to challenge. Delegates to factory committees enjoyed legal protections against summary dismissal, but union officials did not. Accordingly, factory committees became an instrument through which the unions obtained some measure of legitimacy within the plant. They served as a legal "cover," but full and frank recognition of a union presence was still withheld.

The law of 1968 changed all that. The unions were at last granted legal status within firms employing more than fifty workers. Union locals were entitled to an office and a bulletin board, and union officials were protected against summary dismissal and authorized to spend a portion of their paid work time on union activities (the exact amount of time depended on the size of the firm). Before 1968 it was illegal to engage in union activity inside the plant gates; now it was a guaranteed right.

The New Norm

Thus labor moved outside the private domain. It became rare to work at home, even for the self-employed. At the same time, working for wages ceased to be thought of as working for someone else within that individual's private domain. Work relations became impersonal and subject to formal regulations determined by collective bargaining in which not only employers but also workers' organizations enjoyed specific rights.

These changes provoked a variety of responses. Private life, expelled from the workplace, returned in a multitude of guises, some of which will be mentioned later. The current conception of work is not fully satisfactory either to workers or to those who rely on their services. What was once seen as protection against incorporation into the employer's private domain is now perceived by some as subjugation to a heartless bureaucracy. People yearn for more personal work relations, and this is even now leading to changes in the way we work, although work itself remains firmly in the public sphere.

Ménilmontant, a decaying working-class neighborhood of Paris, in 1957. The children play in the street, which is an extension of the home.

ᴥ The Family and the Individual

AT first glance the evolution of the family seems simple: it gave up its "public" functions and retained only "private" ones. Some of the tasks once entrusted to the family were taken over by cooperative organizations. The socialization of these functions left the family with no other role than to further the development of private life. Hence we may speak of a "privatization" of the family.

While not inaccurate, this analysis does not go far enough. The modern family, exclusively concerned with private functions, is no longer the same as the family that once performed public functions as well. The change in function has brought about a change in nature. In fact, the family has ceased to be a powerful institution; its privatization has amounted to a deinstitutionalization. Society is moving in the direction of what might be called "informal" families. At the same time, however, it is within the family that individuals have won the right to an autonomous private life. Private life has assumed two interconnected forms: within the private life of the family the private life of the individual unfolds. An extreme form of this tendency can be seen in households consisting of a single individual, in which domestic life is reduced to nothing more than one person's private activities.

THE SPACE OF PRIVATE LIFE

In theory the wall of private life encloses the entire domestic universe, the family and household. This frontier appears to be more sharply defined in France than it is in England or the United States. The English "bed and breakfast," an arrangement under which paying guests are taken into private homes, is unknown in France. Nineteenth-century French par-

ents sent their children to schools with dormitories rather than
board them in the homes of teachers and other families as was
done in Germany. What went on in a French home was thus
strictly private.

An End to Overcrowding

In a very real sense the twentieth century has been characterized by the conquest of space, but not by astronauts. It
is living space that has been conquered, as more and more
people acquire the room without which a full-fledged private
life is impossible.

Until around 1950 the homes of the well-to-do differed
markedly from those of the poor. The wealthy had spare
rooms for receiving guests, a kitchen and other service rooms,
a bedroom for each family member, and often additional
rooms as well. Different parts of the house communicated via
corridors and a foyer. Working-class housing bore little resemblance to the grand apartments of the bourgeoisie. Workers
and peasants often lived cramped into one or two rooms.

Many rural homes consisted of a single room used for

both cooking and sleeping. Physicians investigating health conditions in rural housing in Morbihan and Yonne around 1900 described common rooms that contained as many as four beds, each occupied by two people.[1] Only the most prosperous farmhouses included a separate bedroom. As the prosperity of the peasantry grew after 1900 and especially between the First and Second World Wars, families frequently added a bedroom or two to an existing farmhouse. In addition to the number of rooms, the size of rooms reflected the income of their inhabitants. A farm laborer might occupy two tiny rooms; a wealthier peasant might live in a single-room but quite ample farmhouse. Rooms generally were quite small, however, considering the variety of activities that went on inside them. In Yonne the average farmhouse contained a mere 270 square feet of living space.

Urban dwellings were less uniform. Many consisted of a single room, while others had a separate kitchen. In 1894 some 20 percent of the population of Saint-Etienne, 19 percent of the population of Nantes, and 16 percent of the population of Lille, Lyons, Angers, and Limoges lived in one-room apart-

Left: a middle-class salon in 1958. A maid is serving coffee amid books, paintings, an oriental rug, flowers, and—a rare prize at the time—a television set. Below: the one-room dwelling of a farmhand with several children near Moyon (Manche). Note the new stove, a cabinet for storing food attached to the wall, and the fake mantelpiece behind the stove.

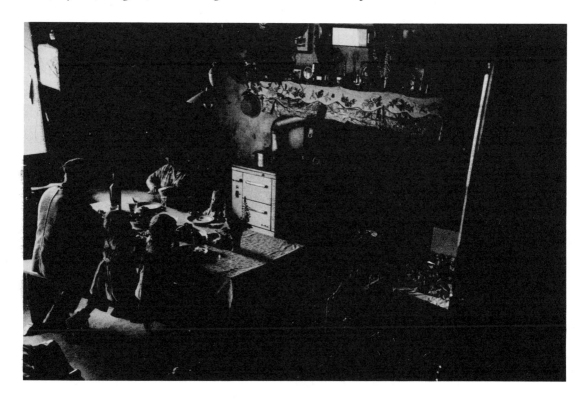

ments. Jean Guéhenno's description is typical: "We had only one room. There we worked, ate, and on some nights even entertained friends. Along the walls we had to find space for two beds, a table, two armoires, a buffet, and a gas stove, as well as room to hang pots, photos of the family, and pictures of the czar and the president of the Republic . . . Lines stretching from one corner of the room to the other always held the most recent laundry . . . Beneath [a high window] we installed the 'workshop,' my mother's sewing machine, my father's bench, and a large bucket of water in which arches and soles were always kept soaking."[2] And this was a home of recent construction in a small town, a relatively favorable situation. Older apartments in big cities were even less spacious.

Overcrowding, which Bertillon defined as a density of two or more persons per room, was the rule. According to the 1906 census, 26 percent of those living in cities whose population was over 5,000 lived more than two to a room; 36 percent lived more than one to a room; 16.8 percent one to a room; and only 21.2 percent less than one to a room.[3] At the end of the nineteenth century miners' housing offered more space and a larger number of rooms. The Anzin Company, for instance, typically offered its miners three-room homes with 760 square feet of living space.[4] Though quite basic, these houses were designed by upper-class architects to standards that they took for granted, so it is not surprising that they were more spacious than the typical urban apartment, where overcrowding and lack of privacy were the rule. As the workplace moved outside the home, living quarters became less cramped.

Generally speaking, the conditions just described persisted through the first half of the twentieth century. Michel Quoist's description of the Saint-Sauveur district of Rouen in 1949 is reminiscent of Léon Frapié's account of Belleville in 1900 and of the findings reported by Jacques Valdour from a survey conducted just after World War I. The explanation is simple: very little housing was constructed between 1919 and 1940, no more than two million dwelling units all told. Rent control, adopted after World War I to protect tenants and hold down rising prices, resulted in rents so low that landlords had no incentive to build new rental units other than apartments for the well-to-do. Public housing might have offered a remedy, but the nonprofit housing agencies set up by the government in 1912 were never funded adequately to meet the demand. Some projects were undertaken, however. Under the Lou-

The public fountain was still widely used in 1956. If there was no running water at home, it was the best place to wash clothes.

cheur Law (1928) some 200,000 low-cost apartment units were built; high-rise apartments were constructed in Villeurbaine; and low-rent apartment buildings went up on what once had been the site of Paris's urban fortifications. In general, however, the issue of housing for the poor, which had been raised as early as the end of the nineteenth century, by 1950 had yet to be resolved. The twentieth century got off to a slow start in the area of urban housing.

Between 1900 and 1950, consequently, there was little improvement in home comfort and appliances. The only major development was the availability of electricity. By 1939 electric power had come to most villages and urban buildings. Running water was not universally available, however. More than half (1,300 out of 2,233) the buildings in the Saint-Sauveur section of Rouen were without it as recently as 1949.[5] Hence public fountains and hydrants were still much used. Half the streets in the district lacked sewers. Hygiene was rudimentary at best. There were of course no baths or indoor toilets in buildings where washbasins lacked even cold-water taps. There was no central heating, either, and in some buildings no heating at all.

A Leap Forward

The 1954 census yields a striking image of the primitive state of French housing. Of 13.4 million homes, scarcely more than half (58.4 percent) had running water; only one-quarter (26.6 percent) boasted indoor toilets; and only one in ten (10.4 percent) were equipped with a bathtub or shower or central heating. Even allowing for the fact that the rural homes included in these figures were particularly backward, it is hard to believe that we are describing a situation that existed only thirty-five years ago.

Since 1950 French housing has undergone unprecedented change. New housing was built at the rate of 100,000 units per year in 1953, 300,000 in 1959, and 400,000 in 1965. From 1972 to 1975 more than 500,000 new units were constructed annually. During those four years, in other words, more new housing was completed than during the entire period between the two World Wars. From 1953 on home construction received powerful encouragement from the government. This continued until the mid-1960s, when rising rents once again made private investment in housing profitable. Government subsidies required that new housing meet certain minimum standards in regard to size, number of rooms, and equipment.

Although these standards were changed several times, their general tenor is clear. No room could be inhabited unless it was at least 98 square feet in size. Apartments were required to contain a kitchen, a living room, a master bedroom, at least one bedroom for every two children, a water closet, a bathroom, and central heating. These standards were applied to the vast apartment complexes that sprang up on the outskirts of major cities. For millions of French families unable to afford a home of their own, the new apartment buildings represented a veritable leap into modernity. They extended to the bulk of the population advantages previously enjoyed only by the wealthy, who of course continued to enjoy distinctions with respect to status, location, and furnishings. Nevertheless, the sweeping changes of the 1950s and 1960s democratized housing on a vast scale.

The improvement was spectacular. In 1973, less than twenty years after the distressing results of the 1954 census, the average French home contained 3.5 rooms; the average room was 218 square feet, and the average person possessed 267 square feet of living space. Admittedly workers were housed less well than the average, but even they disposed of more than 200 square feet of living space per person. Contrast this with the figure of 152 square feet per person that P.-H. Chombart de Lauwe established in 1953 as a minimum ac-

An urban working-class apartment in 1955. The beds are crowded together, but everything is clean and well-kept. The double bed is of the sort sold by the Galeries Barbès; above it hangs the couple's wedding photo. The radio stands permanently on a shelf of its own. This apartment has at least one more room.

ceptable standard. At that time he found that only one Parisian working-class household in ten met or exceeded that minimum.[6] Within twenty years the average worker's situation had progressed to well beyond the minimum.

Modern comforts became widely available at the same time. By 1973, 97 percent of all homes had running water, 70 percent had indoor toilets, 65 percent a bathtub or shower, and 49 percent central heating; by 1982 the three last-cited figures had increased to 85, 84.7, and 67.5 percent, respectively. The percentage of units equipped with running water, indoor toilets, and at least one shower increased from 9 in 1953 to 61 in 1973. Once again the average was depressed by the inclusion of homes occupied by elderly persons and farmers. Since 1973, moreover, progress has continued.

These quantitative changes led to qualitative changes. When individual living space increases, the nature of that space changes, as does the way people use it. As apartments became larger, the number of rooms increased, and certain rooms were designated for special functions. As the configuration of do-

Courtyards of two working-class apartments, 1959. Left: Roubaix; above: Paris, 19th arrondissement. The walls are in ill repair and the paving stones are uneven. The communal outhouses and a number of washbuckets and bicycles are visible.

Above: Auvergne, around 1960. The furniture (four-poster bed, night stand, clock) suggests a fairly well-to-do home, but the walls look shabby, and salt pork hangs from the beams of this room in which a bedridden man lies.

Lower left: a woman in Chalon-sur-Saône does her wash in the river in 1956. Left: another woman uses a large washing machine that barely fits in the kitchen. Below: the ideal was the functional and hygienic "laboratory kitchen," with formica countertops and a variety of appliances.

mestic space evolved, each family member acquired the right to a certain privacy, which, among working people at any rate, was a major innovation.

The Lack of Intimacy

Prior to this revolution in housing, individuals enjoyed privacy only in common with others who shared the same living space. Domestic space and public space, family and strangers, were separated by walls, but within those walls there was not enough room for each family member to experience truly individual privacy, except among the well-to-do. Private space was nothing more than the public space of the household.

Today it is difficult to imagine how family pressure affected individual members. It was impossible to be alone. Parents and children lived in close proximity throughout the day. Each had to wash and dress in the presence of others, who when necessary to preserve decency averted their eyes. Before mining companies installed showers, for instance, the

As recently as 1960 people were living in incredibly cramped quarters. Here there are three children to a bed.

miner returned home to a wooden tub in the family room and a kettle of water that his wife had heated on the stove. With her help he then bathed in the tub. It was the same on the farm: on the rare occasions when people bathed, they did so in the common room or outside and never washed the whole body at once.

Nor did anyone sleep alone. People slept several to a room and often several to a bed. Michel Quoist, writing of the years just after World War II, recalls the astonishment of poor children arriving at summer camp and discovering their beds: "Look at that, one for each!" He notes that "often there was only one bed per household, occupied by two, four, sometimes five or more people."[7] In the country it was no different: Pierre-Jakez Hélias shared a curtained bed in the common room with his grandfather. In 1947 two anthropologists studying a village in Seine-Inférieure found similar conditions and, applying the prejudices of their own culture, disapproved of the fact that a four-year-old child slept in the bed with its parents.[8] Many more examples could be cited.

Under these conditions it was difficult for a person to keep private belongings anywhere but in a pocket or purse. It was hard to find even a niche of one's own when space was at such a premium. And it was impossible to hide anything from one's relatives. The slightest indisposition was instantly revealed, and any attempt to be alone drew immediate attention.

Intimacy was an almost meaningless notion. Sexuality, taboo where there was ample room for private lovemaking in a boudoir or alcove, could hardly be kept secret when everyone lived in one room. Even the menstrual periods of the women of the house were public knowledge, and in miners' families the dates were marked on a calendar tacked to the kitchen wall. Sexual activity was either relegated to the semi-public realm—the woods behind a dance hall, say, or a thicket at the edge of a field—or exposed to view at home. "Morality does not suffer from the fact that nearly everyone sleeps in one room," one specialist in rural housing wrote in 1894. "On the contrary, a sort of mutual surveillance develops . . . Only decency suffers, but this hindrance is less serious than one accustomed only to private rooms might imagine."[9] Léon Frapié mentions one couple that lived with its children in a single room. Before engaging in lovemaking, this couple sent the children out into the stairway, where they waited quietly until their parents allowed them back into the apartment.[10]

The fact that Frapié presents this couple as a paragon of decency and tact suggests that most parents did not closet themselves away for the purpose. It may be worth noting that the issue of sex education for children and adolescents did not arise before 1960.

Thus, at the turn of the century the private lives of most French men and women were indistinguishable from family life. The poor had few personal belongings, and most of those were generally objects received as gifts: a knife, a pipe, a rosary, a watch, a jewel, or a dressing case. These often modest objects took on great symbolic value, since they were the only things a person could truly claim as his or her own. A similar exclusive bond developed between peasants and their animals: a cow, a dog, or a horse had a name and a master. This was not much of a private life by today's standards, perhaps, although it is difficult to believe that a modern pet owner's feelings toward his cat or poodle could be more intense than the affection a peasant felt for the animals that kept him alive.

Secrets

Secrets offered another refuge for private life. Family secrets were hidden even from the children. Personal secrets included dreams, desires, fears, regrets, and fleeting or persistent thoughts that remained unspoken. Persons outside the family in a position to serve as confidants therefore assumed great importance. The doctor was unlikely to be chosen, however; the poor rarely called on his services and still more rarely went to visit him in his offices. He made house calls in case of serious illness, but the circumstances on such occasions were hardly likely to inspire confidences. People sometimes confided in nurses and social workers, and the dispensaries that became common in the first half of the twentieth century provided a suitable setting. The most likely confidants for family secrets, however, were the notary and the priest. The notary learned the family strategies of all from the lowliest peasant to the grandest bourgeois: matters of marriage, acquisition, sale, leasing, inheritance, and donation. The priest heard confessions, especially of women, and had no compunctions about asking the most intimate of questions. The very poor, who, being propertyless, had no family strategy, nonbelievers, and believers unwilling to allow the priest to meddle in their private affairs (one of the root causes of anticlericalism) kept their secrets to themselves and wrapped their private lives in the silent monotony of unremitting labor.

The private life of the wealthy exhibited a greater variety. For one thing, they had more room. Each person had his own bed, his own room, his own dressing table, perhaps even his own bathroom. A wider range of possible confidants was available: servants; the family doctor, who knew each family member as an individual and who could be consulted in private; and an extensive range of family connections and friends. There was time to visit an uncle, an aunt, a godparent, or an old school friend. Shopkeepers and artisans had less time and less space. Despite their growing economic advantages, their private lives were more like those of workers and peasants than those of the well-to-do. By contrast, the petty bourgeoisie of office and clerical workers, bookkeepers, schoolteachers and the like may have earned little more than laborers, but they enjoyed a fuller private life. They constitute an intermediate category about whose habits we would like to know more.

It is no exaggeration to refer to the improvement in French housing since 1950 as a revolution. In multiroom apartments equipped with running water and central heating, each member of the family can now claim a space of his or her own. The forty-hour week and paid vacation, fruits of the Popular Front period, have given people leisure time to enjoy this newfound space. Family life proper is now concentrated at specific times, such as mealtimes and Sundays, and in specific places, such as the kitchen and what since World War II has come to be called the living room. Lives are divided into three unequal parts: public life, meaning essentially work; family life; and personal life.

The diversification and expansion of private life in the second half of the twentieth century has not been limited to the household. Private life is on the move. Automobiles are now widely available: 88 percent of all households owned at least one automobile in 1981, and 27 percent owned two (for semiskilled laborers the figures were 84 percent and 17 percent). Cars have liberated people from their homes and have elicited a surprising, in some cases excessive, degree of personal attachment. The automobile and other forms of transportation have allowed people to enjoy their free time in an ever-expanding variety of locales and with all sorts of other people. Everyone now can enjoy places and activities once accessible only to the wealthy. The ability to make friends at ski resorts or to enjoy a summer romance on the beach is open to all—one of the great changes of the twentieth century. In a

Sarcelles-Lochères, 1961. People envied the comfort, appliances, and modern construction of high-rise apartments; above all, they wanted the space.

paradox that we will have occasion to explore further, private life has moved beyond the home into certain once public places.

PRIVATE LIFE VERSUS THE FAMILY INSTITUTION

If there is one new idea in France, it must be that individuals have the right to lead their private lives as they see fit. For the first half of the twentieth century private life was in most respects subject to communal controls. The wall that was supposed to protect individual privacy was a privilege of the bourgeoisie.

There is no more striking illustration of this class difference than social attitudes toward the night of marriage. What could be more private than the wedding night, the wedding chamber, and the wedding bed? Among the bourgeoisie the wedding night venue is a secret as closely guarded as the honeymoon destination. Among peasants and workers, by contrast, the custom in most regions of France is for members of the wedding party to visit the newlyweds in their bed in the wee hours of the morning and to present them with a concoction known as *la rôtie,* a mixture of white wine, eggs, chocolate, and biscuits delivered in a chamber pot. This ritual embodies the community's control over the most private of all acts. In a society where domestic values occupy a central place, it is essential that the marriage be consummated. When the family is the basic social cell, the union of husband and wife must be made public.

The family used to exercise fairly strict control over its members. The husband was the head. A married woman needed her husband's written authorization to open a bank account or manage her own property. All parental authority was vested in the father. Not until the passage of new marriage laws in 1965 and a new law on parental authority in 1970 was the legal inferiority of women eliminated from French codes. No doubt reality was more egalitarian than the law in some segments of society and some regions. The anthropologist Susan Rogers found that in the villages of Lorraine, but not in Aveyron, the real power was wielded by women, who determined not only whom their children would marry but also whether or not their husbands could run for mayor. The condition of this power, however, was that the women in

Power-sharing by Husband and Wife

question always had to pretend in front of children, relatives, and neighbors that the man was "boss."[11]

Such a situation raises questions. Is it true that the division of roles between men and women tends to empower women in the private sphere? That division has for the most part assigned women a role within the family and men a role outside it (in business transactions, representation of the family, and politics), although Martine Segalen has noted certain exceptions to this rule in traditional rural families.[12] Has this division worked to the detriment of women? Some feminists argue that the truly important arena is that of public life and therefore that the confinement of women to the home was a setback. On the other hand, one might argue that, given the central importance of domestic values in a society in which the worth of an individual depended on the quality of his or her family and there was only family, not individual, success, women's power in the domestic sphere was in fact decisive. As far as the history of private life is concerned, the important fact is that the home was incontrovertibly the dominion of the mistress of the household.

Quite often the man returned to what was in reality his wife's home. In the house she was in charge. A man could do nothing on his own without making a mess, breaking something, or creating a disturbance. Hence outside the family there developed an exclusively male society, whose justifications and customs varied with social and geographical setting.

Cramped lodging and lack of privacy often drove workingmen out of the house and into the café. Not until more room became available at home could men enjoy leisure time without going out. One of the most appreciated features in high-rise apartments is the availability of a small room that can be used for tool storage and workshop space. In houses a garage or cellar provides even more space for such purposes.

Men of the upper classes once enjoyed a great deal of leisure time. The club was a place to play cards and read the newspaper. Some even offered discreet apartments away from the family eye. But times have changed. Now women are as well educated as men and able if they so choose to take their place in the working world. They insist on equal rights in the public sphere. Family connections are no longer the chief source of marriage partners; young men and women meet at summer camp or the university. In the wake of these changes the couple, in the modern sense of the term, has emerged. This in turn has led to a reapportionment of powers in the private sphere.

The question of power brings us to one of the major changes affecting private life. If there is some question as to the relative power of husbands and wives before 1950, there can be no doubt as to the power of parents. Children had no right to a private life. Their free time was not their own, it was their parents', and devoted to a thousand and one assigned tasks. Parents closely monitored their children's friendships and were wary even of innocent associations with children from other families. If a child made the slightest overture to another child in the park, he or she was reprimanded.[13] Such exclusivity was not limited to the bourgeoisie. Henri Mendras noticed that the peasant children of Novis were subject to similar restrictions just after World War II; they were forbidden to dawdle on their way home from school.[14] Young people did band together in groups, segregated by sex, but these were a traditional element of village life and subject to public scrutiny.

The supervision of children included monitoring their mail. For parents, reading children's letters was not only a custom, it was a duty. This duty did not end when children were sent away from home; it was simply delegated to others. As late as 1930 letters sent to boarding students had to be signed on the outside so that a proctor could check the signature and make sure that the correspondent had been authorized by the child's parents.

Such practices enabled parents to determine their children's future, and first and foremost their choice of profession. Upper-class parents decided what their sons and daughters would study at school. Working-class parents chose the trade their sons would apprentice in. In a survey conducted by a widely read magazine in 1938, 30 percent of the readers responded affirmatively to the question, "Should parents choose a career for their children and steer them toward it from early childhood?"[15]

Parental power actually went much further. Parents kept a close watch on the private lives of their children. Marriage was a family affair, hence of direct concern to the parents, particularly where considerable wealth was at stake. At the bottom of the social hierarchy, where lack of wealth obviated the need for a family marital strategy, children were relatively free to choose a spouse. Workers could marry without parental interference. Among peasants, office workers, merchants, and artisans, however, if parents no longer chose their children's mates, they nevertheless made their preferences known. Before 1950 it was difficult to marry a person of whom one's parents did not approve. In the bourgeoisie marriages frequently were still arranged by families, and coming-out parties remained the rule.

In theory marriage marked the emancipation of a young man or woman from parental authority at all levels of society. "*Mariage, ménage,*" the saying went: you married and started a household of your own. In some cases, however, children remained under parental tutelage, particularly where parents and newlyweds lived together under one roof. Such a situation was deemed abnormal and scarcely tolerable, but it was not always avoidable.

The Socialization of Education

Progress in education has been a notable feature of the second half of the twentieth century. For one thing, the number of years that a person spends in school has increased. In France education up to age thirteen (twelve for vocational pupils) was made compulsory by minister of education Jules Ferry in 1882. The age at which a child could leave school was increased to fourteen (thirteen for vocational pupils) in 1936 and to sixteen for children born after January 1, 1953 (by a directive issued on January 6, 1959). The average length of schooling increased by three years. In the school year 1950–51, only half of all fourteen-year-olds, a third of fifteen-year-olds, and a quarter of sixteen-year-olds were in school. In 1982–83 nearly all fourteen- and fifteen-year-olds were in school, along with 85.7 percent of sixteen-year-olds and 70.4 percent of seventeen-year-olds. Today, proportionately more seventeen-year-olds attend school than did fourteen-year-olds in 1950. And 44.8 percent of eighteen-year-olds are in school, more than the percentage of fifteen-year-olds in 1950.

Three years more in school hardly constitutes a revolution in family life, and we might be tempted to pass over the phenomenon quickly or to see it as an indirect consequence of the shift of work outside the home. Since children can no longer learn a trade at home from their parents, who work elsewhere, they must learn it outside. The prolongation of schooling cannot be explained solely by a desire to improve the training of the work force, nor by the aspirations of families to improve their social standing in a period of rapid economic growth. The fact that occupational training is now conducted in the schools must also be taken into account. Furthermore, the development of technical and occupational courses is one of the distinguishing features of the French educational system. Two out of three high-school students in the seventeen- and eighteen-year age group are enrolled in such courses.

The prolongation of schooling actually stems from far deeper changes in society. The phenomenon reflects not so much the socialization of apprenticeship as the need for an apprenticeship in the ways of society. In the past this kind of teaching was carried on within the family, and for that reason it was possible to characterize the family as society's "basic cell." Subject to powerful economic constraints, the family was governed by norms applicable to broader segments of society subject to constraints of the same kind. These constraints disappeared, partly because productive labor was transferred out of the home, but partly too because of postwar prosperity and the revolution in housework. If parents became less authoritarian, more liberal, and more permissive, it was partly because their own behavior had changed but above all because the reasons for requiring children to do certain things had disappeared. Parental authority became arbitrary; when it ceased to be employed in the direction of indisputably necessary family chores, it was exercised in a void. Yesterday's parents were authoritarian not only because it was customary but because they had to be. When storm clouds gathered, a father did not solicit his children's opinions about the wisdom of getting in the hay. And somebody had to fetch water, wood, and other essentials. Necessity gave parental commands the force of law.

The liberalization of family education shifted the burden of educating youngsters for their future life in society from the family to the school. The schools assumed responsibility for teaching young people to respect the realities of time and space and the rules of social life as well as how to relate to other people. This socialization, moreover, was not limited to the period of adolescence but extended throughout a child's educational career.

The Child outside the Home

In this regard the extension of schooling beyond age fourteen is less significant than the development of the nursery school. In no country other than France has the nursery school taken on such great social significance. Ever since the late 1950s more and more people have felt compelled to send their children to nursery school, despite the absence of any law

Nursery school, 1930. The school taught hygiene and cleanliness.

requiring them to do so. Previously the norm was precisely the opposite: to keep young children at home as long as possible and even to teach them to read at home. Nursery schools were for the children of the poor, whose mothers were obliged to work. A nursery school was nothing more than a babysitter, a regrettable but unavoidable necessity. Now, however, it is widely believed that it is better for small children to be sent to nursery school than to remain at home with their mothers. Parents of the upper strata of society, especially the urban and the well-educated, have led the way, even in families where the mother does not work. In 1982, 91 percent of all three-year-olds attended nursery school, as did a third of two-year-olds. People have come to believe that the school is better than the family, which is rapidly being supplanted.

This change, which has come about in less than a generation, reflects the family's retreat into private life. If the family has assented to its replacement by the school, it is because it has become conscious of its constitutional unfitness for the job. Since all education is education for public life, the

Municipal day-care center in Rennes, 1980. Children are taught to get along in groups.

Children at a summer camp in Brittany returning from the beach. Because of a belief in the healthy virtues of clean, fresh air, some city children spend vacations away from home with friends rather than with their families.

family, having become a purely private institution, can no longer play an effective educational role. Parents notice the change in more concrete terms when they say they have no idea how to keep their children occupied.

A glance at the role of summer camps confirms these observations. Originally the purpose of summer camps was to promote health. Philanthropists sought to give sickly city children an invigorating dose of fresh air. Today parents choose camps to provide their children with an interesting vacation. The camp, as they see it, offers a richer, more stimulating environment than the home.

Adolescents, it is true, resist going to camp, and since the early 1960s youth organizations have fallen on hard times. The reason in both instances is the same: young people insist on their right to a private life. The shift of educational responsibilities from the family to the school carried with it an implicit recognition by the family of the value of extrafamilial relations. In the past families, believing that they alone were capable of truly educating their children, were wary of outside friendships. The nursery school phenomenon stems from the opposite belief: that it is good for youngsters to intermingle with children from other families. Through such contacts they prepare themselves for life in society.

Children allowed to mix with friends and classmates tend to form groups. Thus, in a seeming paradox, the shift of educational responsibilities from the family to a public institution, the school, gives rise to new centers of private life that compete with the family. Adolescents refuse to participate in highly structured leisure activities, that is, in organizations subject to the norms of public life. They accept institutions such as the schools because they recognize their social necessity, but to them the school belongs to the world of work, hence to the public sphere. The world of leisure is private and therefore unsuited to institutions that enforce collective norms. Camps and youth groups aimed at adolescents must cease to be institutions in order to survive. Their difficulties stem from this intrinsic contradiction.

Parents face a similar problem. If they treat the family as a coercive institution, their children will leave. Yet no family can exist from day to day without certain indispensable rules, which have to be worked out through compromise, adaptation, and negotiation.

Boy Scouts in the Vosges Mountains. Adult supervision and educational programs create a healthy climate for adolescent friendships.

This adjustment is facilitated by another consequence of longer schooling: the increasing influence of the schools over decisions that affect the child's future. Occupational training

LA VISITEUSE D'HYGIÈNE EST L'AUXILIAIRE DU
MÉDECIN ET DES ŒUVRES SOCIALES DANS
LA CROISADE CONTRE LA TUBERCULOSE
ET LA MORTALITÉ INFANTILE.
SOUTENEZ·LA !

The battle against tuberculosis
was a patriotic crusade.

determines many children's place in society, but the choice of such training is not subject to parental control. Under the neighborhood school system, where a child attends school is determined by where its parents live. Testing and selection determine the course of study open to a particular student. Only good students have a real choice; the rest take what they are given.

This elimination of the parents' role is a source of conflict, because selection often becomes an impediment to lofty social ambitions. Yet if selection is often challenged, it is also convenient: responsibility for accommodating to an unpleasant reality is shifted to an outside agency. Before the Second World War parents often chose their children's careers; lately they have renounced this prerogative and conceded their children's right to choose.[16] Nevertheless, the powerful pressures of selection do the parents' work for them, making it unnecessary for them to exert pressure on their children and thus eliminating one source of tension within the family.

Public intervention in education has not been limited to the schools; it has increased in other areas as well. The government takes an interest in the child almost from the moment of conception. Under a 1946 law a woman who wishes to be eligible for child-care allowances must see a physician at least three times during her pregnancy. Medical supervision is required during breast-feeding and in early childhood. Vaccinations are compulsory. The provision of child-care allowances under the law of 1932, the family code of 1939, and the law of 1946 has promoted increased medical supervision of pregnant mothers and of children.

Any aspect of child-rearing potentially involves the scrutiny of public authorities. In the 1920s and 1930s visiting nurses were sent to inspect private homes as part of the struggle against tuberculosis. In some towns, such as Suresnes under socialist mayor Henri Sellier, these visits were systematic and led to the compilation of complete health documentation on every household. Soon welfare agencies were sending social workers out into the field to make sure that welfare money was being well spent. The social workers reviewed family budgets and offered advice. In emergencies families could be placed under official guardianship according to a law of 1942; in such a case the social worker was authorized to spend the family's allotment in place of the parents.

Welfare agencies were joined by health agencies and juvenile courts. Judges were authorized (by a 1958 directive and

a 1959 law) to take children away from their parents and assign them to the care of an approved guardian. The removal of "endangered" children from the home is of course an extreme case. Nevertheless, the fact that a public authority is empowered to entrust the education of children to persons other than their parents reveals the shift that has taken place. France has not yet evolved to the stage of Sweden, where children are allowed to bring charges against their parents for mistreatment, but it can certainly be said that French parents are now only partially responsible for their children's upbringing, and whatever they do is done under the watchful eye of the state. Parents have relinquished to the schools the responsibility for teaching the rules of social life to their children. The responsibility to feed, clothe, and above all love their offspring is still that of the parents, but now the state ultimately judges whether they have adequately performed that task.

Two different worlds confront each other as a medical inspector visits a family in the 1930s. Domestic customs were changing in response to concerns about health and hygiene.

THE CHANGE IN MARRIAGE

The evolution of marriage reveals the profound transformation that has taken place in family life. In the first half of the twentieth century to marry was to establish a household, that is, to lay the foundations for a socially well-defined and collectively understood mode of existence. As recently as the 1930s, when it came to deciding on a mate, professional prospects, wealth, and moral qualities were seen as more important than aesthetic or psychological preferences.[17] People married in order to provide help and support to each other over the course of what promised to be a difficult life (one even more difficult for single people). They also married in order to have children, add to and pass on a family fortune, and contribute to their children's, and therefore their own, success. Family values were central, and individuals were judged in light of family success and their role in it.

This common purpose required a strong legal foundation. A marriage, even if no notary was involved, constituted a permanent contract that could be dissolved only for very serious cause. An 1884 law permitted divorce only in cases where the husband or wife was guilty of grave misconduct. Divorce was rare: fewer than 15,000 annually at the turn of the century and fewer than 30,000 as recently as 1940. Four out of five divorces were granted at the request of the wife,

Marriage, the family event par excellence, was a *mise-en-scène* of two families according to a complex protocol. As the custom waned, weddings became less elaborate.

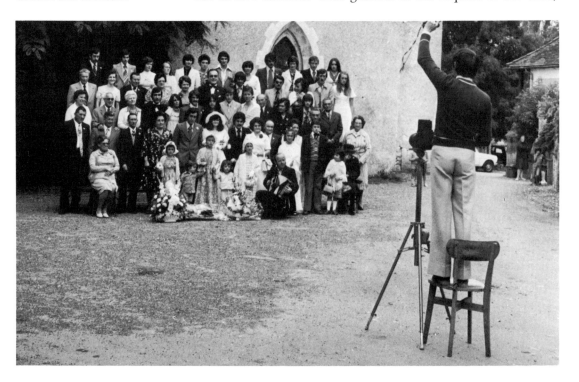

often because an alcoholic husband not only was unfaithful, abusive, and unable to support the household but became a burden as well.[18] Emotional dissatisfaction was less important than material reality.

It is difficult to say anything precise about the role of the emotions in marriage in this period, beyond the fact that love was considered to be neither a prerequisite for marriage nor a mark of success. Marriage required only that a man and a woman like and feel capable of understanding, appreciating, and respecting each other; in short, they had to be suitable mates. This did not mean that they could not love each other prior to marriage, any more than it ensured that they would love each other later on. The institutional aspects of marriage were emphasized, masking the emotional realities. As for what was still referred to as the "physical" rather than "sexual" side of marriage, a 1938 survey of marital happiness found that while physical considerations were important in 67 percent of those surveyed, these were outweighed by fidelity (78 percent), intellectual qualities (78 percent), sharing of authority (76 percent), and sharing of worries and chores (92 percent). To marry was above all to form a team.[19]

Marrying for Love

Things probably began to change in the 1930s, but it is impossible to be precise about the date because the change was at first camouflaged by traditional-sounding rhetoric. Among Catholics the emergence of what was known as "conjugal spirituality" may serve as a convenient milestone. During the Occupation groups of young couples began to form, and a Catholic young couples' organization with its own newsletter, the *Anneau d'or* (Gold Ring), was established. The first issue of this newsletter appeared in January 1945, and the second contained nothing less than a paean to conjugal love composed by a respected churchman. At the risk of making a comparison that may seem disrespectful, the words of this homily were reminiscent of Edith Piaf's popular songs. The question arises whether these observant Catholic couples were behind the times compared with the rest of French society, and the answer, to judge from numerous other signs, appears to be no. In a remarkable article published in 1953, Philippe Ariès drew attention to what he saw as a recent development, a new emphasis on conjugal love in all its forms, particularly sexual (his word). In 1948, he notes, 12 percent of students were married.[20] This figure, he argues, marks a major change, because previously it was unusual for a man to marry before he had established a position in the world; student marriages were love matches.

Social norms, meanwhile, were evolving. Women's magazines published articles by doctors and psychologists who argued that the emotions have their proper place in marriage and who popularized Freudian concepts. Premarital lecture courses were offered at teachers' schools in the Paris area in 1953. In these lectures marriage was depicted as a stage in the process of emotional maturation, which culminated when the desire to have children was finally satisfied.[21] The proper upbringing of children, it was argued, required not only parental love but the love of peers.[22] The term "couple" appeared in such expressions as "the life of the couple" and "the problems of the couple." Henceforth love occupied a central place in marriage, of which it formed the very foundation.

This new norm legitimized sexuality, a term that came into vogue in the late 1950s. Sexuality, which involved the sincere expression of genuine emotions, became the language of love. A Catholic physician, the abbé Oraison, wrote a book entitled *L'Union des époux* (The Union of Spouses), which introduced the new norm into Catholic circles whose traditional attitude toward sex had been ascetic: the sexual act was tolerated as a concession to the weakness of the male and to the need to reproduce the species. Readers of a magazine with a very different outlook were treated to the story of a "woman of marble" whose husband had failed to make "a real woman" of her and who discovered pleasure in the arms of another, only to return to her "onerous marital duty."[23] Elsewhere a woman wrote: "It was more immoral to live in each other's presence without love than to live apart."[24] No longer was the institution of matrimony alone sufficient to legitimate sexuality; love was now essential.

The tie between love and marriage was not yet severed, however, because sexuality remained tied to procreation. Not that contraception was unheard-of at the time, but it was primarily the man's responsibility, whereas pregnancy and its consequences were of more direct concern to women. Public opinion became more tolerant of premarital sexuality provided that the engaged couple were in love and wished to make a life together. Disapproval of unwed mothers remained harsh, however, and young women continued to deny sex to their young men unless marriage was in the offing. The number of premarital concepts rose steadily through 1972, while the percentage of illegitimate births remained stable. Couples slept together sooner than before, but sex remained firmly linked to marriage and childbearing.

But life-styles were changing. Feminism found a new following, whose ranks were swollen by the events of 1968. The procontraception movement evolved into the family-planning movement, which promised control over the rhythm of childbearing and the unfortunate consequences of unwanted pregnancies, as detailed in the preamble to the Neuwirth law of 1967. Abortion was legalized in 1975 under the Veil law, passed after debate in which the right of women to control their own bodies was frequently invoked. Subsequently it became increasingly common for women to use contraceptives, and the tie between sexuality and procreation was severed.

Thereafter marriage slowly ceased to be an institution and became a formality. As education evolved, young people obtained a large measure of independence within their families. No longer was it necessary to marry in order to escape parental power. Nor was it necessary to marry in order to have regular relations with a member of the opposite sex, because those relations remained without consequence as long as the partners wished.

Living Together

The number of unmarried young couples living together increased.[25] Seventeen of every hundred couples who married in 1968 and 1969 were already living together; by 1977 the figure had increased to forty-four of every hundred. Gradually the public came to accept the idea of young couples living together. Parents of young people who lived together sought to avoid estrangement by refraining from criticism. Parents were informed of the situation 75 percent of the time, and 50 percent of them helped the young couple out financially. They did so because they looked upon cohabitation as a kind of trial marriage and hoped, often justifiably, that marriage would be the eventual outcome.

This state of affairs reveals how deeply the institution of marriage had been shaken. Getting married changed nothing in the life of the young couple that already lived together. It brought no additional social recognition, because cohabitation was already treated as marriage by family and friends. As far as the welfare and social security authorities were concerned, a duly attested cohabitation was the equivalent of marriage.

Cohabitation has become a life-style. Here such conventions as tables, chairs, and most furniture have been discarded.

The couple that lived together gained nothing by marrying. On the contrary, they often experienced a sense of loss: to marry was to make a commitment, to devote one's life to a purpose. Couples that lived together were content with present happiness and wary of the future. The wager seemed risky. Was not marriage a renunciation of freedom, a sacrifice of possibilities, a curtailment of the self?

At a more profound level, couples feared that marriage might affect their relations for the worse. They were afraid that true feeling would degenerate into mere habit or routine. Marriage meant growing old and turning bourgeois. Young people felt that love under contract was an impossibility. If affection was promised, did it not become obligation? The young wished to be loved for what they were, not because it was their due. And they were determined to preserve the spontaneity, freshness, and intensity of their relationship; some even believed that the absence of commitment and institutional stability was what guaranteed its quality.[26]

Thus, as people individually staked their claims to private life, they chipped away at the institution of matrimony from within. The couple became the primary focus of individual self-development, a purely private affair of concern to no one but the two people involved. As the legal status of marriage was weakened, the frequency of marriage decreased. A 1975 law permitted divorce by mutual consent. Even before passage of this law, the number of divorces had risen sharply: 28,600 in 1960; 37,400 in 1970; 54,300 in 1975; and 79,700 in 1980. The frequency of divorce in the early years of marriage also rose sharply. Undeniably marriage became more and more fragile.

It also became less common. In 1971 a record 416,500 were celebrated. Ten years later the figure had dropped by 100,000. The number of unmarried individuals increased: 16 percent of men and 35 percent of women between the ages of thirty and thirty-four were officially listed as unmarried in 1981. At the same time couples lived together for longer periods without getting married. In 1981 some 11 percent of all couples in which the man was less than thirty-five were living together outside wedlock, compared with only 5 percent just six years earlier. Cohabitation and the avoidance of marriage increased among managers, professionals, and white-collar personnel. The new mode became a way of life among

An urban family, exemplar of a new way of life and a new culture.

educated and cultivated city dwellers. According to the 1982 census, more than half of all households in Paris consisted of a single person.

The family too was shaken. No longer did the typical household consist of a couple and its children. Single-parent households became increasingly common. In 1981 some 10 percent of children were raised by a single parent—in three out of four cases, the mother. In addition to divorcées living with their children we find a growing number of mothers who remained single by choice. The percentage of children born out of wedlock doubled between 1970 and 1981, to one in eight, but more than half of them were acknowledged by their fathers, compared with only one in five before 1970. With the advent of contraception, the seduced and abandoned young mother has been replaced by the single woman who chooses to have a child without marrying and who assumes sole parental authority even though she maintains relations with the child's father. The bond between mother and child has tended to become the only stable and durable family tie.

The Ascendancy of the Individual

Such extreme cases remain atypical, and the trend may yet be interrupted or change course. Still, the transformation of domestic space, the socialization of work and of much of education, the alleviation of everyday constraints, and the decisive evolution of life-styles have brought about genuine change. A half-century ago the family took precedence over the individual; now the individual takes precedence over the family. The individual once was an intrinsic part of his or her family. Private life was secondary, subordinate, and in many cases secret or marginal. Now the relation of individual to family has been reversed. Today, except for maternity, the family is nothing more than a temporary meeting place for its individual members. Each individual lives his or her own life and in doing so expects support from a now informal family. A person who considers his or her family suffocating is free to seek more rewarding contacts elsewhere. Private life used to coincide with family life; now the family is judged by the contribution it makes to the individual private lives of its members.

THE INDIVIDUAL AS KING

There is no more telling sign of the primacy of individual life than the modern cult of the body. At the turn of the century the status of the body depended in large part on social background. Workers valued bodies that served them well and bore hard labor without complaint. They respected physical strength, fitness, and endurance. The bourgeoisie had a more aesthetic attitude. Because it was important for members of this class to display their social superiority, physical appearance was more highly valued than it was by workers. But the body was not shown unadorned. Distinguished people wore hats and gloves and revealed little more than their faces, except for women, whose evening gowns were generously décolleté. When Boy Scouts first donned shorts in the 1920s, it caused a scandal, because they showed their legs.

At all levels of society one strain of Christian tradition cast doubt, not to say anathema, upon the body. The biblical contrast between the flesh and the spirit was translated into an antithesis between body and soul. The soul was said to be imprisoned in the body or fettered to it. Worthless, the body kept man from realizing his full potential. To be sure, it deserved respect; certain attentions were indispensable. But too much attention to the body opened the way to sin—especially sin of the flesh.

Hygienic Practices

Grooming was therefore quite limited. Water was in short supply among peasants and workers, and difficult to transport. It was also widely believed that water turned the body soft, while, as Guy Thuillier and Eugen Weber have shown, dirt signified health.[27] The face and hands—the visible parts of the body—might be briefly washed, but rarely more than that. Historians have rightly called attention to the importance of primary schools in spreading information about cleanliness and hygiene, but the standards they touted, though in advance of local practices, today seem old-fashioned. Thuillier notes that in Nièvre before 1940 it was often impossible for children to wash their hands at school.

Washing the whole body was not yet a normal part of the daily routine. At the Dijon Academy prior to World War I, four upper-level boys' dormitories were equipped with showers but a fifth was not, nor were two upper-level girls' dormitories, fifteen lower-level boys' dormitories, and thirteen lower-level girls' dormitories. Students took footbaths once a week. At the time a progressive local government was building new showers, but taboos remained unshaken. On the eve of World War II, when a school principal in Chartres pointed out to a woman of the people that her daughter had

A luxurious bathroom of the 1950s, with double sink, bathtub with shower, and toilet. The towels are warmed by water passing through the pipes on which they are hung.

begun to have her menstrual period, the woman indignantly responded: "I am fifty years old, Madame, and I have never washed down there!"[28]

The bourgeoisie and petty bourgeoisie washed more extensively. By the end of World War I they often lived in apartments equipped with bathrooms and tubs; where there was no bathtub, a portable washtub was used. There was often a dressing room off the bedroom, and from the diary of a chambermaid that Octave Mirbeau has given us we learn of the maid's irritation that her mistress would not allow her to enter this inner sanctum.[29] Running water, sinks, and bidets expanded the range of possible ablutions. Infants were washed daily and bathed thoroughly once a week, usually on Sunday. In short, cleanliness habits varied widely with social class.

Social differences are clearly evident in the spread of bathrooms to lower-class housing. The postwar construction boom made it possible for families of modest means to move into apartments equipped with all the modern conveniences. People of the upper classes used to joke about workers in low-rent housing who used their bathtubs to store coal or keep rabbits. It took time for the new residents to accommodate to modern customs.

These differences were by no means systematic. The popularity of sports, youth hostels, and vacation spots had familiarized younger workers with new attitudes toward cleanliness. Such differences as there were can be explained by the existence in different social classes of very different attitudes toward the body. For the upper classes, the period between the two World Wars was one of physical liberation and of a new attitude toward clothing. Previously clothing had hidden the body and held it prisoner. For men the change, which can be traced back before 1914, was modest: stiff collars and top hats had given way to soft collars and homburgs. Replaced by the sport jacket, the waistcoat became a ceremonial costume. For women the change was more marked. Corsets and girdles were discarded in favor of panties and bras; dresses were shortened, and stockings drew attention to legs; softer fabrics discreetly revealed the body's lines. A woman's physical appearance depended more than in the past on the body itself; that body, therefore, had to be kept in shape. Women's magazines alerted their readers to this new need and began to include regular columns on daily exercise. Women

The New Concern with Physical Appearance

The first issue of *Marie-Claire,* March 5, 1937. The cover set the tone for the new woman.

were exhorted to stretch their abdominal muscles in regular workouts. A lighter diet was recommended, with emphasis on grilled foods and green vegetables. Menus were simplified, and even at formal dinners the classical triad of appetizer, sauced meat or fish, and roast gave way to the simpler fish followed by meat. A round belly ceased to be a mark of respectability in men and became a sign of neglect. Excess weight causes fatigue. Svelte tennis players in flannel pants and open shirts offered a new model of elegance that appealed to the young.

Women could now openly avow a desire they might previously have kept secret: the wish to remain attractive. New women's magazines, such as *Marie-Claire,* first published in 1937, urged women to maintain their looks if they wanted to hold on to their husbands. That this was a new idea is indirectly demonstrated by a reproach addressed to the editors of *Marie-Claire* by an older reader, who complained that the magazine asked too much of women. Keeping one's looks had not been part of the marriage contract a generation earlier.[30] Beauty treatments, makeup, and lipstick, no longer limited to coquettes and women of easy virtue, became respectable means of emphasizing charm.

How did these new attitudes spread? The research needed to answer this question remains to be done, but let me hazard a few guesses. The new model, which first gained a foothold in the 1920s and 1930s, was initially adopted by Parisian socialites who frequented coastal resorts and spas. This modern-minded group, much influenced by English and American life styles, frequently launched new fashions. The provincial bourgeoisie, rooted in tradition, did not change until around the time of the Second World War. Catholic Action movements, Boy Scouts, and Girl Guides all may have played an important role in legitimizing the new fashions.

In other segments of society the new habits were slow to catch on. Clerical workers adopted them before workers and peasants, and women preceded men, in every case under the impetus of a growing consumer society. The advertising revolution hastened the widespread adoption of practices that physicians and social critics had been advocating since the turn of the century. Following the successful marketing of a suntan lotion in 1937, firms like L'Oréal resorted to massive advertising campaigns to sell shampoo, perfume, deodorants, creams, and sunscreens. The manufacturers of undergarments, lingerie, bathing suits, and mineral waters quickly followed suit. Suggestive photos in magazines supported the advertisers' message, which was also trumpeted by the movies and above all by television. To sell a shampoo or toothpaste, companies now sought to sell the public an image—a star's hairdo or gleaming smile—to reinforce the idea that it is essential for everyone to wash their hair and brush their teeth. Similarly, suntan lotion could only be sold after people had been convinced that it was a social requirement to come home from vacation with a tan. Merchants did as much as health professionals to popularize new attitudes toward the body.

Since the mid-1960s the focus has been on grooming, diet, and physical fitness. A 1951 poll conducted by the magazine *Elle* caused a furor when it was revealed that 25 percent of the women questioned never brushed their teeth, that 39 percent bathed only once a month. In 1966 and 1967 time-use surveys conducted in Paris and six other cities showed that the average woman spent an hour a day caring for her body, the average man slightly less. By 1974–75 the time devoted to such grooming had increased by 30 to 40 percent for women and 20 to 30 percent for men. Eight to nine hours a week

Jogging in the Bois de Boulogne—and even in the streets of Paris. Such running no longer is seen as ridiculous.

were being devoted to grooming. Male executives were a little below average in this regard, but female office workers were well above average (nine and one-half hours), and women in middle management were highest of all (nearly ten hours). Grooming, more careful and more varied than ever before, took much more time than in the past.

Although workers remain partial to fattening foods, meals generally have become lighter. Between 1970 and 1980 the weight of the average French woman decreased by more than two pounds, and among males the average height for a given weight has increased by more than half an inch. Since changes in physical size usually take centuries to reveal themselves, these differences over no more than a decade are eloquent evidence of increased concern for the body on the part of the average man or woman.

Sports

Changes in the area of physical fitness are also evident. Women's magazines, as I have already mentioned, began recommending regular exercise before 1940. But it was difficult to follow such advice. It is impossible to say how many women did so, but it seems likely that many tried, only to give up in discouragement. Powerful encouragement was needed to get men and women to exercise regularly, and that did not happen until people enjoyed a greater opportunity to show off their bodies. Advertisements in the mid-1960s for fancy apartments often showed a young man and woman in bathing suits lying next to a swimming pool with a tennis court in the background. The vacation habits of the upper class now extended into daily life. With the award of a third week of paid vacation to all workers in 1956 these habits began to spread to other segments of society as well. Only four out of ten French citizens took vacations in the mid-1960s, but the enormous popularity of camping put the seaside within reach of young people of all classes. In 1956 one million people went camping; by 1959 that number had increased to three million, by 1962 to nearly five million, and by 1964 to more than seven million. Within a period of less than ten years a veritable revolution in vacations had taken place.

The last ten years have seen a growing concern with more regular forms of exercise. People flock to gyms and enroll in aerobic dance classes, while health club advertisements in the tonier daily papers remind executives of the need to keep in shape. Social clubs and organizations for the elderly foster

regardez-vous...

la forme, ça vous regarde!

l'exercice c'est la santé

Réalisée par LES GRANDES CAUSES NATIONALES

The waistline has become a national cause as exercise is equated with health.

similar concerns in a very different group. In the late 1970s jogging became popular, and individual sports have attracted growing numbers of participants. Participation in team sports such as soccer and rugby has remained constant, while participation in tennis increased from 50,000 in 1950 to 133,000 in 1968 and 993,000 in 1981; the number active in judo went from 200,000 in 1966 to 600,000 in 1977. Above all, sports that yield a heady sensation of speed and mastery of the elements have enjoyed unprecedented popularity: graduates of skiing schools increased threefold from 1958 to 1978, and the 686,000 current graduates represent only a fraction of the millions of skiers in France.[31] In just a few years windsurfing has developed into a major sport. And in recent years other new sports have been invented, developed, and popularized.

As a result, the pursuit of physical fitness has acquired a new status. Combining pleasure with health benefits, it is no longer merely tolerated but enthusiastically prescribed. It has become a duty for anyone who wishes to be up to the minute to be athletic. Personal tastes no longer enter into it. One sign of the times is that sports apparel, once confined to specific times and places, is now commonly seen on city streets. Sportswear has gained in popularity since 1976; the parka has replaced the raincoat, sales of which have declined by 25 percent.[32] People now wear sports outfits to the office and in the street—a sure indication of the new status of sports.

DEVELOPING THE BODY

The rehabilitation of the body, one of the most important aspects of the history of private life, has changed the individual's relation to self and others. People who use makeup, do gymnastics, jog, play tennis, or go skiing or windsurfing treat their bodies as both ends and means. In physical labor and certain other kinds of activities, the body is a means, not an end. In cooking, the dish is the means, the body the end. What is new in the late twentieth century is the widespread popularity of physical activities whose purpose is to improve the appearance, health, or skill of the body itself. To feel comfortable with one's appearance has become the ideal.

Changes in dancing exemplify the new attitude. Dancing always involves partners, and sensuality, however discreet, is always a part of it. But turn-of-the-century dances such as the waltz and quadrille were complex rituals; dancing revealed mastery of the relevant social codes. After World War I couples

Club Méditerranée has popularized the three S's: sea, sun, and sex.

began to dance more closely together; moralists denounced the tango as lascivious. Before World War II the Charleston was danced only by small numbers of people; after the war jazz rhythms such as boogie-woogie, bebop, and other new sounds found their way into popular dance tunes. Dancers could enjoy the vigor and grace of their movements in fast dances, while slower steps allowed couples to dance cheek-to-cheek without having to contend with the complexities of a dance like the tango. In rock and disco dancing a person can even dance alone, without a partner. Once a social ritual, dancing became a ritual for couples and ultimately individuals. It evolved in three phases: from formal group to couple to celebration of the individual body.

Concern for the body thus came to occupy an important place in private life, and people began to search for a variety of sophisticated new gratifications. The pleasures of swimming, dressing, and physical exertion are in part narcissistic, the satisfaction of self-contemplation. The mirror is not a twentieth-century invention, but its widespread use is a novelty of this century. What is more, people do not look at themselves in mirrors as another person might look at them, simply to make sure that they are properly dressed. They look in a manner not permitted to others, examining themselves in the nude, without makeup or clothing.

The narcissistic satisfactions of the bath are freighted with dreams and memories. The body is prepared as if a gift were to be made of it. Clothing, jewelry, and decorations no longer suffice. Today's clothes must either be functional, that is, comfortable and practical even in defiance of tradition, or else they must disclose the beauty of the body, suggest, enhance, even reveal its form. People make a show of their tans, their smooth, taut skin, their supple bodies. Modern managers affect an athletic style to make themselves seem dynamic. And more and more of the body is exposed to view. Each stage in this progressive baring of the physique initially caused a scandal, only to be taken up subsequently by large numbers of people, especially the young, thus widening the generation gap. The miniskirt of the mid-1960s was received this way, as was the "monokini," seen on the beach a decade later. It is no longer indecent to show thighs or breasts. In summertime men can be seen in cities wearing shorts and open shirts or no shirts at all. The body has been not only rehabilitated and accepted but, even more, trumpeted and displayed.

Judged by the standards of the 1920s and 1930s, nudity has reached the stage of indecency or at any rate provocation. By today's standards, however, nudity is the most natural thing in the world, just one more way of feeling at home with one's body. Casual attire is evident not only in public places but also in the home. During the summer people wear bathing suits while working around the house or dining. Naked parents go back and forth between bedroom and bathroom without concealing themselves from their children. How widespread such behavior may be is difficult to say; age and social class no doubt make a difference. But the mere possibility of such things attests to a change in community standards.

The first miniskirts caused a scandal, but soon long skirts were considered anachronistic.

The body has become the focal point of personal identity. To be ashamed of one's body is to be ashamed of oneself. Compared with previous generations, our contemporaries feel less responsible for their thoughts, feelings, dreams, and longings, which many accept as though imposed from without. But they identify with their bodies. A social identity may be a mask or sham; ideas and convictions are weak and subject to manipulation; but the body is the real essence of the self. Hence the body is involved in every aspect of private life. Real life is no longer the social life of work, business, politics, and religion; it is the life of leisure, during which the body is free

The Body and Personal Identity

and unfettered. One high-school senior captured this new attitude when he defined an animal as being like a human but free. So did the slogan that appeared on walls in 1968: "Under the streets, the beach."

THE BODY THREATENED

Every threat to the body assumes a new gravity. Consider violence. Contrary to conventional wisdom, violence today is on the wane. It remains important on the fringes of society, among those not well integrated into the social structure. On the whole, however, the decline of violence is undeniable. Take political violence. To measure the decline, one has only to compare the Paris riots of February 6, 1934, which resulted in sixteen deaths, with the events of May and June 1968, which claimed only five victims throughout France.[33] The presence of specially trained riot police is of course part of the reason why lethal confrontations were avoided in 1968; but beyond that, the very idea that a demonstration should lead to anyone's death has become intolerable. Ordinary street violence also has declined, as Gilles Lipovetsky's figures make clear.[34] Between 1875 and 1885, the rate of conviction for assault and battery was 63 per 100,000 in the Seine département and 110 per 100,000 in the Nord département. In 1975 the comparable figures were 38 and 56 per 100,000. Deaths by homicide in Paris numbered 3.4 per 100,000 in the period 1900 to 1910 but dropped to just 1.1 per 100,000 in 1975.

Given these figures, one cannot refrain from asking why people today are convinced that violence has been steadily on the rise. The gap between fact and opinion is problematic. No doubt the attention paid violent crime is partly responsible. And it may be that less serious forms of violence have increased. It is also clear, however, that people have become more sensitized to violence. Any physical attack is keenly felt as a violation of an absolute. Extrapolating, people have come to feel that violence toward animals is cruel, not because of what such acts reveal about those who commit them but because they cause the animals to suffer, as if their bodies were in every respect analogous to human bodies. The law now punishes such acts as crimes. In short, respect for the integrity of the body now stands at the top of our hierarchy of standards.

Threatened from without by violence, the body is threatened even more from within by illness and old age. People seek to slow the inexorable injuries of time, and with undeniable success. Today's forty-year-old men and women bear little resemblance to the forty-year-olds of two generations ago. Hygiene, diet, and physical exercise are not the only weapons in the war against aging; the whole cosmetic arsenal has been mobilized. There is a brisk trade in antiwrinkle creams, royal jellies, and mud baths, as people seek to exorcise the fear of aging by digesting seemingly scientific claims and alluring advertisements. Hair loss is combated. Luxurious clinics promise miracle cures on the shores of Lake Leman or the Mediterranean. And if they fail, there is always plastic surgery to get rid of pouches under the eyes and shore up sagging breasts.

The Battle against Aging

Plastic surgery is a remedy normally used only by a minority of film stars, politicians, and others constantly in the public view. The less wealthy and famous rarely go so far. But the popularity of facelifts has increased in recent years, demonstrating the lengths to which our contemporaries will go in the denial of aging. One is supposed to look young, and the personality is so bound up with the body that it has almost become necessary to remain young in order to retain one's identity.

Resignation to growing old is no longer considered a virtue, resignation to disease even less so. At the turn of the century disease and death were familiar companions: one child in five died before the age of five. Pneumonia, diphtheria, and infectious disease claimed many lives; tuberculosis was a major scourge. After 1945 antibiotics (including penicillin, for which Fleming received the Nobel prize), blood transfusions, and advances in surgery changed all that. Child mortality declined dramatically, and the life expectancy of children born in 1985 exceeded that of children born at the turn of the century by twenty years.

Fear of Illness

It now seems shocking that anyone should die young. To die before reaching a ripe old age seems abnormal. Naturally sudden deaths occur: traffic accidents claim the lives of healthy people; heart attacks strike without warning. Cancer, which afflicts men and women in the prime of life as readily as the

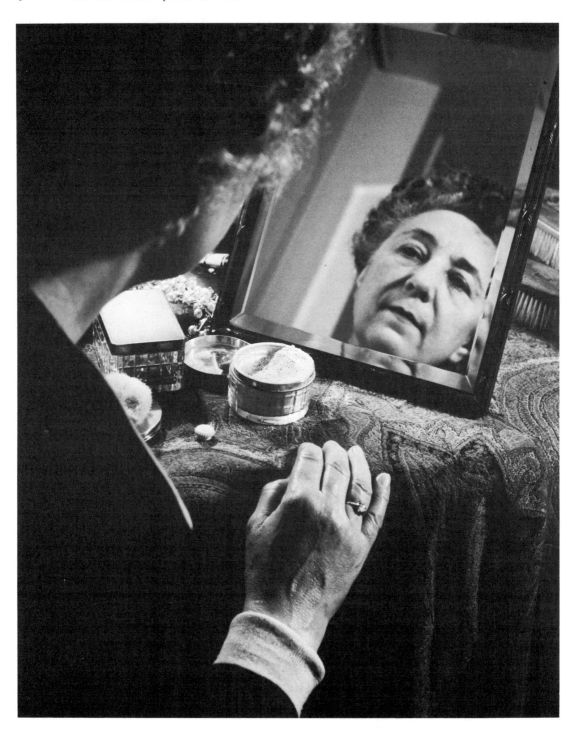

elderly, is often detected too late. It is therefore feared as a curse, and people are sometimes reluctant to call it by name. Now that most diseases have been conquered and the chief threat to the body is the wear and tear of age, to live is no longer considered a stroke of good fortune but a right.

Along with grooming and fitness, then, one of the principal concerns of private life today is to protect the body from disease. Fear of disease surrounds us. It has expanded the clientele and enhanced the prestige of doctors, inflated the sales of pharmacists, and ensured the success of medical laboratories. At the first hint of trouble people turn to doctors and drugs. Scientific progress has fostered a perhaps excessive confidence in medicine, whose limitations have done nothing to encourage resignation. The desire to seek treatment is so powerful that the inevitable ultimate failure of normal medicine, for all its greatly increased therapeutic efficacy, has led to the development of alternatives. Quacks and faith healers flourish against all probability, while homeopaths and acupuncturists serve a greatly expanded clientele. Health is a constant concern, a topic of conversation and subject of countless news-

Facial care for two generations: not only is the mirror larger, but the meaning is different. The feminine gestures of an earlier era have been replaced by a more clinical technique.

paper and magazine articles. Meanwhile, modern biology, a far cry from the natural science of an earlier era, has joined physics at the pinnacle of the scientific hierarchy.

Ironically, however, sickness, a central concern of private life, has become the focus of much public policy. Nothing is as private as health, yet nothing is so readily made the responsibility of the public authorities. Health is now a public as well as private affair.

Public Health Policies

When any issue takes on this much importance, the government inevitably steps in. Public health concerns made a state role in health imperative. Once effective therapeutic and preventive measures existed, it was no longer acceptable for a sick individual to compromise the health of his neighbors. Health regulations proliferated, and in 1930 the government established a ministry of public health. Smallpox vaccinations were made compulsory, and all unvaccinated schoolchildren received one. Anyone who wished to marry was obliged to submit to a premarital medical examination to detect possible communicable diseases and diagnose Rh-factor incompatibility. Under the Popular Front the government introduced maternal and well-baby clinics. Women who agreed to three examinations during the course of their pregnancy became eligible for prenatal allotments and could bring their newborns to the clinics for treatment. Parents were urged to keep health records for children. Summer camps were subject to health inspection. Public health policy burgeoned into a complex system of governmental regulations.

The state was not content simply to supervise and prohibit. It sought to make the medical system accessible to the entire population. In addition to promoting free health care through a network of clinics, the government attempted to eliminate cost as an obstacle to obtaining the best available treatment. Private health insurance, though more widely used than ever before, was a long way from covering the whole of the population. In 1928 and 1930 the legislature approved laws establishing a system of national health insurance, which went into effect the same year that the ministry of health was established. After 1945 the ministry of social security assumed responsibility for and expanded the health-insurance program.

The health of French citizens thus became dependent on the huge governmental agency that financed the health-care system. Because of the great importance attached to health by

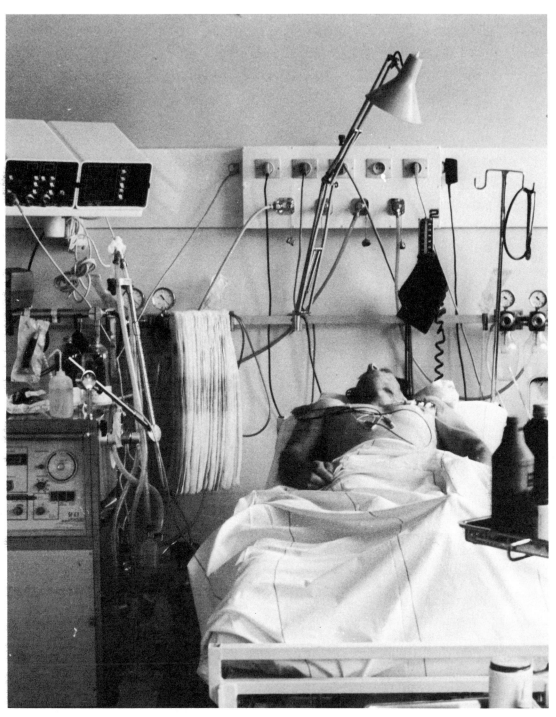

Heroic measures, the ultimate in medicalization. Restarting stopped hearts is high-tech medicine, and the technology is reassuring.

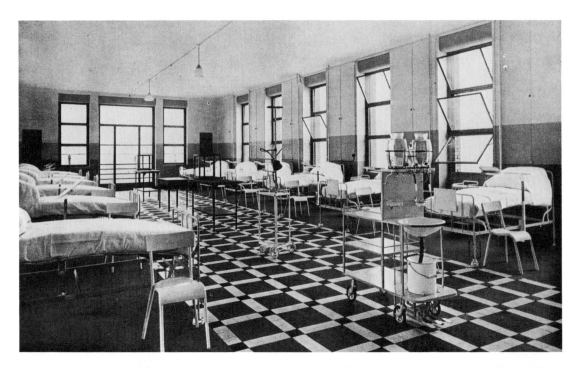

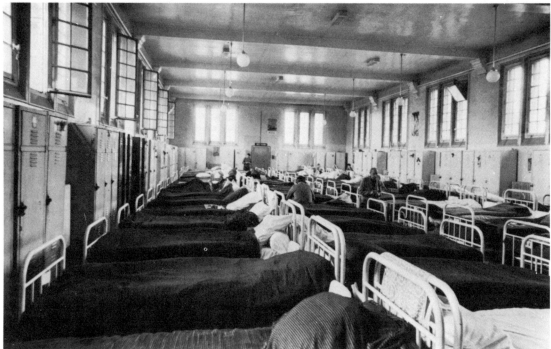

Originally the ward was large and well-ventilated—modernity incarnate. Over the years, however, new beds were added in response to increased demand. Today's call for privacy spells doom for these open wards.

the general public, coupled with the growing complexity of medical technology, health-care costs have risen more rapidly than individual income or the government budget. In 1950 direct and indirect (third-party) payments for health care accounted for 4.5 percent of household expenditures; by 1970 that figure had risen to 9.4 percent and by 1982 to 12.4 percent.

At the same time the position of the hospital has changed. Prior to recent medical and surgical advances, hospitals cared for the poor; they were charitable agencies. But as medical treatment has become increasingly sophisticated, the hospital has become the temple of medicine, the only place where patients can be treated with the full arsenal of modern scientific therapeutics. Accordingly, patients have flocked to hospital beds. They go not only in order to receive the best treatment when truly ill but also in order to avoid complications in relatively routine matters such as childbirth. Prior to 1940 most women gave birth at home; today nearly all births occur in hospitals. When the body is in jeopardy, treatment is no longer administered in the private sphere. The burden of health care—in the physical and emotional as well as financial sense—has been assumed by public institutions.

There is a glaring contradiction between the desire to experience what is an intensely emotional situation in private and the public setting in which health care is dispensed. Physicians, whose incomes rose after national health insurance guaranteed the ability of their clientele to pay, overcome this contradiction by insisting that medical care is still essentially a private matter between doctor and patient.[35] Though many physicians are employed by state hospitals, they consider themselves independent practitioners and continue to believe in the doctor-patient dialogue as both a reality and an ideology.

For the first time in history, people are born and die in hospitals. All want the best care, and it is difficult for families to assume the entire burden. Thus the most important of life's moments, times when the meaning of existence and identity are most clearly revealed, have been removed from the familiar and relatively spacious setting of the home and moved into the antiseptic and functional but anonymous setting of the hospital room. The old wards, once good enough for homeless charity cases, no longer seem tolerable. Over the past twenty years older hospitals have been renovated, and wards replaced by private or semiprivate rooms.

The neighborhood serves as a transitional space between public and private. Although no provision was made for such transitional zones in early high-rise apartment complexes, new towns such as Cergy-Pontoise are rediscovering their importance.

The Transition from Neighborhood to Metropolis

THE transition from private to public can be brutal, as many of us discover each morning. The moment a person leaves home, he or she is caught up in the world of work with its obligations and requirements. Punctuality is essential. Leaving home, the commuter, suddenly plunged into an alien, not to say hostile, public environment, squeezes into a crowded railway car, only too happy to arrive on time. Such a journey is not a transition but a leap.

This picture is not atypical of today's large cities. More than half the French population (50.7 percent in 1982) lives in cities of more than 50,000 inhabitants. This degree of urbanization is a novel feature of the late twentieth century. Since people no longer work at home, they must travel to their jobs. The workday begins with a commute, either by public transportation or, in an effort to extend private life and ease the transition into the public sphere, by private automobile. The traffic jam is one consequence: even private vehicles must use public roadways, and individuals in their cars are perfectly anonymous and isolated.

Contrast this modern world with the old neighborhood and village, which constituted a kind of transitional space. A neighborhood is a subjective matter, defined by where people go when they leave home—on foot of course for the neighborhood is defined by walking, just as the metropolis is defined by motorized transportation. The space of the neighborhood or village, open to all, is governed by a communal code, but its focus remains the enclosed space of the home. It is an outside defined with reference to an inside, a public space whose center is a private one.

The Neighborhood

103

In this space people know one another. Details of private life are known to casual acquaintances, people who are not chosen, as friends are, and yet who are neighbors rather than strangers. Proximity affords a degree of mutual knowledge; outsiders are considered strangers. One thinks of the unforgettable passages in Proust's *Remembrance of Things Past* in which the narrator's aunt discusses with Françoise, the maid in her Combray home, the identity of a dog "with whom she is not familiar" or the source of the asparagus she sees a neighbor carrying in her basket.

Neighbors not only know about each other's lives but participate in various forms of social interaction. Anyone willing to pay the price can enjoy the benefits of living in a neighborhood: smiles, hellos, friendly greetings, an exchange of pleasantries—things that make a person feel alive, known, recognized, appreciated, and respected. Neighbors are even more solicitous toward people in special circumstances. They may, for instance, look in on an elderly widow if she does not appear at the usual time to fetch her bread. In order to enjoy these benefits, however, one must observe the neighborhood rules; one must do what is done and refrain from doing what is not done. Anyone who fails to respect these unwritten rules is subject to unpleasant comments and perhaps even to a kind of exclusion. If you don't play the game, you can find yourself on the sidelines.

Pierre Mayol suggests using the term "proprieties" for the set of rules governing such neighborhood interchange.[1] These proprieties define a transitional space between the private sphere and the public. Underlying the proprieties is the fact that encounters with neighbors are inevitable yet unpredictable. Anyone who leaves the privacy of his or her home is likely to meet neighbors but usually has no idea which ones. A neighborhood encounter is not a private matter. It is not planned, takes place in a public setting, and generally is limited to an exchange of commonplaces. Nevertheless, no one can avoid being personally implicated in such a meeting: the other person knows who you are and where you live. He knows your wife, your relatives, and your children. She even knows the purpose of your venture outside: whether you are running errands, picking up the children at school, or returning home from work. And he or she is full of neighborhood gossip, especially rumors concerning other people's private lives.

The person who ventures into the neighborhood opens himself up. The proprieties regulate, among other things, the

Marseilles. In poor neighborhoods everyone knows everyone else.

way she is to present herself. This transitional space is marked, according to Mayol, by a certain theatricality, and whoever goes there is in some sense on display. It is best to offer a presentable image. Dress immediately is subject to interpretation, because neighbors know what is usual and what is not. A shopkeeper may remark to a customer that she is looking very pretty today, only to tell the neighbors a few minutes later that Mrs. X was in this morning dressed to the nines. Any deviation from customary dress had better be explicable, for it will surely be noticed, commented on, and interpreted. So will visits and personal remarks. Family quarrels attract attention. Occasionally a party to such a dispute will call the neighbors to witness. Any unusual purchases will set tongues wagging. The proprieties might permit, say, the purchase of a bottle of wine from the local grocer for Sunday dinner, but, as Mayol shrewdly observes, the first bottles of whiskey drunk in his home town of Croix-Rousse were purchased in nearby Carrefour, where the anonymity of a large liquor store allowed the buyers to pass unnoticed. The neighborhood is a public stage on which everyone is required to present his or her private life.

The proprieties not only govern the nature of that presentation but to some extent protect the private lives represented. Certain things are forbidden, others regulated. Behavior toward the neighbors' children, for example, is governed by shrewd customs that dictate when to abstain and when to intervene, thus maintaining a delicate balance. What can be said is also regulated. Private life is not only shown but also recounted, yet always with discretion.

Women's Talk

Here the analysis diverges, because men and women tend to converse in different places. In the past, for example, women congregated in the village washhouse, where the talk was exclusively feminine. But even in today's cities, women who shop prefer personal service to the supermarket-style checkout. Shopkeepers who know their clients' tastes and can assist them in their purchases thrive. Stores are chosen not only for what they sell but also for more intangible qualities; not even a bakery with good bread can survive if the woman behind the counter is disagreeable. Merchants have to establish a reputation and win the loyalty of their customers in order to stay in business.[2]

The neighborhood grocer occupies a preeminent place

among merchants because the variety of items purchased in the grocery store is eloquent testimony to the variety of private lives. The grocer knows what people eat, when they are away or ill, when some occasion is to be celebrated, and when a family has fallen on hard times. If the store is not busy, the grocer may engage his or her customer in seemingly innocuous conversation in which a good deal of personal information is nevertheless exchanged. To others such conversations may seem little more than a tissue of banalities, and it is easy to be ironical about them. Nevertheless, Mayol is correct when he notes that with specific knowledge of the context it becomes possible to draw real meaning from apparently stereotyped words. When Mrs. X tells her grocer that "kids will be kids," he can easily infer from his knowledge of the circumstances that her grandson is still living with his girlfriend.[3] While observing the proprieties, it is still possible to say a great deal, provided it is couched in the impersonal form of proverbial wisdom. Precisely because such proverbs have no meaning in themselves, they take on a variety of meanings from the context.

Men's Talk

In France most men's talk goes on in cafés—not the ones that serve transients but real neighborhood cafés, where clients are known by name and have their usual drinks and regular tables. Customers observe weekly and daily patterns. A man on his way home from work may stop off for a drink at a café near his bus stop or subway station. On Sunday mornings between eleven and twelve he may go to a different café to share a glass of white wine with old friends while scanning the racing forms. It would be easy to construct an elaborate typology.

Café conversations are very different from conversations between shopkeepers and clients. There is less talk about private affairs, more about work, business, and politics. When private life is discussed, it is often in conventionally masculine terms. To anyone not in the know, the conversation might seem to consist of comments of the sort that men customarily make about women. But this too is a formalized exchange governed by the rules of propriety, and the ribaldry functions as a kind of code. What is said is not to be taken seriously, and if anyone were to take offense he would be exhibiting a flawed character. Yet many a personal confidence has been exchanged in the guise of such jocular dialogue.

A café frequented by habitués, a center of male social life.

This fact helps to explain the importance of the café in France, a country in which some 480,000 establishments were licensed to sell alcoholic beverages on the eve of World War I and some 500,000 on the eve of World War II—more than one "bistro" per hundred inhabitants. Even the smallest village had more than one café, and in industrial towns their number was legion: one per fifty inhabitants of Roubaix at the end of the nineteenth century. The small size of working-class apartments was part of the reason for the popularity of the café, and no study of workingmen's sociability is complete without a stop at the *cabaret* or *estaminet*.[4] From the middle of the nineteenth until the middle of the twentieth century the private life of the common people spilled over into these public places, which *argousins* (cops) and *rats de cave* (revenuers) kept a close eye on.

In a sense the French of this period spent as much time in their *quartier* or village as they did at home. Colette Pétonnet has traced the daily routine of a woman whom the welfare authorities wished to relocate. Admittedly she lived in a wretchedly shabby room, but she was also at home in the streets of her neighborhood. What good would a modern apartment be if she lost her familiar streets?[5] To draw a clear-cut distinction between a purely private home and a wholly public outside world is a peculiarly bourgeois perception. For the Neapolitans described by Sartre and, to a lesser degree, for the average Frenchman in years past, the opposition was less dramatic. The neighborhood was indeed set apart from private space, but as a kind of protective zone around it. Thanks to the observance of the proprieties, the neighborhood could remain open and public yet still welcome the spillover of private life, which neighbors supported, and also on occasion controlled. It formed a complex transitional zone.

DESTRUCTIONS AND RECONSTRUCTIONS

Recent urbanization has destroyed this subtle interplay of public and private. The "culture of the poor" could be passed on from generation to generation only where the population was relatively stable and there was time to assimilate newcomers.[6] From 1954 to 1968, however, France experienced a period of very rapid urbanization. The percentage of urban dwellers increased from 58.6 percent to 71.3 percent of the population.[7] Subsequently the pace slowed, so that by 1982 the figure had climbed to only 73.4 percent.

The sudden growth of the cities aggravated the housing crisis and led to various attempted remedies. During the first half of the twentieth century the pace of construction was slow, yet another reason for the persistence of working-class neighborhoods and their associated culture. The result was a housing shortage. Large numbers of new buildings were required, and entire sections of older cities needed rebuilding. The new high-rise housing constituted a sudden leap into modernity. Here I am interested primarily in those sections that were entirely reconstructed and then populated with people from other places. There is scarcely any historical precedent for relocation on such a vast scale. Not only did the new residents have no tradition, they even lacked the means to create one. The new populations tended to be homogeneous, all of the same generation and similar family situation. The elderly were sorely lacking. A few grandmothers lived with their children, but there were none of the solitary old people

Modern city planning treats movement as a problem of flow. There is no opportunity for chance encounters, for efficiency precludes idle ambling.

who in older neighborhoods served as repositories of local memories and arbiters of the proprieties and who with sharp eyes observed everyone's comings and goings from behind drawn curtains. When schoolchildren and workers left the neighborhood every morning, the life was drained out.

Modern urban design and architecture have disrupted the space of the neighborhood, making the task of relating public to private even more difficult. Small streets have been eliminated, small shops have been replaced by shopping centers usually reached by automobile. In this functional environment it no longer makes sense to go out for a walk. High rents have driven the neighborhood café out of existence, leaving only the larger, more impersonal cafés to serve their former clientele (although at certain hours when off-track betting windows are open a semblance of neighborhood life may revive).

The Disruption of Neighborhoods

Relations with neighbors have also changed. An elevator is not like a street. In the street you can watch people go by, see where they stop, note differences between buildings. The passengers in an elevator are hidden from view; they enter their buildings through indistinguishable entranceways and exit the elevator on floors that are as alike as two peas in a pod. Similarity engenders anonymity. Yet people still have neighbors, whom they can hear through thin walls even if they cannot see them. A 1964 study examined social relations in high-rise apartment buildings. Sixty-eight percent of the residents had no sustained contact with anyone else using the same entry; 50 percent had no relations with anyone in the entire complex; and 21 percent had no relations with anyone anywhere.[8]

Let us avoid facile nostalgia, however. City planners are not to blame for what is actually the effect of a deep-seated social trend. To be sure, the high-rise designers and slum renovators of the 1950s and 1960s failed to grasp the fact that urban forms fulfill social functions beyond their obviously utilitarian uses in providing housing and promoting commerce and industry. Consequently, they built buildings that make no provision for the development of a transitional zone between public and private. But older neighborhoods have also evolved. As recently as the late 1970s it was still possible for Pierre Mayol to study the rules of propriety that governed life in the streets of Croix-Rousse. But even there, where the old

The retail outlet has become an assembly-line operation, leaving no room for neighbors to meet.

street life was exceptionally well preserved, it was no longer as rich as it once had been and people no longer knew their neighbors as well. Life styles have changed. People are in more of a hurry and spend less time in the neighborhood. Also the rule of propriety was not all positive; constant surveillance, criticism, and malicious gossip were part of it. Modern individualism cannot easily tolerate such close supervision. How can you "do your own thing" when neighborhood gossips are constantly spying on you? Bourgeois norms have not been imposed on the poor just by city planners, public health officials, and housing renovators. They have spread, more widely and more subtly, by contagion to the new middle class of white-collar workers. The young management trainee who moves out of the old neighborhood with its myriad rules and obligations has moved up a step in the social hierarchy.

In some areas the rules of propriety have reestablished themselves, although in more limited, less coercive forms than in the past. Even in supermarkets cordial relations sometimes develop between customers and personnel. These relations are limited, however, by the fact that the store personnel have no independent knowledge of their customers' lives.

The high-rise complex—anonymous, mass-produced housing. Gone are the streets and meeting places of old.

Single-Family Homes

The social life that develops in neighborhoods of single-family homes is more interesting and varied. Again the picture is complicated by regional and social differences. A contrast is usually drawn between the habits of the French, who customarily enclose their property, and those of the Americans, who allow one yard to merge imperceptibly into the next. Indeed, when NATO forces withdrew from France in 1966 and housing developments abandoned by the U.S. Army were sold to French citizens, the new owners' first concern was to build fences. Within a few months a sort of suburban equivalent of the rural hedgerow had sprung up on what had been a continuous expanse of green. It is superficial, however, to interpret the change as a mark of French individualism. On closer examination the way in which space was appropriated turns out to have been quite subtle. True, each resident who erected a fence was staking out the boundaries of what he owned; the fence was an affirmation of private property. Yet the kind of fence that went up depended on where it stood on the property. Fences were higher in the back and on the sides

A new town in which street life has been restored. Neighborhood life may become possible once again.

than in front of the house facing the street. This was because different sections of the yard serve different purposes.

The house divides the property into two distinct parts.[9] The back yard is purely private, an intimate setting where the family can dine outdoors on warm summer evenings. Here the wash is hung out and space may be set aside for an herb and vegetable garden. The front yard, by contrast, is for show. Homeowners are careful to present a good image of themselves. Well-kept lawns and flowerbeds, illuminated statuary, and showy vases contribute to the facade. A low fence or hedge marks the boundaries of the property and restricts access but not visibility; neighbors can talk right over it. The street itself, visible from the windows, is domesticated space. If there is not too much traffic, children can play or ride their bicycles there. Thus a new kind of transitional space has been created in the suburban development, a space governed by its own rules of propriety.

Places for meeting and exchange frequently develop around the foci of private life. The latest architectural trends take the need for such space into account. The functionalist theories that dominated urban planning twenty years ago have given way to culturalist views, and it is now common for architects to incorporate pedestrian walkways and small squares into their designs. The differences between today's projects and those completed no more than ten years ago can be quite striking.

Semiprivate areas also develop outside residential neighborhoods. At work they provide a kind of refuge where informal social exchanges may take place, such as plant or office cafeterias or nearby cafés where people who work together can go during breaks. In some offices there is a lunchroom or coffeeroom where employees can spend a few moments away from superiors and clients. The organization is temporarily forgotten as private life asserts itself in the very heart of the workplace.

Such semiprivate meeting areas give rise to a variety of interchanges. Sometimes the groups that gather are composed exclusively of women, other times of men, although mixed groups are also common, especially in the less intimate environment of a factory cafeteria. People discuss the incidents of the working day, and rumors fly. A kind of workplace sociability develops, and in some companies committees may even organize employee trips, ski weekends, fishing expeditions, athletic events, shows, musicals, courses, or group purchases.

Even in a suburban development like this one, where each family has its own yard, children can play in the streets, for there is little traffic.

Personal matters may be discussed: vacations, children, domestic concerns. Once again the rules of propriety allow people to reveal themselves discreetly to others whom they have neither deliberately chosen nor pointedly rejected. Life today affords greater opportunity for this type of relationship to develop at the workplace than in the neighborhood.

The development of semiprivate zones within the workplace is but one aspect of a more general trend. Private life, driven out of the public world of work, has been quietly finding its way back in. Although the boundary between public and private is more sharply defined than ever before, each may still influence the other across the boundary. The clear-cut division of space and time between work and private life is attenuated on the margins by a complex series of transitions. More than that, it is partially overcome by the interactions between the two.

PRIVATE NORMS IN PUBLIC LIFE

As productive labor moved out of the private sphere, it was subjected to functional, impersonal norms. As jobs and work relations came to be regulated by formal rules, workers

ceased to feel responsible to a single individual. The working world became bureaucratized. Direct, face-to-face relations tended to be avoided, and the power of managers was hidden behind impersonal rules, directives, and evaluations issued from on high. Employees tended more and more to limit their relations to the workplace. In a 1960 study of postal workers Michel Crozier found that they rarely saw each other outside work. A person's involvement in his or her work was strictly limited; real life was private life.

As I have shown, certain kinds of congenial interaction among coworkers developed in reaction to this bureaucratic universe. As workers sought to reestablish warm personal relations within the cold and impersonal workplace setting, the effects spilled over beyond the cafeteria, the lunchroom, and the break period and affected all aspects of the organization of work.

What has been called young people's "allergy to work"[10] reflects not so much a repudiation of effort as a difficulty entering into a hierarchical and purely functional system of relations. A poll conducted by a respected organization in 1975

Young People and Work

A modern office building, functional but impersonal. The individual is a cog in a large machine.

showed that the most important characteristic of a job, for 73 percent of the young people questioned, was that it be tailored to their personal tastes. That the job should be respected, socially useful, or afford an opportunity for independence were less highly valued qualities. This desire for personal growth on the job frequently led to disappointment, which in turn was responsible for a high degree of instability among people in the early stages of their professional careers. In 1974, before the recession hit the job market, one poll found that 43 percent of the young people sampled had already quit at least one job.[11] Admittedly many of these were temporary or seasonal employments, but we may ask whether young workers took these jobs because they were the only ones available or because their temporary nature made them less daunting.

A similar ambiguity surrounds the market for temporary workers. The first agencies to offer the services of temps in France were established in the 1950s: Bis in 1954 and Manpower in 1956. By 1962, 170 employment agencies in the country employed some 15,000 temporary workers. By 1980 there were more than 3,500 employing more than 200,000 people, most of whom were young. Many of these were relatively unskilled high-school dropouts who had grown up in suburban apartment complexes, a background that carried a kind of stigma at that time. Yet while these young people faced a bleak future, they were not without aspirations. The sociologist Bernard Galambaud studied the attitudes of a group of such youngsters from the Paris region in 1975. He found that young temporaries placed an extremely high value on actual workplace experience. When confronted with a choice between very interesting work in a relatively unfriendly environment and less interesting work in a relatively friendly environment, six out of ten chose the latter. The younger they were, the more importance they attached to the work environment: 70 percent of those under twenty made this the primary criterion, compared with 60 percent in the twenty–twenty-five age group and 50 percent in the twenty-five–thirty group.[12] It also emerged that what constituted a good working environment was the existence of authentic personal relations among the employees. When such relations did not exist, 61 percent of those surveyed preferred to change jobs rather than ignore their coworkers, in whom they valued frankness (46 percent) more than intelligence (31 percent) or competence (16 percent). In short, the picture of the workers that emerges from Galambaud's study differs sharply from that of the bureaucratic employee described by Crozier. The behavior of today's younger workers challenges the formal, functional organization of work. For them there is no such thing as work relations, only human relations.

This insistence on the rights of private life within the working environment is not limited to the young. One reason for the major strike that affected the banking industry in 1974 was reaction against the changes in working conditions that followed the introduction of computerized banking systems. The resulting reorganization left many employees feeling that their jobs had become meaningless and their relations with other employees had been destroyed. Taylorism, or scientific management, is not dead yet, but it is increasingly contested. New methods seek to give more autonomy to work groups in order to foster closer relations among workers. So-called quality circles are one remedy that has been proposed to rescue companies hamstrung by rigid formalism. Indeed, the clearest sign of the impact of private values on work life has been in the area of evolving concepts of the organization.

Corporate Authority

Throughout the first half of the twentieth century organization theorists approved of hierarchical systems. Taylorism accorded well with the French tradition of command. The engineer cultivated the image of a commander. He was even called a *chef* until the word fell into disrepute after 1945 because of its fascist connotations (*der Führer* translates as *le chef*). People discussed the "social role" of the engineer much as Lyautey, at the turn of the century, had discussed that of the military officer.[13] The hierarchy of an industrial organization was as clearly delineated as that of an army. In the mines, engineers were provided with a special bathroom and fresh soap and towels; the firm also provided a clean suit of clothes every day and paid for a servant for each engineer. Pit chiefs were allowed a shower stall and assigned an aide to polish their boots; the company paid for brown work uniforms. Foremen had individual showers furnished with soap from Marseilles and received a fresh pair of overalls every two weeks. Ordinary miners had to pay for their own overalls and soap and shared common showers and locker rooms.[14] In the Renault plant at Flins in 1970, "clothes made the boss: blue shirts for team leaders, white shirts for shop foremen and floor managers. Above that rank, managers wore suits, ties, held their heads high, and looked haughty."[15]

Over the 1950s and 1960s this hierarchical conception came under attack as American theories of human relations gained influence. The French style of authority and command seemed stiff compared with American-style management. It was possible for a manager to discharge his responsibilities without putting quite so much distance between himself and his subordinates. It was argued that a less rigid, less formal style that would afford workers greater autonomy might prove more effective. American sociologists were read and translated, and the phrase "democratic leadership" entered the vocabulary of the organization. And terminology is not without significance: a *chef* commands, a "leader" (the English term was taken over into French) shows the way to collaborators who assume an active role.

Psychologists and psychosociologists such as Roger Mucchielli and Guy Palmade conducted seminars for business leaders that gave wide currency to the new ideas. Influenced by the new management techniques, new organizations such as the Association pour la Recherche et l'Intervention Psychosociologiques (ARIP, established in 1959) worked to spread them still further, as did older organizations such as CEGOS (Commission d'Études Générales des Organisations). At a 1966 seminar in Dourdan, two hundred managers crowded into a lecture hall to hear a talk on nondirective management techniques. Theory jostled theory, while certain academic sociologists attempted to bring order to chaos. Missionaries of varying degrees of competence sold business firms on a variety of psychological techniques, with group dynamics (based on the American T-group) perhaps the most widely adopted. In a myriad of ways interpersonal relations assumed an important place on the corporate agenda.

The impact of these new ideas on workplace relations is hard to gauge. Large firms apparently were affected more than small ones, and the service sector more than industry. The creation of on-the-job professional advancement programs can be used as a rough indicator. Even before a 1971 law compelled businesses to devote 1 percent of their total payroll to such programs, companies like Electricité de France, Air France, and Saint-Gobain were already spending more than this amount. Other companies, such as CGE, had set up their own in-house training units. In 1968, when the ministry of national education set up a short-lived office of professional advancement, it chose the director of Renault's training affiliate to be its head.

There is evidence that management attitudes actually did change at around this time. Daniel Mothé has found that a change in management style occurred around 1965 at Renault. Managers began to shake hands with workers at the beginning of each day. "Of the essential laws that have been discovered, the first is that you have to be nice to your employees. So thoroughly has this precept demonstrated its worth that it is universally accepted. Management instills the need to be nice in its foremen, who interpret it as best they can and, in so doing, obtain results that put the authoritarian methods of the old shop-floor despots to shame . . . The second law is: You have to let people express themselves."[16]

Actually talking things over with employees worked better for management than had more authoritarian tactics, because workers were then more willing to follow orders. Thus managers began to implement the recommendations of organization-theory textbooks.

1968: A Protest against Hierarchy

Changes were reinforced and radicalized by the events of 1968—the riots and rebellions of students and workers. Previously the initiative lay with management, which was naturally cautious; now workers included changes in work relations among their demands. Students set the tone by challenging the pedagogical authority of their teachers. Knowledge formed the basis of that authority but could not protect it, for knowledge itself was attacked as abstract, impersonal and irrelevant to the needs of individuals and the community. People felt called upon to speak in the first person, to expose themselves, to say what they thought rather than simply what they knew. Protesters gleefully tore off social masks in search of genuine personalities underneath. In the occupied Sorbonne, students presided over vast assemblies in which everyone was allowed to speak. If a professor or lecturer had something to say, he had to raise his hand and wait his turn like anyone else. To some this was an intolerable affront.

The same spirit of protest soon spread to the factories. While *gauchistes* (left-wingers) attacked the stodginess of union bureaucracies, strike-committee leaders consulted constantly with the rank and file—a notable difference from the factory occupations of 1936. The strike was not aimed solely at achieving wage increases or a change in government. In a confused way the strikers also sought greater responsibility for themselves in the work process and a transformation of hierarchical

Lycée students demonstrating in 1986. The climate was very different from that of 1968: there was no violence, and student autonomy was now taken for granted rather than proclaimed as a demand.

workplace relations. In 1968 socialism could no longer be defined as advocacy of an end to private ownership of the means of production; it had taken on a new libertarian component. Amid the creative ferment of those unprecedented weeks, libertarian aims even gained priority. The protesters insisted on the need to "change life" and to "prohibit prohibition." With a deep yearning for sincerity and joy, everyone spoke and expected others to listen. When such things happen in the name of socialism, socialism ceases to be an economic or even a political doctrine and becomes a secularized eschatology.

The desire to restructure public workplace relations so as to reflect private standards applicable to volitional, reciprocal interpersonal relations can be seen with exceptional clarity in the Lip strike of 1973. To the strikers the most important thing was contact with one another, friendship. "In the course of this struggle many people have changed and are now quite frankly different men, and it's good to work with them and argue with them," according to strike leader Charles Piaget. The secretary of the factory committee echoed these sentiments: "In this struggle 95 percent of the people have been able to discover just how important human values are, and just how much generosity and friendship have emerged. In speaking to one another we no longer use the formal *vous,* we

The strike at Lip was not only a struggle but an opportunity for people to get to know one another.

use the familiar *tu* . . . We have discovered one another." Ordinary workers corroborated him: "Now we all know each other . . . We all call each other *tu* . . . Friendship develops of its own accord . . . I don't think we'll be as anonymous as we were before."[17]

Self-Management as Utopia

It is not difficult to understand the power and appeal of such aspirations, nor is it difficult to see why they failed. Personal objectives can all too easily obscure the facts of the situation. The determination not to surrender any of one's freedom leads to a refusal to delegate authority and thus to direct democracy, instability, and organizational weakness. Work and politics belong to the public domain, which is governed by rules of its own, and it is unrealistic to think that the public sphere can be turned into a meeting place and theater of individual development. Self-management, an attempt to impose private norms on the public sphere, is a utopian notion.

This soon became apparent. The self-management movement that grew out of the events of 1968 attracted only a minority following in the years that followed. The CFDT (Confédération Française et Démocratique du Travail) and PSU (Parti Socialiste Unifié, a New Leftish group founded by Michel Rocard) incorporated it into their programs, but it was rejected by most of the CGT (Confédération Générale du Travail). The newly formed Socialist Party occasionally referred to the term self-management, but in a more moderate context. Recession and unemployment changed the climate after 1973, and self-management largely dropped out of political and union debate.

Uneasiness about important institutions remained, however. Only the form of its expression changed. The unions consolidated their position under the law of 1968 and the Auroux laws, but meanwhile their membership dwindled and recruitment of leaders became difficult. As the unions became more institutionalized, their support declined. Nevertheless, the rigid formalism and hierarchy of public life continued to be challenged, but now behavior rather than organizations became the target. The focus shifted from management and organization to habits and customs.

TOWARD A MORE RELAXED SOCIETY

Slowly and unevenly a measure of flexibility began to be introduced into the formerly rigid codes that had previously governed public life. This change was in fact part of a larger challenge that was mounted to the existing pattern of social roles.

At one time public life was organized in such a way that each individual was assigned a particular status and function; this status and function in turn determined the person's public role. Behavior thus became predictable, but exchanges and contacts were limited and spontaneity was suppressed. More recently status differences have tended to disappear, as if the people who face each other in the public arena, unique and equal individuals, were to be accepted as such, with all their distinguishing characteristics. Fundamentally this refusal to be classified or defined in terms of status reflects a determination to be treated, even in the public sphere, as a private individual. The result has been an attenuation of social roles.

That attenuation probably began not in the relatively grim areas of industry or politics but in the more frivolous ones of sport and leisure activities. There was nothing inevitable about this. In the past in fact the hierarchical organization of scout camps had taught adolescents the nature of social roles. But new kinds of organizations developed, the most significant being Club Méditerranée.[18] Its success stemmed from the difference between the type of social relations encouraged at its vacation spots and those found in everyday life. Club resorts are closed compounds, and the welcoming ceremonies stress the difference between life inside and life outside. Visible signs of social and status distinctions are abolished. Another type of hierarchy is established through sports and games. Once formal constraints are removed, "true" human relations are free to develop. The clubs encourage "encounters, exchanges, [and] opportunities to join groups based on your own affinities." Thus the private self is able to flourish in a public setting.

Vacations: A State of Mind

Seen in this way, vacations are not a time or a place but a state of mind, and valued as such. The function of the club personnel is to help guests discover that state of mind; for that reason, unlike hotel personnel, they share in the guests' activities to some extent. The vacation industry promotes contacts, smiles, and relaxation as norms. The ability to endure ridicule in games, for example, shows that a person is open and friendly, a "good sport." The earnestness of ordinary social life has no place here; it is "square." In Edgar Morin's phrase, the value of vacations is the vacation of values.[19]

A vacation is a break from everday routine, and a trip to a club resort, however idealized, is an escape. The media, particularly radio and television, have done much to popularize a more relaxed everyday life-style. The radio station Europe One, established in 1955, pioneered a new style of programming in which listeners were encouraged to participate in broadcasts. Game shows masked differences in the statuses and roles of participants through the use of first names and a warm if superficial familiarity. The new tone set by such programs became available for the ordinary exchanges of daily life.

The same tone crept into billboard and television advertisements. Ads ceased to convey information; instead they took pleasure in their own frivolity and triviality. The product to be sold was set against an implausible but humorous backdrop. Verbal and visual puns abounded, and seriousness was avoided at all cost. In this connection Gilles Lipovetsky has remarked on the novel importance of humor in today's society.[20] Earlier forms of humor from Molière to Charlie Chaplin featured characters who unwittingly made fun of themselves; the new comedy made fun of *itself,* mocked its own silliness. It was an era much given to deflating the sanctimonious and to revealing the hollowness of traditional social and political figures. This corrosive demystification undermined the very structure of public life.

The events of 1968 marked a major milestone along this path. The protesters who took to the streets in May challenged the belief that people ought to talk and act in a manner befitting their social status. They insisted that everyone, regardless of function, behave "authentically." Old norms lost credibility, because their legitimacy could no longer be taken for granted. Anyone who remained "in character" was dismissed as "conventional." Those who continued to play roles became identified with the much-denounced institutions they served; they acquiesced in their own alienation.

The Success of Feminism

The role traditionally ascribed to women was subjected to particularly vehement attack. Feminism did not originate in 1968, but the movement then gained momentum that it retained for several more years. In 1972 militant feminists mobilized to win legalization of abortion. After that was granted in 1975, they continued to work to ensure that the new law would be enforced. At a deeper level, the success of feminism has had much to do with the movement's insistence on complete equality between women and men. The battle has been not a war of the sexes but a struggle against sexist discrimination that has garnered wide support extending far beyond the younger generation, where tenets of the women's movement are accepted as self-evident. Simply being a woman is no reason for doing one thing and not doing another; in itself sex requires no specific behavior. Sex roles are outmoded because they stand in the way of self-affirmation and self-expression.

Changes in dress reflect the weakening of familiar statuses and roles. The decline of the skirt is a sure sign of the obliteration of traditional sex roles. In 1965 for the first time the number of women's slacks sold exceeded the number of skirts. In 1971, 15 million dresses were sold, compared with 14 million pairs of pants. Blue jeans have become ubiquitous, the number manufactured having quadrupled between 1970 and 1976. Young men allow their hair to grow long and wear bracelets and neck chains; young women hide their figures beneath voluminous sweaters.

"Women, you are not rabbits." Women demanded autonomy for themselves within the family and, if necessary, against it.

The rules of dress have become less rigid. May 1968 marks a break with the past and the end of old taboos. In girls' *lycées,* where students were once forbidden to wear makeup and female teachers were not allowed to wear slacks, a wide variety of dress is now acceptable. In the university an ancient idol was smashed when the necktie was abandoned; foulards and turtlenecks are a clear sign of liberalization. Beards abound. Executives wear sport jackets and open shirts on warm summer days. Lacoste shirts are seen in offices as well as at resorts. Even politicians have hastened to show that they are not stuffed shirts or sticks-in-the-mud. Valéry Giscard d'Estaing appeared on television in a sweater while serving as a government minister. During the ceremonies marking his inauguration as president of France, he walked up the Champs-Elysées in a suit rather than the traditional morning coat, out of place in the new relaxed France.

In fact the whole system of fashion began to fall apart. The fashion industry reached its apogee in the early 1960s. By then the vast majority of women would await the arrival of new fall fashions—not just the small minority of fashion-conscious society women who had sustained the industry fifty years earlier. The essence of fashion is change; old clothes become obsolete, so new ones must be bought. Those who follow fashion are set apart socially from those who do not. Yet even as fashions change, dress continues to convey an intelligible message. Different styles refer to different social situations. There are sweaters to be worn by the fireplace, clothes for the hunt, outfits for an autumn walk in the woods, others for an evening on the town or for cocktails or an afternoon's shopping or a late-night party.[21] To dress fashion-ably and well, one must not only have taste but also demonstrate a mastery of the social codes governing appearance at such public occasions.

The very success of the fashion industry has been responsible for its demise. As the appeal of fashion reached an ever-growing number of women, it began to affect some unable to afford a different outfit for every occasion. A secretary or typist had to be able to wear the same dress or skirt to the office that she wore to the movies and still be considered well dressed. The accent shifted to accessories and outfits: one skirt worn with a variety of blouses could serve many purposes. By changing belts, gloves, shoes, scarves, handbags, and jewelry a woman could work endless variations on the same basic theme. Rules of dress became increasingly sophisticated.

Dressing is no longer a matter of conforming to social codes but a form of self-expression.

A Subtler Dress Code

Further change has complicated the issue. It became fashionable to make fun of fashion and to wear clothes that were strictly speaking out of place: exotic Indian and Mexican costumes, clothes that were either too much or too little for the occasion or too young or too old for the individual wearing them. Dress lost its conventional and customary meaning. People twisted the codes, investing them with personal meaning. Change was still of the essence, but being fashionable ceased to mean following fashion. The point now was to use fashion to demonstrate that one was not fashion's fool. Thus dress ceased to demonstrate the adaptation of the individual to public life and became a way of demonstrating publicly one's unique personality.

Does this mean that private norms and values entered the public sphere? I think not, for two reasons. The first has to do with the nature of the new norms. The relaxation of forms of address, the use of first names, the attenuation of traditional roles, the importance of humor and fashion—all these things represent an effort to restore individual particularities in the public setting. Nevertheless, public life was not thereby transformed into private life. Today's society may be held together by more flexible modes of regulation than in the past, social codes may have become more subtle and discreet, but rules remain. One cannot say whatever one pleases to a superior or colleague, nor can one dress however one wishes. A person

The clothes in this scene are less interesting than the postures and their meaning.

who wishes to express him- or herself in public must conform to social codes more complex but just as real as those that existed in the past. The person who, on grounds of authenticity, voices some feeling at work in the same terms as that person might do at home will very likely be misunderstood. Social rules may have changed, but they have not disappeared.

The second reason has to do with the evolution of private life itself. The changes just analyzed have been offset by countervailing changes: public life has infiltrated and transformed even the most intimate of private refuges.

The Impact of the Public on the Private

The Media: Press, Radio, Television

Recent years have witnessed a prodigious burgeoning of the mass media. At the turn of the century there was only one way for public opinion to breach the walls of the domestic fortress: through print, primarily in the form of newspapers. Newspapers created a distance between the news and their readers; the mediation of the written word was abstract, and it took time for news to reach its destination. Here, however, I choose to focus on other aspects of the print media.

Originally French newspapers were essentially local journals. In 1912 there were more than 300 daily papers in France: 62 in Paris, 242 in the provinces.[22] Ninety-four provincial cities had daily papers. In addition there were some 1,662 provincial weeklies and biweeklies, often more widely read than the dailies. Broadly speaking, the press in the early 1900s was a local press. Although local papers reported the national and international news, they were rooted in the same environment as their readers. They provided a window on the world, while at the same time they respected local proprieties.

World War I created problems for these local papers, which were not well placed to report news from the front. More than one paper ceased publication during the war, only to find it impossible to resume in the troubled economic climate that followed. By 1922 the number of provincial weeklies had dropped to 982, and by 1938 it was down to 860.

By the latter date the print media had to contend with a new competitor: radio. The first broadcast station in France began transmitting in 1920; in 1922 a second station began broadcasting from atop the Eiffel Tower. Their audience was limited, however, by the poor quality of the crystal receivers

available at the time. Radio did not really catch on until the introduction of the vacuum tube, which made receivers easier to tune and permitted the use of loudspeakers. By 1930 some 500,000 receivers were in use throughout France. Four years later, in 1934, there were 1,400,000 sets in use, though most French people still learned of the events of February 6 via the newspapers rather than the radio. But during the Munich conference of 1938 people stayed glued to some 4,700,000 radio receivers throughout France. A year later the number of radios was up to 5,200,000, and in June 1940 countless French men and women heard Marshal Pétain announce that he would seek an armistice with Germany. Few people heard de Gaulle's June 18 appeal to the French to continue their resistance, but during the Occupation many spent their evenings listening to BBC broadcasts from London.

The early vacuum–tube sets were large and heavy and required external antennas. They occupied a place of honor in the kitchen or living room. Listening to broadcasts was a

Television makes its tempting début. Radios have been reduced in size but not yet transistorized.

Three eras in the history of radio. 1942, a vacuum tube radio at home; 1964, a transistor radio on the beach; and today, the Walkman. The first two were suitable for group listening, the latter only for individual listening.

family activity, and in many homes people gathered around the dinner table to hear the news. After the war people continued to buy radios, and until 1958 there was little change in the nature of radio listening.

By that date some 10 million radios were in use in France, and more than 80 percent of all households had at least one. The spread of radio listening seemed to have leveled off when technology came to the rescue: the solid-state revolution began with the invention of the transistor. These tiny devices replaced the power-hungry tubes of an earlier era, making it possible to build relatively low-cost, lightweight units that could run on batteries. By 1959 half the radios manufactured used transistors, and by 1962 nearly all did. French soldiers in Algeria were among the first to buy transistor radios, as the officers who staged a would-be coup in 1961 discovered to their dismay. Cheap and portable, the transistor radio quickly became an individual listening post. The manner in which the radio was used changed. Once a family affair, listening now became individualized. Young people bought radios so that they could listen freely to music their parents disliked. Receivers moved into the bedroom and bathroom. Private space was opened up to sounds from the outside world. The clamor of the entire world could now be heard in the most private sanctum of the home.

Simultaneously the television set supplanted the big family radio. Images were first transmitted over the airwaves in the 1930s, but these early experimental transmissions were over short distances only. The first televised news program in France was broadcast in 1949, at a time when there were only 300 television receivers in the country. Progress was slow. In order to broadcast programs nationwide, a costly network of relay stations had to be constructed. As recently as 1956 only half the population, occupying just one-third of France's land area, could receive television broadcasts.[23] In 1959 the first national television network in France began operations. At that time there were some 1,400,000 TV sets in the country, and just over 10 percent of all households had at least one.

With the invention of the transistor, television sets became smaller and cheaper, and more and more households acquired one. In 1964, when a second national network was created, there were 5,400,000 sets in 40 percent of French homes. By 1968, 62 percent of all households had a TV, and by 1974, when the second network began color transmissions, 82 percent did. Today, depending on social level, anywhere from 88 to 96 percent of homes have a TV set, two-thirds of which are color.

The presence of radio and television sets in nearly all homes is a social change of major importance. The average person today watches television sixteen hours per week: twenty-four minutes of television per hour of work. TV sets are still too expensive for each member of the family to own one. The family watches television together, while individuals listen to the radio alone. Together, these two media are capable of filling every minute of leisure time, and many people today rely on the radio to put them to sleep at night and wake them up in the morning.

The other information media have suffered from the competition. The number of daily newspapers in Paris dropped from 36 in 1946 to 19 in 1981, and in the provinces from 184 to 75. The decline in circulation is just as precipitous: from 370 papers per 1,000 population in 1946 to 197 in 1978.[24] To be sure, news magazines have expanded, and televised news documentaries are increasingly popular. Television and radio now dominate the news business; the print media fill in the gaps by providing in-depth information, specialized reporting, and local news. But the broadcast media get the news out more quickly to more people.

This has been more than a change in medium. The news

broadcast by radio and television is not the same news that used to be carried in the newspapers. The very function of the news has been transformed.

LIBERATED CONFORMISM

The turn-of-the-century press was oriented entirely toward public life. The subject might be politics or the local county fair, but it was public, not private. The papers did not tell readers about themselves. They gave advice about farming or politics but avoided personal topics. Advertising was relatively unimportant. When present at all, it was limited to texts and slogans, with few pictures. It conveyed a message, not a subliminal suggestion. A newspaper was not a looking glass.

Admittedly, even before World War I the movies offered private idylls and melodramas to urban and suburban audiences. In the period between the two World Wars, movie-going was the primary diversion of the general public. Some people deplored the fact that the movies were not exerting a proper moral influence on the working-class families that flocked every week to the local theater.[25] But the films portrayed another world. They might stimulate dreams and encourage identification, but everyone knew that what they depicted was not real life.

The popularity of film affected the print media. Films were not all make-believe: weekly newsreels showed the news as it was happening. As the technology for printing photographs improved (heliogravure, 1912; phototelegraphy, 1914; offset printing, 1932), newspapers began to include pictures, not just line drawings possibly enhanced with color but actual photographs, which lent authenticity to the news.

Pictures, legitimized by their use in reporting the news, soon found other uses, most notably in advertising. A whole new branch of publishing came into existence: the women's magazines. First came the fashion magazines, the most famous of which was *Le Petit Echo de la mode.* This and other weekly magazines contained advice concerning the latest fashions but little else. On the eve of World War II a new type of woman's magazine emerged: *Marie-Claire* appeared in 1937, followed by *Confidences* in 1938. Both quickly achieved circulations in excess of one million. The most successful of all was *Elle,* which began publication in 1945. In addition to recipes and patterns for knitting and sewing, these magazines offered con-

Women's Magazines

Magazines are advisers as well as mirrors, combining escape with everyday life.

fident but friendly advice on grooming, makeup, interior decorating, pleasing husbands, and raising children.

In an effort to personalize this advice, the magazines conducted reader polls to find out what women were thinking. Letters from readers aroused tremendous interest. Those written by readers of *Confidences,* Evelyne Sullerot discovered, contained a "frightful outpouring of distress, suffering, illness, and vice, appeals for help of every variety . . . The flood of letters demonstrated all too well the real need for such an anonymous form of the confessional."[26] Columnists such as Marcelle Auclair, Marcelle Ségal, and Ménie Grégoire, who answered readers' letters, became confessors to the nation. New moral authorities, they dispensed intimate advice to millions every week.

The Onslaught of Advertising

Advertisers were intrigued by the success of the women's magazines. As early as 1932 manufacturers of perfumes and cosmetics discovered the virtues of advertising in *Votre beauté.* Advertisements with color photographs not only lured buyers to new consumer products but spread new norms and values. Ads for lingerie, cosmetics, and summer resorts encouraged new adulation of the body. Ads for fruit juice and yogurt changed eating habits. Refrigerators, washing machines, stoves, and other major appliances were depicted in ads that made kitchens look like laboratories; second-hand furniture stores were filled with old cabinets replaced by new formica countertops. Radio and television further multiplied the power of advertising. Soon people were not only in touch with the most remote corners of the world but inundated with publicity touting a new way of life, perhaps even a new ethos.

Advertising as decoration.

Advertising contributed greatly to the erosion of rules that once had governed private life. Since it existed for one reason and one reason only—to sell new products—advertising was obliged by its very nature to break down resistance. Often that resistance was justified by tradition: "That's not the way things are done." Advertisers quickly learned how to make such attitudes look quaint: "Up-to-the-minute people don't do things the old-fashioned way." Or they appealed to vague longings: "Have it your way." Or they extolled independence and nonconformity: "I make my own rules."

Quietly and subtly, advertising shapes the way people live. Each person feels that he or she is acting independently, but all these independent decisions add up to an expanding market for the latest mass-produced product. People feel more individualistic, but meanwhile tastes and fashions become more and more standardized. The illusion of independence gives rise to conformity.

Liberated conformism is not limited to life-styles and consumer purchases; it also affects values and ideas. The great principles of the moment are quietly propagated by the media. Believing themselves well-informed, everyone hails the liberation of Cambodia, only to discover a few years later the bloody atrocities committed by the regime of Pol Pot. People who believe they are thinking for themselves repeat the views of the latest opinionmaker. Intimate gossip is broadcast over the airwaves. Even our dreams are filled with images that come to us via the media. What historian can say how much the way we love has been affected by the movies?

None of this is the result of behind-the-scenes machinations; it is simply the way our society works. No Machiavellian decisionmakers sit dreaming up ways to impose their ideology. Those who run the media and create the advertising have no such intention. They are in any case a nebulous group, whose membership is constantly changing and in which no one person holds real power. Each is simply doing his or her job. But the nature of the media is such that no conspiracy is necessary: everyone takes an interest in the same subjects at the same time and forms the same opinions. The listening, watching, and reading public supports them and assures their success. Journalists believe that they are dealing with issues that interest the public; so long as they are not boring, the public believes them. In order not to be boring, journalists personalize their reporting.

News used to be information: public issues were presented as such, in their generality and exteriority. Now we have communication: we are all supposed to become personally involved in the issues of the day. General problems are cast in the form of particular examples with which one is supposed to identify; issues are dramatized and emotionalized. We watch the events of the day unfold "live" on the screen as if we were actors rather than spectators. The boundary between private life and public life is eroded.

The Private Lives of Public Figures

Consider the way the media treat public figures. People involved in certain kinds of activity, such as sports, show business, or politics, automatically become public figures. Their success is measured in terms of notoriety, of "name recognition." Yet mere recognition is not enough. People want to know more; they want to enter into the private lives of public figures.

This is not new. The public has always been fascinated with the lives of great men. But a barrier existed, one that the objects of fascination themselves could lower in certain circumstances when they wished to place themselves on display. Sometimes that barrier was broken down against their will. Nowadays, though, the tendency is to do away with it altogether. Stars avid for fame welcome journalists, and thus the public at large, into their homes and reveal their likes and dislikes, their loves, their suffering. The media give the public, avid for such fare, what it wants. When the confidential revelations are exhausted, they can always be embroidered with fiction. Stories about celebrities sell well.[27] With telephoto lenses photographers even track them in their private lairs. Things got so far out of hand that a law was passed (17 July 1970) to protect celebrities' rights to privacy.

Professionally and financially celebrities inhabit another

world, but in private they are men and women like everyone else. This combination of proximity and distance transforms them into models.[28] The boundary between public and private is blurred, as the private lives of public figures are served up for popular consumption. It is difficult to say whether the norms thus promulgated are more public, by virtue of their origin, or private, by virtue of their destination.

The blurring is especially noticeable in politics, the public arena par excellence. The media carry the message of politics from one world to another. Political discourse used to be carried on in public by means of after-dinner speeches, dedications, political debates, and schoolyard rallies. Radio and television have brought politics into the private home. Yesterday's candidate simply had to capture the public; today's has to touch individuals. In the past he had to master the art of public speaking; now he must learn how to look squarely at the camera and speak to families in their living rooms. The persona of the politician has been transformed. Once he sought

The 1965 presidential elections in France marked the personalization of politics and the intrusion of the political spectacle into the privacy of the home. Henceforth political speech would find itself more at home in the private setting made possible by the television than in public meetings.

to present himself as a statesman; now he appears in posters with his wife and children. Television takes us into the politician's home, so we can see how he lives. The public figure must dramatize his private qualities in order to establish his credibility with the viewing public.

I doubt that the public is entirely deceived. People are dimly aware that, while the rhetoric conforms to a private code, beneath the camouflage it remains public. Not even showing the private lives of public figures has assuaged the public's curiosity to know more. Rumors about the escapades of politicians abound. Reports of illness, usually cancer, crop up frequently in France, where old taboos remain in effect. Unlike their American counterparts, French politicians reveal neither their income tax returns nor their health records. But their reticence fosters suspicions that sometimes erupt in scandal, such as the one that led to the suicide of minister Robert Boulin in 1979. Paradoxically, politicians must appear to be sincere precisely because their sincerity is incomplete. A presidential campaign may turn on the ability to appear genuine when answering certain questions.

Conclusion

No simple formula sums up the history of private life. There has been a growing divergence between public and private. While work migrated from the domestic sphere into public places regulated by impersonal norms, individuals asserted their right to privacy within the family; this broke down the old family structure, and the physical aspects of individual identity gained new importance. Public and private activities formerly had been combined in the homes of much of the population below the very highest strata of society; this old unity has been replaced by a widening gap between an ever more private life on the one hand and an ever more public life on the other.

Social space was never so dramatically divided between factory and office and bedroom and bathroom. Transitional spaces, partly private and partly public, though destroyed by urbanization, reconstituted themselves outside the old neighborhoods. Public and private spheres influenced each other in a variety of ways. The formal organization of public space became less rigid as new, more relaxed norms took hold. Private life was quietly but effectively subjected to the influence of the media and advertising. People today insist on investing their social roles with individuality, while behaving in private in ways suggested by the media. Even politics has begun to speak the language of private life in approaching public issues.

The boundary between public and private, now blurred, has not disappeared, but only become more subtle. Because spaces and situations—public as well as private—have become more and more specialized, the social norms and codes in use in the two spheres have become increasingly similar. Situations and places are no longer specified by public or private codes; it is the other way around. A new equilibrium has been established.

Richard Lindner, *The Secret,* 1960. Engaged in his own occupations, each man preserves his secret. Lindner (1901–1978), a German Jew who had sought refuge in France, was imprisoned when war came, and moved to the United States in 1941, was the painter of total solitude. (Sands Point, N.Y., Joachim Jean Aberbach Collection.)

❧2❧

A History of Secrets?

Gérard Vincent

Oskar Schlemmer, *Four Figures with Cube,* 1928. (Badenweiler, Germany, Schlemmer Family Collection.)

✄ The Secrets of History and the Riddle of Identity

IT is widely, and incorrectly, believed that since 1914 the field of private life has narrowed, that the curtains of secrecy have been lifted, the frontier between what is said and not said pushed back. In the 1920s three authorities continued to preside over private life: the confessor in the spiritual realm; the notary in the material realm (particularly in matters of marriage); and the doctor in the realm of the physical. These three were privy to the secrets of individuals and families. Urbanization has increased anonymity. In the village everyone kept an eye on everyone else. In the megalopolis what is unavowable, hidden, remains unavowed.

In a totalitarian regime all barriers between private life and public life seem to be broken down. Mail is opened, the police may knock at the door at any hour of the day or night, family members are encouraged to denounce one another, and so on. There is nothing new about such practices; they existed in the would-be theocratic societies of earlier times—Spain during the Inquisition or Florence under Savonarola. But to define a totalitarian society as one in which private life does not exist would be to forget the many ruses to which men will resort in extreme situations to preserve their secrets, even if in practice that means no more than choosing the manner in which they will die.

Orwell's *1984* was written in 1949. Rereading it today, one feels that Orwell's bleak pessimism was excessive. In matters of dissidence the human imagination is fertile. Strict orthodoxy has always given rise to heresy. Paradoxical as it may seem, it may be that private life, understood in the very narrow sense of a secret existence, reaches its highest pinnacle

Private Life in the Totalitarian City

147

of development under totalitarian regimes. In the essentially schizophrenic Soviet society described by Zinoviev, every individual leads a double life: as a citizen, he obeys the rules, but as a cautious deviant he flouts them in order to feed himself, satisfy his sexual needs, and maximize his gain. An implicit consensus develops between official institutions, which are not deceived by this discreet lawbreaking, and cautious criminals, who know just how far they can go. Skirting the edges of the law, every citizen is guilty of criminal activity and subject to potential prosecution. Totalitarianism generates more secrets than it ferrets out. As Sartre put it: "We were never so free as under the German occupation."

The problem is more complex in a democratic society. The state does not interfere with private life; an individual's family and friends are not subject to investigation. The media, spontaneously or consciously, operate as a system that works effectively to maintain social peace. Subtly combining the mimetic with the cathartic, the media perpetuate the "star system," especially in the realm of sports, and thus divert people's interests and passions from the field of social conflict. Georges Devereux has analyzed what he calls the "disorientation" of Sparta's helots, by which he means that the helots had no choice but to turn to their masters to understand what they were seeing and hearing and to find out what they could think and say; the same mechanism operates in so-called liberal societies. And even here pockets of totalitarianism subsist: the Mafia and other underworld organizations dispense their own swift justice and enter into relations with legitimate institutions.

The fundamental question is: How much freedom of action do people have in a particular situation? Max Weber maintains that sociology "can be based only on the actions of one, a few, or many separate individuals" and must adopt "strictly individualistic methods." Raymond Boudon echoes this view: "Individual action always develops within a system of constraints, which may be well defined or not so well defined, transparent or not so transparent, strict or not so strict." At its most elementary level behavior is neither absolutely free nor mechanically determined by socialization. If behavior is determined by two systems of forces, what role does each of them play? And if some degree of freedom of choice is the basis of private life, what sources is the historian able to use in order to be able to gauge that freedom?

Félix-Edouard Vallotton, *Study of Trees,* 1911. Even the most realistic painting can give at best a static, simplified image of a tree. The painting is a mere translation, which, if it aims only at reproduction, is unfaithful. (Quimper, Musée des Beaux Arts.)

SOURCES

The Law: Guardian of Secrecy

The historian who wishes to rummage through private papers must circumvent their guardian, the law. In France the law of January 3, 1979, and ordinance of December 3, 1979, extended the period of protection afforded to public papers from thirty to anywhere from sixty to a hundred and fifty years, depending on the law's estimate of the importance of the information contained therein. Papers containing "information pertaining to the personal or family life or private actions or behavior of individuals" are protected for a period of one hundred years, medical information for one hundred and fifty. One writer sums up the situation this way: "Historians, keep your hands off the private lives of the living! . . . The law protects our lovemaking, our suffering, our vices, our illnesses, our manias, our homes, our pictures—everything that it takes to be private . . . It empowers judges to censor texts and seize published works . . . And the dead man who has heirs lives on." In 1970 a superior court in Paris pointed out that "the 'rights of the historian' carried no weight against the heirs of a Sarah Bernhardt fan whom the historian had imprudently accused of having raped the illustrious actress . . . How is history to be written when judges are the arbiters in the conflict between the historian and the law?"[1]

What Is Said and Not Said

Who's Who? is a good source of information about private life. It contains information about the elite that is considered to be avowable or "moral," thus legitimate; what is unavowable—regrettable or shameful—remains hidden. We learn about the positions held by the members of this group—but not about the way those positions were obtained, held, and capitalized on. We read, for instance, that Mr. X was first appointed undersecretary in some cabinet department and then named to the appellate bench as a judge. We are not told whether his promotion resulted from his exceptional talent, opportunism, or selfless dedication to government service. We learn nothing about the way in which diplomas from the right schools are transformed into career success. The data can be loaded into a computer, processed, and statistically analyzed, but the machine cannot tell us more than has been fed into it. No shame attaches to a person born into a family blessed with social, economic, and cultural advantages, who attends good schools and makes all the right educational decisions. Yet our sources omit this information lest they seem to be minimizing the "talent" of the individual. Similarly, marriage is usually described as an affair of the heart, when in fact potential mates are preselected by the system.

Who are the kingmakers? The kings do not tell. Max Weber coined the term bureaucracy (which for him had no pejorative connotation) to describe what he considered a healthy rationalization of the functions of state. Recruited on the basis of universalistic principles (examinations, diplomas, and so forth), promoted in accordance with strict rules, independent of superiors and subordinates, the bureaucrat, Weber believed, would bring forth what we now call civil society. Yet despite the existence of a rationalized bureaucracy in France, personal ties such as friendship, loyalty, gratitude, and kinship continue to play a part. Such ties predated the modern state; they constituted an extensive system of patronage, which facilitated the exercise of power while allowing for some measure of social mobility. In France, where structures of dominance take precedence over meritocratic structures to a greater extent than in other Western countries, these networks of private influence have survived repeated attempts to establish more democratic systems of selection.

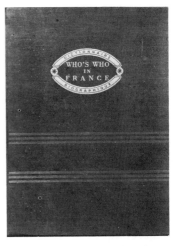

Who's Who? reports only what can be openly avowed. Those providing information present themselves in such a way that their success appears a legitimate reward for their merits.

WHERE THE MONEY IS

Money is more often alluded to than named. Ubiquitous, omnipotent, transcendent, some say that it is fetishized as a God; others say that God is a symbol of money. Whether hidden or flaunted, money is everywhere. It makes its presence felt at every stage of life. The birth of a child? The firstborn is the family heir. First love? People cannot love those whom they do not meet, and they meet only those who belong to their own set. Marriage? Though it may no longer be necessary to work out the financial details with a notary, various social mechanisms perpetuate the confusion between chance and necessity. Death? Tearfully the heirs firmly grip the handles of the casket. The media? The rich are displayed to the poor to teach them the virtues of a patience which they will need throughout their lives. The enigma of good taste is also the enigma of the bank account. World War I profiteers displayed their profits ostentatiously; black marketeers hid theirs.

Money is an essential ingredient of those pockets of totalitarianism that persist in democratic regimes. Organized crime depends on the profits of prostitution, drug trafficking, and gun-running. The repudiation of money by the counter-

culture's alternative societies accounts for the hostility they provoke. Latter-day hippies continue to believe in the words of John Chrysostom: *Pecunia pecuniam non parit.*

Today half of all French families own their own homes. More than 80 percent own a car. All, or nearly all, own a television set. This triad of modernity preserves social peace, despite the gap that still divides the rich from the poor. The last structural revolution in France took place two centuries ago, yet at the least sign of popular unrest people humor themselves by asking whether or not a "revolutionary situation" exists (as they did at the time of the Liberation and again in May '58 and May '68).

In response to a question concerning what was most precious in life, 1 percent of men and 5 percent of women polled in 1947 answered "love," while 47 percent of men and 38 percent of women answered "money." The rampant inflation triggered by World War I upset traditional rules. Deluded about the possibility of returning to prewar conditions, the French poured their money into savings and fixed-rate bonds. Later they adapted to the new postwar situation and learned to invest in real estate, stock, or gold, depending on conditions. According to a 1953 poll, 72 percent of French men and women believe that real estate, jewels, and paintings are the safest investments, while 16 percent prefer stocks and other negotiable securities.

Death often reveals a family's attitudes toward money and forces the courts to intervene. Imagine a wealthy old man who, though he has living nieces and nephews, leaves his fortune to a woman unknown to his next of kin. The family has no recourse but to prove that the deceased was "not of sound mind" at the time the will was drawn up. Its validity depends on the circumstances, and the proof is not simple. Even seemingly solid family ties may not withstand the strain. The veil of secrecy is then lifted as the case passes from the private to the public domain.

Since the face of another person only deceives me when, at long intervals, I turn my intermittent attention to it, why not replace it with an apple? Or embellish it with eyes that see but do not look?

Above: Vavro Oravec, *Kafka.* (Private Collection.) Opposite: René Magritte, *L'Idée,* 1966. (Private Collection.)

THE STATE AND THE LAW

In French statutes and other legal texts the phrase "private life" is used without definition or gloss, as if its meaning were obvious. Article 9 of the Civil Code (1970) states: "Every person is entitled to respect for his or her private life." Article 8 of the European Treaty on the Rights of Man states: "Every

Can Liberty Be Codified?

person is entitled to respect for his or her private and family life, domicile, and correspondence." Article 12 of the Universal Declaration of the Rights of Man states: "No person shall be subject to arbitrary interference with his private life, family, domicile, or correspondence or to attacks on his honor or reputation." There is an ambiguity about the word "private," which *Le Dictionnaire Robert* naively defines as a place "to which the public has no access." But at least some of the public has access to the private rooms of casinos and sex shops. Toilets used to be called privies, even when located in public places. Parents who send their child to "private school" willingly bear part of the costs of teachers' salaries and school operating expenses. Yet some people object to being forced to pay taxes to support public schools. The state, always the focal point of desires as well as the target of criticism, continues to cast its shadow.

The 1970 law prohibits wiretaps and clandestine photography. Since then, however, the French public has become increasingly frightened about criminal activity. In the resulting repressive climate, a majority appears to favor the death penalty and aggressive investigation of potential criminals. How can such investigations be carried out without resorting to wiretaps and hidden cameras in violation of the law? The law of June 7, 1951, establishes a committee in charge of coordinating statistical surveys by governmental agencies. All receiving an official questionnaire must respond accurately within the time period specified. Guardians of privacy protest that this law is an unacceptable invasion of privacy, yet many of them agree that it is important for the government to have its finger on the nation's pulse. In cases of child abuse the public is quick to denounce the silence of neighbors and the inaction of public agencies. Under a 1951 law, family-court judges have the right to order an investigation in cases of suspected child abuse. Such an investigation can be triggered by an anonymous report, a public rumor, or a teacher who notices a child's bruises. The resulting inquiry is surely an invasion of the family's privacy.

The automobile is the symbol of personal freedom. Freed from the constraints of airline and train schedules, someone with a car can go wherever he or she pleases. A car is by law a private place, but the person who buys a car is subject to many legal requirements. He must obtain a driver's license, insurance, and an inspection sticker and observe the traffic laws. Most French people prefer to own their own home. The

George Grosz, *Rich Toads,* drawing for "Brigands," 1922. Is the one-legged survivor of the Great War lost in thought about atrocities endured or committed? There is no resignation in the eyes of the war widow who stands beside her child. Is there any room for remorse in the consciences of the war profiteers who count their cash? Who knows? In any case, the army is still there, keeping an eye on the internal enemy: the poor. (West Berlin, Nierendorf Gallery.)

Don Eddy, painting, 1971.

government has designed policies to encourage home-buying. Social security has helped the nuclear family to replace the extended family. The elderly, once taken in by their children, are now sent away to live in solitude.

Ensconced at home in front of the television set, the car parked in the yard, the nuclear family can lead its secret existence. If discord arrives, a couple may decide to divorce, turning to a judge to resolve a private dispute. Before 1975 divorce implied responsibility, and the legal procedure involved investigations, inquiries, and all the rest. The introduction of divorce by mutual consent has limited the scope of the inquisition, although the final decree remains a public act. Private life can flourish only in a climate of security, which can be guaranteed only by government. People complain about the ever-growing number of incompetent, money-hungry bureaucrats, yet they insist on more and more police. Magistrates do not make the laws; elected representatives do. The legislative imagination cannot possibly foresee the variety of disputes that may arise. Therefore the law is extended by the decisions of the courts. Judges cease merely to enforce the law and begin to make it.

The public fears unofficial organizations. Youth gangs in particular arouse alarm. It is no accident that the "antivandalism" and "security and liberty" laws passed in recent years were aimed primarily at gangs. Young people have long been encouraged to join official groups such as the Boy Scouts and Youth Cultural centers; cities and towns build youth recreation facilities. Land use has always been a bone of contention, but let a building threaten to rob a property-owner of his sunlight or unobstructed view and all hell breaks loose. When a law creating new national parks was passed on July 22, 1960, there was an immediate hue and cry, although many people use these facilities for recreation. Of course properties bordering the new parks immediately went up in value, so not everyone was victimized.

Court Resolution of Private Disputes

People turn to the courts when they are unable to resolve private disputes. It is not the courts that intrude upon people's privacy, but men and women who call upon judges to come into their homes and even their bedrooms. Two examples illustrate this phenomenon. On January 22, 1982, a divorce court judge in Meaux issued an interim separation in which it was stipulated that husband and wife would each retain pos-

session of personal items and the wife would take custody of a dog owned by her. The husband petitioned for "the right to visit and provide shelter [for the dog] on the first and third weekends of each month as well as during school vacations." When his petition was denied, he filed an appeal. On January 11, 1983, the Paris court of appeals again denied his petition on the grounds that Article 254 of the Civil Code, which deals with the custody of children, does not apply to dogs.

On February 22, 1983, an appellate court held that "no court can be reproached for having ordered a divorced woman to return to her mother-in-law a ring received on the day of her engagement, when it has been proven by means of letters that she . . . sincerely believed that the party in question was aware of an obligation to return the item to the person from whom she had received it upon becoming a member of a family to which she would now cease to belong." Indeed the future daughter-in-law (then fiancée) had promised in a letter to return the ring in case of divorce, a prospect which on the

The expensive and deadly automobile. In 1981, 94 percent of families in which the head of household was employed owned at least one car. In 1984, 11,515 people died in highway accidents in France, roughly 35 a day. (Saint-Etienne, Musée d'Art et d'Industrie.)

Pets: In 1980, 9 million dogs
and 7 million cats annually
consume a million tons of food
distributed through 5,000
outlets. Thousands of
veterinarians are among the
most highly paid professionals
in France.

eve of her wedding naturally seemed rather remote (*Gazette du Palais,* December 9–10, 1983). On March 23, 1983, an appellate court upheld the decision of a lower court that a divorced woman was obliged to return certain jewels to her husband's family on the grounds that they were "family jewels," although she had worn them for three decades.

A family jewel is movable property, so the question is in what respect it differs from other jewels. The family jewel is not a routine gift to which no emotional attachment is likely to form, nor is it a family souvenir of the kind to which the courts have attributed "considerable moral value" beyond any possible monetary value. In order for a jewel to be a "family jewel," it must have "display value," that is, it must be to some degree an ostentatious item, hence not without value. "The type of jewel with which the law is concerned is characterized primarily by its preciousness," according to one law-school dean, writing in 1984.

Employer-Employee Relations   Dismissals of employees for reasons relating to their private activities have given rise to a large number of subtle and often contradictory rulings of the courts. Consider these examples. A female psychologist is employed by a facility that specializes in the treatment of disturbed children and adolescents. A divorcée, the woman has been living with the director of the clinic, who happens to be a man of the cloth. After renouncing his vows, this man marries the psychologist and resigns his directorship. The new director, a lay person, fires the young woman on the grounds that her conduct is "in conflict with the aims of the establishment." A court rules against him on the grounds that the clinic is no longer a Catholic charity and the acts alleged to have been committed by the psychologist "introduced no disturbance into the professional setting." A woman employed by a corporation since 1973 was fired in 1976 because of an affair with one of her superiors. The company claimed to have acted "before a scandal erupted to end a situation that had set an example of permissiveness for other employees." The appellate court held that neither scandal nor harm had been demonstrated and deemed the case one of "dismissal without real and substantial cause." A well-known legal reference, the *Encyclopédie Dalloz*, cites numerous cases in which the dismissal of an employee was found to have done harm to that person as a private individual. A man was dismissed after divorcing the company

Television sets: 2.4 million in 1960, 11.9 million in 1970, 20.7 million in 1981 (about half color TVs).

Divortium, the Latin root of "divorce," comes from *divertere,* which means "to go off in separate directions." Meeting is a strictly private affair, but parting requires court action.

president's niece (1965). A woman was fired for refusing to change her hairdo, makeup, and eyeglasses (1973). The female manager of a business was dismissed after a suicide attempt, although it was not claimed that either the business of the firm or its good name was affected.

On the other hand, French courts generally regard incompatibility with the boss as "real and substantial cause" warranting an employee's dismissal. In such cases the burden of proof does not fall on the employer (according to a 1981 appellate decision). Consider two rather remarkable cases. A young woman living with a pharmacist at first volunteered to help in the pharmacy and later was hired as a cashier and bookkeeper. After living together for several years the couple broke up, whereupon the woman was dismissed from her job. She sued for damages on the grounds that her dismissal was without "real and substantial cause." The court dismissed the suit, and an appellate court rejected the woman's appeal on the grounds that "the severing of personal relations between the parties had an impact on relations of employer to employee, which, given the nature of the employment and the business in question, required a mutual confidence that no longer existed" (1984). After two years' employment and despite repeated warnings, a truck driver refused to wear glasses while driving his employer's trucks, even though his license required him to wear corrective lenses. Finally the employer fired the man. The court found that, despite the absence of a prior warning, the dismissal was justified. The appeals court upheld the decision in 1982, because "the recalcitrance of the party in question made it impossible for the employer to trust him . . . in the position of truck driver for which he had been hired."

Suicide and Death

Although suicide is the most impenetrable of all private actions, the courts are sometimes called upon to intervene. On June 15, 1978, a truck driver hanged himself in the cab of his truck during working hours. A court refused to term this a "work-related accident." The judges found that the man in question had had no on-the-job problems, that he had appeared to be in good health, and that certain known emotional problems might account for his action. Although the court recognized that the widow was entitled to a "presumption of responsibility" because the "accident" did occur while her husband was on the job, it found that the act was "deliberate

and voluntary, having absolutely nothing to do with the work performed that day." The appeals court upheld the decision. Another man, injured in a 1977 workplace accident that left him 95 percent disabled, committed suicide on April 4, 1978. This time a court, upheld on initial appeal, awarded his widow a "survivor's pension" on the grounds that the prior work-related accident had been the cause of the man's suicide. But the widow testified that the victim had been greatly affected by the deaths of several family members, so the agency responsible for paying the pension appealed to a higher court. The decisions of the two lower courts were upheld on the grounds that "the party in question had been sorely tried by the prior accident, which left him unable to work for a long period and led to a diminution of his physical and professional capacities. A progressive, reactional major depression ensued, resulting in suicide."[2]

Death can lead to litigiousness. A man who had lived with his mistress for several years, though he continued to visit his legal wife, and his children, was buried in the family tomb. The mistress sued to have the body exhumed and re-buried in a grave of her own choosing. The court found for the defendants, arguing that in the absence of any explicit instructions by the deceased it was their right to choose the place of burial; furthermore, it was appropriate to give pref-

Wearing glasses could be required by law.

erence to the children, who represented certain legally protected interests; finally, "the dead are entitled to rest in peace, and since the remains have lain in the family tomb for more than three years, that fact alone would stand as an obstacle to any proposed exhumation" (1983).

Computers and Big Brother

Today it is a simple matter to interconnect huge data bases. Big Brother can examine our criminal records, health records, military service records, foreign travel, magazine subscriptions, and what have you. On January 6, 1978, the Commission "Informatique et Liberté" (CIL, or Computers and Freedom Commission) was established in France. Various guarantees to protect the privacy of electronic communications and records were made, but one major loophole remained: telephone conversations may be recorded if deemed to be "in the public interest." Early in 1985 some young computer hackers gained access to theoretically confidential files. Despite all legal protections, the confidentiality of electronic information remains at the mercy of the technically competent. Computer security can be increased, but investigators can also resort to more sophisticated methods of penetration.

"Mortals take no less care enshrouding all thought of death than they do with burying the dead themselves" (Bossuet, *Sermon sur la mort,* 1666).

THE IMPENETRABLE

Since such matters as marriage, divorce, suicide, burial, jewelry, and pets can come before the courts, clearly private life cannot be defined as that which falls beyond the purview of the law. Only a unifying thread will allow us to formulate hypotheses. That thread may be the concept of the secret (*le secret*)—not that which is totally secret but that which lies beyond the shifting boundary between what is said and not said.

The word *secret,* which first came into use in the fifteenth century, is drawn from the Latin *secretus,* the past participle of *secerno,* to separate, to divide. Arnaud Lévy notes that the word *secret* "originates with the sifting of grain, whose purpose is to separate the edible from the nonedible, the good from the bad. The separation is effected by a hole, an orifice, whose function is to allow something to pass or not to pass depending on the relation of the object's shape and size to the shape and size of the hole." Hence this sifting process allegedly constitutes "a metaphorical representation of the anal function."[3] The secret, defined as knowledge hidden from others, contains, Lévy argues, three semantic atoms: knowledge (which consists of psychic, behavioral, and material components); dissimulation of that knowledge (through refusal to communicate, inarticulateness, silence, lying); and a relation to others based on that dissimulation (which may yield power over others, as in secret army, secret clique, secret agent, secret file, and so on).

There is no word for the person who is in possession of a secret. Secret is a powerful signifier, as its various associations show. In a "violation of secrecy" is the violation committed by the person who reveals the secret or the person who extorts the disclosure? To be *mis au secret* is to be placed in solitary confinement. Lévy writes: "The divulgence of the secret/content is associated with the notion of incontinence in expressions such as 'to let the secret out' or 'the secret leaked out.'" The secret is associated with the olfactory in expressions such as "to sniff out a secret," or "to stick one's nose everywhere." It is also associated with the sense of hearing: "The secret exploded like a bombshell." An "open secret" is not a secret at all. To be "in on the secret" is to join—or be drawn into—a conspiracy, but "to possess a secret" is to wield the threat of confession. The idea of secrecy is intolerable to the

The Etymology of the Word Secret

person excluded. But a secret may also be intolerable to one who possesses it, so that revelation comes as a "relief." Nevertheless, secrecy bestows power. The man who knows the score can score first.

On Indiscretion

On February 2, 1933, M Lancelin, a lawyer in Le Mans, found the bodies of his wife and daughter, who had been murdered by their servants, Christine and Léa Papin. After their arrest the Papin sisters, shown here, confessed at once, voicing no regrets: "We've been servants for a pretty long time, and now we have shown our strength." Previous employers spoke of the Papins' "impeccable work, perfect honesty, and irreproachable behavior." The investigation found that "after the house was cleaned, Mme Lancelin used to put on white gloves to check whether any dust remained on the furniture."

The only absolute secret is the one that resides exclusively in the conscious—or unconscious—mind of the individual, beyond the reach of the historian. But there are "shared secrets"—those of the family, primary group, village, neighborhood, occupational group, and political party. The word is therefore ambiguous, for it denotes both that which remains completely unspoken and that which is subject to a certain type of communication among initiates. Where a shared secret exists, the historian has a chance of grasping it. The behavior of an individual may imply that he belongs to a particular sect. Communicate, a word in fashion these days, implies an end to secrecy. What is an "intimate" conversation, if not an exchange of secrets and indiscretions? ("I'll tell you, but you've got to promise to keep it secret.") The moment a secret is told, however, it ceases to be a secret. One divulges a secret because it is a burden or an embarrassment, or because telling it enhances one's own importance and may elicit secrets from others. "Everone agrees that secrets must be kept, but people do not always agree about their nature and importance. Usually we consult only ourselves in deciding what we should divulge to others and what we should keep to ourselves. Few secrets are kept permanently, and reluctance to tell is not always durable" (La Rochefoucauld).

The dividing line between family life and professional life is hard to define. If a baker bakes bread, his wife runs the store, and his children deliver pastries after school, there is no division. But a business executive can say to his family: "My work is none of your concern"; and at work he need not disclose anything about his family life. Secrets also lurk within the nuclear family. A man may keep a mistress or a woman may take a lover of course. But there are also more subtle secrets: a wife may be annoyed by her husband's mannerisms or dream of wandering about the world alone. Family secrets are difficult to keep in the poured-concrete apartment buildings built since World War II. Walls are thin, neighbors unavoidable. Members of youth gangs growing up in public-housing projects spread tales from family to family.

In bureaucracies too there are secrets, some of them nec-

essary, others not. Knowing a secret, concealing information, can be a source of power, or of an illusion of power, giving rise to what Michel Crozier calls "zones of uncertainty" in which some bureaucrats naively squander their will to power. Politicians staunchly guard their private secrets. Parliamentary ethics in France forbid any allusion to the indiscretions of fellow deputies, even enemies. Reprisals can easily escalate out of hand, and scandal only strengthens the solidarity of the scandalized.

Sharing secrets—whether among the membership of a club for gentlemen, Freemasons, terrorists, a religious sect, a youth gang, or a homosexual coterie—is a way out of the hell of solitude. It is gratifying to be in the know. The shared secret establishes a community that lives in invigorating fear of a leak. Secrets fascinate. Agatha Christie and Alfred Hitchcock keep us in suspense waiting for the secret to be revealed. Some people are excited by the thought that the CIA or KGB is at work everywhere.

The person with a secret often feels compelled to reveal

"Justice is a relation of harmony that really exists between two things. . . . Men, it is true, do not always perceive these relations . . . Justice raises its voice, but it has difficulty making itself heard amid the tumult of the passions" (Montesquieu, *Lettres persanes* 84). No doubt it is for fear of not making itself heard that the Cour de Cassation of Paris, France's most august institution of justice, resorts to the reinforcement of pomp.

it. Disclosures are made in surprising places. In planes, trains, and taxis people often will say things they keep hidden from their closest friends in the belief that they will never see the person again. One can tell tall tales to strangers or invent a new biography for the sheer pleasure of shedding the constrictions of a unique identity. Since the 1970s telephone hot lines have helped the lonely, battered women, homosexuals, and others. They satisfy the need to confess, which proves that interpersonal relations remain inhibited. The volunteer who answers the telephone, like the priest in the confessional, is anonymous and invisible.

Left: Georg Grosz, Painting. Once homes were constructed in such a way that family secrets could be concealed. But is it possible, in a high-rise apartment building, to avoid the neighbors' "sound and fury"?

THE WORK OF MEMORY

"The root of the past is in the future." Heidegger's statement holds true for collective history: it is impossible to understand the past without knowing how the people who lived then projected themselves into the future. The statement is also true of individual history. We cannot discover who we were without taking account of the future we envisioned. The boundary between private and social memory is poorly defined. Orwell showed that totalitarianism depends on domination of language and memory. In the society he envisions,

For young people Armistice Day means speeches, flowers, and elderly gentlemen with lots of medals. When these last witnesses have gone, little trace of their suffering will remain.

history is constantly rewritten to reflect the needs of the moment.

Even in France the manipulation of history is not entirely unknown. A glance at history textbooks shows that periodization varies with historiographical fashion. When it was believed that history was shaped by great men, periods were marked by illustrious deaths. Then came the vogue of the *longue durée* and the study of demographic and climatic variations and their effects. More recently we have had the history of *mentalités,* or broadly shared cultural attitudes, which unfold according to a variety of timetables. French and German textbooks of the 1930s treated World War I so differently that one wonders whether they were dealing with the same event.

Although the ability to write was much more widely distributed by 1980, the French government nevertheless attempted to reinvigorate the national memory by encouraging Frenchmen, their eyes fixed firmly on the past, to embrace the future of modernization as well. The device for accomplishing this feat was the so-called *année du patrimoine,* the year of the national heritage. We are reminded inevitably of the Vichy slogan: *"Travail, famille, patrie"* (work, family, fatherland). The word patrimony evokes the rural roots of our ancestors and the past glories of France, a country that never tires of commemoration.

Today's family memories are preserved in forms unknown or not widely available in the 1920s. In addition to the traditional library (in cultivated, well-to-do households), we now have photograph albums, slides, records, films, and videotapes—an impressive mass of information. On the other hand, one crucial form of documentation—letters—has been on the decline. People claim that they no longer have time to write. They live longer, start work sooner, retire earlier, take longer vacations, and work fewer hours—yet they find no time to write. Only starry-eyed lovers risk committing their thoughts indelibly to paper.

Memory is idiosyncratic. Two people who live together for decades remember different episodes. When an elderly couple look back on their past, they discover that their memories do not coincide. Even shared episodes are interpreted differently. It is sometimes claimed that photographs and films give proof of what actually took place. But a photograph is not unbiased. The person may have been asked to pose, or the picture may reflect the sensibility of the photographer rather than of the subject.

Years later treasured photographs are reminders of happy occasions, old friends—and younger selves.

Watching a movie on television years after seeing it in a theater is a good way to discover the three stages of memory: what is consciously memorized through repetition; what is apparently forgotten but quickly recalled; and what is "completely" forgotten. In the words of Serge Leclaire: "The operations of the unconscious system cannot be translated or transposed into the grammar and logic of the conscious system . . . The unconscious is a different system, in which neither causality nor contradiction operates, and radically different from the systems we elaborate with our conscious minds . . . It is a different place, a different scene, not subject to the ordering of either space or time."[4] Photographs, films, and tapes satisfy nostalgic yearnings, but do they restore the presence of what they record? When history was static, the question had a simple answer: social structures—and the norms that revealed and perpetuated them—were stable, and people died (at a relatively early age) in the same world into which they had been born. Today things are different. Take someone born at the turn of the century. The year 1985 bears little resemblance to 1900 in science, technology, demography, or culture. No matter how many memories the person may have stored, he cannot reconstruct his past without resorting to autobiographical invention.

THE LAIRS OF THE SECRET: HUMILIATION, SHAME, AND FEAR

The 1980s have been a decade of exhibitionism, of sexual and financial ostentation. Yet the range of the inarticulate remains vast. It is easy to find people willing to listen to boasts of sexual prowess, of thefts in supermarkets, of turnstile-jumping in the subways, but things of which people are truly ashamed remain unspoken. Some people are ashamed of their greed, others of physical deformity. It takes a biographer to tell us that so-and-so was lame or suffered from syphilis. We are ashamed of humiliations inflicted upon us. Even an old humiliation can resurface, reviving forgotten enmity.

What endures, what Pareto would have called a "residue," is uncertainty. In the 1920s there was still uncertainty about the weather, as there is today in Africa, where the climate determines the dividing line between survival and famine. Today, if bad weather spoils a crop, a country like France is not automatically plunged into famine. There used to be uncertainty about health: syphilis, tuberculosis, pneumonia,

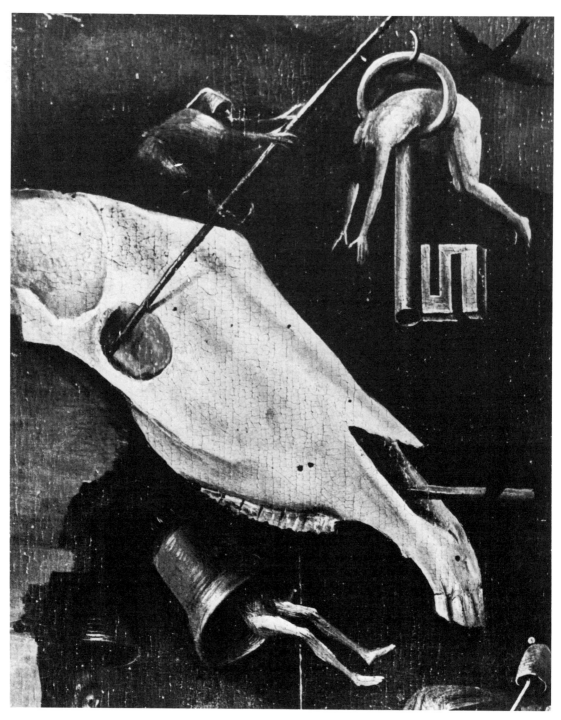

Hieronymus Bosch, *The Garden of Delights*, detail from right panel. The often enigmatic tortures that Bosch imagined for the damned probably were considered real possibilities, indeed probabilities, by his contemporaries, who believed in heaven and hell. (Madrid, Prado.)

septicemia, and other maladies. Now tuberculosis has been vanquished, syphilis brought under control. But there are new areas of uncertainty. How long will a marriage last, or a job? Farmers know that their children will not succeed them on the farm, that soon they will choose to work on assembly lines—if assembly-line workers have not been replaced by robots.

The history of private life is also a history of various kinds of fear. Fear of a nuclear apocalypse, for example. In 1985, the fortieth anniversary of the bombing of Hiroshima, it was reported that the two superpowers possessed weapons with a destructive capacity 500,000 times as great as that of the bomb dropped on August 6, 1945. Paradoxically, people do not seem to have internalized the knowledge that man now possesses the technological capacity to destroy the planet several times over. In the past, when pandemics threatened to destroy humanity (in the wake of wars and the plague the population of France declined from 18 million in 1300 to 9 million in 1400), impressive works of art emerged from the collective imagination. But the possibility of immediate, total destruction has not become an obsession. Nuclear disaster is the subject of "entertainment"—popular books and films. The real fear of the 1980s has been of crime. In May 1984 the security industry staged its first trade show under the auspices of the French Ministry of Industry and Research; burglar alarms, security cameras, and other devices were demonstrated. "Fears were thus brought into the commodity era. The need for security has spawned a profession, and the professionals in turn need no encouragement to stimulate our fears. There is something for everyone here."[5]

Fear has a role to play in protecting secrecy. "I don't want to know." Like lying, denial is a kind of simplification. The godless man needs "charismatic historical figures"; their pettiness, shabbiness, and grudges are no concern of his. Discreet heroism, anonymous generosity, unexhibited works of art—in short, any refusal of ostentation—is perceived as an insult by a public that wishes to sit in judgment.

THE RIDDLE OF IDENTITY

In the first three decades after World War II, although social inequalities remained unchanged, the disposable income of the average French household increased fourfold. This rapid

The Disoriented Person

Hieronymus Bosch, *The Last Judgment,* detail. So strong is the power of narcissism that it limits us to anthropomorphic representation. The demon carrying off the sinful woman has eyes astonishingly like those of Steven Spielberg's E.T. New forms are born not from the imagination but from the demands of science. (Munich, Alte Pinakothek.)

improvement in people's standard of living was unprecedented, so surprising that it was referred to as a "miracle." Other Western economies made similar advances. The old Promethean myth was revived and fostered arrogance. One saw it in economists and technocrats, who claimed to be able to steer government policies in such a way as to produce a steady improvement in prosperity. One saw it among urban architects and city planners, symbolized by the name of Le Corbusier, who hoped to orchestrate the futurist city. One saw it in physicians, as advances in medical science raised hopes that man's life expectancy would continue to increase. Epidemics and meteorological disasters were increasingly subject to human control. Decisionmakers seemed to have the know-how needed to cope with the increasing complexity of social mechanisms. By the 1980s, however, disillusionment had begun to set in. Growing unemployment dampened de-

mand at a time of exponential growth in output. Once-gleaming apartment complexes spawned delinquency and violence. Neuroleptic drugs quieted but did not cure the mentally ill.

At one time people stayed in the same occupation or profession all their lives; a trade often was passed on from father to son. But the introduction of computers, automation, computer-assisted instruction, and similar advances has led to a "permanent revolution" in the production process, so that today's worker must be regularly retrained. Unemployment threatens people in all walks of life. Assembly-line workers are replaced by robots; farmers are forced to sell farms too small to be profitable; small businessmen are driven into bankruptcy by competition from Southeast Asia. A person cast overnight into unemployment, without hope of finding another job in a reasonable period of time, is faced with a dramatic change in identity—an "identity crisis," to use a

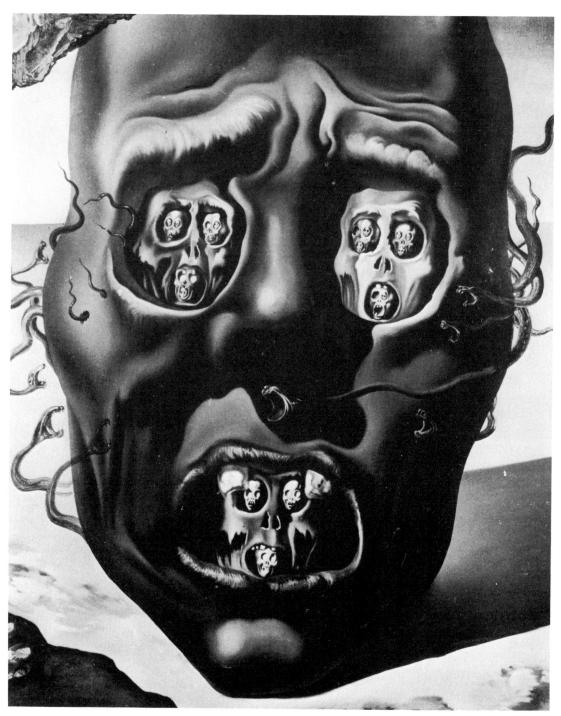

Salvador Dali, *The Face of War*. This painting is an allegory of war and its perpetual renewal, but human atrocity outstrips painters' attempts to represent it. (Rotterdam, Boymans-Van Beuningen Museum.)

common but inadequate description that tends to break down old allegiances. Among young people more and more the watchword is "every man for himself." If a young person gets wind of a job, he keeps that information to himself. Daily life in socialist countries is so difficult it is also every man for himself. Not friendship but complicity guides the search for food and helps people avoid trouble with the authorities. A society that calls itself classless actually encourages self-protective behavior. So does capitalism. In other words, systemic differences have little effect, and man remains what he is, more Hobbesian than Rousseauist, regardless of the nature of the political and ideological system under which he lives. The trauma of unemployment is hard to overcome, all the more so in that it affects people who are not so much rising in the social hierarchy as improving their standard of living. They are people who have taken risks, who have borrowed money to purchase those three indispensable items—a home, a car, and a TV set—and who now are faced with their loss. The decline of self-employment also poses problems of identity, though less dramatic than those associated with unemployment. Until recently, tradesmen and small retailers perpetuated an early capitalist mode of production in which family and production unit coincided. The decline of independent employment destroyed this, altered traditional roles, and introduced the dichotomy of home and workplace.

The problem of identity is exacerbated by the changed relations between urban and rural populations brought about by France's embrace of what, for the sake of simplicity, I shall call the modern model of civilization. Since the beginning of the twentieth century the French people have undergone experiences comparable to those of immigrants. The *poilu* who went to the trenches in 1914 came back (if he was lucky) a different man, with new attitudes toward such things as language, clothing, and diet. The distribution of national media to rural readers reinforced the effects of the mass exodus from the countryside: rural people gradually gave up their regional dialects and identities and absorbed urban, mainly Parisian, norms and fashions.

In reaction to these developments, regionalist movements sprang up in the 1970s. Earlier, in the 1920s and even more with the onset of the Depression in the 1930s, survival—holding on to a job and maintaining a standard of living—had

A Pseudo-World

In *Farrébique,* subtitled "The Four Seasons," a film shot in 1945–46 and first shown in 1947, Georges Rouquier sought to portray life in a Rouergue village where "nothing happens." From the standpoint of the urban media, it was the film of a "nonevent."

been the chief preoccupation of most people. It was only when the standard of living rose that cultural concerns were able to come to the fore. Regional cultures became objects of study and fascination. Young people developed interest in rural dialects that had ceased to be spoken by all but the elderly. Discovering one's roots had become a need as well as a fashion. Tourism played a part in this, but it was a double-edged sword. City dwellers bought country homes in which they hoped to enjoy both today's comforts and yesterday's customs. The locals (one hardly dares call them natives) obliged, giving rise to a variety of "pseudo-revivals."

The Secret of the Analysand

In *Civilization and Its Discontents* (1929) Freud writes: "it is impossible to ignore the extent to which civilization is built up on renunciation of instinctual gratifications, the degree to which the existence of civilization presupposes the non-gratification (suppression, repression or something else?) of powerful instinctual urgencies. This 'cultural privation' dominates

the whole field of social relations between human beings . . . It is not easy to understand how it can become possible to withhold satisfaction from an instinct . . . Since culture obeys an inner erotic impulse which bids it bind mankind into a closely knit mass, it can achieve this aim only by means of its vigilance in fomenting an ever-increasing sense of guilt . . . It can be maintained that the community, too, develops a super-ego, under whose influence cultural evolution proceeds."[6]

Psychoanalysis attempts to ferret out the patient's most hidden secrets, secrets he is not even aware of hiding. Psychoanalysis provoked indignation, aroused enthusiasm, and extended its influence over all aspects of language, as was only natural given that the discipline is based on language spoken and heard. Ultimately it triggered a counteroffensive by sexologists, about whom I shall have more to say later on.

It is important in the context of this book to note the effects of psychoanalysis's revelation of memories that exist in the present but are hidden. Take Freud's celebrated analysis of the "Wolf Man." Sergei Petrov Tankieff lived for ninety-two years (1887–1979). He was twenty-six when he began his treatment with Freud. At age four he began having a recurrent dream in which several white wolves with bushy tails stared at him from the branches of a walnut tree. The child awoke

In *Biquefarre,* shot forty years later in the same locale and with some of the same people who appeared in *Farrébique,* Georges Rouquier shows us what did pass: time. New houses, appliances, television sets, telephones, cars, running water, and so on. The message is that some things remain: husband and wife and love of the land, not altogether exempt from greed.

"Work, above all meditate, condense your thought, you know that beautiful fragments accomplish nothing; unity, unity—that is what is all-important. The *whole,* that is what is lacking in everybody today, the great as well as the small" (Flaubert, *Correspondence*).

in terror. Freud's interpretation was that the dream was a reconstructed version of another "terrifying" memory hidden deep in the boy's unconscious: at age eighteen months, while sleeping in his parents' bedroom, young Sergei witnessed the primal scene: his father, erect, penetrating his crouching mother. The revelation of the secret did not result in a cure. Tankieff, a Russian aristocrat ruined by the revolution, became a ward of the young psychoanalytic community. "Without psychoanalysis," he wrote, "I would never have been able to bear what life held in store for me." This statement was true in every sense. The man lived, preoccupied with his own problems and indifferent to everyone else, in particular his wife, a Jew, who committed suicide in 1938 in terror over the rise of the Nazis. He experienced numerous relapses, which led him to consult many other psychoanalysts, all the while remaining in contact with Anna Freud, who recognized that "this old patient from Vienna is part of [my] heritage."

The patient's secret sometimes eludes the analyst. Charles David recounts the case of a man of forty-five, elegant, sophisticated, reserved, and "highly skilled in the use of language," who came to see him after showing signs of sexual inadequacy with a woman he particularly admired. In twelve

On January 3, 1953, *Waiting for Godot* was performed in Paris. Robbe-Grillet commented: "The two tramps find themselves on stage *without a role*. There they are, and they are free. A useless liberty. The only thing they are not free to do is to cease being there. They will be there tomorrow and tomorrow and tomorrow, alone on stage, standing, futile, without past or future, irremediably present."

Paul Gauguin, "Where Do We
Come From? What Are We?
Where Are We Going?," 1897.
No one has yet answered
Gauguin's questions.
(Museum of Fine Arts,
Boston.)

sessions on the couch, the man told the story of his life: "A
ribbon of words was unreeled before me, forming something
like a screen upon which he projected a film, my only function
being to watch . . . He left no space for any intervention on
my part." For the thirteenth session the man showed up as
usual, lay down, and continued his story. After forty minutes,
"he got up from the couch on his own initiative and immediately paid my fee, at the same time telling me, with his
habitual aplomb, that he had come to a firm decision to end
his story there. The experience, he said, had been most interesting. He even felt he had derived some profit from it, for
his difficulties had abated and the future looked bright. During
no session had he so much as breathed a word of this improvement . . . The flight from analysis set me thinking." In
the remainder of the case study David argues that the patient
had a secret and ultimately kept it. Or perhaps he, the analyst,
had let it escape. "Just as the analysand can hide behind a
secret, so may the analyst hide at the moment of disclosure
. . . Sometimes sharing the patient's secret is the unconscious
equivalent of entering into incestuous relations with him.
Whether hidden or revealed, the secret may be staring us in
the face. If Oedipus had not unraveled the riddle of the Sphinx,
he would have died. Having unraveled it, what Henry James

might call an extraordinary concatenation of circumstances led him to blind himself. Blessed for a moment with clear vision, he would subsequently allow himself to be trapped by fate and never forgive himself."[7]

Women, until recently obliged to change names when they married, may be more concerned than men by the riddle of identity and therefore more likely to unravel it. The birth of a daughter, so often a disappointment for parents who were hoping for a son, is a source of guilt in Judeo-Christian society, for it was through Eve that mankind was plunged into tragedy, helplessness, and illusion. Because women are less imbued with (false) certitudes than men, they are predisposed to denounce the "social" that is masked by so-called nature, which explains why they have set out to expose psychoanalysis.

Henry Moore, *A Family*. "The human figure is what interests me most deeply," Henry Moore wrote. There are four in this sketch; each seems to be in a world of its own. (London, Christie's.)

✺ Family Secrets

REPEATED condemnation of contraception in Christian penitentials proves that it has been practiced for many centuries. The Church declared the use of contraception, even in marriage, to be a mortal sin; punishment was more severe than that meted out for seduction of a virgin, kidnapping, incest, or even acts of sacrilege. The purpose of sexual intercourse was supposed to be procreation, not pleasure. Positions thought to prevent the "female vessel" from retaining the fertilizing semen were proscribed.

Yet even where such elementary contraceptive techniques as coitus interruptus and sodomy were shunned, birthrates fell short of what was theoretically possible. In medieval France women rarely produced more than five or six viable births, owing to late marriage, a high mortality rate (as a result of childbirth especially), and difficulties in nurturing. Only two of these half-dozen infants survived to adulthood, a figure not far below today's average 1.81 children per couple. By the end of the eighteenth century agricultural advances and the decline of epidemic disease combined to create a situation in which two out of every three children born lived to adulthood.

THE LEGALIZATION OF CONTRACEPTION

Responsibility for controlling births passed from the community to the couple. A 1920 law in France made it illegal not only to perform an abortion but also to disseminate information about contraception. Nevertheless, the average couple in the 1920s and 1930s still produced fewer than two children; hence early forms of contraception must have been fairly effective. In the 1880s workers had an explicitly political motivation for limiting births: through a "strike of the wombs" they aimed to deprive employers of an abundant and therefore cheap supply of labor and at the same time to deprive the bourgeois state of "cannon fodder." In 1896 Paul Robin founded the first Neo-Malthusian Association, but few women joined. The most common means of contraception was still withdrawal; if that failed, abortion was the only recourse. Then World War I, which decimated the population, undercut the anarchists' Malthusian campaign.

In 1978 pollsters examined a representative sample of 3,000 women in France between the ages of twenty and forty-four. They found that 28 percent of those questioned used birth-control pills and 68 percent used some other form of birth control. Some who did not had been voluntarily sterilized, while others stated that they wished to conceive. The use of contraceptives was as high as 97.8 percent among those aged twenty to twenty-four. Use of the pill was highest among those between twenty-five and twenty-nine. Above the age of thirty the pill was edged out by coitus interruptus; this was the second most popular method, even with younger women. A follow-up poll in 1982 found that 38 percent of young women between the ages of fifteen and nineteen used either the pill or the coil; the figure rose to 46 percent for those between twenty-five and twenty-nine. Between 1978 and 1982 use of the pill held steady, while use of the coil doubled. (This phenomenon previously had been observed in the United States, where use of the pill dwindled after 1974.) Use of traditional forms of birth control—withdrawal, condoms, rhythm—increased with age.

Introducing sociological criteria further complicates the picture. Among women who were between twenty and forty-four years of age in 1982, 44 percent used either the pill or coil. Of those who held the baccalaureate or higher degrees, 56 percent did. Of women who were top managers or professionals, 48 percent; of women living in the Paris region, 55 percent; of women who attached no importance to religion, 52 percent; of unmarried women, 64 percent. The practice of birth control indicated not an unwillingness to bear children but a desire to decide when. Fewer and fewer couples chose not to have children.

Contraception and Demography

In the short term the consequences of the declining fertility rate were beneficial: fewer maternity leaves; reduced

An enigmatic family photo, with the father missing. The past hangs on the wall: are these portraits of the dead or images of bygone happiness? Whom or what are these sad, sober gazes focused on? The only smiles are on two faces cut from a magazine and fastened to the wall.

medical costs; and fewer children categorized as "class three," those receiving the highest welfare allowances. There were two longer-term consequences: a declining population, which is not necessarily a catastrophe; and a declining youth population combined with a growing number of the elderly, which suggests that "young working people should be prepared to deprive themselves of the fruits of higher productivity in order to meet the needs of a proportionately larger elder population."[1]

Yesterday people took "appropriate" steps to keep from having a child; today they make a "positive decision" to have one. The declining French fertility rate (which has actually declined less than the fertility rate in other eastern and western European countries) can be attributed to two causes: effective contraception, which has reduced the number of what Alfred Sauvy called "unwanted yet unrejected children," and the decision by many couples to have no more than two children.

Still, demography is hardly an exact science, as is shown by the "baby boom," which began in France in 1943, and by a downward turn in the fertility rate beginning in 1965. The French, though late to discover modern contraceptives, embraced them enthusiastically, much as Swedes had done somewhat earlier. A survey conducted in Sweden in the 1960s on a representative sample of individuals of both sexes ranging in age from eighteen to sixty found that 77 percent of those under thirty used modern contraceptives; 57 percent of the men and 44 percent of the women had their first sexual experience before the age of eighteen; 98 percent of married couples had had sexual relations before marriage; and only 1 percent felt that a child born out of wedlock should not enjoy the same rights as a legitimate child.

Toward a Judeo-Christian "Erotics"?

The recent widespread use of modern contraceptive techniques has brought dramatic changes to private life, changes whose magnitude has yet to be fully measured and which are all the more dramatic because, unlike other civilizations, the Judeo-Christian, according to Pierre Simon, "has no erotics." Couples can now plan when to have children. And women, no longer obliged to suffer unwanted pregnancies, can reasonably insist upon full satisfaction in their sexual lives. Society for a long time was willing to tolerate what was considered the "natural" polygamy of the male, but until recently polyandry was restricted by male-dominated values and norms. In recent years, however, these values, along with other aspects of male supremacy, have been challenged. Not surprisingly, it took many years for the idea of contraception to gain legitimacy, or, to put it another way, for medical science to gain control over the reproductive process. Many taboos and prejudices had to be overcome, and victory was by no means assured.

Let us review the high points in the history of birth control in France. In 1953 the Littré Group, an association of French-speaking doctors, mainly obstetricians, met in Geneva to discuss the disturbing spectacle they witnessed every day in the hospitals. Dr. Simon described it this way: "In the hospitals? It's a massacre . . . At the Hôpital de la Pitié (Mercy Hospital), which in this instance failed to live up to its name, I recall appalling scenes in the ward for women suffering from venereal disease. Curettage was practiced without anesthesia, deliberately, in order to punish these women where they had sinned."[2]

Although the group's ultimate goal was the legalization of abortion, members, aware of the obstacles posed by traditional thinking on the subject, looked upon contraception as a first step, the only infringement of the law of 1920 likely to be accepted by public opinion and therefore by legislators. In 1954 the centrist Radical-Socialist coalition, then in the throes of reorganization, filed a bill to abolish the law of 1920. In 1956 Dr. Lagroua Weill-Hallé founded the "Happy Motherhood" movement. In 1959 the MFPF, or French Family Planning Movement, was launched. It soon gained support from teachers, the press, Protestants, and even some Catholics. In 1961 the first regional family planning center was opened in Grenoble by Dr. Henri Fabre, who was summoned to appear before the local medical association after he tied the tubes of a mentally ill woman. In 1963 the coil, developed by a New York gynecologist, was brought to Paris by Pierre Simon. In the 1965 presidential campaign, candidate François Mitterrand stated that he favored the legalization of contraception. The Gaullists took up the cry, and in December 1967 the Neuwirth Law was passed, although it would be five more years before the necessary changes in bureaucratic regulations were approved.

Dr. Pierre Simon, cofounder of the French Family Planning Movement, is not without enemies. In his book he charged that "some Catholic doctors had no intention of saving their souls at the cost of their clientele. Unwillingly, surreptitiously, cautiously, cushioned by prudence, careful lest word leak out, they came around to practicing painless deliveries, rather like those Catholic lawyers who have always been willing to accept divorce cases."

THE LEGALIZATION OF ABORTION

The legalization of contraception was a first step toward the legalization of abortion in France. This became clear on April 5, 1971, when the weekly magazine *Nouvel Observateur*

le nouvel
OBSERVATEUR

la liste des 343 françaises

qui ont le courage

de signer le manifeste

« JE ME SUIS FAIT AVORTER »

Professor Lejeune agrees with
Monsignor Marty that
"abortion is objectively an evil,
a work of death" (January 9,
1975).

published the "Manifesto of 343 Women," all well known,
who stated—indeed proclaimed—that they had undergone
abortions. At last emerged from the shadows, abortion could
now be talked about openly. The manifesto and accompanying
articles totally changed the terms in which the issue was discussed. The customary ethical evaluation was reversed: now
carrying an unwanted child to term was considered "absolutely immoral." The body is not a machine, and to enforce
maternity was to fail to recognize the uniqueness of the life-
giving act. A woman's body deserved respect; so did the body
of the unborn child. Maternal love could flourish only if the
infant was wanted. The choice was not between abortion and
no abortion, but between clandestine abortion and abortion
under medical supervision.

Although credible statistics are hard to come by, the number of clandestine abortions performed in France in the 1970s
has been estimated at around 600,000 annually; of these, some
500 resulted in death and 20,000 in sterility. Gynecologists
were well aware of the risks, because 20 percent of the women
they treated for sterility came to them following botched abortions. The situation was one of absolute hypocrisy: the police
turned a blind eye to the problem, and the courts, defying the
law of 1920, refused to sentence abortionists even if caught.
According to Theodore Zeldin, between 1920 and 1939 the
courts heard only 350 abortion cases a year, and juries often
refused to return a verdict of guilty. In 1945 clandestine abortion clinics were operating in Paris. A 1947 study showed that
73 percent of women who sought abortions were married and
did so with the consent of their husbands.

The "Manifesto of 343 Women," provocative though it
was, actually reflected the government's concerns. Prime Minister Jacques Chaban-Delmas was then promoting his "new
society," and his health minister, Robert Boulin, set up a
commission to study the abortion question. Headed by Dr.
Pierre Simon, it included colleagues of various political affil-
iations; it also sought the advice of Catholic and Protestant
theologians. Legislation seemed imminent when Chaban-
Delmas resigned—or, more accurately, was dismissed—on July
5, 1972. The Chirac government took up where Chaban left off,
and Simone Veil, Chirac's minister of health, shepherded the
bill through to final passage. The law legalizing abortion was
passed on November 29, 1974, by a vote of 284 to 189. By
this time the last of the regulations implementing the Neuwirth Law were also in place, and the Veil Law garnered

Simone Veil, minister of health, argues for the bill to legalize abortion.

widespread public support. In fact, a 1975 poll found that 93 percent of women between 15 and 50 years of age hoped to plan their childbirths; 82 percent approved of the use of contraceptives; and 74 percent wanted their children to receive information about contraception.

The new abortion law was not without enemies. Philippe Lejeune, head of an antiabortion group known as "Let Them Live," accused Dr. Simon of having "hands red with the blood of French infants." Although the Veil Law medicalized abortion, it placed subtle obstacles in the path of women seeking to avail themselves of their new right. Applicants had to have their pregnancy verified by a physician and had to explain their reasons for seeking an abortion. They were then given a "Guide to Abortion," which explained various ways in which the woman might carry the baby to term. The first edition of the guide did not even list approved abortion clinics. Since every abortion had to be reported by the attending physician, we have accurate figures on the number performed: in 1973, 134,173 (18.7 percent of live births); in 1980, 171,218 (21.4 percent of live births); in 1983, 181,735 (21.4 percent of live births). These figures, which are much lower than estimates made prior to passage of the 1975 law, suggest that clandestine abortions may still exist.

THE BATTLE AGAINST STERILITY

The Medicalization of Reproduction

"The learned specialist in contraception," Dr. Simon asserts, "will also know how to treat sterility. The two disciplines are one and the same, two sides of a single coin." One 1978 survey in France showed that 5 percent of the couples questioned were unable to have children; 18.4 percent experienced difficulties in conceiving at one time or another; 10.8 percent had trouble having a first child, but three out of four successfully overcame the difficulties and gave birth. Increasingly, couples who feel they cannot have children have been turning to doctors for help. The entire reproductive process has become highly medicalized: pregnancy-testing kits are sold in pharmacies, prenatal diagnostic techniques such as amniocentesis and ultrasound are widely used, and physicians supervise artificial insemination; some doctors even claim to be able to influence the sex of a child. Sterility is such an emotional trauma that couples are willing to try anything, even to reveal what has traditionally been kept secret.

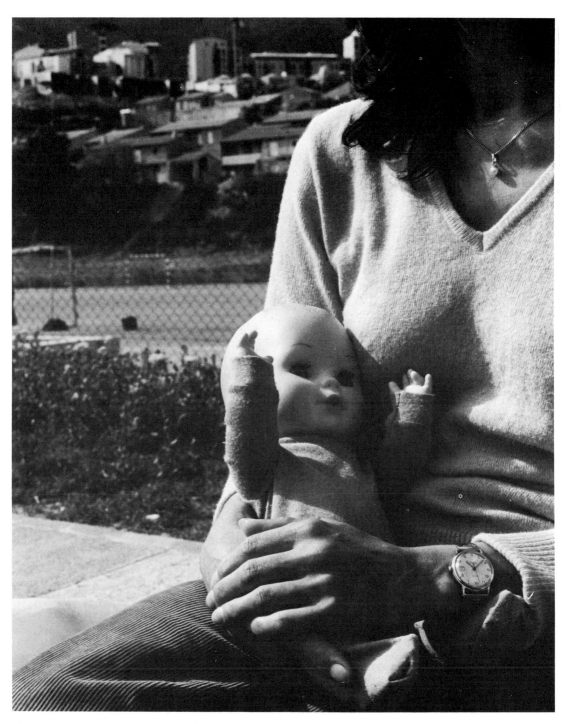

The imaginary child.

The problem of sterility is hardly new. In antiquity a man unable to father children might call on one of his slaves to act in his stead. The same remedy existed in the case of a sterile woman: when Abraham could not have a child with Sarah, he turned to the slave woman Hagar. In the past a social taboo ensured that the cause of sterility would be imputed to the woman; to a man who confused virility with fertility, it would have seemed dishonorable to submit his sperm for microscopic examination. It appears that in one-third of the cases the problem lies with the woman, with the man in another third, and with a mismatch between the two in the remainder. Sometimes the failure to conceive stems from the obsession with procreation itself. Physicians have remarked that many seemingly sterile couples conceive a child after adopting one.

Sperm Donors, In Vitro Fertilization, and Surrogate Mothers

Consider a couple in which the man is sterile and the woman fertile. The woman can be artificially inseminated with sperm from a fertile sperm donor. Since 1975 more than a thousand children in France have been born each year as a result of this method (1,400 out of 749,000 births in 1983). The technique is quite simple: the sperm is collected, preserved by freezing, then introduced into the recipient's cervix. The procedure is supervised by doctors and conducted, in France, under the aegis of the Centers for the Study and Preservation of Sperm. Sperm donors are anonymous and receive no remuneration. The mother is both the biological and legal mother; the father, although not the biological father, is the legal father.

Consider next a couple in which the man is fertile but the woman is infertile owing to an anomaly in her Fallopian tubes; her ovaries, however, function normally, and the uterus is normal and capable of supporting a pregnancy. Some 3 percent of women fit this description. Surgery to correct the defect in the Fallopian tubes is possible but difficult, with success in roughly one out of four cases. Another possibility is in vitro fertilization. An egg is removed from the woman's body either by surgery under general anesthesia, coelioscopy, or transvaginal incision with ultrasound monitoring. Once removed, the egg is fertilized in vitro with sperm taken from the male of the couple. The resulting embryo is then implanted in the uterus of the woman from whom the egg was taken. The result—the so-called test-tube baby—has proved to be a fascinating subject for the news media. In such a case the mother is both biological and legal, and so is the father. The Antoine-Béclère Hospital in Clamart, which specializes in this type of operation, performed as many as eighty a month in 1985 and boasted a two-year waiting list. Only 20 percent of the operations result in pregnancy, and a quarter of those end in miscarriage. The technique is complex and costly and involves the risk of extrauterine pregnancy. Between February 1982 and May 1985 one hundred children in France and fifteen hundred throughout the world were born as a result of in vitro fertilization.[3]

Consider a third case, one in which a woman who cannot ovulate is capable of a normal pregnancy. An egg obtained from another woman could be fertilized in vitro and implanted in the first woman's uterus. Thus the mother would be legal, though not biological, and the father legal and biological (if he provided the sperm) or not (if the sperm came from another donor).

Or consider a couple in which the woman is incapable of supporting a full-term pregnancy. An egg fertilized by that couple might be implanted in another woman who would carry and give birth to the child, then presumably turn it over to the original couple.

In another situation a woman might agree to become a surrogate mother for a couple in which the woman is sterile. The surrogate would then be artificially inseminated with sperm from the male of the couple. In this case the father is the biological father, but the "mother" is not; the surrogate is. The legal status of the individuals involved has yet to be resolved.

LEGAL AMBIGUITIES

The problem of sterility increasingly has become an issue for medical science. It has also become an issue for the courts. The physician—no longer the "family doctor" of old—and the judge have become participants in private life. In fact they always were, but to a lesser degree. People believed that the "law of the family" was rooted in nature and summed up customary practices essential to any human society; it therefore transcended the diversity of man-made laws. Today, such great strides have been made in genetics and biology that science, which claims mastery over nature, is seeking to establish a new law made by men and adapted to human needs.

But legislation must contend with the old requirements

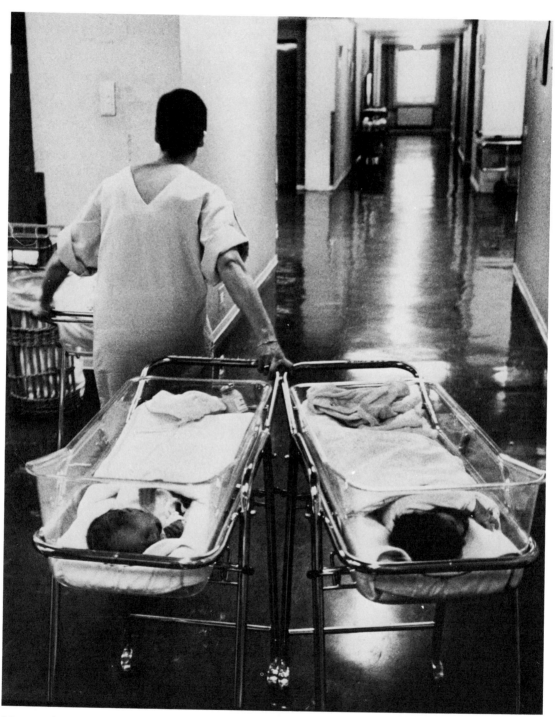

Mama, where are you? And where are they taking us?

of natural law in their new modern guise. The biological situation is unprecedented, the laws to cope with it inadequate. Whenever existing law contradicts widespread attitudes and customs, judges have the option of either enforcing the law or circumventing it in creative and intelligent ways. Take one example: since 1975 artificial insemination has been not only legal but available free of charge in French public hospitals. A husband agreed to allow his wife to take advantage of the program. Shortly thereafter, for undisclosed reasons, he filed a petition to be allowed to disavow paternity of the child. On June 30, 1976, a court in Nice granted his request on the grounds that "kinship cannot be renounced." In this particular case it was clear that the child's biological father was not the mother's husband. Was the child born in these circumstances legitimate, illegitimate, or the fruit of adultery? Under the terms of a 1972 law the legal status of an illegitimate child was the same as that of a legitimate one, although the legitimate child continued to enjoy preferential treatment with respect to inheritance.

Suppose a surrogate mother had been involved. Would the surrogate and the couple seeking her services be bound by a contract as defined in the Civil Code: "Legal agreements take the place of law for those who have entered into them. They cannot be revoked except by mutual consent or for reasons authorized by law. They must be executed in good faith." As the law now stands, the answer would be negative. The agreement between the surrogate and the couple would not be regarded as "legal," hence it would not constitute a binding contract. Nor would it constitute a donation, since a donor is legally bound to carry out his pledge. A surrogate mother can always change her mind and have an abortion or refuse to hand over the child. By the same token, the couple might decide not to accept the child if by some misfortune it turned out to be abnormal. Can a surrogate mother receive payment? To make contact with the couple she may have relied on the services of an intermediary, a newspaper perhaps or an agent of some sort. On this point the law is explicit and provides for punishment of "anyone who, for purposes of monetary gain, acts or attempts to act to bring about the procurement or adoption of a child." Moreover, "Those guilty of abducting, receiving, or concealing a child, or of substituting one child for another, or of imputing a child to a woman who has not given birth, shall be punished by imprisonment for a period of five to ten years." But unless, as has actually happened, a family member is willing to serve as surrogate, who would agree to work without compensation?

These issues were discussed in January 1985 at a conference on Genetics, Procreation, and Law. It was proposed that pregnancy be considered a form of "labor." Every pregnant woman is entitled to a government stipend. A surrogate mother performs a service over a period of nine months, during which her life is changed. She must refrain from doing certain things and runs certain risks. The Committee on Ethics therefore recommended that the surrogate mother receive not remuneration but an indemnity in compensation for abiding by the prescribed restrictions. This subtle distinction made it possible to offer surrogate mothers compensation without violating the law.

In 1979 Pierre Simon had raised a key issue: What about a widow who has herself artificially inseminated with sperm left by her late husband? In 1984 a woman asked a court in Créteil to allow her to be artificially inseminated with sperm left by her husband, who had died three years earlier. The court authorized the insemination, in a decision handed down in August 1984, on the grounds that, "since one purpose of marriage is procreation, there is no offense against natural law in the way in which the decedent's sperm was preserved or handled or in the insemination of his widow." The dead man's paternity is implicitly acknowledged. In this case, in the absence of legislative action, the judges permitted themselves to "make law." The decision was clearly open to legal challenge: the child could not possibly be legitimate, since at the time of its birth no marriage existed owing to the prior death of the husband. The judges went far beyond the letter of the law in finding that a dead man could father an orphan.

At the opening of the Genetics, Procreation, and Law conference a message from the president of France raised the issue of the need for legislation in this area: "What principles can we rely on to guide us now at a time when the contours of life are being altered and many are invoking the rights of the unborn? . . . Now that mankind can control reproduction and rule heredity . . . man finds himself at a point in time when he himself must choose his own rules." Is legislation the answer? Or would it be better, as Dean Carbonnier proposes, if, when faced with a choice "between two solutions, always to prefer the one that requires less legislation and leaves as much as possible to custom and morality"? Robert Badinter, an eminent legal scholar as well as minister of justice, minimizes the legal complexities of dealing with surrogate motherhood. In his view, to "hire a womb" is simply to adopt a child in advance of its birth; the child's interests are no more in jeopardy than they would be in an ordinary adoption. Georgina Dufoix, minister of social affairs, disagreed, as she made clear in a statement broadcast on April 24, 1985: "I cannot allow a market to develop in wombs for hire . . . People's views on this subject differ, and differences exist even within the government . . . No one can claim that he is today in possession of the just solution, because the problem is too new." Dr. Coutant had this to say: "The paradox is that, because of an irresistible urge to fit in by having children, these sterile couples have chipped away at the foundations of the very social structures of which they wish to become a part."

Experts are still asking questions rather than proposing answers. The European Treaty on the Rights of Man states that "every person's right to life is protected by law." The constitution of West Germany states that "every person has a right to life." But when does the human person come into being? Is the fetus a person and therefore entitled to the protections of law? An affirmative answer would rule out abortion. Some people believe that a human being exists from the moment of conception. Others hold that life begins when the fertilized egg is implanted in the uterus five to seven days after conception. Some insist that no person exists until the fetus begins to resemble a human being in roughly the sixteenth week of pregnancy. Others say that life begins when the fetus begins to move; still others, when it becomes viable (twentieth week). And, finally, there are some who hold that human life does not begin until birth. Since women now have the right to have an abortion, why deny them the freedom to choose whatever mode of procreation they please? If unmarried women are allowed to adopt children, why deny them the freedom to procreate as they wish? Medical science has developed technologies for prolonging life that have altered the definition of death; now it is developing technologies that call for a new definition of life.

GROWING UP: PARENT-CHILD RELATIONS

It was not until the nineteenth century that children were   *Families and Households*
perceived as something other than adults-to-be. Monsignor

People dressed in their Sunday best to be photographed (1930).

Félix Dupanloup wrote a six-volume treatise on *Education;* his book *L'Enfant* (1869) is considered by some to be a veritable summa of childhood. His conclusions were challenged by Compayré's 1893 work, *L'Evolution intellectuelle et morale de l'enfant,* which challenges the notion of original sin and offers a picture of the child more innocent than Dupanloup's. The 1920s and 1930s saw numerous works on childhood: Dr. Paul Robin produced a twelve-volume work in which he argued that children should be accorded greater freedom. In 1926 Henri de Montherlant saw what he called "adolescentism" as a rival of feminism. A poll conducted in the 1950s found that people considered the Fifth Commandment, "Honor thy parents," the most important of all. Of those surveyed, 70 percent felt that discipline was a crucial factor in education, and 52 percent wanted no sex education in the schools.

A 1983 poll conducted by Alain Girard and Jean Stoetzel found that the family still enjoyed a very positive image: 72 percent of those questioned stated that they were close to their fathers and 80 percent that they were close to their mothers; 75 percent felt that parents must always be respected, regardless of their faults; 50 percent favored divorce and abortion, while 85 percent felt that "for a child to grow up in a happy environment, both father and mother must be present." Nevertheless, 61 percent expressed approval of single women having children if they so desired. The economic crisis triggered by the 1973 oil embargo helped to keep children in a situation of dependency: according to a 1978 survey, 85 percent of young people aged eighteen or nineteen lived at home; for the twenty to twenty-one age group, the figure was 72 percent; for those twenty-two to twenty-three, 63 percent; and of youths aged twenty-four, 53 percent. Seventy-five percent of business executives provided financial assistance to their children in the eighteen to twenty-four age group.

Economic Growth and the Declining Fertility Rate

Polls conducted in the 1980s showed that the typical French envisioned the ideal family as one with 2.7 children; in bed, however, the average couple produced only 1.81 children. Workers were slightly more prolific than executives and professional people and considerably more so than middle managers, artisans, and merchants. Large families were rare. In the eighteenth century the average woman bore five children, but child mortality was so high that only two and a half survived to the age of five.

The large-family model was embraced for only a brief period of demographic history, when the fertility rate and frequency of religious practice were high and the mortality rate was in rapid decline. Contraception, abortion, cramped housing, working women, and lack of day care all worked against large families. But even more than these factors, a revolution in people's attitudes, probably linked to a decline in religious practice, led parents to limit family size in order to assure a more comfortable life for their children. Children have become a focal point of their parents' hopes and dreams; they have to be supported during long years of education. Not so long ago even young children contributed to the family's upkeep. Nowadays children are a drain on family finances until the age of twenty or beyond. The family's hopes of social advancement are invested in the children. By contrast, immigrant workers, without hope of social advancement, exhibit a high fertility rate. The children survive thanks to medical advances and welfare allowances.

Children complete the education of their parents and grandparents. This grandmother (or great-grandmother?) explores the world of Astérix (a French comic-strip hero) as attentively as the children.

Children are beaten every day. In 1985 a senatorial investigative committee found that every year some 50,000 French

Child Abuse

children suffered psychological, physical, or sexual abuse. Some 400 died. Yet few charges were filed: 1,611 in 1982, about 600 of which resulted in prison sentences or fines. This relatively lenient treatment is the result of what the author of the senate report called a "conspiracy of silence." Family members tend to conceal out of fear, shame, or remorse. A 1971 law released physicians and social workers from their obligation to maintain confidentiality in cases of abuse of minors under the age of fifteen. Yet many still do not report such crimes because they believe that it is best for the child to remain with the family, regardless of the conditions.

Child abuse often is a class phenomenon, a consequence of alcoholism, substandard housing, and "social and emotional underdevelopment." Abusive parents were almost invariably abused as children, and most abused children were either unwanted or products of a previous marriage. The law provides for punishment not only of abusive parents but also of people who fail to report cases of abuse. Bills have been filed to increase the penalties for these crimes, but even stiffer penalties are unlikely to stem the tide.

Obedience

Relations between parents and children have changed greatly since 1920. In the past even wealthy families were wary of spoiling their children. Toys were rare, gifts for special occasions. Discipline was strict. Children were to be "corrected" so as "to shape their characters." They were forbidden to protest. Crying was not allowed. "We were not placed on this earth to enjoy ourselves. Other children are less fortunate than you. During the war your father saw children who . . ." Feelings of guilt were instilled at an early age. Bedwetting was a sin, soiling one's bed unthinkable. The value of work was unquestioned, for girls as well as boys.

Girls were supposed to keep their hands constantly occupied, as Yvonne Verdier recounts: "When my grandmother saw us doing nothing, she would say, 'Here, girl, here's a piece to hem.'" Even while tending cows in the fields, little girls would knit standing up. At age twelve they would embroider their names in red on little canvas squares for their trousseau, a practice called "marking," which in Old French also meant to menstruate. Menstruation marked a rite of passage, at which point the almost-adult young woman would turn to other activities: "I milked the cows, fed the chickens and rabbits, and in the morning did a little housekeeping. We

In the 1930s a young woman was never to remain unoccupied. Time was not made to be wasted.

had a dozen cows, and mama and I had to take care of them. I could milk four an hour, mama maybe five. During the summer I always rose before dawn. From noon until two we hoed the beet and carrot patch. I was doing all this work by age twelve." Such was the schedule of a twelve-year-old girl in 1920. Her virginity would have been subject to close scrutiny. "I assure you, no boy could come near me. My father wouldn't let them. When I went dancing in 1925, he was always around, and when he called me, I had best not dawdle. If I was dancing, I left the boy standing there and ran, because my father had already left."[4]

Above: Georges Pompidou between the first and second rounds of the presidential election that would take him to the Elysée on June 15, 1969, with 57.5 percent of the vote, compared with 42.5 percent for Alain Poher—a better showing than General de Gaulle's 54.5 percent in 1965.
Below: The "modest" home of Pompidou's peasant grandfather. The farmer's son became a teacher and his grandson president of the Republic—a striking example of upward mobility.

Deviance

Every society is structured by norms, and to some extent everyone deviates from norms and their subsidiary rules. Indeed, no system can function properly without some deviation, as is illustrated by the type of job action in which workers, by adhering strictly to established rules, actually slow production. If no one deviated from social norms, if everyone followed the rules that derive from them, social life would be impossible.

The deviant is a disturbing figure because he is defiant and contemptuous of legitimate values such as health, work, career, property, and so on. Dynamic, "organic," possibly anomic industrial societies are subject to constant challenge by intellectuals and by the underprivileged. Depending on their intensity, such challenges may be viewed as misconceived, insulting, or even criminal, but ultimately they are integrated into the fabric of society itself. Liberal society, as described by Robert Merton, is distinguished by its ability to endure precisely by absorbing all that occurs on its margins. Deviants may assume a political or religious identity. Sometimes they refuse to compromise with prevailing norms and are excluded from society altogether. A system capable of evolving by absorbing hostile perturbations is ultimately stable, as Durkheim realized: "There must be room for innovation. To make room for the idealist who dreams of transcending his time, there must also be room for the criminal, who is beneath his time. You cannot have one without the other."

Alcoholism

The two most prevalent forms of substance abuse are alcohol and tobacco addiction. These abuses stem from (but are not explained by) three factors: personal problems; dependent personality traits; and, looming in the background, substantial financial interests.

Alcoholism is a recent phenomenon. The average per-capita consumption of alcohol in France rose from 51 liters per year in 1848 to 77 in 1872 to 103 in 1904 to 136 in 1926. Since 1960 the consumption of wine has been declining steadily. The customers of fast-food restaurants, 60 percent of whom are between sixteen and twenty years of age, drink water, soft drinks, and fruit juices. By contrast, the consumption of highly alcoholic beverages such as whiskey, perceived as a status symbol, has been on the increase. Estimates for 1985 suggest that 1,740,000 alcoholics (1,690,000 of them men) consumed an average of seven glasses of alcoholic beverage (roughly 70 grams of pure alcohol) per day. There is alcoholism among the poor, there is alcoholism in high society. There is also an insidious solitary form of the disease, which forces a person's family and friends to keep anything with alcohol in it under lock and key. Victims of alcoholism seek help from detoxification programs and other forms of treatment.

Drug Abuse

Tobacco and alcohol are consumed openly, but drug use, the bane of parents everywhere, is covert. The youth who abuses drugs does so in secret, and if his or her parents stumble onto the secret, they do not talk about it.

At a 1972 UNESCO conference on drugs Dr. Olievenstein stated the fundamental issue: "It is obvious that the motivations of Hindus and Indians for using drugs are not the same as those of young people in Western countries . . . In the underdeveloped countries young people take drugs to allay their hunger, and there is reason to ask what hunger those who take drugs in the developed countries might be seeking to allay . . . It is possible that somewhere in these new experiences there is an attempt to send a message." Implicit in this view is the notion that drug abusers have difficulty communicating. What is new and devastating since 1970 is the widespread use of drugs by children. Apart from psychotics, whose use of narcotics may be a way of avoiding psychotic episodes, specialists agree that there is no such thing as a born addict, that addiction is the product of a certain disposition in contact with a certain social and cultural environment.

According to Olievenstein, the disposition to use drugs is usually a combination of two things. First, a rejection of the father, the figure invested with power and money. By using drugs the son "outstrips" the father by experiencing a form of pleasure to which the elder man has no access. Second, the drug addict enters into a special relationship with his or her body. No longer is the body an object of "exchange," as in heterosexual or homosexual encounters. Rather, it is wholly eroticized; pleasure is experienced throughout the body, not only in the genitals. Olievenstein claims that drug addiction proceeds through two phases. The first is the "drug honeymoon," in which pleasure alternates with craving. In this phase the person on drugs feels like a god while high, whereas being down is a form of self-punishment that is tolerable only be-

"Drugs—let's talk about them." But can we talk about them so as to discourage rather than encourage their use?

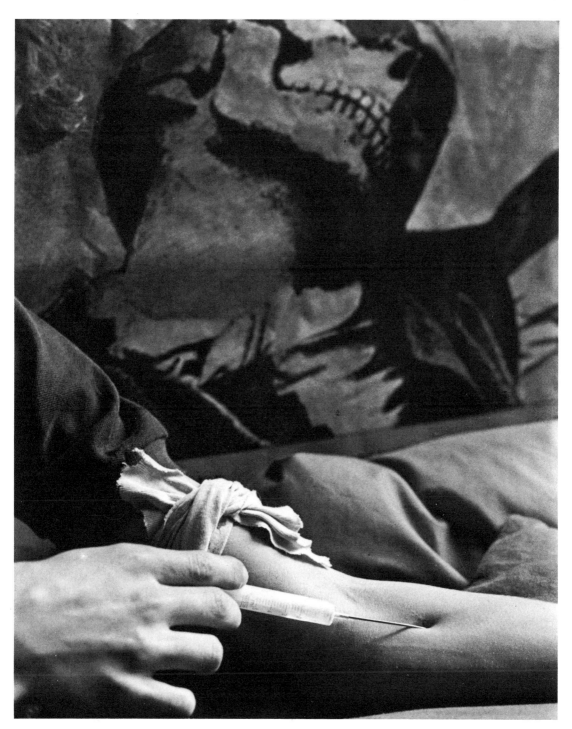

The loneliness of the drug user.

cause the person knows he will soon be high again. The ability to "do it again" is the big difference between the addict and the potential suicide, whose act is irrevocable. Yet drug abuse always ends in failure, because the honeymoon phase does not last. When the "rush" disappears, the addict turns to drugs not for pleasure but to alleviate the craving for drugs.

The fundamental question is why young people are willing to accept this suffering, to reject society, to throw away any chance of a career, and to embrace a life of crime or prostitution to support their habits. Olievenstein's answer is that "the rush is like an atom bomb. A person can spend his or her whole life trying to recapture the pleasure or mourning its loss. Unlike recovered alcoholics, they always feel nostalgia for it." The intravenous injection that causes the rush brings about a "fundamental libidinal severance" that reshapes the personality. If the person who has had such an intense expe-

A fair-sized crowd attends the funeral of Lucky Luciano.

rience no longer desires sex, it is a sign not of impotence but of indifference toward what is regarded as a lesser pleasure. During the drug honeymoon the substance abuser never seeks help. If taken to a drug rehabilitation facility by the police or by his parents, he or she will refuse treatment and run away. He will seek treatment only after the rush has disappeared and nothing but craving and dependency remain.

LIVING TOGETHER

The word *concubine* comes from the Latin *concubina,* "who lies with." Since the word today carries a pejorative connotation, French census-takers chose the more neutral *cohabitation* to refer to couples who slept together. The pollsters were interested in "young" couples, but their questionnaires did not specify specific age limits. Living together out of wedlock is not a recent phenomenon, nor is the fact that unmarried couples sometimes produce children. In the middle of the nineteenth century such children accounted for 30 percent of all births in Lyons, 32 percent in Paris, and 35 percent in Bordeaux; comparable figures for the 1890s are 21, 24, and 26 percent, respectively. Since 1975 cohabitation has increased rapidly: 445,680 couples in 1975 (3.6 percent of all couples), compared with 809,080 in 1982 (6.1 percent). "Illegitimate" births increased from 7 percent of all births in 1970 to 14 percent in 1982, at which time 50 percent of the children were recognized by their father compared with 20 percent in 1970. Cohabitation is primarily an urban phenomenon: in 1982, 22.7 percent of all couples living in the greater Paris area were unmarried, compared with 4.8 percent in rural areas.

The growing prevalence of cohabitation has not compensated for the decline of marriage and the increase in divorce. Between 1975 and 1982 the percentage of people under thirty living in couples declined. So the dwindling marriage rate cannot be imputed exclusively to the growing appeal of cohabitation. If we are entering an era of solitude or of single-parent families, other factors have played a part. Foremost among these is a growing awareness of the difficulty of maintaining a couple over a long period, perhaps because, in their evolving attitudes toward marriage, Western societies have attempted to reconcile two incompatible requirements: romantic love, which is ephemeral, and property considerations, which presumably are not. Be that as it may, over the past ten years many people appear to have become convinced that cohabitation is good preparation for the formidable difficulties of marriage. In 1968, 17 percent of young married couples had lived together prior to marriage; by 1977 the figure had increased to 44 percent.

A Training Ground for Marriage?

Times change so quickly that the recent history of cohabitation can be summed up by examining three surveys. In 1975 and 1976 some 2,765 individuals between the ages of eighteen and twenty-nine were asked to fill out questionnaires. It was found that 38 percent approved of cohabitation by young couples; 86 percent of those actually living together approved. Seventy percent felt that marriage was the result of "direct social pressure." For them, a couple was a private matter, not a social phenomenon. Of the parents, 15 percent were unaware that their children were living together, but 70 percent saw their children and their children's partners regularly. Twenty-five percent of unmarried couples received financial assistance from their parents; 80 percent of the men and 60 percent of the women had careers. Half of the couples pooled their income. Sixty percent claimed to have a view of life "somewhat different" or "very different" from that of their parents, but 22 percent denied feeling any hostility toward their mothers and fathers. "Real but minor" differences with their parents were reported by 40 percent; only 25 percent

(Photo from Aline Issermann's film, *L'Amant magnifique,* 1986.) The new sexual morality has reduced the length of the waiting period.

claimed to feel "strong hostility." Half of the unmarried children living with their parents said that they had "frequent" or "very frequent" conversations with them about "big problems." Their ideas were "generally similar," and parental control was "weak or nonexistent" for 75 percent. Another 30 percent disapproved of "communal living," and 45 percent claimed it "did not interest" them.

From these results, Louis Roussel, who supervised the survey, concluded that the couple remains a fundamental value because living together allays fears of solitude. Thus, cohabitation only appears to violate social taboos; in fact mutual respect, confidence, and affection remain honored values. Sexuality is of relatively minor concern (only one in five felt that sexual harmony is a decisive element in love). Since young people rapidly settle on a single partner, sexual freedom leads, paradoxically, to shortening what Roussel circumspectly characterizes as a period of "sexuality without stable commitment." In his words: "Once this rather turbulent period of youth is over, everyone returns to the traditional order. Admittedly, there is greater freedom prior to marriage. In the end, however, people do marry . . . Marriage is not obsolete." Rather than enter impetuously into marriage, young people first go through an exploratory phase, a period of "trial marriage" such as Léon Blum advocated at the turn of the century. Ultimately, however, they find themselves walking down the aisle.

Another set of questionnaires was administered in 1978 to 2,730 people between the ages of eighteen and twenty-four. The results confirm those obtained by Roussel. Of those questioned, 28 percent stated that they were living or had lived with another person before marriage; the percentage was highest (36 percent) for the children of executives and professionals and lowest for the children of farmers (15 percent). Paris was still in the lead: 50 percent of young people there had cohabited, compared with 14 percent in rural areas. Catherine Gokalp, administrator of the survey, notes that cohabitation is "therefore not a marginal phenomenon but a form of behavior found in all segments of the population." Those who believe that "society must be changed" are twice as likely to cohabit as conformists. Only 10 percent of practicing Catholics engaged in cohabitation. Cohabitation is not so much a form of social protest as a reflection of the desire of young people to allow themselves time to consider marriage before taking the plunge. Thus it is more often an anticipation of marriage rather than an outright rejection. In eight out of ten cases the only experience of extramarital cohabitation is living with a future spouse. There is some correlation between probability of cohabitation and parental divorce: children of divorced parents are more likely to live together than children of couples that have remained together (44 versus 26 percent).

Having It All

Hermaphrodite. Hermaphrodite, child of Hermes and Aphrodite, was so handsome that he inspired an irresistible desire in the nymph Salmacis. He rejected her advances, but when the fifteen-year-old youth went swimming, she took advantage of the opportunity to couple with him in the lake and obtained from the gods the favor that their two bodies should never be separated. Could Hermaphrodite be the symbol of the egalitarian couple? (Rome, National Museum.)

In the early 1980s, when cohabitation among the young was widely viewed as preparation for marriage and as no threat to the established order of things amorous, investigators sought to understand the success of this new rite of initiation. André Béjin argued that cohabitation marked a tentative synthesis of traditional marriage (with its threefold purpose of duration, procreation, and transmission of wealth) with extramarital love, in which people could explore their ambiguous passions for intensity and diversity (while taking precautions against pregnancy).[5] Cohabitation, according to him, is a way of satisfying "the modern obsession with 'having it all' and leaving no possibility unexplored." He compares cohabitation among the young with legitimate marriage and its extramarital adventures, tolerated in husbands but not in wives, and finds these differences: cohabitation is more durable than the "affairs" of yesteryear but is not seen as permanent; cohabitation is "semiconsecrated by society"; like marriage in the past, cohabitation protects the partners against loneliness and boredom, but sexual concord, optional in marriage, is here oblig-

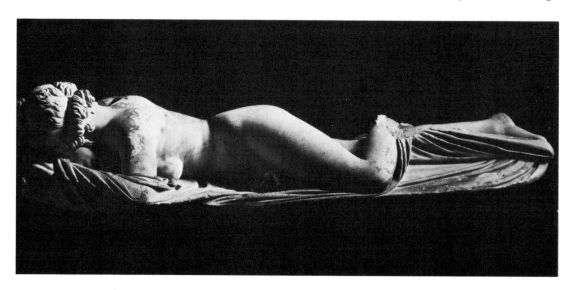

atory, for in its absence one of the partners may choose to look elsewhere; the age-old "roles" of husband and wife are rejected in the name of equality. Hence the partners must either agree to be faithful or must consent freely to outside physical relations, provided that such affairs are openly avowed and emotional investment in them is limited. In other words, the effect is to push back the boundaries of the secret. Everything must be verbalized—not only outside sexual adventures but even fantasies, including masturbatory fantasies. "It is quite a heavy burden," Béjin remarks, "to have to be for one's partner not only lover but also spouse, friend, parent, sibling, confidant, and confessor." In traditional marriage some things could remain unspoken. If a husband said he had spent the previous day at his club, his wife asked no questions; perhaps none even occurred to her. Is it not utopian to dream of transparent interpersonal relations? Is not some kind of secrecy ultimately necessary? Underlying the restless search for alternatives to traditional marriage is there not an element of that yearning for unity that has been called "hermaphroditism"? In Béjin's words: "It is as if the overgrown adolescents who aspire to an 'egalitarian' relations with the opposite sex were seeking both to find the other and to find themselves in the other. Equal, each is reflected in his or her *alter ego,* and each magically discovers the other blessed with that little difference, that missing element needed to complete the self-sufficient and stable figure of perfection, the androgyne, liberated from the need for self-perpetuation."

The Rejection of Marriage

Detailed study of the 1982 census and subsequent surveys challenge the notion that juvenile cohabitation in France is merely a prelude to marriage. In 1982 there were 800,000 unmarried couples, and the percentage of unwed couples was roughly the same for all occupational groups with the exception of farmers. Of those couples in which the man was under thirty-five, 456,000 were living together without benefit of matrimony in 1982, compared with 165,000 in 1975. Most of these unmarried couples lived in the cities. One young couple in five in the greater Paris area lived out of wedlock. In Paris itself more than half of young couples without children were living together.

Cohabitation often followed the breakup of a marriage. After failure in matrimony, people hesitated to entangle themselves again in legal bonds. A 1982 survey of unmarried couples found that in 280,000 cases at least one partner had been divorced. The number of marriages performed each year dwindled steadily: from 346,308 in 1965, the number rose to a record high of 416,521 in 1972 before dropping to 387,379 in 1975, 334,377 in 1980, and 285,000 in 1984. Many couples were having children without marrying. In more than half the cases the fathers recognized their offspring, who were born as the result of a deliberate choice, not an accident. Childbearing no longer implies marriage. Cohabitation, no longer a youth phenomenon, has evolved into a kind of free union. In 1982 some 56 percent of French men and women deemed cohabitation "normal," compared with 37 percent in 1976; 70 percent of cohabiting couples stated that they had not encountered difficulties with friends or relatives or experienced problems of any kind because of their living arrangements.

Is the decline of marriage merely a passing fancy that conceals an underlying conservatism? In my view the answer is no, because the decline reflects underlying economic changes. In the past, marriage was based on the exploitation of inherited wealth, be it large or small, from the loftiest noble to the humblest peasant, artisan, or shopkeeper. Things began to change when growing numbers of men and, even more important, women began to work for wages, when society began to offer protection—once the responsibility of the family—against some of life's major risks, and when it became easy to obtain "modern methods of contraception that permit women to control reproduction, in contrast to the great Malthusian revolution in nineteenth-century France, which relied on male initiative."[6]

Yet as cohabitation gains wide acceptance, it more and more resembles marriage. Motivated by a wish to keep church and state out of matters of the heart, the reaction against traditional marriage ends up by appealing to the services of the state, because couples are unwilling to forego the protections offered by society. The "privatization" of marriage thus leads not to a revolution in mores but to changes in the law, which, as we saw earlier, has followed rather than anticipated changes in popular attitudes. The law makes fewer and fewer distinctions between living together out of wedlock and legal marriage or between legitimate children and illegitimate ones. Some people believe that too many rights have been granted to unmarried partners; others believe that they have too few. The question is whether these changes in the law threaten to undermine marriage as an institution.

There may not be as many brides as in the past, but they still wear white.

CHALLENGES TO MARRIAGE

In what was intended as a devastating critique, France's Economic and Social Council attacked legislative measures intended to protect married couples while also encouraging cohabitation. Noting the decline in the number of marriages, the increase in divorce, the decrease in the number of divorced men and women who remarry, and the growing proportion of children born outside of marriage, the council's report maintains that "over the years countless laws and other measures have done more to hinder marriage than to help it. Certain people enjoy tax advantages accorded to single and divorced individuals while at the same time receiving the social benefits of marriage recently extended to unwed couples." Evelyne Sullerot, who drafted the report, found it paradoxical that the legislature should intervene to establish rules governing those who, in repudiating marriage, were explicitly trying to avoid such rules. Napoleon, she said, had correctly proclaimed that "since concubines forgo the law, the law takes no interest in them." In the 1950s most unwed mothers worked as domestics, menials, or farm workers, but today's single mothers are relatively well-educated inhabitants of large cities, hence members of the avant-garde that people of lower social status imitate.

Sullerot expressed outrage that laws passed between 1965 and 1982 "abandoned or weakened the principles of sacred marriage, of respect for the patriarchal hierarchy, of respect for the institution, and of the importance of legitimacy in matters of kinship and inheritance, as well as the idea of marriage as a solemn personal commitment."[7] The law now specified that, in the event of a death in an unmarried couple, the surviving partner could remain in the couple's shared apartment, provided that occupancy was established six months prior to the date of death. Sales of property between unmarried partners were valid, but not sales between husband and wife. An unwed partner was entitled to health insurance, family allotments, and maternity allowances as well as to death benefits from the social security administration. The council's report found it paradoxical that a 1975 law permitted divorce by mutual consent, but custody of any children had to be awarded to only one of the parents, in 90 percent of the cases the mother. Before 1970 parental authority over a child born outside marriage belonged to the parent who recognized the child, and if both parents did, then to the one who did so first; after 1970, however, the mother had sole authority re-

During the week I live with Mother, who does the cooking. On weekends I go to Dad's, and I do the cooking.

gardless. The child, once "the property of the father," became "the property of the mother" at the very time when, on grounds of equality between the sexes, men were being urged to avail themselves of paternity leave in order to experience the joys of child-rearing.

Sullerot found it outrageous that a man and a woman, both earning the minimum wage and living together unwed, paid no income tax, while the same couple, if married, was liable to tax. She wondered whether it made sense to speak of "family," given the phenomenal variety of living situations: young, unwed couples; certified common-law marriages; divorced couples with and without children; divorced people living together; youths sharing apartments; unmarried couples living with their families; and so on. Furthermore, it is misleading to suggest that separation is easier for unmarried couples than for married ones. Lawyers have become accustomed to drawing up agreements between unwed couples detailing what items belonged to each prior to the relationship or were subsequently acquired by one party alone. In the name of equity and virtue, Sullerot anxiously asked if France was on its way to accepting the "Swedish model," under which 40 percent of all marriages end in divorce and 40 percent of children are born out of wedlock.

In an otherwise bleak picture there are two bright spots. According to Louis Roussel, divorce may result in additional children: after having two children with a wife and then divorcing, a man may decide to have another with his new partner. And married couples, unstable though they may be, live more communally than in the past: 70 percent of them have joint bank accounts, and 80 percent intend to leave their property to the surviving spouse.

THE CHOICE OF A MATE

Alain Girard and Louis Roussel have shown that people tend to choose marriage partners from their own social group. The same is true of the choice of partners for cohabitation. One way to get an idea of what social, moral, and physical characteristics people look for in prospective mates is to examine the notices placed in *Le Chasseur français,* a monthly magazine that includes advertisements for spouses. First published in 1885, the magazine attained a circulation of 400,000 in 1939 and 850,000 in 1970 only to decline in subsequent years. Its readership, originally composed mainly of peasants

Choosing a Husband.

and provincial petty bourgeois, expanded in the 1950s to include the urban middle classes. In 1903 the magazine began to include a marriage section among its classified advertisements. The number of marriage advertisements averaged 10 per month in 1903, 67 in 1922, 444 in 1930, and 1,000 in 1977, by which time marriage ads far outnumbered all others.

Marc Martin has studied these advertisements for the period 1930 to 1977, focusing on the "part of the message in which the advertiser describes him- or herself and proposes marriage." In 1930 most of the men who advertised were in the colonial administration or the military; most of the women were postal workers or schoolteachers. Marriage was conceived of primarily as a financial transaction, as evidenced by the fact that nearly all the advertisers, both male and female, indicated either what financial resources they would bring to the couple or what their minimum requirements were. "Property" and "expectations" were key terms. According to Martin, "fifteen years of inflation and monetary difficulties had done little to moderate the petty or middling bourgeois hunger for modest holdings of property and small savings. Devaluation had yet to enter anyone's mind." By 1977, however, people had little if anything to say about "property." The key economic referent was now occupation, and the range of advertisers was considerably broader: many of the women were professionals, business executives, secretaries, or nurses; among the men were executives, engineers, and technicians. In 1930 divorce was so disreputable that divorced women were careful to make clear that their ex-husbands had been found "at fault," hence by implication that they themselves were "innocent." By 1977, however, divorce was mentioned "without further details and without embarrassment." All references to "tradition," "respectability," and Catholicism had vanished. Physical details assumed new importance; many men as well as women described the color of their eyes, their weight, and their physique and mentioned their love of sports. In 1930 the typical woman described herself as "a homebody, affectionate, sentimental, serious." In 1977 she was "gentle, warm, knows how to entertain." She no longer claimed to be able to sing but described herself instead as a "musician" and claimed to take an interest in art, reading, and other cultural activities. Martin notes: "Over the past fifty years, femininity has ceased to be embodied in the figure of Cinderella; the ideal woman is now seen as a sort of homespun muse and model." One thing has not changed: it is disadvantageous to be a foreigner or, worse yet, a member of a different "race," as is clear from ads that end with the words "willing to consider foreigner."[8]

LOVE IN MARRIAGE

In May 1985 in the Indian state of Rajputana, 40,000 *A New Idea* children were married in a twenty-four-hour period. Indians believe that love is an unpredictable emotion that should not be the basis of marriage. Although divorce exists, rural people disapprove of it, so there is reason to believe that these marriages will last a lifetime. By contrast, no one in France today thinks of the family as having any basis other than the love between a man and a woman.

The merging of love and marriage is circumscribed within a limited geographical area; historically it is a new idea. Philippe Ariès has shown that the most widely accepted model of marriage, historically as well as geographically, is one in which a man may repudiate his wife and marry someone else. Indissoluble, monogamic marriage is "the crucial fact in the history of Western sexuality." Until the tenth century marriage among nobles was a contract between two families, a strictly private and secular affair that did not concern the Church. If the woman did not give birth, she was considered to be sterile and sent back to her family or to live in a *moutier*, "a dependency of the castle in which the head of the family kept daughters and widows." The Church was divided between an ascetic model that can be traced back to Saint Jerome, according to whom marriage was a vulgar, almost animal state and no concern of religion, and a different model stemming from Saint Paul, for whom "it was better to marry than to burn."[9]

It was not until the thirteenth century that the Church, through the prohibition of incest, gained a role in the regulation of marriage. Over the objections of the nobility it introduced the requirement of *stabilitas* (indissolubility), although according to Paul Veyne rural communities had accepted such a requirement of their own accord since the end of Gallo-Roman times. After the Council of Trent, marriage, having become a sacrament, began to be celebrated at the door of the church and later, in the seventeenth century, at the altar.

Divorce was allowed for a brief period after the state supplanted the Church, but the principle of indissolubility soon was reinstated. Love had no place in the contract that joined two noble fortunes or two wretched peasants. If love did develop between husband and wife, it was a fortunate coincidence, unless it led to erotic excess of the sort relentlessly condemned by a religious ethic that identified coitus interruptus with infanticide. Love between husband and wife was something to be kept secret, because it was so contrary to the civilized code of conduct.

This state of affairs lasted until the twentieth century. After the couple signed the marriage contract in the presence of the notary, who was often the instigator of the marriage, it would have been indecent, even ridiculous, for the pair to exhibit too much enthusiasm toward each other. Léon Blum caused a scandal when he urged, in his book *Du mariage* (1907), that prospective brides and grooms gain experience with other persons of similar station and background. In a lyrical style he pointed out that "one cannot play the violin without study . . . Do not pretend to take pleasure from a novice, then, without first learning to play." For, "when equality of experience enables both you and the other person to appreciate the reasons for your choice, you may fully savor the pleasure there is in living together." In other words, Blum was recommending that young couples live together some three-quarters of a century before it became fashionable to do so. Abbé Grimaud, in a book entitled *Futurs Époux* that won a prize from the Académie Française in 1920, was more in tune with his times when he recommended that men avoid not only prostitutes but also female intellectuals and working women.

Secrets between Spouses

In the past couples were discreet about passion in marriage. Now that marriages last longer because of today's greater longevity, they are just as discreet about the waning of passion. In times past people accepted the enigma of the other, provided that the spouse did what was expected in his or her social and familial roles. What joins, or even brings together, a couple in which one partner lives for the future and the other lives in the past? How do memories of shared life manifest themselves in old age? What was a high point to one may have been forgotten by the other.

How do couples deal with this less-than-total transparency? When exploring the realm of the secret, there is always some question about the truthfulness of the answers people give, and survey data must be interpreted with caution. In 1969 (after the events of May '68) apparently 41 percent of women wanted a good husband, 20 percent desired a good and harmonious home. Only 22 percent hoped to find love in marriage, although 44 percent believed in "the love of a lifetime." Where did they hope to find it?

The conclusions reached in 1983 by Alain Girard and Jean Stoetzel are more comforting. They found that while the French approve of contraception, most believe that a woman needs children in order to develop to her full potential. The factors contributing to the success of a marriage are: a good sexual relationship, 70 percent; fidelity on both sides, 73 percent; respect for the other person, 86 percent; mutual understanding, 73 percent. The authors sum up as follows: "The family is the focal point of relaxation and leisure. It is the place where people feel happy. They describe their feelings toward the family in terms of security (66 percent), relaxation (61 percent), and happiness (57 percent). On a scale of 1 to 10 satisfaction with home life measures 7.66. The family is seen as a refuge against the assaults of modern life."[10]

This is an optimistic picture indeed, and perhaps some degree of skepticism is permitted. Evidently the questionnaires were filled out by satisfied husbands and wives. In the past prostitution satisfied masculine desire for a variety of sexual partners. Today, although prostitution still flourishes, men also have flings (which sometimes develop into full-blown affairs) with women of their own background and class. Marriage, no longer based on the joint exploitation of two pooled inheritances, now rests on feeling. Someone may agree to run a business for a lifetime, but no one can guarantee that his or her desires will endure forever. Fear of solitude and the conviction that, once the bloom is off, life with another person will subside into the same monotonous routine are the negative factors that hold marriages together. Apparently these have failed to capture the imagination of pollsters.

People organize their married lives in many different ways. François de Singly suggests, quite rightly, I think, that Georg Simmel's definition of socialization aptly describes the family: "A form that comes into being in many different ways, in which individuals constitute a unity on the basis of certain interests and ideals, either temporary or permanent, conscious or unconscious, and within which those interests are realized." François de Singly's research, admittedly focused on families of relatively high social status, has shown that individuals increasingly place development of their own potential and freedom of choice ahead of "the constraints, limits, vexations, and sacrifices implicit in a long-term multifunctional relationship."[11]

This primacy of "I" over "we" in marriage, because it tends to devalue fidelity and permanence in favor of self-fulfillment and personal possibilities, casts marital life in a new light. It is no longer possible to "settle in" to marriage. The married person is aware that his or her partner is a free individual, capable at any moment of insisting on his or her radical otherness. Marriage thus becomes a realm of uncertainty. What is emerging may be a more varied conception of marriage: an initial phase of physical love, fidelity, and procreation followed by a period of mutual freedom and intermittent sexual relations leading to a time of friendship and cooperation, of growing old together and sharing memories.

GUILT-FREE DIVORCE?

Divorce was impossible in prerevolutionary France. Canon law permitted only annulment, of which there were numerous instances. On September 20, 1792, a fairly liberal divorce law was adopted: divorce could be granted not only by mutual consent of the spouses but also on grounds of incompatibility alleged by one spouse only. Under the law of July 11, 1975, divorce for cause continued to be allowed and divorce by mutual consent was reinstated. It could be granted on application either by both spouses or by one spouse if accepted by the other. Divorce was also authorized in case of a separation of more than six years or of a serious change in the mental faculties of one of the partners continuing for the same length of time. A divorce court was established and granted sole jurisdiction in the granting of divorce by mutual consent. It could also determine the amount of compensatory payment (in lieu of alimony) to be made in order to restore financial equity, given the likely prospects of each party—no small task for the judge.

Divorce, Commonplace but Not Painless

In 1960 there were more than 30,000 divorces in France; by 1984 the number had risen to 100,000. Not only had the frequency of divorce tripled in twenty-five years, but the rupture occurred earlier in marriage. It has been calculated that 21 percent of those born in 1975 will experience divorce. In Sweden today 40 percent of all marriages end in divorce, and a marriage that lasts as long as seven years is termed a success.

The divorce rate in France began to increase long before passage of the 1975 law. The legislature had merely sanctioned established fact. When love dies, divorce does no more than reveal a disillusionment previously endured in secret. In the past couples remained together in order to "keep up the front" or "for the children." Nowadays, when sex and companionship give way to marital squabbles, people choose divorce. Two-thirds of all divorces are initiated by the woman, usually before the age of thirty. The proportion of women seeking divorce is the same among service personnel, office workers, and working women in the upper classes.

Has divorce become painless? Can a marriage be dissolved amicably? Not always. Mutual consent works best with couples that have been married for less than three years and have no children or major property acquisitions. If there are children and community property, a quick, low-cost resolution is possible only if both parties agree about custody of the children and division of the property. When women insist on equal rights, men insist on equal privileges, including child custody. Many women prefer the traditional alimony to the more recent compensatory payment. Yet 40 percent of the time alimony payments are irregular or nonexistent. When this occurs the woman has to resort to complex legal procedures to have her ex-husband's wages attached or money withheld from his paycheck. According to the Sullerot Report, even these measures are often ineffective because the men pretend to be bankrupt.

If divorce remains an ordeal, some signs suggest that marriage is too, and of longer duration. Remarriage among divorced individuals is becoming less and less frequent because there is a lasting disaffection with marriage among divorced people. Among women of all ages, 57.1 percent remarried after divorce in 1970, compared with only 49.7 percent in 1978. According to the Sullerot Report, this percentage was continuing to decline. In the 1970s more than 80 percent of those who divorced before the age of thirty remarried, generally within two and a half years after the divorce. For the relatively young divorce "used to be only a transitional phase between two marriages. Few people remained for long in the status of divorced individual." (This suggests that a third party was involved prior to the divorce and perhaps provoked the couple's decision to separate—or insisted on it.) Today, however, people divorce more often and are less likely to remarry. Of 847,000 single-parent families in France in 1982, 123,000 were headed by single fathers and 724,000 by single mothers. Of the latter, the percentage of divorcées was rapidly increasing while the percentage of widows was on the decline.

THE ECLIPSE OF THE MALE

Today increasing numbers of women hold positions once considered masculine preserves. There are, for example, female engineers, although they are more often found in research and development facilities than in factories or on construction sites. Women are admitted to the top science and engineering schools. Men apparently have suffered a relative eclipse in recent years.

Working Women

It has been estimated that the number of hours of free domestic labor in France in 1981 was 53 billion, compared with 39.5 billion hours of paid domestic labor. Naturally most of this free domestic labor was performed by women. Men who work outside the house spend an average of 96 minutes per day working at home, compared with the average housewife's 483 minutes. Domestic labor must not be very rewarding because the 1982 census found that for the first time the number of couples in which both partners worked exceeded the number in which only the man worked. Furthermore, an aging population and lower retirement age have resulted in an increase in the number of couples in which neither partner works. Also, since wives are typically younger than their husbands, in many couples the man has retired while the woman continues to work outside the home. Women at all levels of society and in all occupational groups want to work outside the home, even in relatively unrewarding jobs. The growing role of women in the work force amounts to a veritable cultural revolution.

The Socialization of Female Children

The constant comparison of little girls with boys who enjoy privileges that girls are denied results in reduced self-esteem and thus hampers the girls' ability to achieve their objectives in the battle of life.[12] So charges Elena Gianini Belotti in a study summarizing the results of American and French research. Even in so-called advanced industrial societies most couples still hope for a boy to carry on the family name. Although most mothers are willing to breast-feed male babies,

This young, pretty, pregnant engineer is the boss on this project.

Dolls for little girls, guns for little boys.

they are more reluctant to breast-feed daughters. Toilet-training is instituted for girls earlier than for boys. Mothers tend to show off their naked sons, while encouraging modesty in their daughters. What is considered wantonness in young girls is taken as a mark of virility in boys, in whom aggressiveness is thought to be a positive sign. Little girls are expected to "be good," not cry, watch their language, be neat, interrupt what they are doing to perform an errand, and treat younger children in a "maternal" manner.

Toys contribute to gender differentiation. When a female investigator visited a number of toy stores and asked for a toy for a child of three, she was invariably asked, "For a boy or a girl?" Parents, worried that a boy takes too great an interest in his sister's dolls, will direct the child toward more aggressive and competitive forms of play. One American study of 144 textbooks used in elementary schools found that working mothers were always depicted as typists, nurses, and school-

teachers—jobs traditionally held by women. A French study of children's books found that groups of children were always portrayed as being led by a boy.

Nursery schools in France are called *écoles maternelles*, not *écoles paternelles*. Nearly all the teachers are women. They tend to foster gender differentiation by insisting that girls be "well-behaved" and asking them to straighten up and clean the classroom, activities from which boys are exempted.

Women were slow to achieve career positions with decisionmaking power, ones that carried high cultural status. In 1920, at a time when a woman's average earnings were 31 percent below a man's, women first gained the right to join unions without their husbands' consent. There were 300 women doctors in 1921 and 519 in 1929; 12 women lawyers in 1914 and 96 in 1928; and only 7 female university professors

The Slow Social Ascent of Women

in 1930. In 1936 women earned only 85 percent as much as men, although since 1927 female teachers in primary and secondary schools earned the same as men of equal rank and seniority.

Not until after World War II did women gain access to jobs previously monopolized by men. Even then they still were viewed in sexist terms, as evidenced by the way in which the newspapers allowed themselves to comment on the physical appearance of prominent women. In *Jours de France* (December 1973) Florence d'Harcourt was described as "tall, thin, blonde, and above all a mother." Anne-Marie Dupuy, presidential chief of staff and a member of the Council of State, "loves boating and skiing. Cheerful, brown-eyed, fair-skinned, her brown hair soberly rolled up in a bun, the chief of staff favors traditional suits or rather severe dresses in discreet colors" (*France Soir,* January 11, 1974). Marie-France Garaud "breathes warmth . . . But look at her neck. Powerful and supple, it betrays the warlike Valkyrie burning for combat. Who is this elegant woman? Succinctly put, she is a shrewd, ambitious, and intelligent provincial. She has two children, a husband who sits as a judge on the court of appeals, and, like most of Pompidou's followers, a fierce will to power" (*Le Nouvel Observateur,* December 24, 1973).

Marriage and the Progress of Women	The progress of women toward prominence has affected marital relations. The most highly educated working women seem to be the least satisfied with marriage. Their independence calls for a new definition of married life, a new division of functions and roles, not only within the family but also outside it. Unemployment has forced people at all levels of society to rethink career choices. In families where the husband is unemployed while the wife retains her job, the terms of the "economic alliance" are reversed. As recently as a few decades ago, even highly educated women often gave up their careers when they married. They used their cultural capital to aid their husband's career and educate their children. A survey of medical students in the Marseilles region in the 1970s shows that women often gave up their careers to marry men in the same specialty or else became general practitioners without specialized training, which meant taking relatively unprestigious salaried positions.

Things are different today. More than one couple has broken up when the wife's performance surpassed that of her husband. A new form of jealousy has come into being because the persistance of traditional thinking makes it difficult for a man to contemplate marrying a woman with a more illustrious career than his own. Such career rivalry raises new questions about relations between couples and between parents and children.

Picasso, *Femme au miroir,* 1932. (New York, Museum of Modern Art.)

✒ The Body and the Enigma of Sex

A S a people the French are handsomer than ever before. Statistics prove it. In 1980 the average twenty-five-year-old man was just over five feet eight inches tall, compared with just over five foot seven in 1970 and approximately five foot three in 1914. In the 1930s one saw goiters and club feet, toothless mouths, and dwarfs. No one can deny that people look better today. Yet social inequalities affect physical stature along with everything else: the average doctor or lawyer stands five foot nine, the typical farmhand only five foot six.

Now we have mirrors in which to admire our admirable physiques. The first mirrors in France, imported from Venice in the sixteenth century, were a precious commodity. As recently as the 1930s mirrors were still rare and expensive items. Full-length mirrors were found only in the homes of the wealthy. Working-class and rural homes generally contained one at most, a small shaving mirror fastened above the sink. Borrowing a phrase from psychoanalysis, we might speak of the recent popularization of the mirror as a historical "mirror stage."

The bourgeoisie reached the mirror stage in the 1880s. The bathroom was the most intimate room in the house. In the full-length bathroom mirror it was possible to view the body not as it appeared in society but in total nudity. This experience is now available to people of all classes: in 1980, 80 percent of French homes had bathrooms.

Mirrors tell us nothing about what goes on inside the body, but thanks to X-rays, ultrasound, computerized tomography (CT scan), magnetic resonance imaging (MRI), and positron emission tomography (PET scan), we know. These new technologies, while therapeutically effective, are the source of new concerns. Doctors, no longer content to mon-

Rubens, *The Education of Marie de Médicis,* detail, 1625. Rubens portrays the type of woman's body people admired in an era when thinness symbolized poverty and curves symbolized opulence. (Paris, Louvre.)

itor surface symptoms, want to know the underlying cause of every dysfunction. Exploring the interior of the body does not eliminate anxiety but does alter its focus. Even as I approve of my appearance in the mirror, I wonder whether a hidden microbe or virus might be lurking within.

The history of female beauty is complex. It is an oversimplification to say that where once fat was beautiful, thin now reigns supreme.[1] To be sure, all undernourished societies admire obesity. André Burguière points out that in medieval Italy *popolo grasso* (literally, fat people) referred to the ruling aristocracy, *popolo magro* (thin people) to the poor. While Rubens and Jordaens painted plump women, Cranach captured slim and tempting silhouettes. Prostitutes and courtesans were often thin. Véronique Nahoum has shown that thin, straight-backed women were "originally admired by social elites . . . Verticality was one aspect of the desire to cut a striking figure. The children of the elite accordingly had to work on their bodies."[2]

Before the nineteenth century workers and peasants paid

The Female Body

Various forms of gymnastic exercise attempt to make women's bodies slim and trim.

Samuel Buri, *Painter Painting a Painter in the Act of Painting Himself,* 1974. A self-portrait—an old idea with, in this instance, a very complicated title. The three self-portraits may express the painter's stupefaction at being there.

little attention to their appearance. The ideal of thinness spread from the top down. Pierre Bourdieu considers it a subtle form of class warfare: "The body became the prize in a struggle aimed at enforcing acceptance of oppression (through submission of the body to scrutiny) and social integration. The perceptual norms of the dominant group were imposed on all of society in a process that coincided with the class struggle in that the characteristics of a particular group were extolled as exemplary, awarded legitimacy, and then imposed on others."[3]

The ideal of thinness, characteristic of a society of abundance in which fat is considered to be bad and obesity vulgar, has been promulgated by the media. Women are endlessly exhorted to diet and exercise. All sorts of exercise fads have appeared: aerobics, aerobic dancing, isometrics, gymnastics, body-building, stretching, and what not. The cult of the body demands sacrifice; people may spend less on clothes, but they spend more on keeping up their appearance. The pundits tell us that we all "have the bodies we deserve," so that there is a moral component in the injunction to exercise. When we appear on the beach, we had better have the body required by the fashion of the moment.

The Athletic Body

The purpose of athletic activity is to bring the body into conformity with the new standards. The Olympic Games, first staged some eight hundred years before the birth of Christ and abolished by Theodosius in A.D. 394, exhibited grace and athleticism in a public setting. Today's conception of sport, like the word itself, comes from England. It was around 1830 that Thomas Arnold introduced sports to the public schools, one of his purposes being to channel—that is, to socialize— violence. Pierre de Coubertin, who organized the first modern Olympic Games in 1896, believed that participation in sports helped to develop self-control and thus to shape the individual. In the 1920s people saw sports as a "noble" activity because it was "disinterested"; it was felt that money would spoil the purity of athletics. Since that time powerful financial interests have been drawn into sports by the burning desire, in part, to win. This has led to increased professionalization, and in recent

Lust for money has transformed this athlete's body into a billboard.

years athletics have been dominated by money, medicine, and the media.

The professional athlete has virtually no private life. His body is ministered to by dieticians, trainers, cardiologists, and other specialists. His coach coordinates the work of all these assistants and helps the athlete develop an acceptable media personality. Only by enduring an ascetic childhood and adolescence can the young tennis player hope to attain international rank. Having reached that level, the young champion continues to train under medical supervision and with the backing of a sponsor. Smoking, drinking, and partying are out, for the goal is to make as much money in as short a time as possible on the court. The standard of performance is so high that the champion's career is brief. Björn Borg is praised for the wisdom of his decision to retire from competition at age twenty-six.

Sports play a not insignificant role in maintaining the social order. In Europe a televised soccer match can draw more viewers than a broadcast of top political leaders. The media lend credence to the idea that athletics can lead to social advancement, whether in tennis, boxing, soccer, baseball, football, or basketball. While not untrue, the claim is misleading because success is such a rare exception to the rule. In sports arenas the most extreme nationalism is still displayed unabashedly and without fear of ridicule. At Roland-Garros, where championship tennis is played in France, the crowd applauds every double fault by foreign players as well as every ace by French stars. The satirical newspaper *Canard enchaîné* sarcastically observes that the extreme Right wants to expel from France all immigrants "except Platini," the soccer star. In reaction against the conversion of sports into a branch of the entertainment industry, a more hedonistic idea of athletics has recently gained currency. Many people have begun to participate in jogging, bicycling, and crosscountry skiing, not with any hope of competing but simply to enjoy themselves.

THE FRUITS OF THE EARTH

Cultural Influences

The vocabulary of eating finds its way into all aspects of language. In some African tribes women are forbidden to eat birds because "eating fowl makes a person flighty." A clever detective "grills" his subject, who then "spills the beans." A

Not all Jews in France keep kosher. Some orthodox Jews obey all the rules; other Jews keep kosher only at home; still others eat kosher food only on Jewish holidays.

man may call his girlfriend a "feast for sore eyes." Inspired by the work of Claude Lévi-Strauss, Mary Douglas has taken a structuralist approach to culinary matters.[4] She notes that the ancient Hebrew code of *kashrut* was part of a larger set of rules governing religious ritual, cleanliness, and sexual and marital relations. For the ancient Hebrews, the material world consisted of three elements: earth, water, and air. Any living thing without a precise place in this taxonomy was excluded from the table. Douglas notes that the laws of *kashrut* make sense to anyone who understands that they reflect a total world view, but that taken by themselves they may seem quite meaningless.

Similar observations can be made of other peoples. Douglas reports that among the Lele of Zaire, amphibious animals and others that straddle divisions in the indigenous system of classification are taboo. The French observe a very strict dietary code: they do not, for example, eat carnivorous animals. Hunters eat wild boar and venison but not fox; yet fox meat is prized in some parts of the Soviet Union, just as dogs are eaten in China. From evidence such as this Douglas concludes that the principles that guide human dietary choices are of a cultural rather than physiological order. Culture creates the communicative system that deals with what is edible, toxic, and satisfying. The transition from nature to culture is most apparent at the moment of weaning, which often proves fatal to infants in traditional societies. People try to find something white to feed the infant, white being a symbolic substitute for the mother's milk. In equatorial Africa some tribes use the "milk of ape's bread," a whitish substance obtained from the pulp of the baobab tree, while in the Antilles they use coconut milk.

Social codes determine who distributes food. A woman from Millot told Yvonne Verdier how, at the turn of the century, newly married young couples sometimes had to live with the groom's parents: "When everybody lived under one roof, the daughter-in-law would never dare slice the bread. The mother-in-law did the cooking and served the food, and she waited on the others without serving herself the way women do today . . . When a person was served a very small piece of bread, they would say, 'Oh, so you're giving me the mother-in-law's portion,' meaning that the mother-in-law put herself last and made sure her daughter-in-law got enough to eat . . . The mother-in-law's slice was a sliver, nothing at all . . . And a mother-in-law's fire was a fire that had gone cold, no fire at all. A mother-in-law was a person who looked out for everyone else."[5]

In France today men are still served by women, although nearly all food critics and prestigious restaurant chefs are men. Men claim that some women are "happy in the kitchen," but when sociologists try to locate them they find that most are housewives, dependent on their husbands, who derive emotional satisfaction from their ability to cook and plan meals. Some wives use their mother-in-law's recipes in order to gratify their husband's taste buds with half-remembered flavors of childhood. In any case, while cooking is mainly women's work, eating knows fewer and fewer gender distinctions. In the past honey and sweets were reserved for those "eternal children," women; male virility required the consumption of red meat and alcoholic beverages. Today traditional images of virility and feminity have been largely obliterated.

Sugar has become public enemy number one. It is blamed for obesity, diabetes, hypertension, cardiovascular ailments, and tooth decay. People today eat only a quarter as much bread as a century ago (150 versus 600 grams daily); they turn up their noses at dried beans and potatoes. The average French person consumes more than 80 pounds of sugar a year, and everyone agrees that this is too much. Experts such as Claude

Daily Judgment: The Bathroom Scale

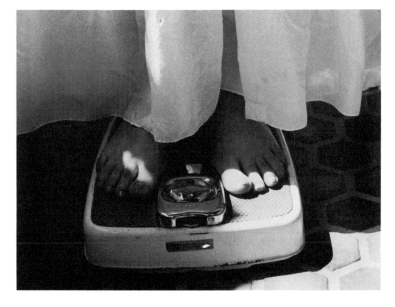

The daily trial of those condemned to a lifetime of dieting.

People today are made to feel guilty about eating. There are so many things to avoid: animal fats, bread, potatoes, sugar, and alcohol—to name a few.

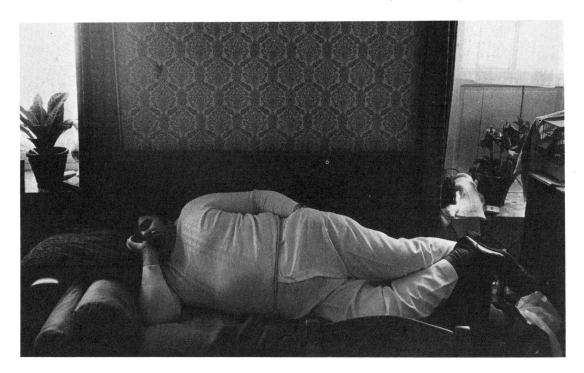

Fischler recommend grilled meats, milk products, and fresh fruits and vegetables. Since our diets are no longer subject to the seasons, "daily, without noticing, we realize the dreams of the connoisseur: meat with all our meals, fruits and vegetables the year round and to our heart's content, a variety of cheeses and sweets, and countless other delights. The old alternation of meat days and lean days is a thing of the past; meat is now our daily bread."[6] Fresh fruits and vegetables come to us from all over the world, as did spices of old.

The need for food suppliers to make a profit has led to a certain monotony. In nineteenth-century France there were eighty-eight varieties of melon compared with only five today, and twenty-eight varieties of fig compared with only three. Anxiety is our compensation. The media exhort us to eat yet enjoin us to stay thin; they send us to our kitchens with calorie-saving recipes; they celebrate gourmet cooking and diet schemes. Today's problem is how to be a gourmet and at the same time have a good physique. Now that France has forgotten the hunger of the Occupation, a flat stomach is à la mode. Fat is reviled; obesity terrifies. Plumpness was a status symbol for the bourgeoisie of the Belle Epoque, and nine-

One of the most unfashionable forms of freedom: being fat.

teenth-century workers were tolerant of the overweight, but in today's jet set obesity is considered almost obscene. In May 1955 *Marie-Claire* ran this headline: "Public Enemy Number One: Pudginess and Pimples." Dietary aids are big business. People pay good money for fat-free cheese and yogurt, by-products that could be had without ration coupons during the war. Many spend several anxious moments every morning on bathroom scales.

Food and Social Class

The average workman spends a greater percentage of his income on food than the average lawyer. What is eaten differs with social level. The so-called *nouvelle cuisine,* a fashion launched by the upper class, is intended to be lighter than traditional French cooking. Much use is made of steam cooking; in order to preserve the "natural taste" of various foods, cream is avoided as much as possible. The lower classes cling to a more traditional cuisine with its familiar sauces. Whiskey is bourgeois; pastis, working class. Champagne crosses class boundaries but is drunk as an apéritif only by the upper class. At the bottom of the social hierarchy wedding banquets go on for hours (sometimes from lunch right through dinner); among the elite it is now customary to serve brunch to family and close friends and lunch to acquaintances.

In 1975 the magazine *Cinquante Millions de Consommateurs* (Fifty Million Consumers) commissioned a poll of some 12,300 households representing more than 43,000 individuals. Analysis of the results has yielded a "social hierarchy of diet."[7] For each food item the experts computed an index in which 100 represents the average Frenchman's consumption for the period 1965–1972. On this scale mutton and lamb consumption by workers was 72, compared with 288 for "industrialists, large-scale merchants, executives, and professionals." In other words, a lawyer or top government official consumes 3.15 times as much mutton and lamb as a worker. "Bourgeois" foods include certain meats, fish, cheese, and fresh fruits and vegetables, in contrast to "working-class" foods such as pork, potatoes, pasta, bread, and margarine. Factor analysis reveals that those who eat leg of lamb, endives, and pears also go to the theater, attend concerts, visit museums, read *Le Monde,* play tennis, frequent auction galleries, own country homes and perhaps boats, and drive a Mercedes, BMW, or Alfa-Romeo. Those who eat potatoes and margarine have never flown on an airplane, drive small Citroëns or Renaults, have

Claes Oldenburg, *Meats*, 1964. Despite its name, pop art is the opposite of popular art. Oldenburg, a Swede, chooses subjects "unworthy of interest." He makes them the point of departure for a critique of society, whose products (from meat to painting) and producers (from butchers to painters) he wishes to ridicule. (Private Collection.)

borrowed money to buy appliances, own no high-fidelity system, and prefer astrology to "hard" science. Adding other variables such as age, sex, number of children, working or nonworking spouse, family background, and region introduces nuances into this perhaps overly schematic picture but does not alter the fundamental conclusion, that status distinctions tend to reinforce one another. French society remains strictly hierarchical. The *Potato Eaters* are no longer those Van Gogh painted; nevertheless, they remain at the bottom of a social ladder up which neither they nor their children are likely to climb more than a few rungs.

Powdered and Frozen

The ritual of dining (breakfast, lunch, dinner) once determined the tempo of family life. Today dining is increasingly affected by work requirements. About a thousand fast-food restaurants in France serve an unknown number of meals daily. The modern, industrial-style restaurant with its scientifically planned, inexpensive menus poses a threat to old traditions of family dining. Working people today grab a quick lunch at the plant or office cafeteria or in a nearby fast-food restaurant; they dine in the midst of coworkers but not *with* them. There is no time, particularly if part of the lunch hour must be used to run errands.

Meals are prepared as quickly as they are consumed: canning, freezing, freeze-drying, and pasteurization have made it possible to transfer to the food-packing plant tasks once performed in the kitchen. Everyone is pressed for time; being busy, even overwhelmed, has become a status symbol. People in a hurry have no time for traditional cooking. Technology to the rescue: companies developed instant coffee, powdered milk, powdered soups, powdered sauces. Frozen foods were another boon, as the magazine *Elle* proclaimed in 1961: "French experts expect a major cold wave to hit the country this year . . . Delighted as we still are by the joys of refrigeration, now we can look forward to the triumph of frozen foods." And so the age of the frozen dinner began, not without resistance in some quarters, as the same *Elle* article was careful to point out: "Many prejudices have yet to be overcome." Eventually, however, resistance was vanquished.

The Body Threatened: From Patient to Client

Diseases of the Past

The French have become not only better looking but also healthier. Theodore Zeldin claims that between the two World Wars some four million people—one-tenth of the French population—suffered from syphilis and that 140,000 died of the disease every year. The same malady was also responsible for 40,000 stillbirths annually. Gonorrhea too was devastating, but not even the founding of a National League Against Venereal Disease in 1924 could do much to stem the tide owing to the lack of effective treatment. Tuberculosis became so widespread that in 1918 the government required every case to be divulged to the authorities. It also built new dispensaries, trained so-called health monitors, and established schools to train visiting nurses. The social control of disease was facilitated by urbanization. Tens of thousands of people died every year of what was vaguely termed "infectious disease" or "influenza." Government action in this area was not without results: there were no major typhoid outbreaks after 1929; the measles epidemic of 1930–31 was controlled; and the construction of new sanatoria reduced the prevalence of tuberculosis.

Some common diseases were kept secret: "syph" and "clap," though widespread, were hidden from view, and tuberculosis was never discussed until the victim's departure for the sanatorium revealed the truth. Physical suffering was a part of everyday life; it was not seen as a failure of medicine. Consumption of analgesics was far lower than it is today, and those who suffered from insomnia made do without sleeping pills.

From Family Doctor to General Practitioner

Between the turn of the century and the eve of World War II, the number of doctors in France almost doubled, from roughly 18,000 to 35,000. Together—at times in jealous competition—with confessor, chambermaid, and notary, the family doctor was privy to many secrets. At the turn of the century "the doctor who ministered to the body also ministered to the soul and looked not just at symptoms but at family history in its emotional and social aspects." The nineteenth-century physician treated not just the patient but the patient's family. Only in poorer neighborhoods did patients go to the doctor's office. Elsewhere the doctor made house calls, just like the hairdressers, manicurists, and seamstresses who served people of "good society." In so doing, Francine Muel-Dreyfus tells us, he gained "knowledge of the interior in which domestic life unfolded and thus of [the family's] secrets, problems, and emotions." What is more, "the doctor took in everything at a glance, all-seeing because it was already all-knowing about such things as the family's social position, its ambitions and defeats, its secret suffering, disappointments, worries, loves, tastes, and melancholia . . . This shared intimacy . . . this unbroken rapport with generation after generation constituted the essence of the doctor-patient relationship as described in nineteenth-century medical memoirs."[8]

The person suffering from a disease was a patient, not a client. The physician presented a yearly bill detailing his *honoraria,* a word that significantly "denied the financial and commercial aspect of the transaction." In some regions doctors did not bill for payment until the patient had died—as if they were sharing in the inheritance.

Specialists, when they first appeared on the scene, were perceived as mercenary because they insisted on being paid immediately. One doctor expressed contempt for the practice in his memoirs: "The physician belongs to a kind of general-

ized family . . . There the specialist has no business, neither as adjunct nor as replacement. He is like a distinguished antique dealer who, when called in to appraise a gold and silver urn in the family's possession, ascribes no value to either the ashes the urn contains or the memories associated with it."

Today the family doctor has been supplanted by the general practitioner, who often finds that the problems to be treated are psychosomatic and that to treat them properly requires knowledge of the patient's family life. If someone requires nighttime emergency service today, the only option is to go to a hospital emergency room or walk-in clinic, where the doctor on call is a stranger. In routine cases he may write a prescription; if the situation is more serious, he will immediately consult a specialist. Muel-Dreyfus observes: "The doctor's services are paid for on the spot . . . The meeting between doctor and patient occurs in a vacuum, based on nothing but the patient's own account of his or her symptoms."

Disease is sometimes admitted, sometimes concealed, sometimes imagined: Hans Castorp, the hero of Thomas Mann's *Magic Mountain* (1924), visits his cousin in a sanatorium and first wants to be, then believes he truly is, ill. During seven years on this "magic mountain" he discovers the insignificance (or nonsignificance) of his person and the vanity of knowledge. (Photo from Hans W. Gessendörfer's film of *The Magic Mountain*, 1982.)

The era of the specialist began in the 1920s. Before this time the various medical specialities were "mere gradations of

Specialists

shading on a single palette, that of general medicine."[9] The nature of medical practice began to change. The number of specialists increased dramatically; new technologies and laboratory tests transformed medical diagnosis; new drugs were discovered and mass-produced; hospital practice was revised; new preventive methods were introduced. In 1980 the number of physicians per 100,000 citizens was 201, compared with 128 in 1970. During the 1970s the number of specialists increased at a 5.7 percent annual rate. In some specialties growth was even faster: psychiatry, 20.8 percent; anesthesiology, 11.1; obstetrics-gynecology, 9.1; dermatology, 9.1; cardiology, 8.2. During the same decade the number of "medium to long" hospital stays increased by 12.3 percent annually.

MENTAL ILLNESS

Although the history of psychiatric nosography cannot be recounted, it tells us a great deal about not only the history of science but also the history of unstated assumptions about mental illness.[10] From the early nineteenth century until quite recently, increasing attention was paid to social rather than intrinsic causes of mental illness. This tendency continued to the point where in the 1960s "the antipsychiatry movement" achieved the status of a reigning ideology. It is remarkable that once unavowable diseases become avowable at the same time they become curable; witness tuberculosis after the invention of aureomycin in the 1940s and cancer today. Perhaps it is because so little has changed in psychiatric therapy that mental illness is still shrouded in secrecy.

Given the current ineffectiveness of treatments for mental illness, man is reminded of his ability to control the creator of his cosmogony, his mind. Somatic medicine is based on empirical evidence: X-rays, ultrasound, tomography, and magnetic resonance imaging enable us to "see" malignant tumors and measure their size. By contrast, psychiatric medicine is based on the patient's own account.

It was no doubt naive to think that monomania (which today would be called obsessional psychosis) would show on a person's face. Shortly before his death at thirty-three, Géricault reportedly said: "If only I had painted five paintings. But I have done nothing, absolutely nothing." No doubt there was madness in this denial of an oeuvre that includes some three hundred authenticated paintings. Facing page: Géricault, *Kleptomaniac,* 1822. (Ghent, Museum of Fine Arts.) Above: Géricault, *The Madwoman,* 1822. (Lyons, Museum of Fine Arts.)

In the absence of clinical evidence, psychiatry wavers between heredity and environment as the key to understanding. It is an old debate. Given a family in which suicides occur generation after generation, how can one decide whether the act of suicide has a genetic or mimetic cause? In order to consider all possible causes of a neurosis a psychiatrist would

The Psychiatrist's Doubts

have to know many things not usually considered within the domain of psychiatry. When faced with choices that may disrupt not just the patient's life but also the life of his family, many doctors prescribe psychoactive drugs, which allow the patient to be treated at home.

The mentally ill raise questions about the identity of those classified as normal. What is the threshhold of deviance? The lunatic, suffering from an inability to communicate, reveals our own inability to communicate because we can neither understand nor respond. The persistence of mental illness demonstrates the shortcomings of scientific research.

AGING

At what age does a person become old? When Mme de Sévigné gave her famous description of Louis XIV's remarriage (*"Madame de Maintenon est devenue Madame de Maintenant,"* Madame de Maintenon has become the Madame of the Moment), she described the king, then aged forty-seven, as "elderly." Old age is a social construct. Indeed, the whole concept of age has changed in recent years. Adolescence has joined childhood and adulthood. Many people can now look forward to two, perhaps three decades between retirement and the onset of the physical and mental handicaps that reduce individual autonomy and therefore define old age. In the past, when man's life expectancy was shorter, the period between the end of work and the end of life was very brief or even nonexistent. Today, millions of retired people remain active and in full possession of their faculties.

The biological facts are clear. People age rapidly. The human body attains its peak of efficiency quite early. The rate of scar formation begins to decrease at age fifteen, and by age twenty-five we are losing 300,000 neurons daily (although billions remain). We notice signs of physical decline: diminished eyesight, slightly impaired hearing, shortness of breath, high blood pressure, and so on. Our mental faculties too suffer. Memory lapses first affect proper names and then recollections of the recent past, while older memories remain intact. Dwelling in the past, the elderly person ceases to be a contemporary of his or her own history. The *laudator temporis acti* can annoy those around, people already irritated by the old person's finickiness (associated with the loss of memory).

Love of comfort and desire for fame and honors come with old age or are intensified by it. As a proselytizer for his own life-style, the elderly person exasperates others by exhibiting what seems to them unwarranted self-satisfaction. Gradually the person enters what is sometimes called "second childhood": a semiliquid diet replaces solid food; the digestive functions become a focus of attention; modesty disappears; and ultimately doctor and nurse become father and mother. A child's dependency gradually decreases as the child progresses toward life; the dependency of the elderly person ends in death. One gerontologist puts it this way: "The elderly person is a caricature of the child, a child without a future. Old age is an empty childhood, an absurd childhood. It is a void ahead and within."

The increasing percentage of the elderly within the population brings an utterly new challenge. Paul Paillat states that "No system of values that advocates respect for one's forebears has had to contend with such rampant proliferation."[11] Of every 10,000 children born, 3,194 males and 5,797 females will survive to age eighty (compared with 1,333 males and 2,399 females in 1936). Men who are eighty today can expect to live for six more years; women, for seven and a half more years. It has been estimated that in 2025 the number of octogenarians will be six times as great as in 1950. According to the 1982 census, 7,500,000 French citizens—some 13.8 percent of the population—are over sixty-five. Of 100 men over the age of sixty-five, 74 are married; of 100 women of the same age, 52 are widows. According to Paillat, "the principal division within the elderly population is therefore gender." The number of men over seventy-five is 1,058,000; the number of women is 2,106,000.

Growing Numbers of Elderly

Thus most of the elderly are women. Those who are not married or who are no longer married have a slightly higher mortality rate than those who are married. Men between the ages of sixty-five and seventy-nine who never married are more fragile than widowers. Nothing comparable is observed among women. Suicide is more common among men than among women. For men between ages sixty and seventy-nine, widowers are three times as likely to commit suicide as married men whose wives are still alive. The frequency of suicide mirrors the social hierarchy: farm workers and other laborers are most likely to kill themselves; white-collar managers are less likely to commit suicide if they have worked in the public sector.

"Hardy old men, or, rather, old women, are to be looked for in such villages, because as one disillusioned old lady put it, 'Men aren't very robust creatures'" (Colette).

People are living longer and retiring sooner. In 1906, 66.2 percent of men over sixty-five were still working, compared with 36.2 percent in 1954 and 10.6 percent in 1975. The average retirement age for managers has dropped from sixty-eight years, five months, in 1950 to sixty-five years, eleven months, in 1972; it will probably continue dropping until it reaches sixty. One poll found that 83 percent of men and 50 percent of women between the ages of sixty-five and sixty-nine suffer from no disability; for the seventy-to-seventy-four age group the corresponding figures are 65 percent and 39 percent. According to Paillat, "men and women today can look forward to an extra twenty years of life, from age sixty to age eighty—a period as long as childhood and adolescence."

Retirement

The disparity between the retirement age and the time when the biological effects of aging begin to make themselves felt is an important social fact. In military parlance "retirement" means withdrawal; it is associated with defeat. One Frenchman complained that "to expel a man from social life at age sixty, when he is still able and eager to work, is an act that must be shrouded in honorable rhetoric so as to hide its ignominious character." The pace of retired life is so different from that of working life that it is wrenching for everyone and disastrous for those not yet ready to retire. Women who have always devoted a part of their time to housework have an easier time than men.

Unskilled laborers (who have the shortest life expectancy of all occupational categories) are usually satisfied to retire at sixty, despite their relatively small savings and pensions. The self-employed often have inadequate savings and can reduce the level of their activity gradually; hence they often prefer to postpone full retirement as long as possible. Farmers have been retiring at an earlier age since the introduction of so-called severance annuities, a form of financial inducement to early retirement. The two groups that work the longest are situated at opposite ends of the income spectrum: "Service personnel, at one extreme, earn low wages, can work flexible hours, are relatively unskilled, and enjoy a favorable ratio of demand to supply. Elderly people without resources (housewives, for example) can find refuge in this job category. At the other extreme are top executives, who like to remain on the job because they find the work interesting and because the pay is high."[12]

Joyful retirement?

Consumer society has encouraged the rebelliousness of "youthful" retirees. *Notre temps,* a magazine created in 1968 to serve this segment of the population and with a current circulation in excess of one million, explains it this way: "They [the retirees] are looking for and can now afford a better quality of life." By the time most people reach sixty, they have inherited something from their own parents and their children have grown; even if parents offer financial help to their children, they are careful not to empty their own pockets. The elderly can afford to participate in sports, travel, and drive fast cars. Today's watchword is to grow old gracefully. *Notre temps* has banished from its lexicon such demeaning terms as "golden age" and "aged" and adopted instead the upbeat "people of leisure." Many advertisers target this group, offering such products and services as hair dyes, facial treatments, plastic surgery, antiwrinkle creams, and skin lotions. Nutritionists offer advice about diet. Sexologists point out that pleasure knows no age limit. By contrast, so-called golden age clubs are of interest chiefly to the middle class. Started in the 1970s, by the 1980s the clubs numbered in the thousands and boasted perhaps a million members. Surveys conducted by the National Gerontology Foundation found evidence of the importance of family life: 65 percent of retirees see their children at least once a week. Many people today live to see their great–grandchildren.

But it does not follow that everyone has access to the "quality of life" extolled by the "leisure magazines." Retirement exacerbates social inequalities. A person's physical and mental condition on reaching retirement depend on what went before, and the disadvantaged suffer numerous handicaps long before their working days come to an end. "In ever growing numbers the poorly educated join those whose health was poor, who worked for many years for low wages, whose jobs were stressful and unsatisfying, who had little time for anything but laborious chores outside work, who led passive rather than active lives, who shunned organizations, and so on."[13] These are the people who turn up in large numbers in homes for the elderly when their physical and/or mental condition deteriorates to the point where they can no longer take care of themselves.

Today in France perhaps 400,000 to 500,000 people fit this description. Those who have always been poor languish in state-run homes and wait to die. It is easier for elderly people in the cities to remain in their homes than it is for those in the country. The elderly vote, so the government has hastened to provide special services and benefits. But who will take care of older people in rural areas, which have been losing population at a rapid rate?

At one time the elderly were credited with special wisdom and knowledge. In so-called primitive societies old age is regarded as an advance rather than a decline. In oral cultures the elderly are repositories of collective memory. When the life expectancy is short, mere survival is enough to command admiration and respect. In dynamic industrial societies, however, change is so rapid that experience is devalued and even experienced older workers must undergo retraining. The elderly are so numerous that they have ceased to be an object of special attention: scarcity creates value.

There is, however, one field in which experience does count and older people play a surprising role: politics. Politicians have gone to extraordinary lengths to exempt themselves from any form of compulsory retirement. The pleasures of power compensate for the pangs of age. Marshal Pétain became chief of state at age eighty-four. General de Gaulle returned to power at age sixty-seven. Ayatollah Khomeini was seventy-eight when he toppled the shah from his throne. François Mitterrand, a politician who fought for a sixty-year retirement age, was elected president of the Republic in his sixty-fifth year.

WHO DIES—AND OF WHAT, WHEN, AND HOW?

Between 1975 and 1980 the leading causes of death among men aged fifty-five to sixty-four were, in decreasing order: cancer, circulatory diseases, cirrhosis, accident, suicide, alcoholism, infectious diseases, and "indeterminate and other causes." In different age groups of course the picture varies greatly. From thirty-five to forty-five years, the number of accidental deaths equals the number of deaths from cancer. Today, thanks to antibiotics, infectious diseases rarely claim lives. The prevalence of cancer confirms Philippe Ariès's observation that "more than the skeletal or emaciated figures of the fourteenth- and fifteenth-century danse macabre, more even than the leper with his clackers, death today is cancer."[14] The life expectancy of a child born in 1900 was forty-eight years; in 1935, sixty years; and in 1981, seventy years, five months, for men and seventy-eight years, six months, for women.[15] The rate of infant mortality was 91 per thousand

births in 1940 but only 12 per thousand in 1978. The mortality rate among children aged ten is extremely low (0.3 per thousand). Indeed the death rate is very low among children generally, except between the ages of eighteen and twenty-two, when there is a high risk of death from motorcycle accidents. In the eighteenth century only five of every hundred newborn children had living grandparents, compared with forty-one in 1973. Some 91 percent of eighteenth-century thirty-year-olds had no living grandparent, and 28 percent had no living parent, compared with 53 percent and 4 percent respectively in 1973. One demographer sums it up this way: "In the eighteenth century one generation succeeded another; generations did not overlap as they do now."

Inequality in the face of death is a statistical fact. Teachers, engineers, civil servants, and professionals live longer than people in other occupations. Most vulnerable are manual laborers, among whom the death rate in the thirty-five-to-sixty age group is 25 per thousand, three times higher than for teachers and engineers. At thirty-five the mortality rate for all men is 2.3 per thousand, but for executives, professionals, and

We saw the first automobiles, the first airplane, the first atomic bombs, the first man on the moon. We have known two World Wars. We have lost all our male friends and nearly all our female ones. Some of our children are dead. We are as lonely at home as in the nursing home. We can recount our memories, not exchange them. Facing page: Gérard Vincent, *Portrait of Madame P.* (Private Collection.)

teachers it is only 1 per thousand, compared with 6 per thousand for laborers and 4 per thousand for farmhands. If the level of employment remains constant, more education means longer life expectancy among both workers and managers.

Work delays death: in all occupational groups the unemployed die younger than the employed. The mortality rate is higher among the retired and semiretired than among employed individuals of the same age. Marriage and family life also seem to provide some protection: the mortality rate among bachelors, widowers, and divorced men between the ages of thirty-five and sixty is twice that among married men. Among women these disparities are less marked: death is not more frequent among unmarried, widowed, and divorced women than among married women. Perhaps, for women, the physical and emotional stress of married life is difficult to bear. In any case, women bear the death of a spouse better than men, notwithstanding the proverbial saying that "there are inconsolable widows but no inconsolable widowers." Urbanization exacerbates inequality with respect to death: in the countryside the mortality rate of farmhands is two and a half times that of schoolteachers, but in large cities the mortality rate among manual laborers is four times that of schoolteachers (five times in the Paris area).

Death, which takes place in a hospital or clinic 80 percent of the time, has been completely medicalized. A representative of the coroner's office must verify the cause of death before a death certificate can be issued. Determining the time of death has become a problem. Death used to be marked by the end of respiration, determined by placing a mirror in front of the deceased's mouth and nose to check for the absence of breath. Later the moment of cardiac arrest became the definitive sign. Today it is a flat electroencephalogram or electrocardiogram. No longer is death a transition completed in a matter of moments; it comes in stages that may be stretched out over several hours or even days. In the words of Philippe Ariès: "Death is now a technological fact, a result of the cessation of treatment. In other words, it is, and more and more is openly avowed to be, a consequence of deliberate decisions by the doctor and hospital staff."

Death and Dying

Death has its fashions. Once there was a vogue for what Ariès called "domesticated death," defined as "a public ceremony organized and presided over by the dying individual

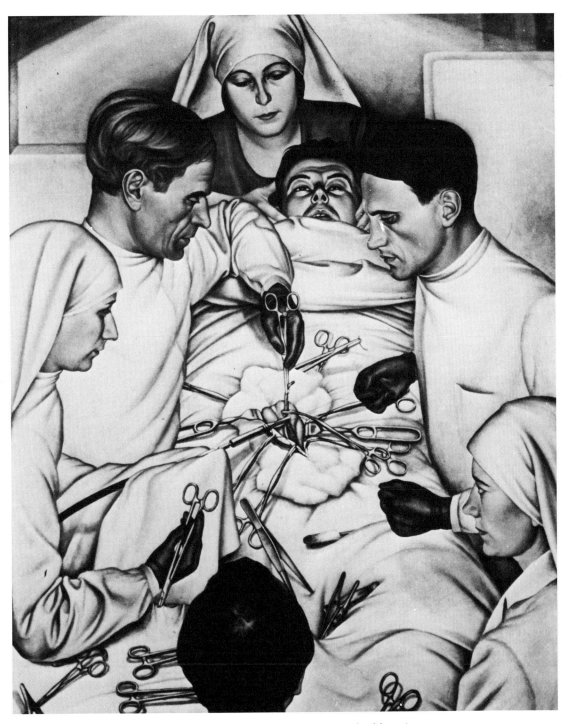

Christian, *The Operation,* 1929. (Munich, Stadtische Galerie im Lenbachhaus.)

and following a standard protocol." Men and women died as they were born: in a bedroom so full of people that the physicians of the time, believing in the "virtues of the air," ordered the crowds out, extinguished the candles, and threw open the windows.

It was not until the 1930s, with the United States leading the way, that people began to die in hospitals rather than at home. With the transfer of death to the hospitals, "all reference to death came to be seen as improper," according to Ariès. "Death being morbid, people spoke as though it did not exist. Certain people simply vanished and ceased to be spoken of, at least for a time, until it could be forgotten that they were dead." He questioned "whether much of today's social pathology does not have its source in the banishment of death from daily life, in the prohibition of mourning and of the right to shed tears over the dead." If yesterday's death was a tragic drama, today's is a lugubrious comedy: the dying person must pretend not to be dying, and loved ones must participate in the deception. The person is deprived of death, society of mourning.

"This death, which some call the most horrible of all horrible things—who does not know that others call it the sole haven from the torments of this life?" (Montaigne).

These are sweeping indictments, and perhaps a measure of skepticism is called for. Death cannot be a "public ceremony organized and presided over by the dying individual" unless the decedent remains lucid to the end and is spared disabling pain. One oncologist says about the terminal stages of leukemia: "I have never heard a dying person utter a historic phrase. Of some 1500 patients dying from leukemia, among them many physicians, I have known only one who dared to look death in the eye." The *belle mort* Ariès finds so enchanting—death in which the victim remains lucid to the end and aware of the imminence of death—surely did exist, and does so today. But to claim that it was universal is to substitute nostalgia for scientific rigor. "Domesticated death . . . is not a model taken from history but an ideal taken from the domain of myth . . . The subject of death has become the focal point of nostalgic and utopian ideas."[16]

Nevertheless, Ariès was on the right track when he borrowed from English the notion of "dying" as opposed to "death." The American authors who have studied the subject take a variety of approaches, but all agree that after initial anxiety and rebellion, the dying person gradually adapts to the inevitability of death.

People today die in hospitals, where the staff behaves as if the person were going to live, administering treatment whose primary purpose is to conceal the imminence of death. Unlike American doctors, French doctors interviewed in 1968 stated that they categorically refused to inform hospital patients that death was imminent. As justification they cited the need to protect the hospital and staff as well as to calm the patient. In the United States, R. S. Duff, a physician, and A. B. Hollingshead, a sociologist, studied forty deaths that occurred in hospitals. Their work calls attention to the tacit understanding that develops between patients and staff. One doctor told them that a well-bred person can grasp the truth without being told.

The silence of a dying patient is hard on the staff, which responds by falling into a silence of its own. One American study shows that two patients in similar physical condition may be classified on admission as curable or incurable depending on their age and social class. If the patient is elderly, a prognosis of certain death may be made even before the doctor arrives. Alcoholics, drug addicts, prostitutes, and va-

Where People Die

grants may be diagnosed as "dead on arrival." According to Claudie Herzlich, the "probability that a person will be considered dead or dying depends in part on that person's place in the social structure."[17] If someone is poor, old, alone, or suffering from numerous other handicaps and unlikely to be an interesting case, one of the kind doctors like to write up for the medical journals—in other words, if a patient is socially and medically unremarkable—he or she is simply swallowed up by the machinery of the hospital. The death becomes one more in a mass-produced series, and the job of the hospital staff is to make the machinery run as efficiently as possible.

Euthanasia

The universe of a dying person comprises three worlds: the medical, the social, and that of family and friends. The question of euthanasia involves all three. In 1968 it was stated that "the physician's task is not to maintain life at all costs; it is not to prevent natural death; it is only to prevent and avoid premature pathological death." And in 1976 the observation was made that "society still has to be organized in such a way as to alleviate the dying person's temptation to commit suicide by surrounding him with love, care, and understanding, by relieving his suffering yet without indulging in therapeutic heroics whose only purpose is to prolong a futile agony."[18] In 1967 a Chicago lawyer proposed that people be allowed to draw up "living wills" in which they could state their preference for "active" euthanasia in the event that they were unable to make the decision themselves. A bill filed in Michigan was designed to allow patients to designate a legal agent "empowered to decide on medical treatment when the person is incapacitated by illness or accident." When a sample of Americans were asked whether "a patient suffering from an incurable disease should be allowed to ask his doctor to let him die rather than prolong his life when no cure is in sight," an affirmative reply was given by 76 percent of Protestants, 70 percent of Catholics, and 75 percent of Jews. The journal *Panorama des médecins* polled 701 physicians, 666 of whom opposed bills that would allow doctors to deny medical care to terminally comatose patients. But another survey of 300 doctors found that 65 percent of those under thirty-five were in favor of "passive euthanasia in cases in which the injured or ill patient has lapsed into deep coma and is *incontrovertibly* beyond hope of recovery." The crux of the matter lies in the adverb "incontrovertibly."

The issue remains in the courts. Judges are bound by law: in France active euthanasia is murder, a matter for criminal prosecution; passive euthanasia constitutes failure to assist a person in danger and is therefore a misdemeanor. Judges (and juries), however, have shown themselves willing to go beyond the strict letter of the law. Consider a few French examples. Mireille Gouraud, who killed her hopelessly ill son, was acquitted of murder charges in November 1966. Seven months after the death of his father, Fernando Carillo killed his mother, who was suffering from incurable cancer; in October 1977 he was acquitted in Aix-en-Provence. Luigi Faita killed his incurably ill brother but was acquitted in January 1982 by a court in Colmar.

In England, Derek Humphrey, a journalist for the *Sunday Times,* revealed on television in March 1978 that, with her consent, he had killed his wife because she was suffering from incurable cancer. He was acquitted. No prison sentence for euthanasia has been meted out in Great Britain for the past twenty-five years. What is surprising, given common preconceived notions about Sweden, is that on September 15, 1978, a court in Stockholm sentenced one Dr. Toss to eight months in prison for voluntary manslaughter; the case involved a patient who in 1974 had signed, in the presence of witnesses, a will asking that no "extraordinary therapeutic measures" be taken to prolong his life.

What is the doctor to do? The dilemma is most difficult when a newborn baby is concerned. An unwritten rule allows attempts at resuscitation to be halted if the infant has not drawn breath after five minutes—by which time irreversible damage to the central nervous system usually has occurred. Yet there are exceptions: some newborns resuscitated after five minutes have developed into normal adults. How should the doctor respond to a mother's request that an abnormal child not be allowed to live? It is likely that passive and active euthanasia are practiced more often than is commonly admitted or believed.

Suicide

The suicide, by repudiating a life deemed unsatisfactory and unbearable, throws down a gauntlet to the living. He throws down a gauntlet to the dead, whom he seeks to rejoin with incomprehensible haste. And he throws down a gauntlet to God, since he denies God's Creation. That is why the Catholic Church declared Judas Iscariot's suicide an unforgiv-

"Suicide Is Nobody's Business." The friend or relative of a suicide victim feels guilty for not coming to the aid of a person in danger. But how can we understand the wishes of one desperate to do away with him- or herself?

able sin. Suicide sometimes elicits scorn ("What cowardice to flee the battle of life!"), sometimes admiration ("What courage it took to go through with it!"). Provocative and visible as the act is, it remains shrouded in secrecy.

Suicide is so shrouded in secrecy that we do not even know how many instances there are annually. What statistics exist record only the "successful" and reported suicides and thus underestimate the actual number. In 1983 there were 12,000 suicides and roughly 150,000 attempts; 10 percent of all deaths in the fifteen-to-twenty-four age group resulted from suicide. A special issue of the journal *Laennec,* published in April 1985, reported that more suicides were committed on Mondays than on other days; almost none were committed on weekends. The months of May and June were favored; suicide in winter was rare. City dwellers were likely to kill themselves in August; and suicide was twice as likely in the countryside as in Paris.

A study published by the Phoenix Association stressed the importance of loneliness due to celibacy, divorce, or death of a spouse. When Claude Guillon and Yves Le Bonniec published *Suicide mode d'emploi* (Suicide: A User's Manual) in 1983, it caused a scandal. One of the authors was indicted for failure to assist a person in danger on a complaint filed by the family of a person who, after several attempts, finally succeeded in killing himself. It is always easiest to blame others. The person who commits suicide condemns family and friends to a lifetime of guilt.

AFTER DEATH

Cremation versus Burial

Philippe Ariès has attacked the excessive "socialization" of death and the excessive "desocialization" of mourning. People now die in impersonal hospitals and are buried "in strict privacy," without the traditional black-clad procession. Young people, forbidden to view the body and excluded from the funeral, have lost all familiarity with death. Quick funerals and shortened mourning periods result in psychological problems. Psychoanalysts tell us that we no longer know how to "kill the dead" and that in the absence of a ceremony to alleviate guilt survivors continue in their fantasies to be obsessed by the deceased.

Ariès points out that the British intelligentsia, "in the vanguard of the death revolution," has turned to cremation, "the most radical means of getting rid of the dead." In the 1980s a sort of promotional campaign in favor of cremation was conducted in France, which faces a shortage of cemetery space. In the February 1977 issue of the municipal bulletin of Talence (Gironde) the municipal councillor in charge of cemeteries, listed the benefits of cremation: not only was it less costly than burial, but it also permitted respect for the religious beliefs of the deceased ("religious music if the deceased was Christian, classical music otherwise"); in addition, cremation is "clean, which is not the case with burial, with its unhealthy vaults, exhumations, and distressing physical decomposition. Ecology would benefit." He proposed that columbaria be dubbed "souvenir gardens."

Nevertheless, burial is still more common in France than cremation. Perhaps the reason is, as Louis-Vincent Thomas suggests, that "the remains are fundamental. Nothing is worse than a missing body . . . What is a body? A presence that manifests an absence." He adds that "the mourning period is also the period in which the body decomposes."[19] Apparently

In contrast to overcrowded French cemeteries, many in the United States are spacious and parklike.

it takes a year for the body to decompose fully, the length of time it usually is assumed to take for the mourner's pain to subside.

In societies steeped in Christianity, Ariès tells us, "the tomb has become the true family home." The cross on the tomb is a symbol of resurrection, and the tombstone represents the dead person. What lies beneath the durable marble headstone that loved ones like to visit and decorate with flowers? A body, says Thomas, a body subject to unpleasant changes that no one wants to think about. Attention has been shifted, in a kind of metonymy, from the contents to the vessel. How can the memory of the deceased be preserved while the state of the decomposing body is forgotten? With photographs, films, and tapes—the modern ways of preserving information. In the future, Thomas tells us, there may be libraries of memories, just as today there are libraries of books. There people will be able to trace the memory of their loved ones. In so doing they will help to preserve the memory of the past, without which no person or society can live.

Inequality in the face of death, inequality after death: a spectacular public funeral contrasted with a quiet village ceremony.

Nostalgia for the socialization of mourning should not be allowed to obscure the fact that death involves inheritance.

Inheritance

Today three generations often coexist, and even a four-generation span is no longer exceptional. Thus inheritances are deferred, and more and more people are responsible for supporting elderly parents who choose to retire earlier than ever before. Consider two extreme examples. A man of sixty may be in line to inherit a large fortune, but if one or both parents remain alive he may have received none of it. Another sixty-year-old may have been forced to retire while still responsible for a parent and one or more unemployed children.

Jean-Claude Chamboredon rightly argues that "a sociology of death not based on a sociology of types of inheritance risks being overly idealist and abstract." More and more parents, aware that their children will not come into their inheritances before they reach the age of retirement, are choosing to make gifts of a portion of their estate while still alive. There were 100,000 such gifts in France in 1970, 185,000 in 1983; the average recipient was ten years younger than the average legatee. It has also become increasingly common to make gifts of property in the form of joint ownership: the number of such transactions increased from 28,000 in 1964 to 54,000 in 1977 and has continued to grow ever since owing to a provision in the French tax laws that allows taxes on the entire property to be paid by the person who enjoys the benefit of use. In the past people usually came into their inheritances when they embarked on active life; today many must wait until they are nearly finished working.

There can be no doubt that the tears and lamentations that once accompanied the deceased to his or her final resting place often masked simple greed. But division of the estate is an important part of death, which among other things confirms the position of the decedent's family in society. An estate is more than just property; it is property invested with emotion and family history. The father who saves, starts a business, and amasses wealth so that he may leave his children more than he received from his parents is motivated by more than the desire for gain. Money is an instrument for perpetuating the family name. An estate, a "patrimony," is, as the term suggests, an image of the father. That is why governments—even socialist governments—have always limited the estate tax.

THE SEARCH FOR SEXUAL HARMONY

According to Pierre Guiraud, there are in French some 1,300 words or phrases for coitus, 550 for penis, and an equal number for the female sex organ.[20] The word orgasm, defined by *Robert's Dictionary* as "the highest degree of sexual excitement," is applied to the pleasure of men as well as women, but it is seen as something more difficult for women to achieve than for men.

The rich language of sex is generally expurgated in polite society and ignored by dictionaries. The 1978 *Petit Larousse* defines sexuality as "the set of specific internal and external characteristics of individuals determined by their sex." Such lofty abstraction is hardly likely to inspire fantasies in teenagers. But Michel Foucault urges us to reflect on the loquacity of this silence. Female pleasure preoccupied all the authorities, and a few even dared to talk about it. In the seventeenth century Dr. Nicolas Verrette said that women were by nature "more lascivious" than men, and the *Petite Bible des jeunes époux* (Newlyweds' Bedside Bible, 1885) encouraged the couple to aim for simultaneous orgasm. In the past a woman who experienced orgasm without love was considered a nymphomaniac, whereas a married man who frequented brothels was "normal."

What is historically new is a discourse of women that talks about their sexuality and enumerates their grievances. Masters and Johnson report that in the 1950s their patients were mainly men concerned with such sexual problems as impotence and premature ejaculation. In the 1960s, however, increasing numbers of women came to see them because of difficulties in achieving orgasm. In the 1970s a new anxiety concerning physical inadequacies appeared. Even after psychological problems were resolved, people continued to worry about differences in sexual performance. Sexual harmony became the structural principle of the couple. Imperatives of duty and reciprocal devotion are no longer the guiding principle of the couple, nor is the child an essential feature of its structure. Values have shifted toward greater emphasis on individual and/or conjugal narcissism. The search for sexual harmony is trumpeted by the media and spread by counseling, groups, and other channels.[21]

Orgasmology and Orgasmotherapy

The major event affecting private life in Western societies in recent decades is probably the emergence of an erotics totally alien to Judeo-Christian culture. Sexology came into being in the second half of the nineteenth century. It did not become a legitimate branch of the human sciences, however, until after World War I (Wilhelm Reich's *Function of the Orgasm* was published in 1927); further gains were made after World War II (Kinsey's *Sexual Behavior in Man* was published in 1948). In 1950 Masters and Johnson, in a bold new use of the laboratory, for the first time observed male and female genitals during the sexual act. After years of observation they described the human orgasm in *Human Sexual Response,* published in 1966. The female orgasm was analyzed in terms of physiological, psychological, and sociological factors. The myth of the clitoris, supposed analogue of the penis, was destroyed, and the distinction between clitoral and vaginal orgasms was shown to be illusory. *Les Mésententes sexuelles* (Sexual Problems, 1971) proposed a nosography of sexual dysfunctions that became the basis of the new disciplines of orgasmology and orgasmotherapy. Unlike psychoanalysts, sexologists insist that their work is based on experimentally verified scientific data and results in cures. Two years before his death Freud wrote "Analysis Terminable and Interminable," a title that can perhaps be interpreted as an admission of failure; by contrast, the orgasmotherapist claims to produce results in a limited period of time.

Sexology takes its inspiration from behavioral therapy, whose practitioners hold that neurotic behavior is "learned." The sexologist's job is to help the patient unlearn his or her dysfunctional behavior. "The goal," we are told, is "to eliminate *present* symptoms (as opposed to *past* repressions) by deconditioning and reconditioning the patient's body. There are two possible approaches: eliminate the anxiety associated with the behavior to be learned, or stimulate anxiety in connection with the behavior to be unlearned."[22] The treatment, which lasts two weeks, is conducted by two therapists, one male and one female, one a physician and the other a psychologist. If successful, the treatment is followed up by five years of posttherapeutic monitoring, generally by telephone. Statistics of success and failure are periodically revised and published.

Masturbation plays an important part in the treatment, which may remove from onanism the pathological stigma it has long had to bear. After millennia of condemnation it is emerging from the realm of the secret to become, the sexologists tell us, the best way of preparing for a sexual encounter with another person. David Cooper, in *Death of the Family* (1970), writes that "we cannot love another person unless we love ourselves to the point of truly masturbating, that is, masturbating to the point of orgasm . . . We move toward

others when we are ready." In *The Sexual Dialogue* (1976)
Gilbert Tordjman writes that "all children of both sexes mas-
turbate from early childhood." At the end of the latency period
it is essential that pubescent youths rediscover their "bad habits" of old, now rebaptized good: "Adolescents who do not
experience masturbation as a stage of maturation are far more
likely to have difficulties in adult life than those who do."

In the past, when marriage was not a consecration of love
but a contract linking two fortunes or two empty purses, the
life of the couple needed a governing rule. Such a rule was
provided, Jean-Louis Flandrin tells us, by the notion of a
"marital obligation" that was to be repaid "in bed and out,
but perhaps most of all in."[23] If husband or wife refused to
participate in the sexual act, the other spouse could turn to
the confessor, who would then admonish the recalcitrant and
perhaps refuse absolution and communion. Today a woman
bedded and respected, but unsatisfied and therefore frigid, may
choose to consult a sexologist. A man may do the same if he

From Confessor to Sexologist

Sexologists now hang out their
shingles like other specialists.

Sexuality is a source of eternal dissatisfaction. In 1986 the walls were covered with ads urging people "to call Sophie" or "type Geraldine" (on the French phone company's Minitel computer network). A "hot" voice on the other end of the telephone line thus became an object of desire that existed nowhere but in the imagination.

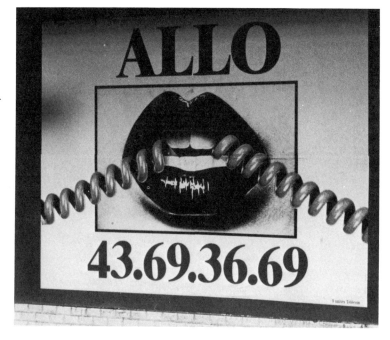

has difficulty having an erection or suffers from premature ejaculation or cannot ejaculate at all. Like the confessor of old, the orgasmologist is ready to share the couple's secret. "In the realm of ethics," Béjin says, the sexologist "establishes a simple rule: the orgasmic imperative, that is, a sexual contract, a hedonic quid pro quo that inaugurates a sexual democracy. In the realm of technique, he teaches his patients orgasmic self-discipline."

Thus the couple has been a three-way affair, involving a man, a woman, and a third party (confessor, psychoanalyst, sexologist). The state was unable to ignore the situation. In 1976 the French ministry of health established a Center for Information on birth control, maternity, and sex. According to one of its brochures, citizens could "call in by telephone to establish a personal yet anonymous relationship with an information specialist." It was like going to a confessor in another town in order to restore the secrecy of the confessional. Requests for information exceeded, if not the ministry's hopes, then certainly its expectations. In 1980 the Center stopped offering this kind of information. In 1983 a television network broadcast a program called "Psyshow," on which a couple was invited to air its sexual and emotional problems in the presence of two journalists and a psychoanalyst. Outraged, the magazine *Elle* called the show a "televised striptease," while *Confidences* denounced it as "vulgar, scandalous, shameful." The producer defended it thus: "The reason the thing works is that we're in a TV studio. Each member of the couple uses our presence to reclaim his or her freedom from the other. They feel safe." Karima Dekhli sums it up this way: "The on-camera suffering, the hysterical public display, the forced transparency of the program—all these things forcefully call to mind the mechanisms of public confession."

HOMOSEXUALITY

Considered a perversion by the Church and later termed a disease, today homosexuality usually is considered a legitimate form of sexuality. Some even see the homosexual couple as a prefiguration of what the heterosexual couple will become in the future. The time is long since past when the mid-nineteenth-century Dr. Ambroise Tardieu could write: "Would that I could avoid sullying my pen with the infamous turpitude of pederasts!" The taboo on homosexuality persisted

In Rome "it was proverbially held that sex with boys procures a tranquil pleasure unruffling to the soul, whereas passion for a woman plunges a free man into unendurable slavery" (Paul Veyne). Times have changed, as these homosexual marchers show.

until the middle of the twentieth century. Dominique Fernandez argues that homosexual writing was full of hidden clues, a genre developed to a high art by Proust and Gide. Out of this came a form of literary expression that suggested the existence of a secret but said nothing explicit about its content. The *Kinsey Report* claims that, under laws now in force, 95 percent of all Americans should be in prison for sexual crimes. The report states, among other things, that one in four men has had an "extended" homosexual experience.

Homosexuals are now free to come out of the closet and claim their right to be different yet still normal. Sexologists reassure their clients that there is no reason to feel guilt. Masters and Johnson (1980) offer two services to homosexuals: "to restore normal functioning in a homosexual setting for those who do not wish to change their sexual orientation, or to attempt a conversion to heterosexuality for those who feel dissatisfied or guilty about their homosexuality." Now that homosexuals are free to assert their own identity, they no longer have to behave in self-parodying ways, with stereotyped gestures and affected voices. The virile, athletic, leather-

Opposite: Jean-Léon Gérome, *The Slave Market,* 1874; above: *The Snake Charmer,* 1844. Gérome, vitriolic on the subject of Impressionism, which he called "the shame of French art," followed the fashion for "Orientalism." In these two small canvases he unmasked the hypocrisy of a society in which many men had never seen their wives naked. (Williamstown, Massachusetts, Sterling and Francine Clark Art Institute.)

clad homosexual is virtually a dead ringer for the "macho" admired by some women. Michel Pollak states: "Short hair, mustache or beard, muscular body . . . The most common mythical images in the homosexual press and pornographic magazines for gays are the cowboy, the truck driver, and the athlete."[24]

Homosexual Biography

A crucial moment in the lives of most homosexuals is the time of "coming out," or publicly revealing their homosexuality. The difficulty of reconciling homosexual impulses with socialization (especially in marriage) prior to coming out gives rise to what Pollak calls "a schizophrenic style of management." The later the coming out, the more powerful the shock. Suicide attempts are twice as frequent as for others of the same age group. Many German homosexuals interviewed more than a decade ago felt a need to seek "medical treatment" after their first homosexual experience. Once that hurdle had been overcome, however, the suicide rate among homosexuals was reportedly quite low.[25]

The sex life of the average homosexual is considerably more active than that of the average heterosexual. To the question "How many sexual partners have you had in the past twelve months?" 28 percent of the whites and 32 percent of the blacks in a 1978 American study answered "fifty-one or more." In Germany, however, only 17 percent were this active. Contacts are made in specific places such as bars, saunas, gay restaurants and theaters, parks, and so on. Pollak characterizes the life of the homosexual in these terms: "High promiscuity, frequent relations, specialization in certain types of activities." External signs indicate sexual tastes: "Keys worn above the left rear pocket indicate a preference for an active role; above the right rear pocket, a preference for a passive role. The color of a handkerchief allowed to protrude from the rear pocket symbolizes the type of activity sought: light blue signifies oral sex; dark blue, sodomy; bright red, fisting."

Caravaggio, *Saint John the Baptist in the Desert*. The theme of the youthful Saint John the Baptist allowed Caravaggio to paint several canvases that exhibit his sexual preferences. (Rome, Borghese Gallery.)

After coming out, do homosexuals live without guilt? An ancient taboo forced them to separate sexuality from emotion, for they were obliged "to organize [their sexual lives] in such a way as to minimize the risks while optimizing the yield, that is, the orgasmic return." Many homosexuals are drawn to the life of the couple. Sexologists say that many who come to them are often seeking an answer to the problem of how to reconcile sexual freedom with an enduring relationship. The

Sexual militancy leads to political militance. This scene is Christopher Street in Greenwich Village, a New York City neighborhood that is home to many homosexuals.

American study found that 31 percent of the whites and 8 percent of the blacks interviewed had been living in a stable relationship for more than five years. In the homosexual community a kind of equivalent of the extended family is provided through enduring friendships that spring up between ex-lovers, relationships in which resumption of sexual activity is excluded.

Is there any correlation between homosexuality and social status? Census figures cannot help resolve this question. If homosexuals must adopt a "shizophrenic management style" and change roles to suit the person they are with, they acquire talents that may be useful in certain professions. In the upper strata of the ruling class homosexuality is compromising, so homosexuals born into that group are driven to seek careers in intellectual or artistic fields where their homosexuality is tolerated and where it may even be beneficial in a career strategy aimed at exploiting the social capital amassed by the homosexual subculture. Homosexual workers and peasants, however, are likely to be singled out and excluded by their peers.

SEXUALITY AND SOCIAL CONTROL

The socialized sexuality of the nuclear family in which husband, wife, and children are permanently united by ties of love is what Michel Foucault has called a "practice." By this he means that it is the product of a given social state that changes when society changes. It is an idealized practice, to be sure, since love and friendship can die. One of the most important developments in private life since the 1920s has to do with our growing awareness of the emphemeral. In the past, social codes and resulting taboos were so rigid that few dared challenge their permanence. Misbehavior by males was tolerated; they could amuse themselves with a mistress so long as they respected their marital obligations. But as man's life expectancy increased, so did the length of marriage. Changing partners became an expression of man's instinctive sexuality. Monogamy has not always existed or been required; it belongs to a specific historical situation.

The faithful woman married to the fickle husband, the irreproachable wife and her adulterous mate—such a couple is a thing of the past. Western society is rediscovering the sexual potential of women—something Ovid knew about long ago and which is illustrated in numerous Greek and Latin myths.

Various cultures have attempted to attenuate that sexual potential in one way or another: compulsory marriage, segregation of women, excision, infibulation, and so on. Among the French bourgeoisie women were expected to remain virgins until they married. For many the wedding night was experienced as a kind of rape, and subsequent sexual relations were seen as a duty if not an onerous chore.

Can the sexually emancipated woman content herself with one man for fifty years? Sexologists attempt to reassure men and alleviate the guilt of women. They argue that the best way to reconcile the need for social order with the imperatives of sex is to institute a kind of "flexible monogamy"— one or more stable relationships over the course of a lifetime, together with occasional brief relationships, or flings.

UNISEXUALITY

Philippe Ariès considered the emergence of a unisex society the most novel development of recent years. "Roles are interchangeable—not only that of father and mother but also that of male and female sex partners. Curiously, this single model is *virile*. The young woman's figure more and more resembles the young man's. Woman has cast off the enveloping forms that so intrigued artists from the sixteenth to the nineteenth century."[26] Is there any truth to this sweeping assertion? In the past of course public places were sexually exclusive: Victorian pubs and clubs banned women; French bistros were exclusively for men, save for a few women of "ill repute"; village washhouses were closed to men, who worried about what women talked about when they were alone.

Today such segregation is a thing of the past. Schools and professions once considered the exclusive province of men gradually have been opened up to women. Conversely, men have made their own into areas once limited to women: the gynecologist has replaced the midwife; husbands participate in the delivery of children; men diaper babies, cook, wash dishes. Men and women both dress in blue jeans and strive for athletic figures. Early sexual activity has tended to break down barriers. When young women were expected to remain virgins until they married, they discreetly exchanged sexual fantasies, while young men went to brothels in groups and shared advice about coping with venereal disease. Today young couples go to the hospital hand in hand to seek treatment for gonorrhea.

Lucas Cranach, *Cupid Complaining to Venus.* Associated with fecundity and milk, the breasts are symbols of maternity, softness, and security. The tomboy figures favored by certain advertisers today have always been found in painting. (London, National Gallery.)

The Girard-Stoetzel study of French values found "a very high level of agreement between the sexes." Although women are more religious and conservative than men, the reason, say these authors, has to do with the age structure of the female population: octogenarian males are just as conservative as women of the same age group, but their number is relatively small. Young women employ the same crude, even obscene, slang as their friends, lovers, and husbands. When it comes to finding a man, they may take the initative. Advertising today makes objects of men as well as women. Nevertheless, we may still ask whether the trend toward unisexuality is irreversible.

Somewhere in *Sodom and Gomorrah* Proust says that the future of mankind depends on absolute separation of the two sexes, that men and women cannot help following radically divergent paths. Yet in France male and female roles still seem to be divided much as they were in the past, along lines laid down by tradition. How many women are key decisionmakers in the economic and political spheres? Has France yet had a female head of state, prime minister, defense minister, interior minister, or minister of foreign affairs? The leaders of youth gangs are nearly always boys. A glance at such men's magazines as *Lui* or *Penthouse* shows that the androgynous model has yet to captivate the masculine imagination: the women portrayed in the nude in these magazines come closer to those painted by Rubens than to those painted by Cranach or portrayed in modern sportswear advertisements. It has always been man's ruse to impute to "nature" what was in fact due to "culture." The feminine and feminist counteroffensive has yet to win a decisive victory. Clothing has changed and statistics show that women have made headway in traditionally masculine professions. This suggests that the rise of women is irresistible and that they are claiming an ever-growing share of life's monetary, social, and cultural rewards. But we must not confuse masks with faces, fictions for realities.

Has friendship, that little understood and difficult to maintain relationship between two human beings, disappeared or changed profoundly over the past few decades? Has it perhaps been killed off by the "cult of the couple," which tends to exclude outsiders? Ariès notes that "today emotion is absorbed by the family. In the past the family held no monopoly, and friendship therefore played an important role. Men were bound by feelings that went beyond friendship, even taken in its broadest sense. Those feelings gave life to many forms of service that are regulated today by contract. Social life was based on personal ties of dependency, patronage, and mutual support. Service and work relations, once man to man, evolved from friendship and trust to exploitation and hatred."[27]

Love has become a prerequisite for a successful marriage. When the ardor of desire subsides, friendship takes its place. Marriage either evolves or ends in divorce. Family relations are increasingly intimate, even between generations. In the past differentiation according to status, function, and role was strong, not only between sexes but also between parents and children. Studies now agree that parents and children have never been so close. Mothers have become the favorite confidants of their children. Greater homogeneity has made it easier to cross boundaries.

Problems of cultural adaptation are especially difficult for Muslim immigrants from Africa. At school the children learn French; at home they speak a different language. (Paris, Goutte-d'Or section, 1986.)

3

Cultural Diversity in France

Gérard Vincent
Perrine Simon-Nahum
Rémi Leveau
Dominique Schnapper

In the 12th century the number of sacramental rites was reduced to the symbolic number seven: baptism, confirmation, communion, penitence, extreme unction, marriage, and ordination. The Council of Trent conferred the status of dogma on this list. (Ordination at Notre-Dame in Paris, June 1985.)

❧ Catholics:
Imagination and Sin

Gérard Vincent

IN exploring the private lives of French Catholics I focus on what I term "the secret." A few statistics from religious sociology will help set the stage. In 1913 there were 59,000 Roman Catholic priests in France; by 1965 the number had dropped to 41,000, and by 1985 to 28,000 (more than half of whom were over forty). It has been estimated that by the year 2000 there will be no more than 16,000 priests in France. A 1985 Harris Poll on the clergy's place in French society sent out 19,000 questionnaires.[1] The 1,700 responses received and answers from 609 priests interviewed showed that, though poor (with an average monthly income of just $600), 82 percent of the priests considered their financial resources adequate. Our situation, one said, "gives us the right to talk about poverty." Sixty-three percent saw nothing wrong with priests' holding other jobs. Half lived alone: "A can of sardines eaten alone at noon on Christmas Day has a dreadful taste of solitude."

Priests are a varied group politically. In 1986, 36 percent planned to vote for the UDF (a center-right coalition party); 18 percent for the Socialists; 10 percent for the RPR (a party of the right); 2 percent for the Communists; and 1 percent for the extreme right-wing National Front. A left-wing priest described his politics this way: "I went from a priori respect for the established order to a priori distrust of the established order." Conservatives attack "the aimlessness, decadence, and rot of contemporary society." In 1980, 215,700 marriages were celebrated by priests, compared with 334,300 civil marriages; the number of church weddings per hundred civil weddings declined from 79 in 1954 to 64.5 in 1980. Of the seven sacraments, marriage suffered the most precipitous decline: in

A seminarian come to witness the pope's visit. "An almost imperceptible tremor which resembles that of inward joy, a joy so profound that nothing can lessen it, like a broad, calm sea beneath stormy skies" (Georges Bernanos, *Diary of a Country Priest.*)

1952, 37 percent of French people who called themselves Catholics never went to confession; by 1974 the percentage had risen to 54 percent.

A 1981 survey conducted in nine countries yields additional interesting results.[2] Of those questioned, 26 percent said they had no religion. Among Catholics, 10 percent attended mass weekly. Sixty-two percent of the French believe in God, 46 percent in the reality of the soul. But 42 percent doubt the reality of sin. Some 35 percent believe in life after death; 22 percent believe in reincarnation, 27 percent in heaven, 15 percent in hell, and 17 percent in the devil. The place of religion will diminish in the future, according to 40 percent, while 35 percent believe it will remain the same. Religion brings "strength and comfort" to 37 percent, and only 10 percent declare themselves "convinced atheists."

Those responsible for the survey point to the secularization of morality: while only 11 percent of the French believe that religion must be taught to children, 76 percent believe that children ought to be taught to be honest. For 21 percent the distinction between good and evil "is not always clear," and 43 percent "have sometimes or frequently felt remorse." When rules are broken, 28 percent want "the guilty party to pay," but 39 percent favor prevention and reeducation. "Every person should have an opportunity for a full sexual life, without restriction," 27 percent believe. "Marriage is an outmoded institution" for 29 percent, but 42 percent believe that the "ideal" number of children per family is three; nevertheless, practicing Catholics, among whom divorce is rare and wives are less likely to work, are the only ones who actually seek to achieve this ideal. The conclusions of the survey's authors can be summarized thus: materialism is not a dominant value in France; all the major religions are felt to contain "fundamental truths and meanings"; the French do not consider their civilization the "bearer of a universal and superior message"; they are tolerant and understanding.

A brief survey of French Protestants shows them similar to Catholics in many ways.[3] Some 1,800,000 French citizens, 4.2 percent of the population, claim some "affinity with Protestantism." Of these, some 800,000 are affiliated with a church: 400,000 belong to the Calvinist Reformed Church of France; 280,000, mostly in Alsace and the Montbéliard region, to the Lutheran Confession of Augsburg; and the rest to various evangelical churches (Baptist, Pentecostal, and so on). Church membership reportedly has held steady for more than

In 1963 an old peasant couple listens deferentially to what the priest has to say. Are these dark-clad figures an allegory for a dying Church, or will the young boy in white socks and Sunday suit carry on?

Medieval mystery plays depended on community. For days on end the populace would recreate Christ's passion or the life of a patron saint. There was no distinction between actors and onlookers. In 1437, during a representation of the Passion at Metz, the priest incarnating Jesus nearly died on the cross, and the one playing Judas was cut down from the gallows at the last minute. Father Guy de Fatto attempted to revive the mystery tradition in Nevers Cathedral in November 1985. Could he do this while using a microphone?

a century. The failure to grow lurks behind the following remark by the Reverend André Dumas: "Sociologically, this standstill amounts to a decline, because the rural breeding grounds of Protestantism have become depopulated; youth and adult movements that were still vigorous at the end of World War II have collapsed; and the faith is no longer passed on as readily as it was in the days when families were prolific in offspring, traditions, and vocations." Of church members 57 percent are women and 43 percent men; 39 percent are fifty or older, compared with only 13 percent between the ages of thirteen and twenty-four. One report found that "a relatively small proportion, around 15 percent, of Protestants participate regularly in religious activities, and this figure is only slightly higher than the most recent figure for weekly mass attendance among Catholics." To these troubling figures Reverend Dumas adds a rather puzzling comment: "Historically, French Protestantism has shown itself capable of engendering distinctive characters but less capable of forging a distinct and united people."[4] This apparent de-Christianization, as measured by the decline in the number of clergy, is not limited to France.

In the United States the number of seminarians decreased from 49,000 in 1965 to 17,000 in 1975; the number of nuns decreased by 25 percent, monks by 30 percent; and 45,000 nuns and 10,000 priests left their positions and in many cases quit the Catholic Church altogether.

As its ranks have shrunk, the clergy has been transformed. In prerevolutionary France younger children in certain families were destined from birth for the pulpit or convent. Today a religious vocation is a choice, one that requires perseverance and acceptance of a certain way of life. But the audience of the Church and of religious discourse in general exceeds the number of churchgoers. Statistics abound, but they are devoid of meaning; almost any hypothesis is conceivable, even this one: that a resurgence of religiosity may be accompanied by a decline in practice.

The Christian Imagination

Everything we do in this world is subsidiary. What are our few years on earth compared with the eternity that awaits? Yet what we do on earth is decisive too, for the use we make of our freedom determines whether we are saved or damned. Such is the traditional obsession of the faithful, but what Catholic in France today shares it?

Unimaginable Eternity

Eternity? Does anyone today take time out from work, vacation, or television to think about it? Yet it was not so very long ago, at the end of the last century, when preachers tried from the pulpit to wrest youthful minds from the ephemeral pleasures of the moment to remind them of what eternity means. Listen to the Jesuit father preach to Stephen Dedalus in James Joyce's *Portrait of the Artist as a Young Man:* "Try to imagine the awful meaning of [eternity]. You have often seen the sand on the seashore. How fine are its tiny grains! And how many of those tiny little grains go to make up the small handful which a child grasps in its play! Now imagine a mountain of that sand, a million miles high, reaching from the earth to the farthest heavens, and a million miles broad, extending to remotest space, and a million miles in thickness; and imagine such an enormous mass of countless particles of sand multiplied as often as there are leaves in the forest, drops of water in the mighty ocean, feathers on birds, scales on fish, hairs on animals, atoms in the vast expanse of the air; and imagine that at the end of every million years a little bird came to that mountain and carried away in its beak a tiny grain of that sand. How many millions upon millions of centuries would pass before that bird had carried away even a square foot of that mountain, how many eons upon eons of ages before it had carried away all? Yet at the end of that immense stretch of time not even one instant of eternity could be said to have ended. At the end of all those billions and trillions of years eternity would have scarcely begun."

And hell? The horrendous paintings of Hieronymus Bosch and Luca Signorelli are picture postcards compared with the sadistic evocations of the Irish Jesuit: "In hell . . . one torment, instead of counteracting another, lends it still greater force; and, moreover, as the internal faculties are more perfect than the external senses, so are they more capable of suffering." And it never gets better: "But in hell the torments cannot be overcome by habit, for while they are of terrible intensity they are at the same time of continual variety, each pain, so to speak, taking fire from another and re-endowing that which has kindled it with still a fiercer flame." And even this physical suffering is as nothing compared with the regret and remorse that afflict the conscience: "In the lake of all-devouring flame the proud king will remember the pomps of his court, the wise but wicked man his libraries and instruments of research, the lover of artistic pleasures his marbles and pictures and other art treasures, he who delighted in the pleasures of the table his gorgeous feasts . . . The miser will remember his hoard of gold, the robber his ill-gotten wealth . . . the impure and adulterous the unspeakable and filthy pleasures in which they delighted. They will remember all this and loathe themselves and their sins . . . How they will rage and fume to think that they have lost the bliss of heaven for the dross of earth, for a few pieces of metal, for vain honors, for bodily comforts, for a tingling of the nerves."[5]

Since the beginning of the nineteenth century Rome had urged confessors to refrain from instilling fear and an obsession with damnation. In 1828 they were ordered to avoid "a harshness of language likely to close the hearts of penitents" and to refrain from "rigorism, the common fruit of youth, inexperience, and perhaps our traditional instruction." Any "exaggeration in the portrayal of terrible truths" was said to be dangerous, whereas "a warm welcome might sow in the heart the seeds of a happy return to the fold." After the middle of the nineteenth century confessors were increasingly free to

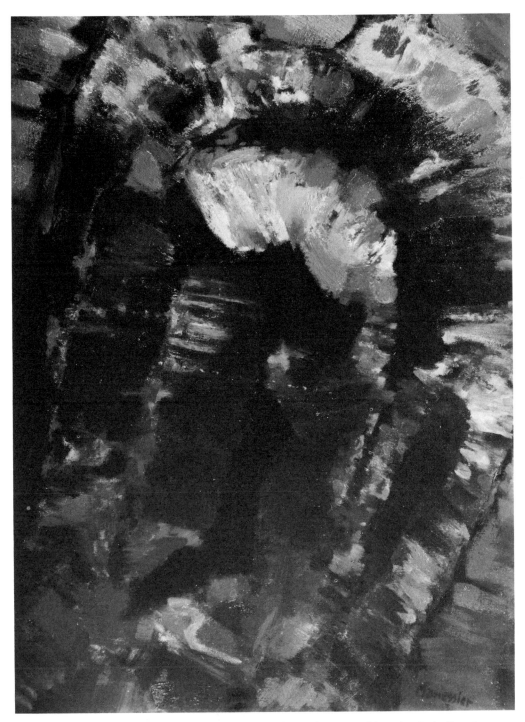

Alfred Manessier. Depicting the face of Christ has always been a problem for Catholic painters. This work by a student of Roger Bissière, Manessier, a Catholic convert, is a lyrical medley of forms and colors that allows the viewer to confront the enigma of the "holy face." (Galerie de France.)

make their own decisions, and the fear of hell began to wane. The dreadful tortures of damnation had always been difficult to reconcile with God's supposedly infinite goodness and mercy.

But if hell does not exist (or is reserved for especially wicked criminals), why subject oneself to vexing tasks and deprive oneself of pleasant activities? Cynical Napoleon observed: "A society cannot exist without inequality of wealth, and inequality of wealth is intolerable unless religion asserts that later, and for all time, things will be divided up differently." If such a view is incompatible with "true" religion, why not acquire as many honors and possessions as possible here and now? The elderly protested, for they had taken so much trouble to accumulate merits in this world on which they hoped to capitalize in the next. "We went to church a lot so that we would not go to hell," said one farm wife. Another stated: "Either there is nothing or the rewards are handed out indiscriminately, so they must not be worth much, because nobody gets something for nothing." But if there is no such thing as original sin or mortal sin, if there is no hell and no purgatory, no tempter and no divine punishment, then "the traditional underpinnings of Christianity are in jeopardy, in particular the theodicy of suffering and the soteriology of redemption."[6]

Paradise on Earth?

The misery of working-class life in France before the middle nineteenth century was described in volume IV of this series. Malnutrition, promiscuity, incest, prostitution, child labor, and alcoholism were among its many scourges. But the absolute pauperization of the working class predicted by Marx never came to pass. For thirty years after World War II France experienced steady economic growth, which, while not eliminating class distinctions, brought new prosperity to all classes of society. With a "decent" house, a "modest" automobile, and a television set, along with the added blessings of the welfare state and modern medicine, everyone could enjoy, if not paradise on earth, at least a tolerable existence. In the past the poor in France lived and died in a world much like the one they had been born into. Upward mobility was unthinkable, so the imagination fastened on the hereafter. Today's dreams are short-term: everyone wants the new trinity (home, car, TV), and even the poor can have it provided they are willing to settle for the bottom of the line. Consumer society has eradicated eschatology, but it has not been able to give meaning to life.

What to Preach?

What, then, should the Church preach? "Certainly no one is required to aid his neighbor by depriving himself of what he or his family needs or even by giving up any of what is decent or proper" (Leo XIII, *Rerum Novarum*). "Religion bestows its warmest consolations on the unfortunate by inspiring in them the hope of immense and immortal goods in proportion to the length and forbearance of their suffering" (Leo XIII, *Auspicato Concessum*). "Christian democracy, precisely because it calls itself Christian, must take the principles of divine faith as its basis. It must minister to the needs of the humble . . . Nothing should be more sacred to it than justice. It must protect the rights of property and ownership from any and all infringements and must maintain the distinction between classes that is an integral part of any well-constituted state" (Leo XIII, *Graves de Communi*). "Willingly accord to masters the respect they deserve and furnish the labor that is their due; do not disdain domestic life, so rich in rewards of every variety; above all, practice religion and turn to it for certain consolation in difficult periods of life" (Leo XIII, *Graves de Communi*). These papal pronouncements were promulgated less than a century ago, but what priest could read them on the pulpit today? When interviewed by Yves Lambert, one farmer had this to say about Sunday sermons: "They've been forced to water things down, because otherwise nobody would show up." More than half of churchgoing Protestants look upon their pastor as a spiritual adviser, and less than 40 percent regard preaching as the most important aspect of a ministry. Even preaching must conform to the iron law of the media system: it must meet the audience's expectations.

CONFESSION, CONTRITION, CONVERSION

An Obsolete Sacrament?

Confession was and still is an opportunity to convey a secret in the knowledge that it will not be divulged. Preserving the secrecy of the confessional has been a point of honor for the clergy and a matter of respect for the faithful and for the rules of the sacrament. Not even twentieth-century anticlerical propaganda has accused confessors of indiscretion. In the past priests were martyred for refusing to talk. From bishops who

Confession no longer resembles a court appearance. The priest, who in the traditional confessional was almost invisible, now sits in a pew and converses openly in his church, or *ecclesia,* that is, "assembly," which here joins the child and the man together with Christ.

moved among the elite to vicars who moved among the humblest of parishioners, what was said in the confessional remained inviolate. "Auricular confession belongs to an oral culture that placed particular emphasis on human contact, on an act of speech performed before the eyes of God alone at a specific time and place. For the purposes of historical research, the pentiential interview is the ideal place to explore the mysteries of religion."[7] But the history of confession cannot be written, because it has no archives. The most famous nineteenth-century confessor, Jean-Marie Vianney, curé of Ars, canonized in 1925, took with him to his grave the secrets of thousands of private lives. Of the two hundred-odd letters he wrote to Monsignor Devie about difficult cases, virtually none have survived. After the turn of the century the clergy recommended frequent confession: "Medicine is not pleasant either, yet you take it in order to preserve the health of your body. Why should you have less courage when it comes to your eternal salvation?" (from a 1913 parish bulletin). Catholics were well-advised to be prepared lest death catch them by surprise: "Will God take seriously those who attempt to clear things up at the last minute?" Countless sermons counseled the faithful to prepare themselves for God's judgment: "In 1922, on Halloween, children equal in number to the number of people who had died that year, whose names were read out, were dressed some in black, others in white, and still others in black and white, to illustrate the preacher's words: those dressed in white were going to heaven, those in black to hell, and the rest to purgatory. Thus sin was not an abstract notion but something to be represented in a concrete and emotional way." In the small Breton parish of Limerzel in the 1920s groups of people made Easter confession in unison. Half the residents confessed on the first Friday of the month (though women outnumbered men); schoolchildren went to confession by class. Did all these people believe in hell? Perhaps, but usually for other people. Confession made up for overzealousness in instilling guilt. One penitent told a taverner: "I came in for a glass of wine because afterward I'm going to clean myself up and this way it won't hurt as much." The rules of confession gradually were eased. Hours became less strict: in Quimper from 1710 to 1851 confession was not heard "before sunrise or after sunset except on Christmas night." The power to hear confessions was expanded: in 1830 only village priests were allowed to receive penitents; teachers were given the right in 1895 and hospital chaplains in 1940.

Absolution (granted if not after the first then after the second confession) brought with it virtual certainty of God's forgiveness, thus easing anxieties about damnation. Confession gave rise to many humorous anecdotes. One concerns a thief who stole bundles of faggots. When the priest asked how many bundles he had stolen, the man replied: "Ten, but let's say twenty, I'll get the rest on my way back." Another priest questioned a man who had stolen a rope: "A long rope?" he asked. "No, not very long," the man answered, "but there was a cow on the end of it." The faithful were quick to protest disparities in punishment. In Brittany, dancing in public could lead to denial of absolution, but alcoholism was tolerated. One merchant, guilty of having danced to a jazz tune at a wedding in 1933, became outraged at this difference, so much so that he attempted to blackmail the priest: "If you don't grant me absolution, I'll never come back." The priest, conciliatory, said: "All right. Leave, think it over, and come back in a few minutes."[8] Yet this priest was the most feared authority figure in the village.

After World War II confession fell on hard times. In 1952, 15 percent of Catholics went to confession at least once a month, while only 3 percent never went at all. By 1974 only 1 percent confessed as often as once a month; 54 percent never did. Priests devoted less and less time to hearing confessions. In the diocese of Quimper the number of "confessor-days" was thirty-four in 1934, twenty-four in 1954, thirteen in 1960, and seven in 1974. What few young priests there are, are overwhelmed with other jobs and unenthusiastic about taking on a chore that many find distressing and "embarrassing." Yet auricular confession, which Marcel Mauss called an "individualized instrument of inquisition," was one of the cornerstones of clerical power, perhaps the most important of all. It was a symbolic power, to be sure, since it rested on secrecy and involved no physical exertion, but it was still both frightening and feared because the man who wielded it could judge and absolve, and from his judgment there was no appeal except in the other world. Limiting clerical power initiated a process whereby morality ultimately achieved autonomy from religion; it simultaneously increased the power of laymen within the ecclesiastical organization itself. Traditionalists claim that it also undermined the traditional economy of salvation.

No sacrament has given rise to more disaffection than confession. Its decline is linked, I believe, to a waning of the belief that man is by nature sinful. The curé of Ars (1786–1859) heard confession seventeen hours a day during the summer and thirteen hours a day during the winter; some five hundred letters or notes addressed to him have survived. During the lifetime of this prodigious confessor theology began to take notice of what was called the "status" of the penitent. Thomas Gousset's *Théologie morale* (1845) gives this advice: "The confessor is required to impose a penance proportional to the number and seriousness of the penitent's faults, with due regard for the individual's *status* and dispositions" (II, 296). A chapter of the second volume of this work is entitled: "On the Duties of the Confessor to Those Who Are Not Sufficiently Instructed in the Truths of Religion, or Who Are Ignorant of Truths Relative to Their Status."[9] By status the theologians meant what we would now call social position, and the admonition to confessors was intended to urge them to take into account the social causes of sinful behavior. Whether the object under consideration is sin, neurosis, or criminal behavior, the evolution in thinking since the late nineteenth century is similar: the status of the sinner, lunatic, or criminal has increasingly had to be taken into account in measuring the individual's "responsibility."

The story of Sister Marie-Zoé, recounted in an unanswered 1858 letter to the curé of Ars, sheds further light on the notion of status. Too poor to feed their daughter, Marie-Zoé's parents sent her to live with an uncle, who abused the girl and stole her "innocence" at age fourteen. After two years in boarding school, she returned to her uncle's home, and sexual relations with him resumed. Although she felt no calling, she entered a convent as a novice and was seduced by a priest. "Our hearts were joined in a dangerous friendship," she wrote, "and when we saw each other we kissed and did similar things. This went on for a period of three years." When this relationship ended, Marie-Zoé clung to her "bad habits," and at age twenty-nine she wrote to the illustrious confessor about her fear of damnation. Her inability to follow the rules filled her not with a desire to protest but with feelings of guilt. Philippe Boutry remarks: "She judged herself in terms of an interpretation of events based on a vocabulary identical to that found in moral theology textbooks." According to the

Theology and the Notion of "Status"

In the 1950s more than a hundred French priests chose to live as workers. Their purpose was not so much to convert their fellow workers as to define and live a new kind of priesthood. In January 1954 the episcopate ordered them to avoid trade-union activity and to work no more than three hours per day. Half of them accepted these conditions, marking the end of an experiment that may have inspired priests in the 1980s such as Father G. Gilbert, who set out to share the lives of marginal youths, even going so far as to dress as they did.

textbooks, there are occasional sinners, repeat offenders, and habitual sinners. At first Marie-Zoé was an occasional sinner. The word occurs twice in her account. After her stay with her uncle, she writes: "My parents took me back home with them, and there at least I had no further *occasion* to sin." Later she adds: "When I arrived as a novice, another *occasion* awaited me: a priest conceived an affection for me, and I, being a woman of strong passions, gave in once again." The girl's second stay with her uncle and her time in the convent made her a repeat offender, and masturbation made her a habitual sinner: "I think that I'm damning myself by not sticking with my vocation." What she wants is a change of *status*. Only married life (a less perfect status) could quench "the fires of lust." The confessional cannot do the job, because, apart from "two extraordinary confessions," she has never admitted her bad habits. At the time, however, return to lay status for such a reason was unthinkable. Sister Marie-Zoé's fate seems to have been to live with her fears of eternal damnation.

Today guilt has been displaced, and the hierarchy of sins is no longer what it was. A 1983 poll found that 12 percent of French men and women over the age of eighteen believed that "it is the role of the Church to teach the moral requirements of sexuality and marriage"; 33 percent felt that "the Church should limit itself to giving advice"; 51 percent maintained that "it is not the role of the Church to concern itself with sexuality and marriage." When asked "Do you personally take account of the Church's recommendations concerning sexuality and married life?" 19 percent answered "Yes, as far as possible"; 69 percent answered "No"; and 12 percent had no opinion. Another survey found that even among women who attended church regularly, only 25 percent condemned the use of contraceptives by married women. A 1985 poll revealed the attitudes of the clergy: 98 percent of the priests questioned approved of John Paul II's position on the rights of man, but only 56 percent agreed with papal declarations on sexual morality and the family. In other words, many priests and laymen reject part or all of the Vatican's teachings regarding sex. Though aware of the Church's recommendations, their consciences reject them.

As for Protestants, 63 percent favor free use of contraceptives. In other countries sexuality has similarly shed its former association with guilt. In the United States, Andrew Greeley has found that 50 percent of Catholics reject papal teachings concerning divorce (compared with only 15 percent

Tim, Drawing. A high percentage of French women, including practicing Catholics, use the birth-control pill.

who approve), and 63 percent of Catholic women practice "illicit" forms of birth control. According to Michel de Certeau, the papal encyclical *Humanae vitae* led to a dramatic decline in Catholic practice in the United States. In Poland, despite the special esteem in which John Paul II is held, the birthrate is one of the lowest in Europe. When one French priest expressed surprise at this fact, several couples responded by telling him that there was no problem: "We go to confession afterward." When the pope visited France and denounced "permissiveness," he was cheered by a crowd of 100,000 young people in the Parc des Princes. It seems plausible, even likely, that many of those who applauded the pope were young couples who lived together without children.

This new attitude toward sexuality brings up the question of priestly celibacy. The Catholic Church has made chastity a value and claims that it yields spiritual benefits. But a survey of the French clergy found that 29 percent favor allowing priests to marry; 36 percent favor allowing women to enter the priesthood; and 92 percent agree that nonordained Christians should be allowed to officiate at burials. Many priests say that they "chose" the priesthood but that celibacy was "imposed" on them. The decline in the number of vocations,

Another Conception of the Priesthood?

Beati pauperes spiritu, "Blessed are the poor in spirit" (Matthew 5:3). The priest, no longer above others, is now one of them. Above: Priest Alain de La Morandais. Facing page: Father Christian.

the example of pastors and rabbis, and above all the number of priests who have left the priesthood have raised new questions not just among the clergy but among Catholics generally. Some of the comments gathered by Lambert indicate the depth of the concern: "Would you believe that they heard confessions right up to the last moment!" "Abbé X ran off with a nun! Why go and confess our foolishness to people who are even greater fools!" "They forbid us to divorce, but they run off without even asking anybody."

Now that women are being admitted to positions previously reserved for men, does continuing to ban them from the priesthood suggest that the Church clings to traditional views of the inferiority of women? Michel de Certeau maintains that "women are once again taking possession of their bodies, which can no longer be controlled or defined by the ideas or wishes of male theologians."[10] Sister Marie-Zoé could argue that her responsibility was diminished by the fact that the occasion for sin was connected with the unfortunate fact of male power (in the form of her abusive uncle and the seducing priest). What right has man to claim a judicial monopoly? Sexual discrimination in the Church is becoming increasingly difficult to maintain, especially since the decline in the number of vocations has forced church officials to allow lay persons to perform tasks once limited to clerics. What is more, many priests claim to have found comfort and support in Christian households, acknowledging that they "evolved" with the help of the very people whom they were supposed to be serving as guides. One curate put it this way: "One used to be a priest *for* other Christians; today one is much more a priest *with* other Christians." A sixty-year-old priest summed up the responses of many others: "My ordination in 1948 placed me 'above' other people. It gave me 'powers' and conferred on me a certain 'knowledge.' . . . Since then I have found my inner self. Less certainty and less authoritarianism are my rules. There are others who know more than I do. I have been forced to revise my estimate of what I thought I knew . . . I have come to realize that faith today is as much fidelity to our world and to man as it is to Christ." Another priest put it more succinctly: "We are in the process of becoming Christians."

Another Ritual of Confession

Vatican II reformed the penitential ritual. Priests were urged to initiate discussion with penitents with a warm wel-

come and mention of God's love and mercy. They might read a passage of gospel before pronouncing absolution and end the interview with a prayer of thanksgiving. In some parishes confessionals have been replaced by so-called *chambres de réconciliation,* rooms in which priest and penitent can hold a private conversation. Collective ceremonies of repentance have become more common; these have the advantage of allowing individual Christians to renew the bonds between themselves, God, and the religious community. Nevertheless, the sacrament of confession (instituted in the eleventh century) is increasingly neglected. In 1952, 15 percent of French Catholics confessed at least once a month; by 1983 only 1 percent went to confession that often, and 69 percent said that they never confessed. In this and many other areas of Catholic practice Pope John Paul II wants to restore tradition and "convince the faithful of the need to seek forgiveness personally, fervently, and frequently" (papal address delivered at Lourdes on August 15, 1983).

A NEW SENSE OF GUILT

Certain Encyclicals

The scope of conscience (considered the secret place in which our choices originate) changes with time. Father Daniélou observes in a homily: "Christianity is in history, but history is in Christianity." Cardinal Suhard puts it this way: "The Church at all times must both *be* and *become*. It must *be* changeless in its invisible reality, and, century by century, it must *become* in its visible reality." At the beginning of this century the pope prescribed the private lives of Catholics in the strictest terms. On September 8, 1907, the encyclical *Pascendi* condemned doctrinal modernism and required theologians to take an antimodernist oath. In a letter dated August 25, 1910, Pope Pius X (canonized in 1954 by Pius XII) condemned *Le Sillon,* a Christian-Democratic journal of opinion and ideas; its editor accepted the pope's judgment and ceased publication. The same Pius X encouraged frequent communion, devotion to the Sacred Heart, and the cults of the saints and of Mary. Nevertheless, the scientific, technological, political, social, and cultural upheavals of the twentieth century ultimately affected the relation between the Church hierarchy and the bulk of the faithful, who were obliged to improvise responses to constant and unprecedented challenges. Such a change was nothing new in the history of the Church. The rebellion of Saint Francis of Assisi against his father and against the mercantile culture of Assisi was redirected by Innocent III into channels sufficiently innocuous that Honorius III was able to legitimize the order of Friars Minor in 1223.

What was new was the rapidity of change. The population of the world, for instance, increased from 1.7 billion in 1900 to 3.6 billion in 1970 and is expected to reach 6.2 billion by the year 2000; developing countries are doubling in population every twenty-five years. The world's oldest bureaucracy had to adapt. John XXIII, who knew that bureaucracy well because he was a product of it, understood that in order to bring about change he would need the support of the Church's periphery against its center. Before the first session of Vatican II he issued the encyclical *Mater et Magistra;* although promulgated on July 15, 1961, the encyclical bore the date May 15, the seventieth anniversary of *Rerum Novarum* and the thirtieth anniversary of *Quadragesimo Anno.* The subject of the new encyclical was the "contemporary evolution of social life in the light of Christian principles."

John XXIII, during his brief pontificate (1958–1963), did everything in his power to ensure that the Church would change without ceasing to be the Church.

I shall consider just two of its many themes. The pope took an innovative position regarding the Church's presence in the world: "The most important problem of our time remains that of relations between economically developed and developing countries. We are all jointly responsible for the malnourished. Consciences must be trained to recognize the responsibility that falls on everyone, but especially on the most favored." As for preserving the transcendence of the Church, the pope renewed the condemnation of all sexual activity other than for the purpose of procreation: "Realized through a deliberate and conscious act, the transmission of life is subject, as such, to God's sacred, immutable, and inviolable laws." The encyclical *Pacem in Terris* (April 11, 1963) was addressed, not as usual to all Christians but to "all men." In it the pope rejected the traditional misogyny of the Church and pronounced himself a strong advocate of a role for women in public life: "Increasingly conscious of her human dignity, woman is no longer willing to be considered an instrument. She demands to be treated as a person both at home and in public life."

John XXIII, elected pope on October 28, 1958, on June 18, 1959, sent a lengthy questionnaire to all bishops, nuncios, and superiors; more than 2,000 responded. On February 2,

From Vatican II to the Synod of December 1985

1962, he announced that a council would be held beginning on October 11 of that same year. The complex history of the council's four sessions (October 11–December 8, 1962; September 21–December 4, 1963; September 14–November 21, 1964; November 14–December 8, 1965) cannot be recounted here. The decisions taken introduced major changes in Catholic practice: the obligation to attend Sunday mass was extended to include the whole weekend; the vernacular replaced Latin; a new rite replaced the mass of Saint Pius V; communion, which laymen could now legitimately dispense, could under certain circumstances be given "in both kinds" (that is, both bread and wine). The pope agreed to convoke an episcopal synod at regular intervals in order to reconcile the diversity of local churches with the unity of the universal Church. Within each country bishops worked toward two ends, described by Michel de Certeau: "Clerics mobilized to produce a religious vocabulary in each language; and the conscience of the various Christian communities was alerted to issues of social justice."

Dom Helder Camara visiting a poor section of Recife, Brazil, in 1962.

Two prominent figures played a key role in informing bishops about the growing misery of the Third World: Monsignor Helder Camara, then auxiliary bishop of Rio and secretary-general of the Brazilian episcopacy, and Monsignor Larrain, bishop of Talca in Chile. Both prelates were concerned to break the alliance between the Church and conservative forces. How could a priest to *favelas* or *poblaciones* preach a latter-day Sermon on the Mount? "Love your enemies, bless them that curse you, do good to them that hate you, and pray for them which despitefully use you and persecute you . . . For if ye love them which love you, what reward have ye?" (Matthew 5:44–46). How was it possible to teach God's infinite goodness less than twenty years after the Holocaust, in a world where plenty averted its eyes from want and millions of children suffered from hunger?

Vatican II was intended to demonstrate that the Church is the people of God, not a hierarchy at the top of which the pope sits enthroned. In the council the Church temporarily forgot about its intense interest in its internal problems and

Opening of the second session of Vatican II, 1962. Vatican II was not content simply to modify Catholic liturgy. Two solemn declarations on religious freedom and on non-Christian religions, particularly Judaism, and a decree on ecumenicism demonstrated that Church councils were no longer purely internal matters.

The abbé Pierre, who has devoted his life to traditional charitable work, has lost none of his plainspoken bluntness. "Poverty makes people stupid, and wealth makes them idiotic," according to this apostle of evangelical poverty.

recognized that it had a great deal to learn from "others," meaning those who professed other faiths or even who had no faith. This search for others, which led to the discovery of the physical and moral suffering of the Third and Fourth worlds, gradually superseded individual feelings of guilt. The sense of sin and fear of hell gave way to a feeling of social culpability, of joint responsibility for the world's woes. Violations of human rights, no matter where they occurred, compelled Catholics to engage in the great political debates of the day.

The Reaction

Although the Church chose to "stand with the poor," its choice was couched in such cautionary rhetoric that its force was sapped. In 1972 the conservative hierarchy of the Latin American Church took control of CELAM. The organization's president, Monsignor López Trujillo, followed a prudently progressive neoconservative line and launched the first attacks against so-called liberation theology. In 1979 John Paul

II put in an appearance at the Puebla conference, where bishops stood firm to preserve what had been won at Medellín. In 1985 the pope returned to Latin America, where he delivered forty-five speeches, all carefully balanced and clearly addressed to all Catholics. He denounced social injustice as "intolerable," declared himself in favor of a "Church based on human rights and according priority to the poor," and advocated "a new evangelism." But he continually warned against "Marxist contaminations," asserting that it was up to the hierarchy "to direct this energy, this strength, this absence of passivity" that was welling up from the poor. In other words, the pope attempted to trace a middle course that would combine the message of the gospel with social action and Roman primacy.

The media system, which consists not only of radio and television but also of Catholic preaching and newspapers, has forced the Christian conscience to confront the two faces of the Church: inquisition and liberation. Catholics today are aware of two tendencies within the Church: one conservative, in which a part of the hierarchy joins with certain laymen; the other, more ready to embrace the world and to seek greater

Liberation Theology

Meeting of a grass-roots Christian community at Crateus, Brazil, 1983.

Théodore or Jean Théodore de
Bry, Illustration. The Spanish
missionary Las Casas described
the destruction of the Indians.
At age forty he charged that
"what is being done to the
Indians is unjust and
tyrannical," and he spent the
remaining fifty-two years of his
life defending them.
(Bartolomé de Las Casas,
*Narratio regionum indicarum per
Hispanos,* Frankfurt am Main,
1598, illustrated by the de
Brys.)

justice, led by laymen in conjunction with other elements of
the hierarchy. Although the 1971 synod was composed exclusively of bishops, it recognized that the "fight for justice" was
an integral part of the gospel's message. When liberation theologians assert that "without commitment to the poor there is
no Christian life," they are merely repeating the message of
Saint James. In 1542 Bartolomé de las Casas, in his *Brief
Relation of the Destruction of the Indies,* wrote these simple and
distressing words: "The Indians are dying before their time."

Liberation theology, though rooted in Latin America,
transcends its origins. It is, in the words of Peruvian priest
Gustavo Gutiérrez, a "reflection on God, an attempt to find a
language in which to speak of the God of love to the disin-
herited Christians of this continent. Liberation is a complex
term that affects the social, political, and human order—total
liberation of the person and not simply a change of structures.
To speak in biblical terms, it is liberation from sin, because
sin is nothing other than the failure to love thy neighbor, with
God."[11] In reviewing the questions that "nonpersons," that
"less-than-nothings" ask of theodicy, he adds: "We are obliged
to ask ourselves how we can make those who consider themselves to be less than nothing, those who suffer, believe that
God is love? How can we sing the Messiah when a people's
pain stifles its voice in its throat?"

In the nineteenth century Walter Bagehot maintained that no pain could compare with that caused by a new idea. It is hardly surprising, therefore, that Vatican II's decision that the Church should work preferentially on behalf of the poor without sacrificing the rich should have irritated many traditionalists, as did various strands of liberation theology. Many French Catholics cherished fond memories of the liturgy of their childhood—a liturgy in Latin, which few of them understood. When traditionalists began to demonstrate against the changes, a part of the hierarchy was not displeased: the innovations had been pushed through, after all, by a minority of clerics with support from laymen and non-Catholics, and forced on a majority that had little desire to change its old familiar habits. From 1975 until 1980 the traditionalist bishop Monsignor Lefebvre was the symbol of this resistance; as such he was lionized by the French media. Paul VI, a complex man torn between the heritage of John XXIII and the injunctions of the Congregation for the Doctrine of Faith, eventually was forced to issue a mild condemnation of the traditionalists.

Traditionalism

Subversive by virtue of excessive traditionalism—that is the paradox of Monsignor Lefebvre, who in 1970 founded the Fraternité Sacerdotale Saint-Pius X at Ecône (Valais), shown here in 1975. Since 1971 he has ordained several priests. Suspended by the Holy See on 24 July 1976, he has persisted in his activities, with the support of some French Catholics.

Toward Ecumenicism?

In 1940 the pastor Roger Schultz acquired a large property at Taizé (Saône-et-Loire), where he offered shelter to Jews pursued by the Nazis until, sought by the Gestapo, he was forced to flee to Switzerland. In 1949 seven novices pledged themselves "for life and to the service of God and our fellow man in celibacy, community of property, and obedience to authority." Taizé serves as a retreat for tens of thousands of young Christians annually.

A declining number of priests; an increasing role for lay persons; a tendency for even practicing Catholics to ignore the pope's prescriptions in sexual matters; contemplation of the possibility of priestly marriage and ordination of women; a conviction that everyone is jointly responsible for the evil, whether located in the Third World or in the suburbs of big cities; and a greater familiarity with the Bible, which is now read and commented upon in the vernacular—these apparently irreversible tendencies are at work in the Catholic Church today. Will they lead to greater ecumenicism and, in particular, to a rapprochement with Protestantism?

The Mehl report cited earlier noted a strong ecumenical movement within Protestantism. To the question "Do you wish to see unity among the various Protestant churches?" 74 percent answered "yes." The same poll showed an attenuation of anti-Catholic sentiment: 69 percent wanted to see "closer relations" with Catholics, and 23 percent felt that there had been some rapprochement under John Paul II, compared with

Ecumenical Center of Saint-Quentin-en-Yvelines. From the time he was elected, John XXIII made it clear that one of the crucial missions of the council he planned to convoke would be to deal with ecumenical hopes. He set up a secretariat for Christian unity and insisted that non-Catholics be allowed to play an active role in the work of the council. On 4 December 1965 (four days before the formal closing session), Paul VI officiated jointly with non-Catholics at a farewell ceremony for the observers.

The pilgrim, *peregrinus,* is both the foreigner and the one who goes on foot. A *peregrinatio ascetica* makes the pilgrim a different person who meets others. This community of walkers (a pilgrimage is a prayer on foot) is not supposed to end when they reach the cathedral at Chartres; it is supposed to remain indelibly engraved in memory.

12 percent who felt that the two religions had moved farther apart and 44 percent who found no change. Mixed marriages are surprisingly common: only 20 percent of the Protestants who responded to the survey have Protestant wives, 50 percent have wives who are Catholic. As far as the marriage of children is concerned, 23 percent approve of mixed marriage, 45 percent are neutral, and only 2 percent are "fairly strongly opposed." Mehl finds this indifference worrisome: "For a small community like the Protestant community in France, the increase in the number of mixed marriages is undoubtedly a danger."

Will the Church soon become a "seamless fabric" again? Probably not. Protestants tell this story: "For Catholics the Church is a mother; for the Greek Orthodox it is a wife; for Protestants it is an old bachelor who says no." Protestants, though pleased that John Paul II heralds the gospel to all mankind, point out that "it is the gospel that gives force to the pope's words and not the reverse." These are the words of the Reverend André Dumas, for whom the Church should never be "a possession or screen but an annunciation and service."

Protestant practice can perhaps be defined as an amalgam of earnestness and liberalism. Eighteen percent of those who call themselves Protestants refuse to give religious instruction to their children. "What people love most of all in Protestantism," Mehl tells us, "is the freedom of mind it allows." But, he adds, there may be today "a group within the Church that is unduly concerned with nondirective guidance and respect for the child's freedom lest the child be manipulated before he or she is capable of making an adult decision." The Catholic hierarchy has no such scruples, but many Catholic parents are troubled by the issue of manipulation. Regular reading of the Bible scored much higher than did regular churchgoing in the survey mentioned. Perhaps religious sociologists should focus on this new tendency to keep the faith but to abandon formal religious practice.

"The desire for prayer is already a prayer and God would never think of asking for more. If prayer were really a kind of chatter, a dialogue between a maniac and his shadow, or, worse still, a futile, superstitious request for the goods of this world, why would anyone believe that thousands of people find in it a harsh, bracing, fulfilling joy?" (Georges Bernanos, *Diary of a Country Priest*).

Communist Party posters in the Nord-Pas-de-Calais during the 1986 legislative elections.

Communism as a
Way of Life

Gérard Vincent

THE importance of the Communist Party cannot be understood without reference to the Judeo-Christian heritage. The shift from eschatology to teleology is explained by nostalgia for monism, for a single principle capable of accounting for the diversity of observed phenomena. For centuries thinkers have hoped that humanity could be shaped by the deliberate decision of a few men aware of pertinent causes and effects. The Church sought to make a morality of necessity. With meticulous care it constructed a hierarchy that endured for centuries, a hierarchy of functions symbolized by colors: black for the lower clergy, purple for bishops, red for cardinals, white for the pope. This hierarchy did not so much control natural forces as it followed in their wake. In the offices of *L'Humanité,* the newspaper of the French Communist Party, a line from Gabriel Péri is said to have hung on the wall for years: "I have practiced my profession as a kind of religion, in which writing my daily article was a nightly ritual."

In the *Critique of Hegel's Philosophy of Right* Marx wrote: "Religion is the fantastic realization of the human essence, because the human essence has no true reality. Religion is the soul of a heartless world as well as the spirit of a spiritless world." A symbolic expression of the human and social drama, religion, Marx maintained, is an illusory effort to rejoin the other in an "other world." Its aim is to substitute for a communication it deems illusory an actual interpersonal relation in this world. In such diverse creations as Goethe's projected "Wandering Jew," Dostoevsky's Grand Inquisitor, Eugène Sue's Samuel, and Edgar Quinet's Ahasuerus we find a recurrent theme: the Church is sinful, it has betrayed Christ's teaching, and the Christian people are always ready to crucify Christ again. There is a heritage that explains why so many

Otto Griebel, *The International,* 1928–1930. "For the worker, work is not a part of his life; it is a sacrifice of his life" (Karl Marx, *Communist Manifesto*). (Berlin, Museum für Deutsche Geschichte.)

communists are converts from Christianity: for certain Christians the proletariat became the vehicle of redemption. "The one truly committed philosophy is the Marxist philosophy. The communist is the conscience of the proletariat . . . In him thought and action are perhaps most intimately united." So wrote Jean Lacroix in the Catholic magazine *Esprit* (December 1944). Lyssenko's ideas about the heritability of acquired characters were believed to be true because they "proved" that man could transform nature, just as the Davydov Plan would convert vast areas of Siberia into a fertile breadbasket by reversing the flow of great rivers.

The Judeo-Christian tradition laid the groundwork for the atheistic materialism of the cult of personality. The Church, while continuing to be what its etymology indicated (that is, an assembly, from the Greek *ekklesia*), placed Saint Peter's successor on a throne and burned incense before him. Narrative history, which establishes no laws but simply notes coincidences, suggests that all revolutions end in Bonapartism, whether Bonaparte be called Caesar, Cromwell, Napoleon, Stalin, Mao, or Fidel. It is as if the toppling of structures compelled men to rediscover their identity in a figure like Stalin, "the man we love more than any other," or Mao, who was to bring forth the "new man" from the communes of China as God brought woman forth from Adam's rib.

The French Communist Party (abbreviated hereafter as PCF) also had an idol: Maurice Thorez was described in a somewhat "retouched" biography as an authentic coal miner. Thorez lacked the global experience of communism of his Italian counterpart, Palmiro Togliatti, an intellectual who had taught in various universities. He also lacked Togliatti's adaptability. A rigid Stalinist during the Spanish Civil War, the Italian leader later became the leading exponent of a communist movement with multiple centers and still later a vigorous critic of simplistic efforts to explain the "excesses" of Stalinism in terms of Stalin's psychology. Thorez lacked what Dominique Desanti has termed the "pessimistic experience" that Togliatti owed to service in the highest ranks of the Komintern.

Many people joined the Communist Party in 1944 because of the tremendous prestige of the Red Army. The French understood that one reason the Allies were able to land troops in Normandy just thirty-one months after the United States's entry into the war was that the Nazi war machine had been destroyed on the plains of Russia. The first three five-year plans were remembered mainly for their effectiveness: they had endowed the USSR with an army that, contrary to all expectations after the disastrous summer and fall of 1941, was able to mount massive counteroffensives on Rostov and around Moscow, thereby reversing the military situation and ultimately leading to victory. People even began to doubt the truth of the great purges of 1937–38, during which half the top-ranking officers in the military were liquidated. If such a thing had happened, how could the Red Army have made such a dramatic comeback? Not the least surprised was Hitler, who had just transferred 400,000 men from the Eastern Front to the West to begin preparations for the assault on England. Many in France wondered if they had been duped by "bourgeois" propaganda. Meanwhile, Stalin offered a simplified textbook version of the history he claimed to be making. His works reveal an astonishing talent for interpreting difficult issues of nationalities, Marxism-Leninism, linguistics, and economics in a way that ordinary readers could understand.

The Prestige of the USSR in 1944

From the basic texts of Marxism he took clear statements that satisfied not only relatively uneducated workers but also intellectuals tired of abstruse commentaries and hungry for action to change the world.

The Communists and the Resistance

Zhukov, Koniev, and Rokossovski attacked Berlin on April 12, 1945, with 180 divisions, 41,000 cannon, and 6,300 tanks. On May 2 General Weidling, with 70,000 German survivors, surrendered to Shchuikov, the defender of Stalingrad. Here the Soviet flag flies over the Reichstag.

The PCF also benefited from its actions during the Resistance. To be sure, the party was quick to style itself *le parti des fusillés* (the party of those shot by German firing squads); it exaggerated the number of Communists executed and said nothing about the period of uncertainty between the Nazi-Soviet pact and the German attack on the Soviet Union. Nevertheless, the party's role in the Resistance was substantial. Accustomed to clandestine action, it became effective the moment it ceased to see the war as a struggle "between greedy imperialists" and began to see it instead as an antifascist crusade. The Communists also managed to avoid becoming bogged down in various intrigues involving rival Giraudists and Gaullists. They opted immediately for the Gaullists, and Fernand Grenier was the first to pledge a party's support to General de Gaulle.

Exploitation had led the proletariat to join the Communist Party. In late-nineteenth-century Prussia, Bismarck had adopted a daring two-pronged policy, strengthening traditional institutions such as the administration, the army, the courts, and dynamic sectors of industry while at the same time instituting a series of social reforms that were quite bold for the times. By the 1920s French social legislation lagged well behind what had been accomplished in Germany. Even Hitler won over a substantial segment of the German working class by instituting a system of "social protection" that went well beyond anything achieved in France by the Matignon Accords, which settled the general strike in 1936. Social mobility in France was limited in the 1920s as well as in the 1950s; the Communist Party promised social upheaval and with it the possibility of significant advancement, whereas the established powers, with few exceptions, promised little more than continuation of the status quo. One milling machine operator summed it up this way: "Just because you're a Communist doesn't necessarily mean that you're a great guy. I know some Communists who are jerks. Obviously . . . you've got to do what you can with them. But unlike other jerks, these are Communist jerks . . . Idiotic as they are, they are taking part in the transformation of society."[1]

After French Socialists and Communists split into two parties at the Congress of Tours in the 1920s, the PCF sought to win over members of the "bourgeois intelligentsia," whose "objective conditions of existence" did not predispose them to join the Communist Party. To gain the trust of intellectuals the party evinced great respect for such writers as Jean Jaurès, Romain Rolland, and Anatole France. The writer Henri Barbusse joined in 1923. Although he had little knowledge of Marxism, he founded the Clarté (Clarity) movement, which published a journal of the same name. Other writers, such as Georges Duhamel and Jules Romains, were thus attracted to the party. In 1928 Barbusse founded the review *Monde,* edited by Jean Guéhenno. In 1927 five surrealists, including André Breton, Louis Aragon, and Paul Eluard, joined the Party, which apparently received them rather coldly. Other intellectuals and artists joined over the years: Georges Politzer, Henri Lefebvre, Paul Nizan, Fernand Léger, Pablo Picasso, and Frédéric Joliot-Curie.

After World War II countless young intellectuals of bourgeois background joined the Communist Party, a decision that

Reasons for Joining

Picasso, sketch. Many intellectuals, including Sartre, joined the League for the Rights of Man in defense of Henri Martin, who was freed in August 1953.

often led to a break with their families. They were fascinated by the figure of the worker and hoped not to supplant the working class but to explore ways in which it might discover and play out its revolutionary role. A text written by Sartre in 1948 captures the enthusiasm of the moment: "Totally conditioned by his class, his wages, the nature of his work, conditioned right down to his very feelings and thoughts, [the worker] himself will decide what his and his comrades' condition means, will decide whether the future of the proletariat will be one of unremitting humiliation or of conquest and victory, depending on whether he chooses to be resigned or revolutionary." With the exception of Aragon, the role of these intellectuals was not to make decisions but to spread the good word. Artists would no longer allow their style of writing or painting to be dictated to them. In March 1953 *Les Lettres Françaises* published a portrait of Stalin by Picasso (Stalin had died on March 5) on its front page. This irritated top PCF officials, who found Picasso "vain and petty-bourgeois." They preferred Fougeron's *Portrait of Marcel Cachin,* because it was faithful, offered a good likeness, was authentically "revolutionary," and did not concern itself with questions of "form."

Above: André Fougeron, *Portrait of Marcel Cachin* (*L'Humanité,* 20 September 1944). Opposite: Picasso, Portrait of Stalin (*Les Lettres Françaises,* 12–19 March 1953).

Militancy

"Man is neither completely good nor completely bad," Machiavelli wrote. Georges Lefebvre argued that what makes a class revolutionary is the conviction that it is serving both its own interests and those of the community at large. In order to understand why large numbers of "bourgeois" intellectuals joined the PCF after World War II we must keep in mind that the party was a kind of subsociety able to offer fairly young people important posts, a level of responsibility to which they could aspire only at a much later stage in life in the wider—and largely gerontocratic—society. It was gratifying for a young man of twenty-five to lead battalions of Communist students in the huge May 28, 1952, demonstration against Eisenhower's successor as commander of U.S. Forces in Europe, General Matthew Ridgway—"Ridgway the plague," as he was called in signs carried by the marchers. It was just as heady an experience for a young student to become a top reporter at *Ce soir* (an evening paper with a circulation of 600,000) and to travel through eastern Europe. Jean-Toussaint

Careers in the Communist Subsociety

Desanti recalled the postwar climate this way: "You get back an immediate echo, which repeats your own words but with enormous amplification, and that is flattering . . . You cease to be a solitary intellectual and become the interpreter of a group." But as to the question whether the party delegated any real power to these young intellectuals, Desanti is quick to respond that it was only "sham power."[2]

Political activists have their own myths and their own pressures to deal with. The least naive and best informed of the 1950s militants (those who had read Victor Serge and Boris Souvarine) were aware of the merciless nature of Stalinist repression. But the "communist family" was untroubled. Whatever difficulties there may have been in the Soviet Union had been "transcended." The case rested on three arguments. First, the capitalist world had no right to give lessons in human rights in view of the methods it used to hold on to the shreds of power in its colonial empires. Second, the need for a coercive system in the Soviet Union could be accounted for by "objective" historical conditions unique to this vast, sprawling land. Third, the communist goal was to create a "new man." Christianity had worked toward the same goal for two thousand years only to arrive at Auschwitz; therefore it had better direct its criticisms inward.

Thorez and Socialist Realism

When Stalin was the best beloved of the masses, in France Maurice Thorez was the "most admired." In the 1950s mining still ran in families from father to son, and at age fourteen the "pit boy" went down into the mine for the first time, proudly claiming his hereditary right. As example and myth, the miner was featured in three "artistic" works: *Le Mot mineur, camarade* (The Word Miner, Comrade, 1949), a collection of short stories by André Stil; *Le Point du jour* (Daybreak, 1949), a film by Louis Daquin; and *Le Pays des Mines* (Mining Country, 1951), a show of paintings by André Fougeron. At that time 80 percent of France's energy came from coal, and more than 300,000 people were employed in the mines. The miners who had dared to go out on strike from May 27 to June 9, 1941, symbolized working-class resistance to Nazism.

Maurice Thorez inaccurately portrayed himself as a miner and the son of a miner in order to benefit from this myth: "What grandeur there is in this fierce struggle with matter, in the continuous hand-to-hand struggle in which man, who must crouch or often lie in all the positions of combat, wrests

the coal from the grip of the surrounding rock" (*Action*, March 22, 1946). Courageous, heroic, united, disciplined, responsible, virile, and unconquerable, the miner, far from being crushed by destiny, transformed it into a radiant future. He was the new man, the communist man whom Louis Aragon described in these terms: "He who puts man above himself . . . who asks nothing and wants everything for man."[3] Even more, he embodies "a new type of intellectual," whom Laurent Casanova described as if he were viewing a statue: "Each of the miner's acts reflects a sustained and elaborate effort of thought, an innovative method of reasoning developed by millions of proletarians . . . The worker already moves on a level of thought well above that attained by any ideologue trained in and still bound by the bourgeois disciplines."[4] Whether he knows it or not, every miner is ontologically a communist. He is the ideal type of proletarian, and invariably he makes the petty-bourgeois intellectual feel guilty.

The miner would become the central figure in the party's new iconography. Laurent Casanova set forth the party's cul-

"The phrase 'Maurice Thorez's party' is regrettable . . . I must say that I have protested its use many times to the politburo and to *Humanité*. I regret that it was not reported sooner to the General Committee . . . Demonstrations of affection and confidence should not be mistaken for a cult of personality"—so spoke Maurice Thorez in a speech to the Central Committee, 10 May 1956.

tural policy in 1947 at its Eleventh Congress. In painting, allegory and symbolism were condemned as relics of a decadent ideology. Portraits, industrial landscapes, and historical frescoes celebrating the class struggle were honored. It was explicitly stated that the painter should align himself "with the political and ideological positions of the working class." Formalism, defined as primacy of form over content, was denounced. The important thing was the argument of a work, the perfect fit between signifier and signified. Zhdanov's peremptory assertion was invoked: "Every true work of genius is accessible, and the more accessible it is to large masses of people, the greater a work of genius it is." Socialist realism was supposed to portray reality in its revolutionary aspects, to depict not only the sense of the struggle but "the ineluctability of victory." André Fougeron's *Les Parisiennes au marché* (Parisian Women at the Market), shown at the Salon d'Automne of 1948, fulfilled this canon perfectly. The "new real-

André Fougeron, *Le Pensionné,* 1950. "The essence of socialist realism lies in fidelity to life's truth, as painful as it may be, all expressed in artistic images envisioned from a communist point of view" (*Philosophical Dictionary,* Moscow, 1967). (Bucharest, Museum of Fine Arts.)

ism" reached its height in 1951, when the Bernheim-Jeune Gallery showed a series of Fougeron's paintings in an exhibition entitled Mining Country. Harsh criticism from *Le Monde* proved to the PCF that it was on the right track, because the work so outraged the "bourgeois" press. At the 1951 Salon d'Automne came the ultimate accolade: the police confiscated seven canvases accused of "insulting national feeling." From then on Fougeron was the embodiment of the French communist painter. In his column in *La Nouvelle Critique* he explained that bourgeois artists sought refuge in abstraction because reality was unbearable to them.

Like any subsociety, the Communist Party was a mutual admiration society so long as one remained orthodox. One canvas in the Mining Country show drew these comments from Jean Fréville: "We come to *La Trieuse* (Girl Separating Coal): a young girl from coal country but with the face of a Florentine virgin, in work clothes, wears a cap that protects her from coal dust, while we observe her calm courage and a gaze in which sadness mingles with dreams of happiness . . . She resembles the coal sorter who, when beaten by the police in the 1948 strike, shouted: 'Smash my skull if you like. You'll never get what's inside.'" Another painting, *Le Pensionné* (The Retired Miner), showed an emaciated old man living in a modest cottage: "He gave his toil and his health, his lungs and his blood, to make the lords of the mines wealthy. After a life spent at the bottom of the mine, he no longer has the strength to enjoy the sunshine, nor does he have a pension large enough to provide him with medical care. Suffering from silicosis, an invalid, prematurely old, weighing less than a hundred pounds, his face marked by past and present suffering, he huddles in the corner next to a small stove, awaiting death, while the eyes in his battle-hardened veteran's face continue to burn with an ardent flame."

Neither the coal sorter nor the retiree were resigned to their fate. Despite the miserabilism of the style, the paintings conformed to the rules laid down by Maurice Thorez: "We need an optimistic art oriented toward the future . . . To bewildered intellectuals, lost in a maze of questions, we shall bring certainties, possibilities of unlimited development. We call upon them to turn away from the false problems of individualism, pessimism, and decadent aestheticism and to give meaning to their lives by linking them with the lives of others."

After Stalin's death the PCF withdrew its advocacy of

"socialist realism." The Thirteenth Congress questioned the wisdom of Zhdanovite cultural policy, and the adaptable Louis Aragon was the first to criticize Fougeron's art.

Denial of Reality

Here I will deal only with the Cold War period. The militant Communist of the 1950s knew, or could have known, the truth about the liquidation of the kulaks, the Moscow Trials, or anti-Semitism in the USSR. Boris Souvarine, whom Alain Besançon has described as "a communist for eight years and an anticommunist for sixty years," was expelled from the PCF in 1925; since then he has been a constant critic of totalitarian Stalinism and its methods. His biography, *Stalin,* published in France in 1935 with the subtitle "A Historic Look at Bolshevism," went almost unnoticed; it was dismissed as a hysterical pamphlet. Later, however, when it was reprinted in 1977, the historian Emmanuel Le Roy Ladurie would call it "one of the greatest books of the century." The writings of Victor Serge, along with innumerable eyewitness accounts of the liquidation of the POUM and of the Trotskyists during the Spanish Civil War, were available to all. The January 1950 issue of *Temps modernes* contains an article signed by both Sartre and Merleau-Ponty in which one can read the following: "It has been shown that Soviet citizens can be deported for an unlimited period while still under investigation and prior to any judgment . . . It has also been shown that the repressive

Picasso, *The Korean War,* 1951. Picasso, one of the most illustrious members of the French Communist Party, could not remain silent; nor did he submit to the dictates of Zhdanovism. (Paris, Musée Picasso.)

apparatus in the USSR has increasingly become a power unto itself . . . It is likely, given the magnitude of the work on the Baltic–White Sea Canal and the Moscow–Volga Canal, that the total number of prisoners is in the millions; some say ten million, others fifteen." The Rassemblement Démocratique Révolutionnaire (RDR, Revolutionary Democratic Coalition), founded in February 1948, made disclosure of the truth about the Soviet camps one of its missions. David Rousset, a Resistance fighter who had been deported by the Nazis and who was, along with Sartre and Camus, one of the founders of the RDR, published damning documents concerning the USSR. The Communist press branded him a liar. Some people simply did not want to know.

Paradoxically, the major postwar trials (of Rajk, Slansky, and others) actually helped French militants become more Stalinist than ever. As Dominique Desanti recounts: "According to Stalinist logic, there could be, as Savarius put it, 'no honest contradiction of the wisdom emanating from the concentric circles centered in Moscow.' I honestly believe that it was through the trials and the public explanation I gave of them that I became totally and profoundly Stalinist." She goes on to say that she wrote *Les Staliniens* (The Stalinists) "to show how and why, when the need to believe exists, one can refuse any information that might destroy or tarnish the faith." She asks herself: "If *The Gulag Archipelago* had appeared at the time, would I have found it convincing?" And she answers: "No, I would not have believed it, because no one is willing to shed a faith simply because it has been proven necessary by inexorable logic. The USSR remained our savior, our myth. The Nazis were different: we had seen them up close."[5]

In January 1955, while a strong economic recovery begun the previous year was still under way, Maurice Thorez published *La Situation économique de la France, mystifications et réalités* (The Economic Situation of France: Mystifications and Realities), in which, against all evidence, he leveled his critical guns at the "absolute pauperization" of the working class. Denial was thus at the center of this addendum to the Communist vulgate. The pauperization was continually harped on for the next ten years: "Experience has verified, has fully confirmed, the law of absolute and relative pauperization." "In France today, hourly wage-earners have roughly half the purchasing power they enjoyed before the war." "The Paris worker eats less meat than did workers under the Second Empire." These repetitive assertions by the secretary-general were backed by the party's economists. In *Economie et Politique* (January 1965) J. Kahn "proved" that from 1956 to 1962 average purchasing power had declined 6 to 8 percent annually. The INSEE (the French bureau of economic statistics) provides the following figures for workers' households: the percentage owning automobiles increased from 8 in 1954 to 61.1 in 1969; those owning television sets went from 0.9 percent in 1954 to 71.3 percent in 1969; refrigerators, 3.3 percent to 80.5 percent; washing machines, 8.5 percent to 65.5 percent (all for the same period). "Pauperized" France had begun to drive automobiles and own homes. Workers began to buy on credit, something that worried the party: the need to make monthly payments might well decrease the worker's willingness to fight. What is more, attendance at cell meetings and rallies began to drop off in the 1960s owing to competition from television.

Communist militants were not the only ones denying reality. Denial is an essential part of private life: people refuse to see the infidelity of a spouse; they "do not want to know" that their child is taking drugs. And politically, to take just one example, it took stubborn protest by the "mothers of May" to impress upon the consciousness of the West the fact that "order" in Argentina was based on torture and terror. People deny what stares them in the face, not so much to convince others as to reassure themselves. "The moment you sense that the Other, the Enemy, has arguments that can damage you, you react by becoming sectarian and violent. That is why sectarianism was at its most virulent during the Cold War," according to Jean-Toussaint Desanti.

The Communist as the Indispensable "Internal Enemy"

Hirelings in the pay of foreigners, guilty of having cost France her empire, bent on brainwashing or beating an entire nation into submission, devoid of all political morality (since the ends justify the means), hostile to any reform likely to demobilize the working class by improving its condition, determined to stamp out Christian humanism and to impose Sovietization on the entire planet, taking advantage of socialist naiveté to plot Prague-style coups—all these charges and more were leveled against the French Communist Party. The rest of the nation united against the party, which was portrayed as the embodiment of evil. Branded the party of lies, the PCF performed the miraculous feat of convincing millions that no

Maurice Utrillo, *Rue des Saules in Montmartre*. This street seems almost empty because there are no cars. Today, traffic and parked cars would prevent us from seeing the pedestrians and would obscure the neighbors' views. (Oslo, M. N. Bungard Collection.)

Raoul Dufy, *Sunday, Music in the Country,* 1942. Dufy multiplies signs of leisure in an unreal rural setting. This space, which has a center but no boundaries, is neither workplace nor home; we are somewhere else. Leisure, initially an escape, an evasion, does not yet have an assigned place. (Paris, Musée d'Art Moderne.)

Pierre Bonnard, *Toilette* or *Nude at Her Mirror,* 1931. The atmosphere in this painting belongs to the past. There is no separation between the dressing table and the room, between the body, displayed in its glory, and the various fabrics, bibelots, and other trinkets of intimacy. The bathroom established a barrier and set nudity in a different ambiance. (Venice, Modern Art Gallery.)

The suntan, a commercial injunction to bask in the sun. A gilt, naked body became the ideal of beauty, legitimatized by health concerns that today are considered health hazards. (Advertising poster for Ambre Solaire, 1937.)

Leonardo Cremonini, *In the Mirror of Desire,* 1966. The enigma of sex may be reflected in many ways. (Private Collection.)

Jacques Villon window, detail of the Crucifixion, 1957. "And with him they crucify two thieves; the one on his right hand, and the other on his left." (Mark 15:27). The power of Christianity remains strong in an increasingly secular world. (Metz, Saint-Etienne Cathedral.)

Edouard Pignon, *The Dead Worker* (preliminary study). The surrealist Paul Eluard wanted this work called "The Murdered Worker," but Pignon insisted on this title. Christian workers youth groups saw it as a "laying to rest." The painting and its preliminary studies were exhibited at the 1952 Salon de Mai and at the Galerie de France.

Gunhild Kvist, *In the Land of the Fairies,* 1976. The northern land of Sweden continues to fascinate—and puzzle—the rest of the world. (Private Collection.)

Mimmo Paladino, Untitled, 1982. Masks and elongated forms are among the many things featured in the work of the Italian painter Domenico "Mimmo" Paladino. Here the skull-like face of the male figure is counterposed with the blue face of the woman. (Cambridge, Mass., Fogg Art Museum.)

Karl Horst Hödicke, *The Welder,* 1978. Hödicke, a member of the new generation of German artists, has painted urban life since the mid-1970s. (Cambridge, Mass., Busch-Reisinger Museum.)

Edward Hopper, *Nighthawks,* 1942. In portraying the "essential solitude" of American society, Hopper casts a cold but fascinated gaze on America's internal exiles trapped in empty, disquieting, yet familiar places. (The Art Institute of Chicago.)

Milton Avery, *Still-Life with Woman,* 1946. This woman, painted by Avery during a trip to Mexico, might be considered the expression of today's woman, pondering her choices in a changing world. (Cambridge, Mass., Fogg Art Museum.)

matter what it said, the opposite was true. When the party claimed that accepting the Marshall Plan would turn France into a minor power within the American sphere of influence, its adversaries had to deny it simply because the Communists said it was true. Since the PCF is the "foreigner's party," its enemies must constitute the party of France.

The truth is that the PCF, like all parties, said some things that were true and others that were not. If it denied the existence of the Gulag, it also pointed out that the war in Indochina was something other than a series of assassinations carried out by a few fanatics trained in China and paid by Moscow. If it denounced "absolute pauperization," it was also the only party to take a serious look at the roots of anticolonialism. At the time, however, the Communists were the "enemy" that France needed to hold itself together. The whole nation came to see itself as a threatened community. As Herbert Marcuse rightly remarks: "Free institutions vied with authoritarian institutions to make the enemy a lethal force *within* the system . . . The enemy is always there . . . It is lurking about even when things are normal. It is always threatening in peacetime as well as wartime (and perhaps even more threatening in peacetime)."[6]

An entire volume could be filled with statements reflecting this fundamental hatred. Early in 1954 Georges Duhamel wrote: "Morocco, Tunisia, Algeria . . . Everything in these countries is working against France: the forces of Islam as well as those of communism" (*Le Figaro,* February 5, 1954). Who was to blame for the 1954 uprising in the mountains of Algeria? "A nationalist agitation associated with communism" (*Le Figaro,* November 12, 1954). "The people have been handed a scourge with which to flagellate themselves in the name of freedom" (a *Figaro* journalist upon his return from the USSR, January 6, 1947). "An occupation by Mongol and Tartar hordes would be crueler than an occupation by Hitler's legions: crimes, rapes, arsons, thefts. Deportation to labor camps would be applauded by collaborators like [Communist leaders] Duclos and Lecoeur, worthy successors to [Vichy officials] Laval and Henriot. Communist voters, be logical. Pack your bags and get ready to do your Compulsory Labor Service in Siberia" (*Le Populaire,* April 16, 1951). And in *Le Figaro* for January 23, 1948, the writer François Mauriac warned: "The conquering Russians, whose kingdom is chillingly of this world, take advantage of the hold that Marxism

"How to vote against Bolshevism?" This poster may have been intended to stiffen the courage of property owners.

can exert over the mind to further their domination over bodies and material things . . . We must fight this ideology with all our strength, because it is in the service of pan-Slavism."

Control by the Communist Subsociety

The Communist subsociety likes to portray itself as "one big family." It is based on the family. There is no firm boundary between party life and private life. Marriages between party activists are common. The moral asceticism of communism is an extension of Judeo-Christian asceticism. Couples do not necessarily have to marry, but they must be stable. Adultery is condemned, and divorce is accepted only if one of the partners is not a Communist, in which case it is conceded that married life is impossible. Woman-chasing is considered a contemptible, petty-bourgeois activity that places sexual and emotional considerations above the purpose of the party, which is revolution. Party authorities keep a close eye on the morality of members. "Since I knew very few party cadres, I still had no notion of the inquisition to which their private lives were subjected: love affairs were ended on party orders, officials were demoted to the rank and file because they engaged in a dangerous dalliance or simply because the wife happened to be a good Communist and complained to higher-ups about behavior unbecoming a party member."[7]

Family life was subordinated in every way to party requirements: the Communist's schedule was filled from morning till night, and it was difficult if not impossible for a non-Communist to remain married to a person whose commitment was so total. "People look upon the Party as a big deal . . . Actually, it's little jobs . . . It takes more than one person to get the Sports Arena ready for a rally of 100,000 people on the Common Program. We built steps."[8] The puritanical marriage of Maurice Thorez and Jeannette Vermeersch was held up as an example to thousands of Communist couples. Jeannette Vermeersch, the daughter of an alcoholic miner and a mother who took in washing from "bourgeois" families, was fond of saying: "When your childhood came right out of a Zola novel, let me tell you you remember it. For me, *Germinal* was not fiction." As Maurice's idealized companion, she spoke out enthusiastically on behalf of the new painless childbirth technique from the Soviet Union, but she strongly opposed contraception on the grounds that it would encourage free love, a typical petty-bourgeois failing unworthy of a Com-

POUR QUE LA FAMILLE
SOIT HEUREUSE

VOTEZ
COMMUNISTE

Parti Communiste S.F.I.C. Elections législatives 1936. Imp. Schuster. Paris.

Vu : Le Candidat.

The Nazi rise to power led to a drastic change in the strategy of the Third International. The slogan "class against class" gave way to the "popular front against fascism." This poster from the 1936 legislative elections was intended to present communism in a reassuring light: the (postponed) revolution would respect the family.

Maurice Thorez, Jeannette Vermeersch, and their four sons. "Every family generates its own inward boredom, which drives its members away (while a little life still remains). But it also has an ancient and powerful virtue, which resides in the communion around the evening soup, in the feeling of being at home and without airs, as one really is. It follows that the family is a milieu in which a minimum of pleasure coexists with a minimum of trouble" (Paul Valéry, *Suite*).

munist. Jeannette and the party resolutely favored large families: Communist couples were expected to produce future party members. In this area Jeannette said nothing to contradict the pope's *Humanae Vitae.*

Here we touch on the most subtle contradiction of the Communist subsociety: it was isomorphic to the larger society and not in contradiction with it. Numerous accounts by former members agree on this fundamental point: the militant was expected to be a competent professional, a good husband and father, a "normal," conformist member of society. The goal was "to change the established society by requiring militants to conform to established norms. The 'characters' found in such large numbers in anarchist groups—bastards, hunchbacks, homosexuals, butterfly collectors, drug addicts, fetishists, people obsessed with personal problems, cultural, sexual, and philosophical minorities, aficionados of music, film, or camping—were not comfortable in Communist organizations."[9]

Conformism plus seniority entitled a party member to consideration for an official post in the hierarchy. Once in he had to maintain his conformist behavior or risk being demoted to the rank and file, which also meant returning to a regular job in a trade he had not practiced for years. The PCF hierarchy was quite different from that of other French organizations. Here there were no cautious graduates of the top schools taking a few years' leave from government service and certain that they could always return to a good post. Many party leaders were former workers, in whom the prospect of returning to the factory was unlikely to arouse enthusiasm. This reluctance to risk demotion no doubt accounts for what Annie Kriegel calls the "blasé endurance" that enabled party officials to absorb endless changes in the party line. Philippe Robrieux, a one-time Communist militant who left the party to write a critical biography of Maurice Thorez, notes this significant feature of the party: "the monarchical and religious cult of the leader, [who is] presented as a new supreme guide and raised above all other party militants."[10]

The Communist subsociety is isomorphic with the larger society but not integrated into it. Its history contradicts the view of Georges Sorel: "Experience soon showed that the anarchists were right and that revolutionaries who joined bourgeois institutions adopted their spirit and were transformed. All deputies know that there is nothing quite so like a representative of the bourgeoisie as a representative of the

"Before we unite and in order to unite us, we must first resolutely and deliberately set ourselves apart from those who are not with us" (Lenin).

proletariat."[11] The Communists were not swallowed up by bourgeois society, but the subsociety they formed offered party officials sufficient rewards that they were ultimately wooed away from the "final goal" of revolution. Though accused of being "in thrall to Moscow," the PCF is actually quite French in its syndrome of denial, its preference for the vulgate over the original text, its fondness for hierarchy, its belief in the infallibility of the supreme hierarch—all of which are characteristics of French Catholicism as well as Communism.

Carrying the analysis one step further, we can see how the core of private life shapes the history of thought. The clearest indication of the isomorphism between the Communist subsociety and the larger society is the PCF's embrace of the Stalinist vulgate and its elimination of every last vestige of Marx's dialectic. The French are allergic to the dialectic. Although they are forever asking whether "the situation is revolutionary," they reject the idea of a revolutionary process, that is, a passage "from the inferior to the superior" via a sudden and chaotic emergence of contradictions. Long before

Martin Malia put forward the notion of a "universal ideocratic bureaucracy,"[12] Henri Lefebvre wrote: "The Russian Marxists, who, between 1917 and 1920, were left in conditions of indescribable chaos to pick up the debris of social and political reality in a predominantly peasant country, made use of Marxist ideology in a new, unforeseen, yet fruitful way. A doctrine that proclaimed itself the accuser and negation of the status quo became a justification of the current situation, which was in fact truly novel yet not what was expected in the radical critique of the previously existing situation."[13] If one agreed with Stalin that the first five-year plans had established a socialist society, one also had to admit that that socialist society bore within it the seeds of a still more perfect society—a communist society—and that this new society could only be born (according to Marxist doctrine) through a painful delivery. Like all dictators, Stalin was a man who believed in order. That is why he wrote this in his *Economic Problems in the USSR,* a sort of political testament: "Under socialism there will be no conflict between the relations of production and the forces of production, because society will have had the time to bring about the necessary correspondence between the backward

La Courneuve, September 1962, festival of *L'Humanité.* So long as "the age of necessity" lasts, the time that precedes—and perhaps heralds—"the age of freedom," the festival is an interlude that suspends "solidification" and possibly "produces man himself along with the other in freedom."

La Seyne-sur-Mer, June 1982, preparations for the festival of the Communist Party Federation of the Var.

relations of production and the character of the productive forces." In other words, the law of perfect correspondence is tendential in a socialist regime. It has become a normative category, no longer a descriptive and critical one as in Marx. An extraordinary importance is attached to the superstructure; a political decision can change the relations of production, as was "proven" by the collectivization of agriculture. We are asked to believe that this came about "without conflict"—proof that Stalin was not without black humor and a sense of understatement. Stalin's ultimate conclusion is that the development of the Soviet Union under socialist leadership will be steady and irreversible. His idea of "progress" is the same as that of the French Encyclopedists and utopian socialists. The death of the dialectic was explicitly announced in a 1954 Soviet textbook on political economy: "The economic law of development of socialist society is the law of necessary correspondence between the relations of production and the character of the forces of production."[14] Reduced to a schematic and "progressive" empiricism, this kind of Marxism held little appeal for French intellectuals, but it was so close to conservative thinking that it facilitated their exit from communism: "I am a conservative in order to conserve what is good," Disraeli said, "and a radical to change what is bad."

LEAVING THE PARTY

The "bolshevization" of the revolutionary party, as theorized by Lenin in *What Is to Be Done?* and as imposed on the PCF by the Third International three years after the split at Tours, was entirely alien to the French socialist tradition as defined first by Louis Auguste Blanqui and later by Jean Jaurès. That tradition allowed considerable scope for the spontaneous expression of working-class sentiment as well as for the possibility of alliance with certain "bourgeois" parties to improve the condition of workers. Eugène Varlin, who called himself an "antiauthoritarian collectivist," rejected the model of a "centralized and authoritarian state, which appoints the managers of factories, businesses, and retail outlets, who in turn choose their own assistants, foremen, and so on, [thus leading to] a top-down hierarchical organization of labor in which the worker is reduced to little more than an unconscious cog in the machinery, bereft of freedom and initiative."

This is not the place to examine in detail the polemic between Marx and Bakunin in the First International or its continuation in the controversy between Lenin and Rosa Luxemburg, who repeatedly insisted that the views put forth in *What Is to Be Done?* would lead to a totalitarian bureaucracy. In Luxemburg's *The Russian Revolution,* written in a Berlin prison in 1918, we read: "Freedom is always the freedom of someone who thinks differently . . . The dictatorship of the proletariat should be the work of the class and not of a small minority ruling in the name of the class."

Antonio Gramsci, for whom Marxism was *praxis* (by which he meant the unity of theory and practice), noted that the last vestiges of freedom had been eliminated in Italy by fascism and in the USSR by bolshevism at roughly the same time. With great daring he wrote the leaders of the Soviet Communist Party, urging them not to destroy the democratic dialectic within the party through excessive measures.

Bolshevik Elitism

Rosa Luxemburg, whom Fritz Mehring called "the greatest genius Marxism has produced since Marx," was beaten to death and thrown into a canal in the Tiergarten in January 1919.

After the Congress of Tours, the majority of French socialists chose the new Communist Party over the SFIO (French Section of the Workers' International). To many activists the "bolshevik graft" seemed a way of avoiding the fate that had befallen German social democracy—integration into "bourgeois" society. Yet French socialists did not feel at ease in the new communist subsociety, where all boundaries between pri-

Class against Class: An Antifascist Coalition

Antonio Gramsci, the theorist who conceived the "organic intellectuals" of the working class, was arrested in November 1926 and sentenced to twenty years in prison; he died in 1937. Bolshevism claimed its victims; it also had its martyrs.

vate life and politics were abolished. Many quit the party. The subsociety shrank to a microsociety or sect: membership fell from 120,000 in 1920 to 28,000 in 1934. The PCF cut itself off from other Left-Wing parties, and Communists were obliged to defend the party's class-against-class strategy at a time when the institutionalization of Italian fascism and the rise of Nazism showed that ultra-bolshevik tactics were ineffective and that what was needed was a broad-based coalition against fascism. In August 1932 Henri Barbusse and Romain Rolland convened the first World Congress against Imperialist War in Amsterdam, and in June 1933 the first European Antifascist Congress was held at the Salle Pleyel in Paris. Meanwhile, the PCF, confined to its ghetto, rehashed the eternal question: "When will we seize power?" Maurice Thorez, who since 1930 had been secretary-general of what was by now a rump party, seized upon the riots of February 1934 as the occasion to replace the party's "unified anticapitalist platform" (which unified nobody) with a new antifascist platform calling for "defense of republican freedoms." This was what many workers had been waiting for, and membership again began to grow. Fifteen months later, in August 1935, the Seventh Congress of the Third International gave its approval to this change of course: the class-against-class strategy was abandoned in favor of alliance with social democracy and the petty bourgeoisie in the struggle against fascism. In the elections of 1936 the PCF reaped the benefits of its new strategy: 1,468,000 votes and 72 deputies (compared with 783,000 votes and 10 deputies in 1932). Membership approached 300,000 in 1936, even though the party had not abandoned what Annie Kriegel calls "its radical strangeness."

A "Revolutionary" Situation?   The Communist Party was indeed a "strange" party, whose members were unlike those of any other political group. Communists carried on political activity right on the shop floor, risking dismissal. They continued their political work outside the factory: attending cell meetings, putting up posters, campaigning door to door, and so on. They politicked even at home, which sometimes led to conflict and division. Above all, without any kind of preparation, the Communist tried to "explain" the directives handed down by higher authority. Party members could hope for no social advancement in the bourgeois society they claimed to be burying. They were accused of proselytizing for a totalitarian society,

"Who's afraid of whom?" Maoism comes to France in the wake of May '68.

but their everyday lives expressed a totality of political commitment.

What kind of person could accept such an ascetic way of life for a long period of time? Was he a precursor of the "new man" that communism was supposed to bring forth? But how could such new men spring from "the dungheap of capitalism" when capitalism was offering workers a steadily growing share in the fruits of consumer society? It is not surprising that there was a high turnover in Communist Party ranks. Every year, and especially with every new "crisis," old members resigned and new members joined. Even during periods when membership remained constant, apart from party officials and a certain hard core of activists, the membership of the party changed from day to day. Leaving the party was a wrenching experience. One lost friends, and there was a question whether they could ever be replaced. There were risks. The sirens of anticommunism were always ready to accept ex-Communists into the fold, provided they confessed their bitterness and suffering.

For General de Gaulle, the Communists were "separatists" in July 1947. The 1947 miners' strike, shown here, followed the expulsion of Communists from the government.

To be sure, Communists felt they were different from other people, and quite possibly superior because their horizon extended beyond the Tour de France, soccer scores, and the pleasures of the table. They were taking part in the redemption of mankind. But when would this secularized Second Coming take place? When would the situation be "revolutionary"? After World War I the revolutionary window of opportunity had closed quickly with the triumph of repression in Germany and the failure of general strikes in northern Italy. In 1936 no revolutionary situation existed: the need to defend the borders of the USSR and the danger of a Franco-style putsch demanded moderation.

What about the Liberation? The presence of Allied troops and directives from Moscow made compromise inevitable. What about 1947, when Communist ministers were dismissed from the government? The Americans were still on the scene with their troops, their interim assistance, and before long the Marshall Plan. In 1958 the political parties were only too glad to let General de Gaulle pick up the burden of resolving the "Algerian problem," and no one was persuaded by the PCF's attempt to link Gaullism to fascism. The year 1968 saw a sham rebellion by spoiled children of the bourgeoisie that had nothing to do with the class struggle. In the sixty-five years of the PCF's existence, the situation has never been "revolutionary." But ultimately the rank-and-file Communist got tired of waiting and could no longer stand the taunts of those "realists" who favored immediate rewards.

The Communist militant had to justify what was taking place in the "fatherland of genuine socialism" and to explain Soviet directives. In the Moscow Trials those who confessed were guilty because they confessed. The Nazi-Soviet pact of August 1939 sowed consternation in the ranks of the party and led to massive resignations. Nevertheless, thanks to its effective participation in the Resistance, the PCF regained credibility. In 1946 it reached its apogee, winning 28.6 percent of the votes cast and 166 deputies in the November legislative elections. The PCF was now the leading party in France in terms of votes and seats. A few years later the new party line was laid down by the USSR: the current situation was described as one of "state monopoly capitalism." The Nineteenth Congress of the Soviet Communist Party declared capitalism to be stagnant, ergo it was stagnant. The crisis of capitalism

The Millennium and "Real Socialism"

For the Communists, as this poster designed by André Fougeron shows, General de Gaulle represented a permanent threat of fascism.

was said to have proceeded through three stages: 1917 saw the birth of a socialist state; between 1945 and 1949 the socialist camp extended its reach from the Oder-Neisse line to the China Sea; the third stage began in 1950 with the anticolonial movement, which pointed the way toward the worldwide triumph of socialism. Capitalism had entered on a period of irreversible decline. Progress in science and technology was finished, production was in decline, the rate of profit was falling.

Then, in 1956, came the Polish October and the Hungarian November. Commenting on the crushing of the Hungarian uprising, *L'Humanité* ran this headline: "Budapest Smiles." Gilbert Mury confessed to Jean-Toussaint Desanti: "But the news can't be true, because if it were, my life, our lives, would lose their meaning. And that's impossible." But it was true, and it was possible. "Everything collapsed," Desanti recounts. "It wasn't a fire, it was an earthquake."[15] Many party members resigned, particularly after learning of the PCF's response to de Gaulle's return to power. In the June 1958 issue of *Cahiers du Communisme* Roger Garaudy observed that "the RPF (Rassemblement pour la France, the Gaullist party) exhibits the social characteristics of a fascist party." In the August issue of the same magazine Maurice Thorez claimed: "since June 1, France has been ruled by a personal and military dictatorship imposed on it by force and threat . . . Those who vote 'yes' on October 5 will be voting 'yes' for fascism." The PCF ordered a general mobilization of its members, asking them to give up their vacations and devote the months prior to the referendum to "the struggle against dictatorship . . . because the future of our people, the future of our country, is at stake." But the people of France calmly enjoyed their vacations, and on October 5 the new constitution was approved by 79.25 percent of those voting. In the November legislative elections the PCF received only 20.5 percent of the ballots cast, and the new electoral law pragmatically imposed by the Gaullists (requiring an absolute majority after two rounds of balloting) reduced Communist representation to just ten deputies. (Independents, who had garnered just 15.4 percent of the votes, held 130 seats.) Two years later the sudden recall of Soviet advisers from China put an end to illusions of "unity in the socialist camp."

In May 1968 the PCF denounced what it saw as probable ties between *gauchisme* (the New Left), the CIA, and technocracy. In the September 1968 issue of *La Nouvelle Critique*

Pierre Juquin wrote: "The *grande bourgeoisie* is expert at ma-
nipulating *gauchisme*. Read *Le Monde*. Listen to Europe One.
News is beginning to leak out about the role of the minister
of the interior and the CIA in the events of May . . . The
interests of *gauchisme* and technocracy are frequently and profoundly the same: this is the case with the PSU (Parti Socialiste
Unifié, a *gauchiste* party) and with the Geismar-Herzberg leadership of SNE-Sup. (a student union) . . . The *gauchistes* are
demagogues, the worst enemies of the people." In a speech
broadcast over the radio at 4:30 P.M. on May 30, General de
Gaulle announced that the National Assembly was being dissolved. Half an hour later Robert Ballanger, chairman of the
Communist deputies' group, announced that the PCF would
participate in the upcoming elections, even though the elderly
general had just told the nation that "in this time of national
despair [the PCF] intends to impose the power of totalitarian
communism." In August 1968 Warsaw Pact troops invaded
Czechoslovakia, ending the "Prague Spring."

Let me make a long story short. The Common Program,
an alliance between Communists and Socialists, was signed
on June 26, 1972, and renounced on September 23, 1977. The
Soviet Union invaded Afghanistan in 1979. Communist presidential candidate Georges Marchais vehemently attacked his
Socialist rival in the first round of the 1981 presidential elections, only to throw his support to Mitterrand in the second
round. Communist ministers agreed to join the Mauroy government but refused to participate in the Fabius government.
With each turn of events, with each new twist in the party
line, party members had to change their tune—or quit the
party.

RESIGN?

Some who once "believed" lost their faith and quietly left
the party. To many of them Stalin, Mao, or Castro had once
been heroes who for years had justified the hope that the world
might be a better place, no longer oppressed by tragedy,
powerlessness, and delusion. Certain members joined the
party in late adolescence, before career worries forced them
to relinquish their vision of utopia. Others found there the
family they lacked. Still others, who had based their identity
on Judeo-Christian ideals, needed a prop to help them through
a period of transition. And some joined the party as an act of
rebellion against collaborationist fathers. But most of all the

party was—and is—filled with workers and sons of workers who know full well that there is little likelihood that they or their children will escape the condition into which they were born.

There are also those who calculated the profits to be made from their former commitments. That Soviet Communism should have exerted a fascination on the French intelligentsia is not surprising. Steeped for so long in Judeo-Christian ideals, intellectuals were ready to embrace a new form of salvation. What is astonishing, however, is that those who made so many errors in the past suddenly laid claim to possession of the truth. As Communists, they had been ready to open the gates of the Gulag to receive those who expressed doubt that the horrors of the moment could be overcome. When they became *gauchistes* in 1968, they combined their newfound anticommunism with their old anti-Americanism to create a new ideology of spontaneity, which, they claimed, would lead to a new and just society. They then rediscovered the sentiments of their fathers and became—as befits prodigal sons returned—the toast of the media, leading many of their peers back to good old "traditional" values, now restored and patched up for the occasion.

Claude Mauriac, whom no one would mistake for a cryptocommunist or a mean-spirited man, wonders why this much-touted sect remained silent for so long, "as if a lengthy blindness, a protracted silence, entitles those who have at long last shed their blindfolds and gags to decide by themselves what is the right path from now on."[16] When a Communist of some notoriety recants, when yesterday's pimp becomes today's flagellant, one can only repeat the words of James Joyce: "Had Pyrrhus not fallen by a beldam's hand in Argos or Julius Caesar not been knifed to death? They are not to be thought away. Time has branded them and fettered they are lodged in the room of the infinite possibilities they have ousted. But can those have been possible seeing that they never were? Or was that only possible which came to pass? Weave, weaver of the wind."[17]

"Happy as God in France"? Are French Jews today still a group apart in either their public or private roles?

✎ French Judaism

Perrine Simon-Nahum

JEWISH culture has survived thousands of years of diaspora and persecution, including the genocide of World War II. Given the need of communities to adapt to their environment in order to survive, it is in the limited sphere of private life that the essence of Judaism has been preserved over the centuries. Of course private space is always subject to the surveillance of the inevitably hostile dominant culture, yet it is also a space where an irreducible measure of freedom remains, freedom based on a kind of secrecy. Bossuet saw the "hardening" of the Jewish community as a "scandal," a view that is one of the underpinnings of anti-Semitism. The hostility and sympathy that French Jews arouse are unlike the hostility and sympathy aroused by other communities.

Certain kinds of private spaces are unique to Judaism. The traditional physical and cultural boundaries between public and private are reinforced by a third boundary, this one political (in the broad sense of life in a civic community). "Jew at home, citizen outside," people used to say in nineteenth-century France, where differences between Jews and other Frenchmen were less pronounced than in some other countries and where, even before the political emancipation accomplished by the French Revolution, it was in private life that Jews perpetuated an identity threatened by assimilation and exclusion.

Some questions that arise are not easily answered. How many Jews are there in France? According to recent estimates, the number is between 535,000 and 700,000. But arriving at any precise measure of the Jewish "community" (if it is a community) is no easy matter. The figures are unreliable, and there are many different definitions of the word "Jew" (from religious to sociological to anti-Semitic). For convenience I shall call "Jew" anyone who considers himself or is considered to be a Jew. The variety of definitions reflects the many ways of relating to Judaism. Anyone wishing to study this diversity confronts a major obstacle: there is a dearth of sources for the years between the two World Wars. During this period both Jews from old French families and Jews recently immigrated from other countries had little desire to display their "differences." Private expressions of Jewish identity were so discreet as to be almost invisible. After the war Judaism became more readily identifiable; for a while the genocide silenced the anti-Semites. To put it another way, the complex history of the Jewish minority (or minorities) in France is inseparable from that of the larger society, which may, at one time or another, tolerate, ignore, or reject the Jews or even close its eyes to their annihilation.

Terrorist attacks on the synagogue on rue Copernic in October 1980, on a delicatessen on the rue des Rosiers in 1982, and on the Jewish Film Festival in March 1984, along with desecrations of tombstones such as the one in the Bagneux cemetery, reminded the French Jewish community that, despite its size and high degree of integration, it was still vulnerable.

When Jews talk about themselves, they often spontaneously adopt the language of sociology. When anti-Semites—covert, overt, or unconscious—talk about Jews, they stress differences. When Jews lived in ghettos, they moved in a

Jewish space where public and private were fused. Once emancipation took hold, however, the French Jew came to be defined primarily by the place Judaism occupied in his private life.

A Private Life Dominated by Religion?

It is tempting to speculate that in contemporary Judaism the private is, in its very essence, religious. One might argue that interpenetration of the sacred (the inviolable domain of religious feeling) and the profane (that which is "outside the Temple" and therefore alien to religion) is what makes Judaism unique. Yet even an agnostic or atheist may participate in certain religious practices or observe certain dietary prohibitions. The content of these intermittent practices is secularized, yet they still signify an ineradicable attachment (transcending time and space) to the "chosen people." Ritual observance thus protects the nearly assimilated Jew from imagining that he has been truly accepted by the host society.

Tradition and Modernity

Jewish law lays down rules and limitations, but it never aims for radical suppression. Rejecting both asceticism and mortification, it seeks an equilibrium. Moderation and free will are the basis of an ethic of responsibility, ubiquitous in the Jewish religion, which has no notion of dispensation. Duty is a consequence of "chosenness." If the Jews are a "chosen people," it is because they have special duties, not because they claim special rights. Judaism is a religion of effort, in which each individual is responsible to the community for his actions. The relation to God is first of all enacted in the relation to others, an idea that has been explored by the philosopher Emmanuel Levinas.

This primacy of the religious originates in a dialectic between tradition and modernity that preserves the central place of the Bible. Because there is also an oral Law, the written prescription can be adapted to changing conditions; thus the teachings of the Torah never can become obsolete. Central to this dialectic is the practice of discussion. Discussion may take the form of commentary on the Law. Even if the argument is sometimes more apparent than real, a mere camouflage for the reiteration of certain norms, discussion of those norms becomes a process of deduction, and the new laws take on a character as sacred as the revealed Law itself, of which they are an emanation.

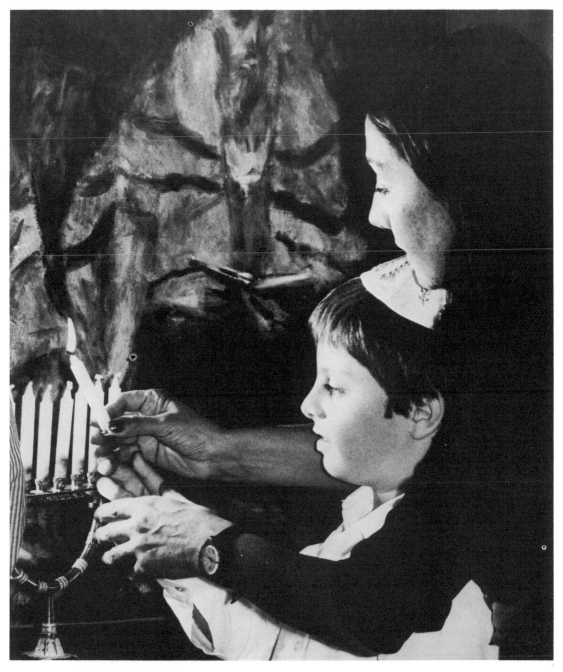

Lighting the Chanukah candles. Memory is a fundamental component of Jewish thought. "Hear, O Israel," says the fundamental prayer known as the Sh'ma. Beyond memory there is also observance. This bipolarity between reflection and action is resolved in teaching.

"If your son is born to a Jewish woman, he shall be called your son, but if born to a non-Jewish woman, he shall be called her son" (Kiddushim, 68b). The Talmud holds that the child's identity is determined by the mother.

This relation to the biblical text bestows the mark of religion on every manifestation of membership in the Jewish community. Even the agnostic or atheistic Jew who registers his belonging to the community thus participates in a rite that either expresses the faith or simply—and secularly—celebrates the vitality of the reassembled group. Of course Jewish religious practice is not exempt from the decline of zeal that has afflicted other monotheistic religions, Islam excepted. Nevertheless, an essential "distinction" remains: the Jew who has "lost the faith," who no longer practices, is still a Jew, both for others and for himself.

French census questionnaires have not asked about religious affiliation since 1872, so it is impossible to say exactly how many Jews identify themselves as religious. A survey conducted in the 1970s estimated that less than 20 percent of the Jewish community based its ritual of observance on religious belief, while an equal percentage did not practice at all. For the rest, observance was apparently more a social than a religious matter.

Private expressions of Judaism take many forms. As long ago as 1919 religion had already ceased to be the universal expression of French Judaism. Although the orthodox are only a minority, they are the most distinctive group within the Jewish community and exhibit many specifically Jewish features in their private life. There are, however, many other ways of participating in Judaism. Rather than attempt to explore these in detail, I shall simply mention a typology first proposed by Dominique Schnapper, who distinguishes between *practicing* Jews, whose faith is religious and metaphysical, and *militant* Jews, who are politically committed to the support of Israel. Schnapper also considers a third category of fully assimilated Jews, whose observance of Jewish tradition is generally limited to celebration of the Bar Mitzvah, the rite of passage from childhood to adolescence.[1]

The private sphere is a symbolic space important to the survival of the group; it is also subject to external surveillance and control. As a people "chosen" by God, the Jews are collectively responsible for their fate. The Jew enjoys total freedom of will within the limits of the Law, but he remains subject to the scrutiny of the group. Freedom and surveillance are merged in the family, the cornerstone of social life.

The figure of the "Jewish mother" dominates the family's

Private Life in a Collective Mode

"And thou shalt shew thy son in that day, saying, This is done because of that which the Lord did unto me when I came forth out of Egypt" (Exodus 13:8).

private life. A symbol of excessive love and guilt-inducing self-denial, the Jewish mother is the heroine of the Jewish family. She is responsible for one of Judaism's fundamental concerns: the transmission of the Jewish heritage from generation to generation. In what Joëlle Bahloul calls her "kitchen-gynecaeum," subject to the same rules of purity as a holy place, she reconstitutes the sacred order of the world. The kitchen is not just a functional but also a social space in which the foundations of a collective order are constantly recreated. There, protected from male curiosity, women exchange intimate secrets along with family recipes. One of the strengths of Judaism lies in the fact that it is taught directly by the parents—especially the mother—without a mediator.

At the dinner table the Jew learns of his "difference" and of the history of his people. Every dish and every flavor is an element of sacred memory. The dinner table is the school where the religion of narration is taught. Holidays are reminders of important events in the history of the Jewish people. Different dishes represent those events. Thus, at Rosh Hashanah, the Jewish New Year, the bread and wine are blessed and then apple dipped in honey is eaten to symbolize the desire for a sweet new year. Dates serve as a reminder of God's goodness as reflected in his readiness to thwart the designs of Israel's enemies. Pomegranate and fish are signs of prosperity. And lamb evokes the sacrifice of Isaac. The Passover meal, or *seder* (order), is designed to recall the bitterness of slavery in Egypt and the haste of the departure.

Every male Jew who has reached the age of religious majority marked by the Bar Mitzvah is expected to offer prayers on behalf of the community. If the mother is the priestess of the home, the rabbi is more teacher than priest. Prayer and study are merged in religious celebration—a significant fusion of sacred and profane. The group occupies a place of paramount importance. There can be no Jewish service without a *minyan,* a group of ten males above the age of religious majority. Study too is a group activity, and in Jewish tradition the elect are usually envisioned as scholars. Studying the Law and its 613 commandments (248 positive, 365 negative) is of practical as well as spiritual value. In this religion of active redemption, whose mission is to transform the world, action is no less valued than study. Study is an invitation to commentary and constant questioning. There is no prohibition against thinking: as Edmond Jabès put it, "A Jew is a man who responds to one question by asking another."[2] The unity of the Law does not require unanimity of interpretation. Commentary is not a paraphrase of the Book but a recreation in the light of both tradition and modernity.

Prayer, Study, Action, Time

"Bent over a text he questions relentlessly because the truth resides within, he needs a lifetime to explore his chosen field of study, not only because there is always more to learn but also because what has already been learned helps him to formulate the next question" (Edmond Jabès, *Judaïsme et écriture*).

The time allotted to the Jew (his lifetime) is to be used for the twin purposes of transforming and sanctifying the world, hence devoted to study and action in a proportion to be determined by the nature of each individual. Time is not to be wasted—an injunction that must be taken in the most profound sense. Included in it are the profane time of history, a sacred time that transcends history, and perhaps an intermediate time marked by repeated threats and persecutions, that of the history of the "chosen people." Within the realm of this third kind of time the Jew may legitimately acquire the profane knowledge on which his and his community's survival depends. The Jew knows that the "other" is a constant threat and potential betrayer (as the Occupation proved). He must therefore possess that which no one can take from him except by murder: knowledge—or perhaps a violin, something easily transportable. Where public and private spheres intersect we find the Jew involved in a secularized form of the traditional religious study: the "people of the Book" place a remarkable faith in higher education. Because of the threats facing the community, the Jew must anticipate the hostility that is all too likely to arise by conceptualizing the world and by mentally embracing its vicissitudes. He must be both in the world (in order to feel it) and at a distance from it (in order to judge).

Jews transposed traditional virtues such as respect for labor and unbending morality into lay terms to justify their participation in French culture. In the 1870s the focus of Jewish intellectual activity shifted from the synagogue to the Ecole Pratique des Hautes Etudes and the Ecole Normale Supérieure. This photograph depicts the latter institution's class of 1878, which included Bergson, David, Durkheim, and Salomon.

Group prayer and collective study are a religious expression of Jewish solidarity, which has enabled the Jewish communities of the Diaspora to survive centuries of persecution. Until the Nazis put an end to all exceptions, there were always some Jews less vulnerable than others and ready to help their imperiled coreligionists. Ultimately such solidarity may lead to the eradication of all private life, as is the case in Hassidic communities in which the usual boundaries of privacy (the home, the family circle, and so on) are virtually nonexistent. In such cases it is permissible to speak of a collective dimension to private life.

The most visible index of community influence on private life in twentieth-century France is the prohibition against marrying non-Jews. Exogamic marriage imperils the cohesiveness of any minority. The prohibition against such marriage, though certainly religious in origin, also reflects concerns about community identity. To marry in the synagogue is to give public proof of one's attachment to the community. According to a survey conducted in France in 1973 by Albert Memmi, 82 percent of the Jews questioned had had religious marriages. The proportion of mixed marriages, while on the rise, has increased less rapidly than in other minority groups. What increase there has been reflects a desire for integration into the larger national community. Take, for example, a community as highly structured as the Jewish community of Strasbourg, in which 60 percent of marriages in the 1960s were mixed. The non-Jewish spouse was not automatically converted, because rabbis working under the authority of the French Consistory, unlike those of the Liberal Synagogue, refused to accept the non-Jew into the congregation. Today there are roughly ten conversions to Judaism each year in France, while Christianity annually has more than four thousand converts.

Marriage and conversion, both private acts, are subject to scrutiny by the group. Of course there may still be a secret sphere protected from communal surveillance. People must live—and survive—in the present, hence there is always some deviation from the norm: religious authorities in Israel authorized a female astronaut to participate in a 1984 space flight on the grounds that the sabbath does not exist in sidereal time. More down to earth, dietary laws are often ignored because they complicate social and professional relations with non-Jews. Such violations of the rules have a positive side: members of the Jewish community living on the margins of the

A hut built to celebrate the holiday Succoth (this one in the Hasidic Saint-Paul section of Paris) reminds the Jew that, even at home, he is in exile. These particular Hasidim came to France from North Africa, but their traditions stem from eastern Europe. They dress in traditional clothing, wear hats and beards, and are scrupulous in their observance of Jewish rites.

group have been able to support more orthodox Jews through their professional activities. Other practices, however, remind members of the community that spiritual time is superior to profane time: the sabbath marks the weekly cycle; Rosh Hashanah and Yom Kippur mark the yearly cycle.

Jewish private life in France has been shaped in part by the Jewish community's relation to the national community. Judaism played a relatively large role in the private lives of those Jews victimized by the rampant anti-Semitism of the 1920s and 1930s; it played a smaller part in the lives of Jews more fully integrated into French society.

THE JEWS BETWEEN THE TWO WORLD WARS

Jews of French Extraction

The arrival of persecuted Jews from eastern Europe disturbed the serenity of the Jewish community already established in France. Judaism had flourished under the French Republic, which had granted Jews full citizenship, and which they in turn staunchly defended. Although echoes of the Drey-fus Affair could still be heard, the rehabilitation of Captain Dreyfus in 1906 in Jewish eyes stood for the victory of the universal values of the French Revolution over the arbitrary power of the state—even the republican state. Speaking of the "fortunate Jews" of pre-1940 France, Dominique Schnapper writes: "owing to a historical miracle, for which they thanked Heaven and France, they were able to maintain the memory of a Judaism to which they remained loyal out of dignity while establishing firm French roots, which enabled them to rec-oncile the singularity of their patriotism with the universality of the values of the Revolution. The France of the Rights of Man and the emancipation of their ancestors resolved the problem of their identity, Jewish by memory and French by passion, and of their fidelity to past and present."[3]

The years 1919–1939 were two decades of profound changes. Jews from central and eastern Europe came to France and joined, but did not identify or merge with, the existing Jewish community. Apart from official contacts, the tradi-tional community remained aloof from if not downright hos-tile to the new Diaspora. The two groups had little in common. They were separated by demography, wealth, and culture, and each lived by a law unto itself. The French Jewish community confronted the crisis of the 1930s riven by severe internal tensions.

It was at this time that French Jews coined the term *Israélite* to mark their distinctiveness from the new arrivals. Israélite connoted a successful fusion of the French nation with its own established Judaism, to the exclusion of new immi-grants. French Jews were determined not only to set them-selves apart from the newcomers but to set them a model of assimilation. The new definition of French Judaism invoked both the connection of French Jews with the soil of France and the relation of Judaism to French national history. The Israélites rewrote the origins of French Judaism in terms of their own genealogy; they concealed their foreign forebears and emphasized only French ancestors. Within the Israélite community there was even an implicit hierarchy in which families with roots in the Comtat-Venaissin, Bordeaux, or Metz were regarded as superior.

These families were joined by other Jews who had arrived in France after 1870 but had fought in World War I. In August 1914, 10,000 foreign Jews volunteered for service in the French army, 4,000 of them being allowed to enlist in the Foreign

The "pope's Jews," authorized to live in the four communities of Cavaillon, Carpentras, Avignon, and L'Isle-sur-Sorgue, enjoyed many privileges. Emancipated on 28 January 1790, the Jews of the Comtat Venaissin constituted a sort of aristocracy throughout the 19th century. The synagogue of Cavaillon, a reminder of the years in the Comtat, illustrates the symbiotic relationship that developed between Provence and its Jews.

Legion before being authorized to join French battalions. French Jews suffered in combat and shared in the joy of victory; even Maurice Barrès (a writer known for anti-Semitic views) hailed their patriotism.[4] Thus Jews of old French stock, who before the war had distinguished themselves from more recently arrived Jews, after the war joined in forming the Jewish community that called itself Israélite.

Although Jewish traditions had no place in public life, nevertheless they influenced social and family relations. Relations among Israélites were closer to relations among the previous generation of French Jews than to those of the Catholic bourgeoisie of the period. Although Jews played a part in all aspects of French life, their relations with other Jewish families in the community were of paramount importance. French Judaism between the two World Wars was parochial in nature and more social than religious in character. Life revolved around the synagogue, but more as a meeting place than a house of worship. Jewish social life revolved around weekly attendance at synagogue and participation in charitable endeavors, and in this respect it was not very different from the social life of the Catholic bourgeoisie. The number of Bar Mitzvahs and religious weddings declined. The rabbis of the Consistory (who numbered thirty in 1905, seventeen in 1931) officiated at eight hundred burials and four hundred marriages annually. Nevertheless, intermarriage was rare, even among the nonreligious. This was partly for religious reasons, partly because the community was so small. Those who, like Julien Benda, recall meeting non-Jews among their parents' acquaintances are rare. Still, within the Jewish bourgeoisie social barriers were less rigid than within the Catholic bourgeoisie; the prestige of education compensated for lack of wealth. Bergson, the son of a Polish-born musician, married the daughter of a director of the Rothschild Bank. Lucien Lévy-Bruhl, the son of a salesman, became the son-in-law of a wealthy jeweler. Arranged marriages and double weddings (in which two brothers married two sisters) were still common. In Paris, where there were many Jews, it was relatively easy to marry within the faith; in the provinces it was more difficult. In an attempt to overcome this obstacle, families from provincial towns attended Jewish community gatherings to which other Jews from the surrounding region and elsewhere were invited.

The chronology of Jewish private life does not coincide with that of France as a whole. World War I accelerated the process of assimilation that had been temporarily halted by

the Dreyfus Affair. Jewish religious practice began to decline early in the Third Republic as a result of urbanization, which gradually destroyed rural communities. Although Jews ardently embraced the Republic, they did not reject their religious traditions, which were kept alive within the family but hidden from the public eye. Here we must recall the role of Catholics in the anti-Semitic furor surrounding the Dreyfus Affair. Of 106,000 subscribers to Drumont's anti-Semitic paper *La Libre Parole,* 30,000 were priests. To a bourgeois Jew who supported the Republic and entertained a secular outlook, it must have seemed contradictory for anyone to claim allegiance to the liberal Republic while at the same time professing religious convictions. But if Judaism maintained a discreet silence in the public arena, it was perpetuated in the private sphere by the Jewish mother, more attentive than ever to her duty of transmitting Jewish tradition. Jules Isaac observes: "If I was Jewish, it was primarily because of my mother." In this respect, the generation that came of age in the 1920s and 1930s followed in its parents' footsteps.

The central Consistory, quasi-official representative of French Jews, is still controlled by Jews of Alsatian descent; between the two World Wars its membership consisted of barely 6,000 families. The synagogues of the Consistory, attended mainly by Jews of the Parisian bourgeoisie, observe a highly Christianized ritual. Music is played on the organ, and rabbis deliver patriotic sermons in French.

From their religious childhood these assimilated Jews remembered some of the traditional practices in which they had participated with their parents. *Shabbat,* or sabbath, was different from other days, and at Friday night dinner dishes not eaten during the rest of the week were served, although even these meals were not strictly kosher. Such meals drew the family together. Similarly, as Proust recounts, the "ancestral jargon" that was avoided in the presence of strangers retained its strong emotional value when spoken among family. The holidays Yom Kippur (Day of Atonement), Rosh Hashanah (New Year's), and Pesach (Passover) were celebrated but not in accordance with orthodox ritual. At the Passover meal, or seder, the head of the family would simply read a few prayers and ask those in attendance to reflect on the history of the Jewish people.

This privatization of Judaism was encouraged by the shortcomings of religious teaching, which was neglected by French rabbis who had lost touch with the tradition of biblical exegesis. Hebrew school teaching was at best mediocre: "You went two or three times a week to a rabbi but learned very little. I had trouble learning to read the texts."

In effect, the traditional values of Judaism were reworked to bring them into harmony with the principles of republican ethics. But we must be careful about the meaning of "assimilation." Biblical virtues were recast in secular form and imparted to young children, who were taught to respect learning, work diligently, and behave righteously. French Israélites perpetuated the religion of culture characteristic of pious families. Claude Lévi-Strauss remembers: "In my circles cultural values predominated. Culture was sacred . . . I grew up in a family of the book." This adaptation of traditional virtues to republican values explains why the Zionist movement was relatively unsuccessful in France. Of 94,131 immigrants to Palestine between 1919 and 1926, only 105 were French. If World War II had not intervened, what would have become of this observance of Judaism as a token of fidelity to the past? Would it have survived among French Jewish families, or would it have disappeared over several generations and thus have ended in assimilation in the full sense of the word?

Because French Jews conceived of Judaism as a private practice, it was impossible for them to resolve the problems posed by the immigration of additional Jews and the rise of anti-Semitism. In order to respond politically and publicly to what was going on, they would have had to renounce the ideology of assimilation bequeathed by the Revolution. The difficulty was compounded by the fact that French Israélites underestimated the scope of anti-Semitism. But who could have foreseen the dimensions it would take? Events moved too rapidly to allow the community to adapt. The private practice of Judaism had convinced French Jews that emancipation was possible, and after 1930 this conviction became their illusory defense against anti-Semitism. Some Israélites felt bitterness toward the new arrivals, whom they regarded as too "visible" and therefore likely to incite the animosity of anti-Semites. It was not until 1933 that they began to be concerned by the influx of more than 60,000 Jews from Germany and Austria, Jews thought to be "assimilated" like themselves, whose exile pointed to the failure of assimilation.

The younger generation, born after 1910, rejected the ideal of assimilation, which they blamed for the failure to find a solution to what was now being called the "Jewish question." Young people expressed their Jewish identity by forming youth movements, the most important of which, the *Eclaireurs Israélites de France* (French Jewish Scouts), was founded in 1923. But events moved at such a rapid pace that this new form of Jewish organization had no time to develop to its full potential.

Jewish Immigrants, 1920–1939

In the 1920s and 1930s France was a place where Jews came not merely to stop on their way to other countries but to settle. Between 1920 and 1939 approximately 80,000 Jews came from central Europe and another 15,000 from the Middle East. Although this influx amounted to only 2 percent of the total immigration, it represented such a large change for the Jewish community that parts of that community reacted with hostility.

The few Sephardic Jews who came from North Africa posed no problem. They quickly gave up speaking Ladino in favor of a French they learned in French schools or at the Alliance Israélite Universelle. Culturally they had more in common with the Mediterranean inhabitants of southern France than with their coreligionists from central Europe, and they did not really constitute a distinct community. In 1907 some 37 percent of the Mediterranean Jews in Paris were living in sections of the city where the Jewish population density was low. Their institutions were affiliated with the Consistory.

I will focus on the Ashkenazy Jews who came from central and eastern Europe. Their integration into French society was complicated by the fact that their Judaism had national aspects, even though many of them had been relegated to a marginal position in the societies from which they came. Habits acquired over generations of life in the *shtetl* (Jewish ghetto) had to be abandoned in France. Boundaries between public and private had to be redrawn. Traditional allegiances had to be adapted to meet the hostility with which the new arrivals were greeted. Some immigrants had left for political reasons, others for economic reasons, still others for both at once. No matter what the reason for leaving, however, the immigrant had taken a step away from his traditional community and from his identification with its future. Hence the decision to emigrate justified some deviations from community norms, although the shock of being uprooted initially resulted in a heightening of traditionalism. But once settled in France, many immigrants soon reached negative judgments about the societies they had abandoned. They embraced the myth of the French Revolution as "liberating and progressive" even for Judaism, and this belief rendered them impervious to Zionism. Their future, they believed, henceforth lay in France.

Whole families immigrated. In this respect the Jewish immigration differed from that of Polish and Italian Catholics, where the husband often went ahead and sent for his family later. Thus the family, as the guardian of Yiddish values, was the place where the break with the shtetl was most keenly felt. For some it led to total abandonment of all forms of Jewish practice. Of the 769 Jews who converted to Catholicism between 1915 and 1934, 43 percent had been born abroad. Women in the ghetto were inclined to accept "modern" habits. Although the conception of the role of women in the couple did not change, the image women had of themselves did. Attitudes toward the body evolved considerably. Women shed their heavy fur-lined coats and hats and were no longer content to hide their bodies. They took pleasure in making themselves attractive to men. Those who still wore wigs changed their cut and color as fashion dictated. Men abandoned their prayer shawls and sacrificed their studies for business. Children were sent to public rather than religious schools, which had been the main means of transmitting community norms from generation to generation. In 1939 Paris's sixteen Hebrew schools had only 753 students, while 760 other students attended schools where lessons were given in Yiddish. This "Frenchification" created ambivalence in the parents. Though proud

The door of the rue Pavée synagogue in 1927, on the first day of the trial of Scholem Schwartzbard for the murder of a Ukrainian nationalist leader by the name of Petlioura in retribution for the massacre of Jews in east European pogroms. "I walked through the streets of the Jewish quarter in the heart of Paris, and it seemed to me that I was back in Warsaw, in Muranow. I found the same tiny shops, the same modest restaurants, the same excitement. My heart beat faster when I recognized my mother tongue" (Moshé Zalcman, *Histoire véridique de Moshé*).

to see their children succeed in their new country, they regretted the estrangement from their old culture. Yiddish, no longer used in daily life, became a private language for use exclusively within the family (and it was not always well understood).

This westernization affected the structure of the family. The nuclear family began to replace the traditional extended family. The birthrate declined, as Jews born into families of ten children produced only two children in the second generation. Marriage with non-Jews began to take place, although almost exclusively Jewish men with non-Jewish women.

The Ashkenazy Jews were a minority in two senses: they were foreigners and they were Jews. They overcame the difficulties of living in Catholic France by banding together in small communities, in a sense reproducing the ghettos they had left behind. It was easier for the newcomers to make their way in French society than to establish close relations with French Jews. J. Tchernoff recounts: "I came into contact with an elite group, but when we found ourselves in the presence of a Jewish family, my friends and I . . . had the distinct impression that they looked upon us as foreigners, as Jews born in Poland, Turkey, or Rumania."[5] Unlike their elders, post-World War I immigrants found an embryonic Jewish community awaiting them, with its own established forms of patronage, mutual assistance, and charitable aid. Forty-four percent of the immigrants who arrived between 1920 and 1939 initially lived with relatives. Immigrants from different countries tended to congregate in different sections of Paris. Each community was unified above all by language. On rue Sedaine the only language spoken was Ladino, unknown a few blocks away. In the café *Le Bosphore* (The Bosphorus) the dishes served included *koftikas kon arroz* (meatballs with rice) and *avikas* (beans) reminiscent of Turkish cooking. Immigrants met "to play cards, listen to Eastern music, and eat *borrekas,* pastries stuffed with cheese and meat and prepared by one of the women of the community." Rue Basfroi, an extension of rue Popincourt, was the Rumanian section. There Jewish life was less public, but once a year the rabbi slaughtered chickens in a doorway. The La Roquette quarter was fabled, Annie Benveniste tells us, even "in the minds of future immigrants who had heard of it as far away as Istanbul."[6] The avenue Ledru-Rollin formed a border between the Sephardic and Ashkenazy sections. And the "Pletzl," an area occupied mainly by

The Russian and Polish Jews who came to Paris at the beginning of the 20th century opened small shops and stores. The first to arrive rose quickly in the social and economic hierarchy with the help of cheap labor provided by later immigrants from eastern Europe. Facing page: Goldberg family, Vincennes, 1938. Above: Kassis family, Bagnolet, 1934.

Jews from Alsace-Lorraine, became the Yiddish-speaking district after the war.

These various microsocieties helped newcomers to find work. Unlike other immigrant populations, the Jews resisted proletarization and dispersion. They avoided public works projects, mining, and domestic service, jobs eagerly accepted by Poles and Italians. Jews became merchants or craftsmen. In the 1920s they controlled 40 percent of the Paris garment trade. This was due in part to the nature of the business: start-up costs were low and the family home could double as a workplace. Jewish merchants found a ready clientele among other Jews in the community. But this tendency of Jews to congregate in certain sections and trades, denounced by anti-Semites, limited contacts with the outside world. On-the-job relations, which had such a powerful assimilating effect on other populations, were irrelevant here.

Jews from central Europe felt out of place in French synagogues. They were disconcerted by the sight of Jews in religious garb talking business during the service. Upset by the lack of religious fervor and impelled by mystical ardor, immigrants gathered in synagogues of their own, houses of worship and study where the Jewish community gathered. In 1906 new legislation enforcing the separation of church and state put an end to the supremacy of the Consistory. Newly arrived Jews were thus free to found their own houses of worship and pay their rabbis. The result was a religious pluralism previously unknown in the French Jewish community. Ritual in the new synagogues was less solemn than in the synagogues of the Consistory. The synagogue again became a neighborhood meeting place. As a consequence, however, it also became the place where French Judaism and foreign Judaism met head on.

Immigrants from central Europe, having survived repeated bouts of persecution, were more alert than were French Jews to the rise of anti-Semitism. Though drawn to the "Western model," they were prevented from embracing it by an explosion of xenophobia and anti-Semitism during the Depression, an explosion that led to a number of discriminatory measures. Still under the influence of the community model, immigrants were quick to respond to the hostility or threats of hostility that they felt; in keeping with the traditions of the shtetl their response took a political form. Indeed, ghetto politics was a secularized form of community life that straddled the boundary between public and private.

FRENCH JEWS SINCE 1940

Nazi persecution eventually would claim the lives of one-third of France's Jewish population—two-thirds of this total being recent immigrants. Official reports and estimates by Jewish organizations agree on the figure of 75,000 people deported for "racial" reasons. The last convoy for the death camps left France on August 17, 1944. Israélites, who had assumed that they were protected because they were "French," shared the fate of those whom they had attacked before the war as responsible for the rise in anti-Semitism. How can one speak of private life for the four years during which French and immigrant Jews were united in a community of suffering? What does the word "private" mean when persecution, escape, and extermination are the very substance of everyday life? During this period the obsession of Jews was to survive. In the indiscriminate conditions of the camps all privacy evaporated.

Deportees combatted those indiscriminate conditions by chastening their conversation. Sex was never discussed. The ability to maintain a decent physical appearance became the condition of moral survival (self-esteem) as well as physical survival (which depended on aptitude for work). In this time of fear and atrocity man developed his individuality to an extreme degree, yet the human was revealed in all its distress. Georges Wellers remembers that "at Drancy in two weeks you got to know someone better than in fifteen months of normal life."[7] In order to survive people shed all vestiges of private life, including even their identity. Children changed their names and were taken in by previously unknown families and institutions. Life was traumatic for these young people waiting in suspense.

Israélites, who right up to the moment of death clung to their faith in the law, were subject to raids, denunciations, and arrests. Persecution brought home to them the unity of the Jewish people. The promulgation of "Jewish Laws" prior to the extermination demonstrated to those who had dreamed of assimilation that it had always been a myth. The divorce from France led to a new definition of Judaism as an extension of private life, itself a kind of myth that posited the unity of the Jewish people in its rebirth as well as in its persecution. In the words of Pierre Dreyfus, the embodiment of the supposedly assimilated bourgeois Jew, "we Jews lived between 1940 and 1944 in a way different from non-Jews, even the most just,

On July 17, 1942, Joseph Koganowsky, shown here at his Bar Mitzvah, was interned at the Vel d'Hiv along with 4,050 other Jewish children arrested in a manhunt organized by French police. All were deported; few returned.

most kindly, and most well-disposed."[8] The postwar generation of Sephardic Jews has internalized this alleged unity as a part of their history. Since 1940 the genocide has been a part of the history of the entire French Jewish community, whether Ashkenazy or Sephardic.

Another event had a similar dramatic impact on the entire French Jewish community: the Six-Day War between Israel and Egypt in 1967. The fear that Israel would be wiped out mobilized all Jews, Zionists and non-Zionists alike. The magnitude of the reaction, even among those who had never actively supported Israel, cannot be understood without the Holocaust. During those few days of 1967 French Jews lived on Israeli time. The only thing that mattered was the news from Jerusalem, whose reunification excited even the nonreligious. The Six-Day War contradicted many anti-Semitic stereotypes. When General de Gaulle referred to Israel as a *"peuple d'élite, sûr de lui et dominateur"* (an elite people, sure of itself and domineering), it could be read as a compliment. French Jews now had a different concept of themselves because non-Jews had a different idea of Jews.

Tim, Drawing. This cartoon was published after General de Gaulle, in a 1967 news conference, referred to the Jewish people as "sure of itself and domineering."

The bond between French Jews and Israel should be discussed in terms not of dual national allegiance but of its roots in earlier private experience. Dual nationality is recognized under international law; but those who invoke Israel and who feel that they belong to the same "people" as that which inhabits Israel indicate, as Vladimir Jankélévitch suggests, an allegiance to a higher norm. French Jews welcomed the Sephardics of North Africa in the 1960s because they belonged to this "people." These new arrivals were not ostracized as central European Jews had been in the 1920s and 1930s.

Invoking the name of Israel, however, introduced a political dimension and blurred the boundary between public and private. Political activists began to identify themselves as Jews whether or not they participated in traditional religious practices. In 1975 the Zionist movement in France boasted some 45,000 supporters, although fewer than 40 percent took part in any regular Zionist activities. Although the genocide had dispelled any illusions of total assimilation, relatively few French Jews went to live in Israel, a sign of deep attachment to France. Lucien Lazare has studied Jews from Strasbourg who decided to move to Israel. Most who did so, he found, made the choice because of memories of persecution. Those who left were not the "official" Zionists but the most prominent citizens in the community, and it took most of them more than twenty years to make up their minds whether or not to emigrate.[9] From 1968 to 1970 the Jewish Agency recorded 13,300 departures. How many returned we do not know. In 1977, 1,171 French Jews left for Israel. Surveys in the 1980s reported that 30 to 50 percent of those questioned had "given some thought" to moving to Israel, but a far smaller number ultimately decided to go. According to an old saying, French Jews are as "happy as God in France." Since 1945 the French Jewish community may have begun to think of itself as a community of the Diaspora, but in terms of geographical distribution and professional profile it has never been closer to the French population as a whole.

Sephardic Jews and the Return to Judaism

The arrival of North African Jews has lessened the tendency of Jews to congregate in particular professions. Many of the newcomers have jobs in middle management or in the bureaucracy; a large number work as elementary and secondary schoolteachers. Since their inclusion in the Jewish community, more and more Jews work for salaries or wages rather than as independent businessmen.

Paradoxically, French Jews have never before insisted as firmly on their distinctive character as they have done in recent years. This has been the great change since 1945, a result of the survivor's syndrome, which has given rise to an unabashed pride in Judaism. Even the word Israélite has taken on a new meaning: instead of referring to Jews with a rather cool and aloof attitude toward their Judaism, the word is now used to distinguish between the Jews of Israel (*Israéliens*) and those of the Diaspora. Until the war in Lebanon, any public expression of anti-Semitism was taboo in France, a fact that encouraged public avowal of one's private affiliation with Judaism. But a more important source of pride in Judaism was the memory of the extermination.

The genocide has been a matter of public discussion for some time. The discussion itself is not new, but its public character is. Memories of the extermination were for a long time buried in the minds of survivors. In the immediate postwar period a minority of Jews, unwilling to call attention to their Jewishness, avoided all forms of public demonstration, even weddings in the synagogue. Of 2,500 name changes over the past century and a half, 2,150 took place between 1946 and 1958 (280 in 1950 alone). Most survivors, however, felt a need to talk about what they had been through. Because it was impossible to forget, many who had moved away from the Jewish community before the war now returned to the fold. For those who had been deported and imprisoned, the wounds were still so raw that any public discussion was too painful. It was a tragic paradox: whole lives were wrapped up in an experience too painful to communicate. But as time passed and a few voices in France began to question whether the death camps had even existed, those who had known the camps firsthand found the strength to delve into hitherto private memories. Little by little the truth about the genocide found its way into the public eye.

Even more important in the revival of Judaism in France was the arrival of North African Jews, who breathed new life into the Jewish community. This Sephardic immigration, which came in the wake of independence for France's North African colonies, doubled the size of the Jewish population—from 300,000 in 1956 to roughly 660,000 in 1967. Although these North African Jews had been educated in French schools, they had to adapt to a society different from the one into which they had been born. The newcomers left behind the old enclosed Jewish community and suddenly found themselves liberated from the close scrutiny of family and neighbors. Now that they were no longer confined to a Jewish

Benhaim family, Ain-Temouchent, Oranie, 1937. The Jews of Algeria, unlike those of Morocco and Tunisia, had been French nationals since the Crémieux decree of 1870. In 1962 Jews accounted for 15 percent of repatriated Algerians.

quarter, their Jewish identity ceased to be a matter of necessity and became a matter of choice. If their community was to survive in France, it would have to assert its own identity. The external forms of Jewish practice changed.

The broad North African concept of family had to be adapted to the realities of France, where parents and adult children generally live in separate residences. Yet family ties remained strong. Recent analyses of the acculturation process show that the family played an important role in shaping identities and aiding in adaptation. Doris Bensimon-Donath has found that one young person in four regularly spends Friday nights and holidays with his or her family.[10] Arranged marriages between young men and women of the same city are a thing of the past, but in other respects first-generation North African immigrants remain loyal to traditional values. Marriage partners are still chosen within a relatively small community, one of many that the Sephardics have formed in order to preserve Jewish customs in daily life. Claude Tappia has traced the formation of these new communities, which are

Arrival of Jews from North Africa at the Arénas camp, Marseilles, 1961. Jews leaving North Africa chose to go either to Israel or to France, depending on how attached they were to French culture. Those who chose France were mainly from the intellectual and economic elite.

based on traditional types of social intercourse: women meet in the marketplace, men in the synagogue.[11] Communities gather to celebrate holidays together. In Sarcelles, one of the largest Sephardic communities in the Paris region, 47 percent of the families living there chose the location for family or religious reasons. For similar motives four hundred families from Haret-el-Yahoub, a suburb of Cairo, chose to settle in Villiers-le-Bel. Establishing a community in this way was the only way to preserve the way of life of the North African Jew. The whole community celebrates the sabbath and holidays together. Stores cater to the dietary and social requirements of their almost exclusively Jewish clientele. At the bakery, for example, women can select their bread in the North African manner, carefully hefting and examining each loaf.

North African Judaism offered an answer to French Jews looking for ways to revive traditional practices. To be sure, the Israélites' "return" to Judaism predates 1960, but that return was shaped by the Sephardic example. France's Sephardic

Sabbath dinner. In traditional society group pressure encouraged observance of religious customs. After coming to France many Jews clung to these customs and familiy ties.

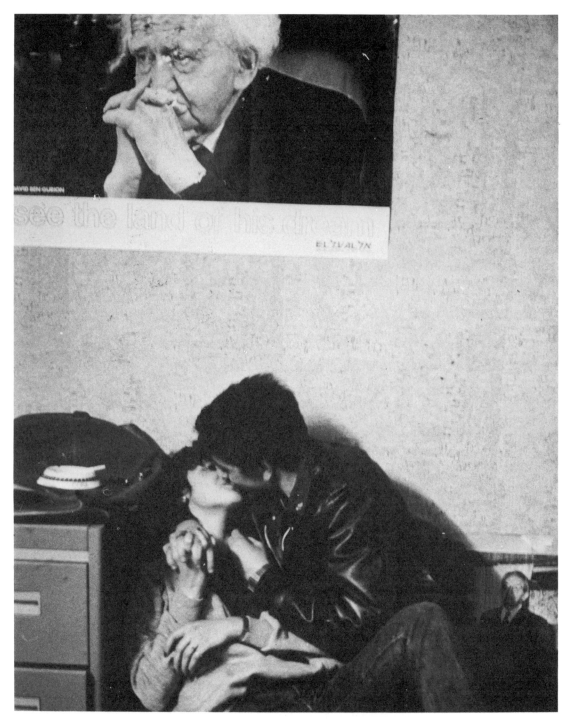

"If I forget thee, O Jerusalem, may my right arm forget me."

Jews are more religious and more traditionalist than its Ashkenazy Jews. They go to synagogue more often, observe the sabbath more strictly, keep kosher more frequently, and fast more completely on Yom Kippur. More than 80 percent have their sons circumcised, and 70 percent choose religious marriages. Their influence increasingly has affected the behavior of Ashkenazy Jews.

The growth of Hebrew studies, increasing enrollment in Jewish schools, and the emergence of a Jewish literary market are all signs of the current revival of Judaism. The self-affirmation of the Sephardic community has contributed to that revival, as has the development of a more decentralized Jewish life based on community centers and youth movements rather than on a hierarchical establishment. If, paradoxically, the importance of religious practice has diminished, Israel continues to play a central role. Young Jews pay close attention to events in the Middle East, and partly for that reason there have been occasional conflicts with young Muslims residing in the same suburbs and faced with similar problems of adaptation to French society.

Tomorrow's Judaism in France

The history of the younger generation of Jews cannot be understood without reference to the genocide. Their newfound Jewish identity represents not so much a return (*teshuva*) in the traditional sense as a revival, born of the private experience of the victims of Nazism. In many ways this revival has been a source of conflict with the previous generation. The determination of young Jews to be clear about the Holocaust accounts for their reactions to anti-Semitic attacks and to criticism of Israel in the media. The Middle East conflict daily reinforces their insistence on defining themselves in terms of difference.

Alain Finkielkraut has called these sentimental and temperamental young Jews "Jews of the imagination."[12] Will their Judaism take a private or a political form in the future? It remains to be seen what place French culture will make for this new arrival.

Expectation, hope, anxiety. Solitary men arrive by train; their large valises, held together by ropes, contain all their personal belongings.

The Role of Immigrants

Rémi Leveau and Dominique Schnapper

I N contemporary France the private domain is distinguished from two public domains, one of work, the other of politics. This distinction is associated with the nature of liberal democracy, under which private life is respected so long as certain conditions are met (most notably respect for the public order). It is also associated with the nature of industrial society, in which the increasing autonomy of the economic sphere leads to separation of home and workplace, of business and personal finances, of economic activity and private life.

For many immigrants the distinction between public and private becomes a source of conflict between their native culture and the culture of the society that receives them. (Culture here is to be understood in the anthropological sense.) North African immigrants to France offer a particularly clear example.

The term "private life" assumes that individuals have the right to organize part of their existence outside the family and community of which they are members. But the concept of an autonomous private life is not readily accepted in an Islamic culture. The distinction made in French society between public and private challenges one of Islam's fundamental tenets. Given that another of its fundamental principles, incumbent upon individuals as well as groups, is to fight for good and against evil, what an individual does is subject to scrutiny and possible correction by the community. Individual behavior tends to conform to the collective judgment. Transgressions are regulated by a complex economy of honor, which ranks individuals and families and thereby controls their behavior. Not all transgressions are pursued with equal vigilance, however; only public transgressions are punishable. A person who drinks wine in secret or who quietly breaks fast during Ra-

madan will not incur community sanction unless the misbehavior comes to light. In practice Islamic culture offers certain
refuges in which private life is possible away from the scrutiny
of family and community. Nevertheless, whatever "right" to
private life exists is not the same as that in the host society.

Private life and family life are not the same. Within the
family group the individual continues to have a world of his
own. But because there are few sources to tell us about individual experience, we shall study private life as if it were
synonymous with family life.[1]

Is not the normal and therefore natural and proper way
to eat, to reproduce, to die, to arrange the house, to address
others, to respect parents, to raise children, and to deal with
relations between men and women implicit in the most deeply
ingrained of the habits acquired through the process of socialization? Emigration, however, challenges these assumptions about what is natural. What was taken for granted is
suddenly thrust into doubt, and the continuity between family
life and life in the immediate and wider society is broken.

Prayer during a break at the
Talbot factory in Poissy, a way
of affirming Muslim identity.
Such "sanctification" of the
workplace is more common in
Europe today than in countries
where Muslims are in the
majority.

Immigrants can neither renounce the internalized habits on which they have built their identity nor continue to observe their native customs in an alien society. Their private lives are subject to voluntary or involuntary transformation and acculturation. The form of that acculturation depends on a variety of factors: date and origin of immigration; historical relations between the country of origin and the host country; the variety of cultures of origin; the evolution of the receiving society, in particular with respect to its ability and willingness to assimilate immigrants.

France has had a steady stream of immigrants ever since the nineteenth century. Owing to a low birthrate during the period of economic development and to the presence of a class of farmers made wealthy by the acquisition of properties confiscated during the French Revolution, the need for manual labor has been constant. In 1930, when prewar immigration was at its peak, there were at least three million foreigners in France—7 percent of the total population and 15 percent of the working class. These figures do not include either naturalized foreigners or clandestine immigrants, whose number Georges Mauco estimates at one-third of the total number of legal immigrants. In addition to those who immigrated for economic reasons, others left their homelands for political reasons. Depending on the period, they fled authoritarian regimes in central Europe, czarist Russia, Nazi Germany and other fascist countries, and, since World War II, various communist states.

The term "immigrant" is imprecise. In France it refers to populations as different as Poles, Italians, Ukrainians, and North Africans. They differ in religion, family and community customs, and political experience. Each group arrived in a different way. In the nineteenth century Italians were recruited in their native villages to work in the steel industry in Lorraine. Groups of Poles arrived to work in French coal mines in the early 1920s. Poor "Levantines," southern Italians, and North Africans came to France throughout the twentieth century, many of them illegally. Algerian families arrived in the 1960s.

The nature of the immigrant experience often shapes attitudes toward the host society. Some central European refugees who came to France in the 1930s dreamed of becoming assimilated into the French population. By contrast, North Africans of several nationalities (though we will treat them as

The Imprecise Concept of "Immigrant"

a single group), who began settling in France with their families after 1950, had no desire to cut their ties to their native countries. They tried to keep their options open, to preserve their right to return as well as their right to stay, even though many obstacles stood in the way of full naturalization, which many saw as a form of conversion, a betrayal of indigenous traditions.[2]

Each group arrived in France at a different stage of acculturation to urban and industrial life. Some immigrants had already experienced some form of urbanization in the country of origin: for example, many of the Italians who left home after 1945. Others came from traditional rural societies: for example, those who came from North Africa in the first wave of immigration, up to around 1950. At any given date one finds in each national group first-generation immigrants, children born prior to immigration (some of whom went to work immediately upon arrival in France, while others attended French schools), and children born after immigration or young enough to have begun their schooling in France. Each of these subgroups has a different relation to the host society and a different type of private life.

The private life of immigrants cannot be understood without understanding the "colonies" (as they were termed in the 1930s) or communities they formed in France. The community exercised social control over its members, helped to maintain norms carried over from the country of origin, and "created a facsimile of national life, a recreation of the atmosphere and ambiance of which [immigrants] were totally deprived."[3]

It is more difficult to investigate the private life of immigrants than to explore that of other segments of the population. Until recently French authorities, employers, and many ordinary citizens have been reluctant to admit that there is any difference at all between immigrants and native Frenchmen in this regard. The differences are often concealed by immigrants themselves and even more by their children, brought up in and through French schools, who sometimes feel ashamed at not being "as French as everybody else."

Broadly speaking, one can distinguish between two types of immigrants on the basis of whether private life did or did not exist. The first Italians and North Africans came to France alone, lived in barracks, hotels, or hovels, and were defined solely by their role as workers; they had no possibility of private life. By contrast, in what might be called a "settlement immigration," workers earned enough to bring their families and to maintain some aspects of the private lives they had led back home. Clearly, the situation of the immigrant bestowed new meaning on private life. Where the outside world was not only different and foreign but hostile, private life became a refuge and protection; it enabled immigrants to settle in to their new homeland. The elimination of private life is the source of all the social problems attributed to the presence of immigrants.

Hospitality and Xenophobia

Despite the traditional notion that France welcomes immigrants and has a long tradition of hospitality, all signs are that the bulk of the population was and is xenophobic. Take, for example, the hysterical proclamations of the extreme right in the 1930s and the almost universally accepted equation of the number of unemployed with the number of immigrants. There is even more striking evidence that French people at all levels of society have never really accepted any immigrants other than those who have become "assimilated," that is, who have ceased to be foreign and become French. Consider this text, published in 1932 by an observer who, though favorable to immigration and aware of the immigrants' contribution to the wealth of the nation, nevertheless displays the characteristic prejudices of the xenophobe: "It is worth noting that in the past foreigners arrived at a rate slow enough to permit a regular fusion. Since World War II the massive influx of new elements, their high density within the French population, and their more fervently nationalistic spirit has made the problem more complex. We have seen that the presence of a foreign population of three million within French borders was not without influence on the country's social and moral life. As a result, the French workers' aristocracy, a settled group, as conservative as it is materially satisfied, now faces an inferior mass of foreign workers without ties to the country. The ignorance of these workers has slowed the evolution of society and may yet trigger a period of troubles. This horde of immigrants, many of whom are rootless and maladjusted, has increased the crime rate in France by one-third and has thus led undeniably to demoralization and disorder. No less pernicious is the shabby morality of certain Levantines, Armenians, Greeks, Jews, and other foreign traders and traffickers."[4] In other words, the good immigrants were those who had lived in France for a generation or more and expe-

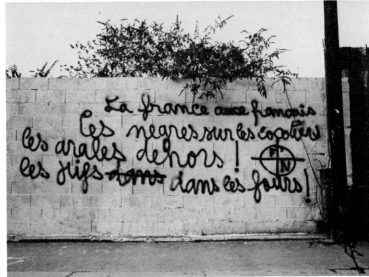

Above: Medical students hold a banner calling for a strike "contre l'invasion métèque," against the foreign invasion, in the 1930s. Below: Offensive slogans spray-painted on a wall in 1980: "France for the French. Niggers to the coconut trees. Arabs out! Jews to the ovens!"

rienced "regular fusion" with the French nation. Xenophobia of this kind was, at least for the generation of immigrants themselves, a reason to preserve a characteristic style of private life, a primary means of self-defense.

Given the diversity of the immigration phenomenon, we shall limit ourselves to stating a few general propositions, illustrated by Poles and Italians in the period 1920–1939 and by North Africans since 1945. It is important to distinguish between the period prior to 1940, when the effects of the Depression were most severe and when assimilation was the stated aim of French policy, and the postwar period, which transformed the economic condition of French and immigrant workers but which also witnessed the disintegration of France's capacity and will to assimilate immigrant populations. Since World War II neither the schools nor the Church nor the army has been able to socialize French children, whether born into immigrant families or not, with the same degree of conviction as prior to 1940.

ITALIAN AND POLISH IMMIGRANTS BEFORE WORLD WAR II

The slums around Paris in the 1930s were no different from slums anywhere else. One often mentioned in the literature is rue Jules-Vallès in Saint-Ouen, where 300 to 350 individuals shared a single water spigot: "The streets are narrow, filthy, and flanked by tall old houses. Sheets and clothes hang from the windows or on lines stretched across the street from window to window. Dirty, barefoot, brown children swarm in every cranny and play with typically southern enthusiasm. The wretched interiors, poorly ventilated and lit, are filled with mattresses. Five or six people, sometimes more, live in one room. Children sleep three or four to a mattress, which in some cases is laid on an earthen floor."[5] Poverty eliminates differences and makes private life uniform.

In the 1920s and 1930s many workers came to France without their families. Denounced as "lawless nomads," they lived in conditions that made private life impossible. No bed ever went unoccupied in hotels for unmarried workers; while the night shift worked, the day shift slept on just-vacated sheets. New arrivals holed up in makeshift accommodations without amenities of any kind. In such living conditions there is a danger that the norms of private life will be forgotten altogether, a danger of "deculturation."

Early North African Immigration

Certain highly structured groups resisted this process of deculturation by limiting contact with the host society to an absolute minimum. The first wave of Algerian immigrants offers a good example.[6] Until 1950 immigrants from North Africa were exclusively unmarried men, sent by their villages to work abroad for a few years so that their families could remain together back home. Many came from poor mountainous regions such as Kabylia and Sousse, inhabited by Berber clans. Their emigration disrupted neither their own society nor the host society. To save money and avoid entanglement in the alien world in which they found themselves, they usually socialized with others of similar background. They chose difficult but well-paid jobs such as miner and worked overtime (adding as much as a third to their base pay) in order to send as much money as possible back home; for themselves they kept just enough to eat. Their private life was limited to infrequent contacts with other immigrants from the same region or village. These North African workers entertained one another and traded news from home, usually brought by trav-

Poor but dignified immigrants, probably Poles, at the Gare Saint-Lazare. The presence of women suggests an organized immigration, with the mines and steel mills of northern and eastern France the most likely destination.

elers since few knew how to write. What they saved in years of austerity abroad enabled their families to hold on to their land and perhaps to repair the big house, purchase livestock, or find suitable spouses for young relatives left behind. When those who had gone abroad returned home, whether temporarily for Ramadan or permanently after five years, they regained their place in the village. Working in the mines or for the colonial army was in many ways the ideal situation for these emigrants. When they returned they could afford to buy land, make good marriages, and perhaps aspire to a higher social status. They also regained their right to a collective private life, whose chief merit was that it was "public" and thus enhanced the honor of both the individual and his family. Men in exile dreamed of their eventual return home, of the visits they would make to relatives, of the wedding invitations they would receive, and of the local holy days and pilgrimages in which they would participate. Such dreams helped them to forget the harsh conditions in which they lived. It is no exaggeration to say that such dreams were the extent of their private life, their only compensation for the long, tiring hours of work and the bleak conditions in which they lived.

In the 1930s many jobs in the mining and steel industry were claimed by groups of Italian and Polish workers who constituted a kind of aristocracy among immigrants. Because they brought their immediate families with them, they were able to maintain a semblance of private life. While the men adapted to the pace and requirements of work in France, the family maintained a private life different from that of French families. Italian immigrants were strikingly successful, not only in the steel industry in Lorraine but also in agriculture in southwestern France. One foreman, speaking of workers he had known in Joeuf and Moutiers, said: "I worked with Italian workers who were better suited to the work than the French." When Italians arrived in the mines, French workers unable to match their pace were driven out: "They were big, strapping fellows, mostly from the mountains, who could load at least twenty wagons. But let me tell you something, the guy who could only fill fourteen was no slacker, believe me! Still, those guys could fill twenty, and there was even one who worked sixteen hours and filled as many as forty. That's what drove down the price and forced out the French."[7] The success of Italian workers in the southwest in the 1920s and 1930s is

Italians and Poles

reflected in the number who were able to save enough to go from being seasonal workers to regular hired hands and then to sharecropping and finally to buying land of their own. Georges Mauco, writing in the style of the period, comments: "Italian farm workers are highly valued and much sought after. They are generally good workers, docile, respectful, and devoted. Many employers prefer them to French workers, whom they judge to be harder to handle and more demanding."

This adaptation to the requirements of the French workplace was not incompatible with the preservation of a distinctive private life; perhaps it was the latter that made the former possible. What has been called the kernel of culture, that which most firmly resists acculturation, probably lies within the family circle, in relations between husband and wife and parents and children.[8] Immigrants clung to traditional styles of interior decoration, diet, and to some extent even clothing and holiday celebration, as women continued to abide by the norms of feminine behavior they had been brought up to honor. Family life in steel-mill and mining towns was punctuated by the thrice-daily wail of the siren that announced the end of one shift and the beginning of the next. There was no avoiding this forced rhythm, but it left plenty of room for the expression of ethnic customs.

Immigrants did not come to France unformed and ready to adopt French ways. They were already socialized in the cultures of their native countries. The requirements of the host society were interpreted according to the norms of the old homeland. Italian, Polish, and North African immigrants did not become "French"; they developed a life-style of their own that mingled aspects of their native lands with features of the host country's culture.

Polish and Italian Communities

This general assertion cannot be applied indiscriminately to different populations. Between the two World Wars the two largest immigrant groups—the Poles and Italians—both stemming from European Catholic countries, preserved traits of their native cultures to some extent. Polish workers were more apt than Italians to settle in organized groups and form communities with their own religious leadership and institutions, which helped perpetuate a Polish life-style and slow assimilation. The Italians, less organized, more dispersed despite their considerable presence in Lorraine, and less subject

to the control of religious institutions, shed native cultural traits more quickly. One obvious sign of this is the rapid decline of religious practice among Italian immigrants. In Auboué, for example, 55 percent of Italian children born between 1909 and 1914 were baptized, contrasted with 80 percent for the population at large. Compared with the French, Italians were less likely to have religious funerals or to participate in Easter services. And the number of common-law marriages between immigrants increased rapidly.[9] Other evidence, including the reports of the Italian Catholic Mission, confirms this decline in religious practice.

By contrast, Polish immigrants who resided in specially built factory towns were more likely to preserve traditional religious and national traits. Each of the company towns built in the 1920s to service the mines of northern France had its church and priest, in some cases provided with housing and paid by the mining company. People turned to the priest for help in coping with the small problems of daily life. He served as an intermediary between the immigrant population and company and government officials and helped to discipline

Athletic clubs known as *sakols* were one of the ways in which the Polish community maintained itself under the authority of the clergy.

the community. Until World War II the priest's flock kissed his hand, and young girls made a quick curtsy when he passed, this in recognition of his role as spiritual and "political" leader of the community. Unlike other immigrant groups, the Poles were allowed to employ schoolteachers of their own nationality. In 1932 there were roughly 150 Polish teachers working in France, 65 of them in the Nord and Pas-de-Calais, about 30 in central France, another 30 in eastern France, and around 20 more in the south and west. Approximately 20,000 children benefitted from their teaching. Nuns also provided charitable assistance. Because the life of Polish immigrants was so structured and institutionalized many distinctive features of Polish culture were preserved right up to World War II.

Workers in Polish factory towns were fervently religious. Attendance at Sunday mass was an assertion not only of religious but also of national identity: "The men wear uniforms with colored caps and ribbons on their chests. Young girls wear white dresses with black velvet bodices. Children wear white suits with red embroidery. The women wear colorful shawls of red, green, and blue . . . Everyone presses into the chapel. Flags and banners bow before the altar and then are set up in the choir. The church is always richly decorated and filled with flowers. Gold and bright colors are naively dis-

Women preserved Polish customs and consciousness by working together in traditional activities such as the one commemorated in this photograph.

played. During the week the women prepare the decorative motifs, and the children scour the woods and meadows for flowers and greenery. The church is often too small to hold the crowd . . . All take part in the ceremony and sing folksongs in their native language."[10]

Other characteristic acts became regular rituals: "Sunday clothes" were put away with loving care; on Saturday they were taken out to be washed, starched, and ironed; the children were bathed that night in the great family washtub. These routines survived emigration. A novelist describes an Italian immigrant as "amazed that the Poles starch everything, even their sheets. They also wash them much better, despite the acrid perspiration of the men. The starch protects the fibers of the fabric from the dirt. They make it themselves by mixing flour with water and then pouring it into a large pot of boiling water (*Knormal*), which they stir vigorously with the top of the Christmas tree, carefully preserved year after year for the purpose. If flour is lacking, they collect the liquid from grated potatoes (*Kiowski Kartoplane*). In either case the mixture is filtered and mixed with the 'blueing' they use to make their linen sparkle."[11] Such practices, passed on from mother to daughter since time immemorial, were preserved with special care by immigrant women; in so doing they affirmed not only their own identity but that of the group.

This preservation of religious fervor, at once personal and collective, played an important part in maintaining traditional norms, and in particular a traditional conception of sex roles. It was no accident that in northern factory towns relations with non-Poles ceased at the end of the working day, while relations with friends and families continued within the group. The rate of intermarriage between Polish men and French women remained low, although it did increase from 5 percent in 1914 to 9 percent in 1924.

It was observed that Polish "homes are clean and well kept, despite the presence of large numbers of children." Women were performing their traditional role. The Polish interior preserved "a special note, an originality that is not dispelled by either the mass-produced housing or the inexpensive furnishings purchased in France. Colorful engravings hang on the walls, usually religious subjects or portraits of famous Poles. Long strips of fabric embroidered with mottoes, greetings, or passages from the Gospel are affixed to the walls

Interiors

Workers recreated a Polish home in the midst of the steel district of Lorraine. Note the impeccably clean quarters, the attentive wife, the embroidered wall hanging on the right, the crucifix and religious icons, and the painted cupboard.

or the backs of chairs. The bed is covered with an enormous down comforter, which sometimes takes the place of sheets. There are many photographs, most depicting organizations to which family members belong."[12]

Keeping a "clean" house was particularly noteworthy because immigrants, like all urbanizing populations, had to endure sordid living conditions. Protests lodged by the governments of Belgium, Holland, Switzerland, and Italy reveal just how woefully bad immigrant housing was, although it was probably no worse than that of French peasants. Even in factory towns electricity was a long time coming. At the time of its construction in 1912 and 1913 the town of Mancieulle was the first in the Briey region to be wired for electricity, and it long served as a model. Workers' homes in Auboué had no electricity until 1928; running water was not installed until 1945, gas in 1955.[13] One retired foreman remembers: "When we arrived from Italy, I was still quite little. We used small oil lanterns for light. Every night, I remember, my mother used to set one to three of those lanterns on the table. I also remember that five of us slept in one bed, the boys at the head, the girls at the foot."[14] Such problems of housing, water, and hygiene were not solved until after World War II.

Ethnic identity was reaffirmed every day in the preparation and consumption of meals. Culinary habits, it has often been remarked, are more resistant to acculturation than any other. In Lorraine factory towns, where workers of many nationalities lived side by side, "cooking odors, more individualized than identity papers, wafted into the streets" every evening.[15] Polish women made sauerkraut in the fall by mincing cabbage and placing it in a barrel with a special brine. Pork and potatoes were also preserved, and Polish delicatessens were quite successful in the Polish colonies of northern France. All observers agree that the rate of alcohol consumption among immigrants was high.

Italians in general preferred a lighter diet. Always worried about the budget, Italian workers often made do with diets inadequate to the work they were expected to perform. When

In this family photo well-groomed parents and children breathe respectability. The school medals worn by the youngest son are tokens of the aspiration toward social advancement in the next generation.

they first arrived in France, Mauco tells us, they frequently ate nothing but vegetable soup, rice, pasta, and above all polenta, made of boiled cornmeal mixed with chestnuts. Holidays were celebrated with the ritual preparation of pasta, which varied depending on the village or region of origin; on the most important holidays meat was eaten. After World War II meat would become the symbol par excellence of material success.

Customs in dress were maintained to different degrees. Until World War II the Poles, better organized and more conscious of their nationality, attempted to preserve their native dress not only for Sunday mass but also for everyday use. While little boys adopted the black smock, backpack, short hair, and beret that was the uniform of French schoolboys at the time, little girls added a Polish apron with embroidered flowers to their black smock, wore a fringed shawl, and tied their pigtails with red ribbons.

If the Italian family could afford it, the children went to school dressed just like French children. Italian workers, who dressed frugally and carelessly during the week, decked themselves out on Sundays and holidays just as they would have done in their native villages. With evident misgivings Camsy observed: "On Sundays and holidays most of them are unrecognizable, and their elegance puts even the best dressed clerks in the shade: they wear suits of fine fabric in loud colors, boots with light fabric tops and polished tips, natty ties, and sometimes even a cane and gloves."[16]

Collective Life and Specific Identity

Within the immigrant colony social relations in off-hours revolved around music, theater, and above all sports. Wherever Poles congregated they formed associations and organizations of every variety. The Union of Polish Workers in France had no fewer than 16,000 members distributed among 182 local organizations. Polish-language newspapers, of which there were some fifteen in 1932, kept the community informed about one another and about France (at a time when television did not exist). Holidays were important occasions for the community to assert its special identity. Among Poles, for whom nationalism and religion went hand in hand, native customs were promoted with particular energy. From one fictional account we know how Christmas was celebrated in a Polish community in Lorraine. Relatives in Poland sent each family a large rectangular loaf like that eaten at the Last Sup-per. These were carefully preserved until Christmas Eve, at which time everyone began a strict fast, consuming only black tea and salt herring. The day was devoted to preparations for Christmas and for the Christmas Eve dinner. The tree was decorated with candles of many colors, with traditional strings, with sugared pastries wrapped in foil, and with artificial flowers. At seven in the evening the whole family, freshly washed and dressed in their finest clothes, gathered around the table. Everyone remained standing. The father lit the candles on the tree and recited a prayer. He then took part of the Christmas loaf, turned toward his wife, and made three wishes, each time breaking off a small piece of bread and eating it. His wife did the same, and then the loaf was passed around as each family member made his or her wishes. Christmas dinner included twelve items: pearl barley, beets, carrots, buckwheat, white beans, sauerkraut, prunes, noodles, mushrooms, salt herring, poppy-seed cakes, and apples with bread. While awaiting the stroke of midnight parents and children sang and prayed. Coffee, cakes, and fruits were shared with Polish neighbors after midnight mass. On Christmas day, in places where there was a Polish school, the schoolmaster would organize brief skits in Polish and lead the singing of both secular and religious songs. Italian families also observed the tradition of eating twelve different dishes during the Christmas meal, and of course they too attended midnight mass.[17]

At Eastertime Italians and Poles felt the same compulsion as the French to clean the house from top to bottom before Holy Thursday. Homemakers in factory towns vied with one another to see who could hang out the most bed linen, beat the most rugs and mattresses, have the shiniest windows. On the Saturday before Easter some Italians sang the *Gloria* while bathing in "holy water" and eating bread or cake moistened with a little white wine. Poles took to their priests to be blessed the twelve food items prepared for Easter dinner: eggs, salt, bread, coldcuts, cheese, horseradish, goose pâté, butter, coffee, milk, sugar, and cake. On Easter Sunday the whole family stood and sang the *Hallelujah,* after which the mother had the honor of blessing the home, the family, and, with a palm leaf divided into twelve parts, each of the twelve foods to be eaten during dinner.

The custom of honoring the dead on All Saints' Day, still very much alive in Italy, was also observed in Lorraine, an observance that was especially apt since, as Gérard Noiriel observes, fatal accidents in the mines were not infrequent: "When I went to the cemetery, candles or oil lamps had been lighted on all the tombstones . . . I do not know if this meant that the dead had come back to life, but it made an impression on me. I was also impressed by the fact that on All Saints' Day people used to put photographs of the dead on a small table with an embroidered cloth, chrysanthemums, and burning candles. We were compelled to watch over the dead."[18]

Immigrants' Children

Until World War II first-generation immigrants preserved many aspects of private life in their country of origin. It was an entirely different story with their children. While the first generation remained essentially a group of foreigners in a country where they had been obliged to settle, their children became French not only in nationality but also in culture, although some maintained emotional ties to their parents' native land.

In 1932 Mauco remarked that girls adapted particularly rapidly to the norms of French society, where they enjoyed greater freedom than at home. The rapid acculturation of immigrant children was the work of the primary schools, authoritarian institutions. This was often traumatic for the children because of the sternness and xenophobia of many teachers. Yet it was quite effective. "All surveys of teaching staff concur that young Italians assimilate rapidly and easily."[19]

School enabled the children of immigrants in Lorraine to become French and aspire to a future different from that of their parents.

ITALIENS DU PAS-DE-CALAIS
FUSILLÉS PAR LES BOCHES

SAIELLI, Verter
de Méricourt-sous-lens
fusillé le 27-1-44
à Bordeaux, à
l'âge de 23 ans

CARSONI
Giuseppe, de Vermelles
fusillé le 14-6-44
à Arras, à l'âge de 22 ans

ATTILIO, Chiarcossi
de Oignies, fusillé
le 28.5.44

SALVADORI
Antonio de Lens
fusillé le 21-2-44
à Paris, à l'âge de 23 ans

SAIELLI, Prodigio,
de Méricourt-sous-lens
fusillé le 28-8-44
près de Trill (M.M.)
à l'âge de 21 ans

LUCARINI
Cesare, de
Pont-à-Vendin,
fusillé le 21.2.44, Paris
à l'âge de 24 ans

MATTEI
Giuseppe, de
Annay-sous-lens
assassiné en prison, à
Chartres à l'âge
de 25 ans

*Ceux
qui sont morts
pour
que vivent libres
et indépendantes
la France et l'Italie*

TOSATO
Prodossimo
fusillé le 1-9-44
à Bruay-en-Artois
l'âge de 47 ans

ORTU
Antonio, de
Fouquières-les-lens
mort en service
commandé en 7.44

The same could be said of young Poles, whose ready adaptation is confirmed by the fact that large numbers of them became priests and schoolteachers. Most immigrant children were thus schooled in the French system, which proved to be an efficient instrument of assimilation. As Jean Willemin observed of Moutiers: "It bears emphasizing that these people assimilated remarkably well. When I look back on it, it seems hard to understand. The old Italians who came here didn't speak a word of French, but their children went to school, fought in the war, and were often taken prisoner. They're almost more French than I am, because they weren't obliged to be but did it on their own. It's a remarkable thing." In 1931 François Mattenet wrote: "The Italians are the most assimilable, the closest to us, no doubt because of our common Latin ancestry. Their children attend our schools, speak our language exclusively, and frequently earn diplomas. They can scarcely be told apart from their classmates with French par-

To combat the suspicion of disloyalty that affected all minorities, the Italians of the Pas-de-Calais reminded Frenchmen of their participation—and death—in the fight against Hitler and fascism.

ents. They share our tastes and our habits, and when they turn twenty they enlist in our army."[20]

The assimilation of Italian, and to a lesser extent of Polish, children was seen in retrospect as an undeniable cultural gain for France. At the time, however, they were frequently met with hostility and labeled with pejorative tags such as "Macaronis," or "Polacks."

NORTH AFRICAN IMMIGRATION AFTER WORLD WAR II

The postwar period marked a new chapter in the history of French immigration. Most of the immigrants now came from different places. The Poles and Italians were succeeded by Spaniards, Portuguese, Yugoslavians, Turks, and North Africans. Today the North Africans constitute the largest group. Even the nature of the immigrant has changed: whereas once immigrants were driven from their native lands by hunger and poverty, many today leave home to embark on a form of social mobility. Some immigrants, particularly illegals, continued to live in the wretched conditions of the shantytowns that persisted in France until the late 1960s. Most but not all of these slum residents were immigrants. The period between 1950 and 1975 was one of unprecedented prosperity for the French economy, however, and living conditions of French workers as well as most immigrants improved dramatically. Better housing and new appliances transformed the daily routine without imposing uniformity on private life. For immigrants who arrived with families and therefore led relatively stable lives, the degree to which private life reflected specific ethnic features depended, as before, on the degree of social control exercised by the community. It also depended on the extent to which an enclave could be carved out within the larger society and apart from the workplace, an enclave within which traditional dietary customs and styles of social, family, and male-female relations could be preserved.

Family Pressure and Individualistic Behavior

The transformation of immigrant life is best illustrated by the North Africans. In an earlier phase of immigration, North African workers had trimmed their own needs to a minimum in order to send as much money as possible back to their native villages to support their families and prepare for their own eventual return. Gradually, however, the situation changed to the point where immigrant workers were

Music and dancing open the Goutte-d'Or, an immigrant neighborhood of Paris, to the rest of the city.

sending back home a bare minimum of family support. They were accused of ingratitude, and various stratagems were employed to strengthen family ties and justify demands from home. It became common for young male workers to marry before leaving for France; the wife and children were kept home as hostages in custody of the young man's father or brothers so as to ensure that regular payments would be sent.

Immigrants, meanwhile, absorbed French culture. Not only did they leave home at a younger age than immigrants of the previous generation had, but they were also better educated. They had become familiar with the French language and French values in primary school. Timidly, they felt tempted to learn more, to break out of the self-imposed segregation of their predecessors—only to discover a different form of segregation imposed by French society. Individualistic behavior asserted itself powerfully enough to create tension with the society of origin, sometimes leading to a partial break, yet not sufficient to constitute a true attempt at integration. Some young immigrants went so far as to reject austerity in favor of consumption. Following the lead of French workers, they invested in dress suits and gradually discovered the pleasures of the city, such as cafés, movies, and Saturday-night dances. Soon, however, many of them would discover a violent racism that forced them to return to their own kind.

The ultimate integration—that of marriage with a French woman—was experienced by only a very few. Often it meant a break both with the local community and with North African friends and relatives living in France. Acceptance by the family and friends of the woman, often a coworker or someone met a union meeting or political demonstration, could be won only at the cost of breaking relations with the other group. Such intermarriage was the great fear of the relatives back home. It meant that less money would be sent, perhaps none at all; it disrupted the émigré worker's emotional ties to his native village; and it made it impossible for the man to return home and reclaim his place in the village social system by making a respectable marriage. The children of such mixed marriages were cut off from their village roots, and for a time at least the man's family would bear the mark of dishonor.

This new phase of immigration, which involved mostly single men who remained in France for relatively long periods, saw the emergence of racism in that country as the immigrants came into contact with French society. Meanwhile they were rejected by their native societies. At home émigré workers wore French clothing, had plenty of money to spend, sometimes drove cars, and perhaps consumed wine or beer—all things that made the émigré seem almost a foreigner in his native village. It became more and more difficult for those who left home to find acceptance when they returned. During brief visits they remained rather aloof from village ways and problems. It was as though they had come back on vacation, that their real lives were situated elsewhere.

Standing outside the group, they came to be seen as models and symbols by educated young people who aspired to escape the constriction of village life and who imitated the returnees' foreign manners, dress, and habits (such as smoking French cigarettes). Families quarreled about material matters. In the first phase immigrants entrusted all their money to the family group headed by a father or older brother, who had sole power to decide how the money would be used. In exchange, the returned immigrant received only a share in the family estate to which his labors had added significantly. Those who emigrated in the 1950s did not object to the custom of keeping the family estate undivided, but they did insist on separate houses for themselves. If they sent money to an elder brother for that purpose, they had the audacity to ask for an accounting of how the money was spent. A man might set aside a few rooms in his house for his brothers and their families, but the traditional division of living space was no longer respected. The man who emigrated tended to assume the role of head of the family, putting himself forward as a rival to his father and older brothers regardless of where he stood in the line of descent.

His eating habits also tended to impose themselves on the group. Instead of adapting to frugal country ways, the returned émigré would order meat and vegetables from the city rather than settling for the items of dubious quality available at nearby markets. Noodles, rice, and fried potatoes began to replace couscous. Meat was no longer limited to holy days. Carbonated beverages and coffee competed with mint tea.

The third phase of North African immigration began when entire families started to move to France. Most North Africans arriving in France today come with their families. The change first became noticeable in the 1960s, after Algeria won its independence. Improved living conditions for work-

The Settlement of Families in France

For many women the television is a window on the world, a language teacher, and a companion during the husband's long working day. Often it is the immigrants' only access to the inside of a French home.

ers, the eligibility of immigrants for low-rent housing, the desire to see their families benefit from better schools and health facilities than were available in North Africa, the growing psychological and social distance that many returned immigrants began to feel between themselves and their native villages—all these factors contributed to the rise of family immigration.

With the arrival of women and children it became possible for North African immigrants to enjoy a private life in the full sense of the word. Married couples developed their own style, different from the traditional extended family life they had known in North Africa. Married life was modeled on the French couple, even though there was little contact between immigrant and French families. Adaptation to the new life was particularly difficult for women. Often they found themselves alone in unpleasant surroundings, isolated by the language barrier, and sorely tried by the French climate. Not a few women were said to have cried for two years before adjusting to life in France. If there were no Arab neighbors, a woman could spend her life in total solitude. If she studied French, it was most likely with her husband and neighbors rather than in school. Radio and especially television played an important role in bringing the French language and cultural models into immigrant households. With these technological aids it was possible to observe French society without being observed and without risking a hostile or racist reaction. Often it took more than a year for women to feel comfortable accompanying their children to school, going shopping, or dealing with the bureaucracy.

Purchases were closely supervised by the man of the house. Women shopped in neighborhood stores run by North African merchants and in large discount stores. While husbands and children usually dressed in the French manner, wives shed their veils but frequently wore moderately long dresses. Some continued to wear the *djellaba* at home but would put on a dress when it came time to go out. European clothing was universally accepted, although attempts were made to limit "abuses" by women and girls. Some men,

Women are allowed to go out in groups or with the men to do the marketing. Such contacts with consumer society are authorized by the community. Shoppers can touch, compare, and converse.

The Emir Abd el-Kader, copper pots, and native dolls recreate something of the village atmosphere.

however, wore Islamic garb (turban and djellaba) instead of a dress suit on Sundays. On the other hand, clothing ceased to play an important part in the affirmation of religious or community identity, although it has recently regained some of its former importance.

Traditional dietary customs were maintained. North African cooking is time-consuming and requires ingredients not readily found in France. Spices were used to lend an ethnic quality to dishes cooked with potatoes, rice, and noodles, ingredients easily obtained in France but unavailable back home. French dairies began producing African cheeses and other products in response to immigrant demand. Meat posed special problems because of the ritual fattening of animals for the slaughter. Economic necessity resulted in the neglect of religious rules except for special occasions, such as holidays. The introduction of freezers made it possible to observe religious requirements and yet still purchase meat at reasonable prices: several families could band together to buy a live animal, then fatten it according to the prescribed ritual before slaughter.

As more and more women arrived and as the number of North African purveyors, some with their own shops, others with market stalls, increased, men rediscovered pleasures of the kitchen that they had all but forgotten except for brief

Once the head of the family has completed the sacrificial slaughter, the women take over—just as they do at home. Holidays recreate the warmth of the native village in all too fleeting moments during which the hardships of daily life can temporarily be forgotten.

visits home or to ethnic restaurants. Mint tea has remained a symbol of conviviality, although now it appears to have a rival in alcohol, at least among men, particularly in contacts between North African and French workers. Alcohol consumption is probably a way to forget difficult living conditions, hard work, daily frustrations, and the fear of losing one's identity. From the earliest days of immigration there have been North African cafés, whose existence has helped to bind the immigrant community together. The French federation of the FLN (the Algerian National Liberation Front) used such places as its listening posts. Usually, however, even immigrants who were alcoholics in France stopped drinking when they returned home to visit or to stay. In immigrant families drinking alcohol is generally prohibited at home, although it is tolerated for men outside the home, so long as they continue to provide for the wife and children.

Home interiors exemplify a compromise between two cultures. Basic furnishings such as table, chairs, and appliances are French, and as soon as there is any money it is spent on

The family gathers for coffee. Despite the differences between the traditional garb of the parents and the jeans and long hair of the young people, there is pleasure in togetherness.

such amenities as a color television or VCR, perhaps purchased secondhand, a radio, and a cassette recorder. Wall decorations symbolize North African life: calligraphy, color posters of Mecca or Algeria, velvet tapestries, and embossed copper plates. In some homes a convertible sofa stands ready to receive a visiting relative or friend, lending an Oriental air to an interior in other respects not very different from that of a French working-class household.

A Renewal of Religious Consciousness

Family life has contributed to a revival of religious feeling. Boys are now circumcised in France, whereas formerly people preferred to wait until they returned home. Many North African parents are trying to strike a difficult balance between Islamic education, which they wish to maintain, and the values inculcated by French schools. Most parents, particularly those resolved to remain in France for a long period of time, accept French preschools and elementary schools despite fears of being absorbed into the French community. In the classroom young North Africans meet French students of their own age and, at least initially, identify with them. Boys who speak French better than their parents are apt to reject paternal authority, which they associate with the despised image of the docile manual laborer. Although they understand Arabic, they refuse to speak it and among themselves use French first names. Before long, however, they discover that they cannot possibly realize their dreams in French society. This throws them back on their North African identity, which, being based in part on fantasy, is of changing content. Meanwhile, their parents continue to view the French schools as offering access to a better life, yet they are critical of the system for not providing the kind of education that would encourage their children to respect family values.

Immigrants view the teaching of religion at home or in community schools as the best way of countering assimilationist tendencies and therefore of accommodating to a lengthy residence in France without renouncing their own identity. Mosques and private associations offer courses in Arabic and the Koran. Embassies sponsor courses in order to maintain contact with their nationals in France. Home instruction in the Koran for the entire family is available on videocassettes that can be rented at Islamic bookstores. To stimulate interest students have been shown commercial films with soundtracks dubbed in Arabic, one such film being *The Message,* in which

The mosque, often a bare room in a basement or garage, is a place for older people to meet. Retirees and unemployed workers attend more frequently than others.

Anthony Quinn plays the role of a companion of Mohammed.

Religious differences pose greater problems than national differences, and immigrants have had to compromise, however unenthusiastically. The renewed interest in religion is exemplified by observance of the Ramadan fast. Immigrant behavior in this respect appears to be related to a new sense that their residence in France is permanent. In earlier phases of immigration it was easier to accept the customs and habits of the host country, provided taboos against the consumption of pork and alcohol were respected. When immigrants returned home to North Africa for Ramadan, they could enjoy the warmth of evening celebrations that were difficult to stage in France without offending neighbors. The regular return to the native land allowed immigrants to compensate for the infractions of religious rules they were forced to commit while abroad. Over the past ten years, however, there has been a tendency toward more open religious observances in France; celebration of religious festivals provides the community with an opportunity to assert its identity. The Muslim family takes cognizance of its specificity and of its distinctive moral code. Anyone who has violated the rules against smoking and drink-

It is not easy to maintain one's identity and one's dignity in a foreign country. This man prays on a doorstep so as not to block the sidewalk. His purchases are placed in front of the man, in the direction of Mecca, so he can keep an eye on them.

ing has an opportunity to quit at Ramadan. The custom of making a fixed charitable contribution, the *zekat,* at the end of Ramadan has been revived. This donation often goes to religious institutions in the country of origin, but an increasing share has been going to religious communities and mosques in France.

Islamic holidays such as Aïd-el-Kebir, which commemorates Abraham's sacrifice, are also celebrated. If possible, immigrants like to return home for these events since certain religious customs pose problems in France. It is difficult, for example, to purchase a live sheep and keep it at home until the time comes for sacrifice.[21] Muslims feel that it is unfair that they cannot obtain leave for Islamic holidays. Although they treat many French holidays simply as days of rest, many Muslim families have adopted the French customs of setting up Christmas trees and exchanging Christmas and New Year's gifts.

Recreation

French society—in the form of television, street life, and shops—has influenced the leisure activities of immigrants. Department stores are more than just purveyors of needed commodities. Weekend shopping expeditions provide an opportunity for families to explore consumer society and the French way of life. The fascinating variety of goods for sale gives an impression of accessible wealth. Off-track betting, the national lottery, and other games of chance assumed an importance in daily life that had more to do with French than with Islamic traditions. Participation in these games even has spread to the middle class back home in North Africa. Immigrants still listen mainly to Arabic music, generally on cassette but today broadcast over small community radio stations as well. Some of these stations also broadcast Friday prayers from Mecca.

Television, like the school, has been a potent instrument of acculturation, all the more so because it is accepted by the parents of young children. At the same time, however, immigrants are fearful of total assimilation. Often the head of the family feels guilty about allowing this to happen. Marriage with non-Muslims is feared as a step toward loss of collective identity. A particular cause of anxiety is the attitude of young Muslim women, who are especially susceptible to the influence of the schools and to the prospect of greater autonomy for women that French society offers.

Music allows young
immigrants to express their
feelings.

Mothers and friends watch as
this young girl performs a
traditional dance.

Matrimonial Strategies

Matrimonial strategies still are largely oriented toward the country of origin, though there is less uniformity than in the past. For men the ideal remains one of marriage to a girl (if possible a cousin) chosen by the family from the village back home. But not everyone gives in to family pressures, and some men marry French women or immigrants from other groups such as Portuguese or Yugoslavs. A more dramatic but perhaps more common form of conflict involves the refusal of young women to return to North Africa to marry and raise a family. Some women have chosen to cut themselves off from their families rather than give in. More intent on succeeding in school than male students, girls often seek to preserve their independence, vehemently rejecting the traditional role that their fathers and brothers try to impose on them. Although Muslim families in France are generally smaller than in the country of origin, they are generally larger than native French families. Family size typically decreases from nine or ten to five or six children in the first generation and to three or four children in the second generation.

Women keep to themselves at a wedding ceremony, as tradition requires. Although European dress is the rule in this wedding party, including even a white gown for the bride, Oriental dances are favored—as long as couples stay apart.

People travel to visit their native lands or those of their parents.

In death as in marriage the immigrant community retains something of its native traditions. Elderly people still long to return home to live out their last days in a large house built near the homes of relatives in their native village. Only in the land of Islam can Muslims feel secure about resurrection. Nowadays, however, returning home to die means cutting oneself off from children and grandchildren. Some of the elderly therefore choose to remain in France, but take steps to make sure they will be buried in their native soil. Still others have come to accept the host country—with its organized Muslim communities, its mosques and prayer halls—as sufficiently sacred to serve as a burial ground.

This evolution in attitudes symbolizes a new relation to French society. North Africans living in France are no longer truly immigrants, nor are they yet full-fledged citizens. They are members of a minority community that aspires to win recognition of its communal existence by French society as a whole. In sum, the participation of these new immigrants in French life is in many ways ambiguous, and these ambiguities are reflected in private behavior. Private life points up the various ways in which populations of foreign origin enter into the French population.

To Die at Home?

As the world becomes smaller, the peoples of its many nations mingle and learn about each other's customs and needs.

❧ 4 ❧

Nations of Families

Kristina Orfali
Chiara Saraceno
Ingeborg Weber-Kellermann
Elaine Tyler May

The ritual skoal, a toast in honor of a guest, is governed by a detailed code of rules.

The Rise and Fall of the Swedish Model

Kristina Orfali

SWEDEN is a country that has long fascinated many parts of the world. In the 1960s a whole generation grew up on clichés of blondness and liberation, on fantasies of a sexual El Dorado filled with shapely Ekbergs and sirenic Garbos—but also with Bergman's anguished heroines. Little by little, however, this fantasy-land metamorphosed into a dark country inhabited by bores, morbid minds, and would-be suicides, a nation of "disintegrated families," "disoriented sex," and "liberated lovers in search of love"—in short, a "paradise lost."[1] The Swedish ideal, once the object of extravagant praise and extravagant denunciation, ultimately was converted into a hyperborean mirage. The idyll was gone. The welfare state, recast in the role of meddling nuisance, no longer was a country to be imitated. Yesterday's middle way (between communism and capitalism) had become a utopian dream. Today it is fashionable on the part of many people to denounce Sweden as a "benign dictatorship" or "kid-glove totalitarianism."

There is nothing fortuitous about either the initial enthusiasm or the subsequent disillusionment. The Swedish model—in part economic and political but primarily societal—did indeed exist (and to some extent still does). The very word *model* (not, it is worth noting, of Swedish coinage) is revealing. People are apt to speak of the "Americanization of a society," of the "American myth" (that "everyone can become rich"), or even of "American values," but when they speak of a Swedish model they conjure up the image of an exemplary society. Swedish society is endowed not just with material or political content but with philosophical or even moral significance, with "the good life." As long ago as 1950 Emmanuel Mounier asked himself, "What is a happy man?" The Swedes, he answered, "were the first to have known the happy city."[2]

More than may meet the eye the Swedish model is a model of social ethics. Insofar as Sweden is a nation above suspicion, a nation that aspires to universality (in the form of pacifism, aid to the Third World, social solidarity, and respect for the rights of man), and a nation whose ideological underpinnings are consensus and transparency, it can perhaps be seen as the forerunner of a new social order.[3] In this respect the distinction between public and private in Sweden is highly significant. Hostility to secrecy, deprivatization, public administration of the private sphere—in all these areas Sweden has shifted the boundary between public and private in noteworthy ways. But the ethos of absolute transparency in social relations and the ideal of perfect communication, both characteristic of Swedish society, are seen in many parts of today's world as violations of individual privacy. The antisecrecy model has come to be seen as an intolerable form of imperialism.

THE ANTISECRECY MODEL

The antisecrecy model affects all areas of social life down to the most private. In Sweden, perhaps more than anywhere else, the private is exposed to public scrutiny. The communitarian, social-democratic ethos involves an obsession with achieving total transparency in all social relations and all aspects of social life.

Money without Mystery

In Sweden money is not a confidential matter.[4] Just as in the United States, material success is highly valued and ostentatiously exhibited. Transparency does not end there. Tax returns are public documents. Anyone can consult the *taxering kalender,* a document published annually by the finance ministry that lists the name, address, date of birth, and declared annual income of each taxpayer. Turning in tax cheats is virtually an institutionalized practice. While the fiscal authorities state publicly (in the press, for example) that informing on cheats is morally reprehensible, they admit that such information is frequently used. Even in the ethical sphere the imperative of transparency takes precedence.[5]

Publication of Official Documents

Another illustration of this imperative is the principle of "free access to official documents" (*Offentlighets Principen*).

Under the free-access law, which derives in large part from a 1766 law on freedom of the press, every citizen has the right to examine official documents, including all documents received, drafted, or dispatched by any agency of local or national government. The law allows for examination of documents in government offices as well as for having copies made or ordering official copies from the agency in return for payment of a fee. Any person denied access to public information may immediately file a claim with the courts. In practice the right of access is limited by the provisions of the secrecy act, which excludes documents in certain sensitive areas such as national security, defense, and confidential economic information. Nevertheless, the rule is that "when in doubt, the general principle [of free access] should prevail over secrecy."[6]

As a result of the free-access principle the Swedish bureaucracy has been exceptionally open. For a long time Sweden has been an "information society," one in which information circulates freely. Computerization has accentuated this characteristic by facilitating the exchange of large quantities of information, in particular between the private sector and government agencies. There are few other countries in which the computers of several insurance companies are closely linked to those of the vital records office. Private automobile dealers may be electronically linked to vehicle registration records; a state agency may make use of a private company's credit records. Since 1974 information stored in computers has been treated just like other public documents and thus made subject to free access.

Sweden was the first European country to establish a central Bureau of Statistics (in 1756). It was also the first to issue citizen identification numbers. Comparison of different databases has been facilitated by this assignment of a personal identification number to each citizen. The practice was begun in 1946, and the numbers were used by state agencies before being incorporated into electronic databases. They are now widely used in public and private records.

If computers make individuals transparent to the state, the machines themselves must be made transparent to individuals. The computer security act of 1973 (amended in 1982) was the first of its kind in the West. It established the office of Inspector General for Computing Machinery with the au-

Any citizen may learn what any other citizen earns simply by consulting the annual directory of Swedish taxpayers.

The state issues a personal identification number to every Swedish citizen. Yet far from being anonymous, Swedish society publicizes the faces of its citizens and remains firmly attached to its traditional communitarian ethos.

thority to grant authorization to establish a database, to monitor the use of databases, and to act on complaints relative to such use. While authorization to establish a database is usually a mere formality, it is much more difficult to obtain when the data to be gathered includes information considered to be "private." Encompassed under this head are medical and health records, records of official actions by social welfare agencies, criminal records, military records, and so on. Only government agencies required by law to acquire such information are authorized to maintain these sensitive files. Finally, any person on whom information is gathered has the right to obtain, once a year at any time, a transcript of all pertinent information.

Some view this computerization of society as a highly effective, not to say dangerous, instrument of social control. Many foreign observers have seen it as marking an evolution toward a police state in which all aspects of private life, from health to income to jobs, are subject to shadowy manipulation. Interestingly, computerization has aroused virtually no protest within Sweden. Everyone seems convinced that it will be used only for the citizen's benefit and never to his detriment. The consensus reveals a deepseated confidence in the government (or, rather, in the community as a whole, which is ultimately responsible for control of the information-gathering apparatus). To Swedes, the whole system—private individuals and government agencies alike—is governed by one collective morality.

A *"Society of Faces"*

We must guard against the simplistic notion that Swedish society is a kind of Orwellian universe, a world of soulless statistics. Paradoxically, this society of numbered, catalogued, faceless individuals is also a society of individualized faces. Every daily newspaper in the country publishes a half-page of photos to mark readers' birthdays, anniversaries, and deaths. Society notes take up at least a full page, and the absence of social discrimination is striking. One obituary recounts the career of a Mr. Andersson, *Verkställande dirktör* (plant manager), while another is devoted to a Mr. Svensson, *Taxichaufför* (taxi driver). Every birthday—especially the fiftieth, to which great importance is attached—is commonly marked by several lines in the paper and by time off work. This mixture of a modern, computerized society with still vital ancient customs is a unique aspect of Swedish society.

The Ombudsman and Public Investigations

Transparency is also the rule in collective decisionmaking. The ombudsman is one Swedish institution that is well-known abroad. The parliamentary ombudsman, oldest of all (dating back to 1809), handles disputes over the boundary between public and private and is especially responsible for protecting the individual's "right to secrecy." He hears complaints, takes action when the law is violated, and offers advice to government agencies. Less well known, perhaps, but just as important is the procedure of public investigation. Before any major law is enacted, an investigative committee is appointed to consider pertinent issues. The committee includes representatives of different political parties, important interest groups, and various experts such as economists and sociologists. After hearings, surveys, and perhaps on-the-spot investigation, the committee transmits its report to the legislative department of the relevant ministry, which then makes public recommendations. Any citizen may also submit advice to the ministry. Thus the most "private" subjects such as homosexuality, prostitution, violence, and the like become the focus of major public debates, on an equal footing with such "public" issues as price controls, the regulation of television, the Swedish book of psalms, or the country's energy policy.

This uniquely Swedish procedure plays an important role in the elaboration of policy decisions and in the achievement of consensus. Its existence demonstrates not only how the most apparently "private" subjects are dealt with by institutions but also how individuals can take part in the various phases of the decisionmaking process. Two key ethical imperatives are highlighted: transparency of the decision process and consensus concerning the results.

Many people are unaware that Lutheranism is the state religion of Sweden and that the Lutheran Church is the established church. (Contrast this with Italy, where Catholicism is no longer the established religion.) It was in 1523, at the beginning of the Reformation, that the Lutheran Church began to function as an integral part of the governmental apparatus. The church played an instrumental role in the political unification of Sweden, since participation in religious services was then considered to be a civic obligation. The strength of the bond between church and state is illustrated by the fact that until 1860 Swedes were not permitted to quit the church—and even then they were required to become members of another Christian community. This requirement was not eliminated until 1951. Any child born a citizen of Sweden automatically becomes a member of the Church of Sweden if either its father or its mother is a member. Thus 95 percent of the Swedish population nominally belongs to the official church.

Sweden therefore remains one of the most officially Christian of states, but it is also one of the most secular. The church is controlled by the government, which appoints bishops and some clergymen, fixes their salary, collects religious taxes, and so on. (A citizen who does not belong to the Church of Sweden still must pay at least 30 percent of the religious tax because of the secular services performed by the church.) The church is responsible for recording vital statistics, managing cemeteries, and other public functions. Thus, every Swedish citizen is inscribed on the register of some parish. The pastor who performs religious marriages is also an official of the state, so a religious marriage also serves as a civil marriage.

The institutional character of the Church of Sweden is reflected in public participation in religious ceremonies. Roughly 65 percent of all couples choose to be married in church. More than 80 percent of children are baptized and confirmed in the Lutheran Church. Some members of the official state church also belong to one of the "free," or dissident, Protestant churches that derive from the Lutheran evangelical wing of the religious awakening movement (*Väck-*

An Established Church

Since 1958 the Church of Sweden has permitted the ordination of women. Although there are today several hundred women pastors, there is still some resistance to their presence in the church.

Anthony Quinn in Richard
Fleischer's *Barabbas* (1962).

else rörelser), most active in the early nineteenth century. Taken
together, the free churches claim a higher proportion of the
religious population in Sweden than in other Scandinavian
countries.

Nevertheless, this formal presence of ecclesiastical institutions cannot hide the widespread disaffection with religion
among Swedes. Fewer than 20 percent claim to be active
churchgoers. In contrast, a tenacious, almost metaphysical
anxiety is a profound trait of the Swedish temperament.
Swedes may not believe in hell, but they surely believe in the
supernatural. To convince oneself of this one need only glance
at the half-pagan, half-religious festivals that fill the Swedish
calendar or recall the importance of trolls and the fantastic in
Swedish literature, folklore, and films. Or consider a writer
as profoundly Swedish as Nobel prize winner Pär Lagerkvist,
author of *Barabbas* and *The Death of Ahasuerus,* whose work is
one long, anguished religious interrogation. André Gide, another tormented conscience, wrote of *Barabbas* that Lagerkvist
had pulled off "the tour de force of walking the tightrope

across the dark stretch between the real world and the world of faith."[7]

The reconciliation of the real with the spiritual is thus more tenuous than it may first appear. The collective religious morality of the past has been transformed into a new morality, still collective but now secular, while literature and film continue to reflect the spiritual world, the metaphysical anguish and tenacious guilt that have left such a deep imprint on the Swedish imagination.

The "Deprivatized" Family

The degree to which the private sphere is open to the public is clearly visible in the evolution of family structure. There is nothing new about the fact that in a modern state "functions" once left to the family have been taken over by the government or community. In Sweden, however, this deprivatization of the family has taken on a rather specific aspect. The point is not merely to intervene in private life but to make the private sphere totally transparent, to eliminate all secrecy about what goes on there. If, for example, an unwed or divorced mother applies to the government for financial assistance, or if a child is born in circumstances where the paternity is dubious, a thorough investigation is made to identify the father. Any man who, according to the woman or her friends, has had relations with the mother can be summoned to testify. Putative fathers may be required to undergo blood tests. If necessary the courts will decide. Once paternity is established, the father is required to provide for the child's upkeep.

The justification for such a procedure is not so much economic as ethical: every child has the right to know its true father. Clearly, however, acting on such a principle may yield paradoxical results. A single woman who wants to have a child and then raise it alone forfeits her social assistance if she refuses to cooperate with the paternity investigation. Although the 1975 abortion law grants women the right to control their own bodies, they do not have the right "to give birth without providing the name of the father." The child's rights take precedence over all others; even if the mother refuses social assistance, all available means (including the courts) will be used to force her to reveal the father's identity, on the grounds that the question is fundamental and that the child will wish to know. In paternity, therefore, there is no secrecy. Kinship is supposed to be transparent and clearly determined. The notion of legitimacy thus sidesteps the family, and the institution of marriage rests on public information, which is guaranteed by law.

Recent Swedish legislation on artificial insemination is also based on the requirement of transparency. Göron Ewerlöf, judge and secretary of the Commission on Artificial Insemination, put it this way: "It is to be hoped that future artifical inseminations will be more candid and open than they have been until now. The objective should be to ensure that birth by insemination is not unthinkable and indeed no more unusual than adoption. In matters of adoption Sweden has long since abandoned secrecy and mystery. According to specialists in adoption, this has helped to make adoptive children happier." Sweden was the first country in the world to adopt a comprehensive law governing artificial insemination (March 1, 1985). Previously, artificial insemination involving a donor had been shrouded as far as possible in secrecy. All information concerning the donor was kept hidden (or destroyed). The chief innovation of the new law—and incidentally an excellent

Two men and a baby carriage. Sweden in 1975 was the first country to adopt a law requiring parental leave. Yet according to a 1981 survey, it is still mainly women who take parental leave in Sweden; only 4 percent of men take off the full allotted time.

Muninn the Troll, hero of one of the classics of Scandinavian children's literature, as shown by Tove Jansson.

illustration of the antisecrecy model—was to eliminate anonymity for donors. Every child now has the right to know who his biological father is and may even examine all hospital data concerning the individual. (Not even adoptive parents have access to this information.) In the past attention was focused on preventing the child from learning how it was conceived. Today it is the opposite: the primary objective is to protect the child's interest, which means not blocking access to any available information about the identity of its biological father.[8] The commission underscored the importance of a frank and open attitude toward the child on the part of the parents. In particular, it recommended (although the law does not prescribe) that at the appropriate moment parents tell the child how it was conceived. The interest of the child was again invoked to justify the decision not to authorize artificial insemination except for married couples or couples living together as though married. It is not authorized for single women or lesbian couples. Thus the image of the standard family—father, mother, and children—has been maintained, even though the number of single-parent families in Sweden has been on the rise. Various psychological and psychiatric studies were invoked in support of this decision. The primary goal is to ensure the child's optimal development. Adoption laws are even more restrictive, and adoption is limited in most cases to married couples.

The Child as Full-Fledged Citizen

The status of the child in Sweden tells us a great deal about Swedish culture and ethics. Children are regarded both as full citizens, and as defenseless individuals to be protected in almost the same manner as other minority groups such as Laplanders and immigrants. The changing status of children is the clearest sign of deprivatization of the family. Since 1973 Sweden has had a children's ombudsman, whose role is to act as a spokesperson for children and to educate the public about children's needs and rights. The ombudsman has no legal authority to intervene in particular cases. He can, however, apply pressure to government agencies and political representatives, suggest ways to improve the condition of children, instruct adults about their responsibilities toward children, and, thanks to a twenty-four-hour telephone hot-line, offer support to individual children in distress. Thus children in Sweden enjoy specific rights and an institution whose purpose is to defend them. The objective is, while respecting the individuality of children, to make sure that they will be integrated as harmoniously as possible into the society.

The same ethic prevails in regard to immigrant children, who are entitled to receive instruction in their native language. Since 1979 the state has allocated funds to provide language lessons for immigrant children of preschool age, and nursery schools increasingly group children by native tongue. Everything possible is done to make sure that immigrant children have the tools they need to learn their mother tongue and preserve their culture by maintaining bilingual competence. Results have not always kept pace with ambitions, however. Many children have a hard time adapting to one culture or the other and a hard time mastering one of the two languages. Integration is envisioned, but respect for the immigrant's native culture is considered imperative.

Immigrants in Sweden enjoy many rights: they can vote in municipal and cantonal elections and are eligible to hold office; they are not confined to ghettos but scattered throughout the society in order to encourage integration; they receive

A course for Turkish children. How are they to maintain a dual cultural identity?

free instruction in Swedish; and they receive the same social benefits as natives. Nevertheless, Sweden has not really been able to achieve a fusion of cultures, a melting pot in the manner of the United States.

Parent-Child Relations   The autonomy of the child vis-à-vis familial and parental authority is reflected in the law prohibiting corporal punishment. Since July 1979 the law governing parent-child relations has prohibited all forms of corporal punishment, including spankings, as well as mental cruelty and oppressive treatment. Examples explicitly mentioned in the law include shutting a child in a closet, threatening or frightening, neglect, and overt ridicule. Admittedly, no specific penalties for violation of these provisions have been set, except in cases of physical injury. Nevertheless, any child who is struck may file a complaint, and the person responsible cannot protest that he believed he had the right to administer a spanking. This once private right, covert yet in a sense symbolic of parental authority, no longer exists.

In various ways the political sphere controls more and more of what used to be private space. The family no longer bears exclusive responsibility for the child. The child's rights are determined not by the family but by the entire national community in the form of legal and social protections. The child therefore spends more time outside the private realm and is increasingly socialized outside the family. Parent-child relations are no longer a strictly private matter; they are governed by the public. The society as a whole is responsible for *all* its children.

This way of thinking is illustrated by the so-called parental education reform of 1980.[9] All prospective parents were invited to participate in voluntary discussion and training groups during gestation and the first year after birth. (Those who attended these groups during working hours were entitled to compensation under the parents' insurance program.) The goal of parental training was to "help improve the situation of children and families in the society": "The community and its institutions should not themselves assume responsibility for children but should try instead to give parents the means to do the job."[10] Interestingly, this parental training, usually administered outside the home to groups of parents, was also a way of encouraging group experience, a way of fostering solidarity among individuals faced with similar problems. Individuals were drawn into group activities, and most who began with a prenatal group continued with a postnatal one. The social reforms helped to reinforce the highly communal nature of Swedish society by emphasizing all the ways in which the individual or family cell is integrated into the larger group or society.

Because the Swedish child is considered to be a full citizen, he or she may, at an appropriate age, take legal action to alter unsatisfactory conditions. This principle applies in particular to disputes arising out of divorce. The child may be a party to hearings to determine custody and visiting rights and is entitled to legal representation. Small children may even be represented by a proxy appointed by the court. In case of separation the child may choose which of its parents it wishes to stay with, even contesting the amicable settlement reached by the parents (although visiting rights are not subject to challenge). In short, the child's opinion may be expressed and defended in exactly the same manner as that of any other citizen.

An End to Marital Secrets

If family life is largely open to public scrutiny, so is the life of the couple. Since 1965 sexual offenses such as marital rape have been subject to criminal prosecution. Since 1981 battered women have not been required to appear in person to accuse their husband or partner; a declaration by a third party is sufficient to initiate proceedings. Of course homosexuality is no longer a crime in Sweden; criminal penalties were abolished as long ago as 1944. In 1970, following a period in which a wave of sexual liberation spread over the country, homosexuals founded the National Organization for Equality of Sexual Rights, or RFSL (Riksförbundet för Sexuellt Likaberättigande).

In 1980 the government conducted a sweeping investigation into the possibility of reforming legislation concerning homosexuals so as to prevent discrimination. The investigative commission not only proposed a series of laws guaranteeing complete equality between heterosexuals and homosexuals but also advocated active support for homosexual culture and organizations. The possibility of institutionalized cohabitation of homosexual couples conferring the same benefits as marriage was also discussed. These proposals stemmed from an official investigative commission.[11]

Paradoxically, the proposal encountered vigorous opposition on the part of certain lesbian groups, which contended that the new laws would have the effect of forcing lesbians to accept the outmoded institution of the family, which deserved no additional support from the government. They insisted that the law concern itself not with couples, whether homosexual or heterosexual, but with individuals, regardless of their relationship. The upshot was that homosexual marriage is still legally impossible in Sweden.

Sexuality

Well before the sexual revolution of the 1960s sexuality had lost something of its totally private character owing to the introduction of sex-education classes in the schools. In 1933 the National Association for Sexual Information, or RFSU (Riksförbundet för Sexuellt Upplysning) was founded.[12] The goal of this nonprofit organization was to "promote a society without prejudice, tolerant and open to the problems of sexuality and to the life of the couple." At the time the chief concern was not so much to liberalize sexuality as to combat venereal disease and abortion. Nevertheless, the effort to make sexual information widely available gradually broke down a series of taboos. In 1938 a new law on contraception and abortion struck down the ban that had existed since 1910 on distributing information about or selling contraceptives. The rules governing abortion were also modified. Abortion was authorized for three reasons: physical disability; pregnancy resulting from rape; and the possibility of serious congenital defects.

In 1942 optional sex education was made available in the schools, and in 1955 it became compulsory. Such instruction initially was quite conservative; students were told that the sole purpose of sexual relations was procreation in marriage. Soon, however, students as young as seven were studying sexuality, or what *Le Monde* in a December 1973 headline called "*la vie à deux.*" It was stressed that "the act of love should be based on reciprocal affection and mutual respect." Nevertheless, matters as intimate as "masturbation, frigidity, homosexuality, contraception, venereal disease, and even pleasure" were discussed. By 1946 the law required pharmacies to stock contraceptives, and in 1959 the sale of contraceptives outside pharmacies was authorized.

Hur du än är skapt finns det alltid en kondom som passar.

"Whatever size you are, you'll find a condom that fits." (Campaign for condoms waged by the RFSU.)

At last sexuality was out in the open, in a quite literal sense. Finally, in 1964, advertising for contraceptives (sponsored by the RFSU) began to appear in newspapers and mag-

Sex-education course.

Se upp för kärleksbacillerna.
Använd kondom. **RFSU**

"Guard against the diseases of love; use condoms." (RFSU campaign, 1986.)

azines. This advertising was meant to be informative, even technical, but frequently it adopted a playful and engaging tone, because its purpose was not only to inform but also to sell. Before long, advertising went far beyond condoms and diaphragms to include all sorts of sex-related products.

The End of Censorship

The demystification of sexuality, which initially grew out of a concern to stamp out disease, misery, and ignorance, in the 1960s came to be associated with debate about censorship. In 1951 the Swedish film *Hon dansade en sommar* (*She Only Danced One Summer*) caused a scandal because in it Folke Sundquist and Ulla Jacobsson, both stripped to the waist, are shown embracing. The film helped establish Sweden's reputation as a sexually liberated country. In 1963 the Bureau of Censorship passed Ingmar Bergman's *The Silence* despite numerous provocative scenes; but it prohibited screening of Vilgot Sjöman's *"491"* (1966) until a scene in which youths force a woman to have sexual relations with a dog had been cut. This act of censorship gave rise to an impassioned debate, until ultimately the uncut version of the film was allowed to be shown. Homosexual scenes began to appear on the screen in 1965.

Finally, in 1967, another Sjöman film, *I am Curious: Blue,* eliminated the last cinematic taboos. It gave rise to a polemic that resulted in its being banned for viewing by children, but the film was not cut. At this point several commissions were appointed to recommend changes in laws that were clearly outmoded. Documentaries on various sexual subjects were issued, including *The Language of Love,* which dealt with female sexual pleasure, and later, in 1971, *More on the Language*

Sweden was the first country to permit nudity on the screen—in Arne Mattsson's film *She Only Danced One Summer*.

A cinematographic milestone was this scene from Vilgot Sjöman's *I Am Curious: Blue.*

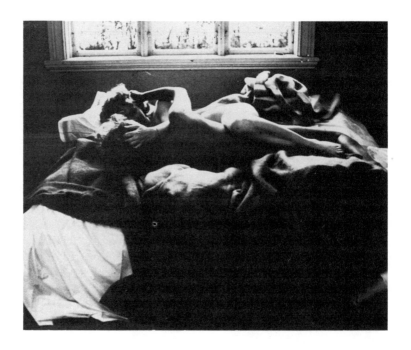

of Love, which, among other things, dealt with male homosexuality and the sexuality of the handicapped. That same year censorship of films was permanently abolished (except for scenes of excessive violence).

Pornography

Pornography was to the sexual revolution of the 1960s and 1970s what sex education was to the 1940s and 1950s. Pornography is perhaps the most immediate manifestation of sexuality since, unlike eroticism, it places no mediator between the spectator and the object of desire. Nothing is suggested or even unveiled; everything is exhibited. It is interesting to note that the Swedish literary tradition contains virtually no erotic novel, no *Justine* or *Histoire d'O,* no equivalent to the works of Bataille, the Marquis de Sade, or even Diderot in *Les Bijoux indiscrets.* Sweden's only frivolous, libertine literature dates from the eighteenth century when the country was considered the "France of the North." Otherwise Swedish literature, particularly in works dealing with sex, is not much given to understatement, suggestion, or indirection. It is either overtly pornographic or resolutely didactic.

Pornography thus represents a certain decline of the fantasmagoric imagination, of the metaphorical evocation of the body. Fantasy belonged to the world of the secret and the possible. Its representation, whether literal (as in peep shows) or iconographic, does away with all mediation, with all work of the imagination, and, ultimately, with all transgression. That may explain why pornographic literature seems so repetitious and anonymous. Sex-education textbooks illustrate sexual techniques; pornographic magazines show fundamentally the same thing together with a few pseudo-perverse variations.

The sexual revolution seemed to sweep away the last taboos. Once the right to sexual information was established, the right to sexual pleasure was next to be proclaimed. No one was to be left out—equality for all: from homosexuality to voyeurism and zoophilia, all sexual practices were equally legitimate. The very notion of a "crime against nature" disappeared from the law and was replaced by that of "sexual offense" (*sedlighets brotten*).[13]

A reaction was not long coming, however. Indeed, when

The Right to Pleasure

"My papa doesn't like pornography." After the excesses of the sexual revolution of the 1960s and 1970s, challenges have been raised to what some people now regard as illusory liberation.

examined closely, the sexual revolution of the 1960s and 1970s turns out to have been partly illusory. Formal taboos were eliminated, but traditional patterns remained largely untouched. At least that is the view of Swedish feminists, who vigorously attacked the portrayal of male-female relations in pornographic literature. One anecdote is worth recounting. The magazine *Expedition 66,* intended to be a female equivalent of *Playboy,* first appeared in 1964. It ceased publication fairly quickly, partly for lack of readers but even more for lack of models. (In a gesture typical of Swedish honesty, the magazine's editor, Nina Estin, refused to use photographs from the files of homosexual magazines.) Subsequently almost all pornography was directed toward men.

Prostitution

An excellent illustration of the reaction against sexual liberation, and in particular of the role played by institutions in that reaction, can be found in prostitution. Rather paradoxically, it was in the early 1970s—at a time when sex ostensibly had ceased to constitute a transgression—that prostitution in Sweden increased sharply. At the peak of this phenomenon (1970–1972) more than a hundred "massage parlors" and "photographic studios" were operating in the Stockholm area alone.[14] At the same time various voices were raised in favor of greater freedom and openness for prostitutes. In 1965 J. Erikson called for the socialization of prostitution, to be paid for through social security.

In 1976 a commission was appointed to study the prostitution question, and a plan for retraining prostitutes was developed in 1980. The commission's report was extremely detailed and analyzed all aspects of the trade: prostitute, client, and procurer. It gave rise to a polemic between those who favored repression (most notably feminist groups) and those who feared that treating prostitutes as criminals would not eliminate the problem but would, by forcing it underground, render control impossible. The commission demonstrated in particular that prostitution in Sweden was closely associated with illicit drugs. Those who championed prostitution in the 1960s have therefore been forced to ask themselves whether it was truly "liberating." Finally, the commission noted that prostitution served exclusively as a means of satisfying male sexual needs. Here too the sexual revolution had not truly "liberated" women.

In the wake of this report, a series of restrictive measures was adopted. Although the new laws did not punish the client (except in cases involving sexual relations with a minor), they did provide for the prosecution of any person owning property used for the purpose of prostitution. Combined with an effective program for retraining prostitutes, the new laws have led to a marked decline in prostitution since 1980.[15]

Laws were also passed against sexual activities involving violence, a common subject in pornographic publications. Peep shows were outlawed in 1982. The commission found that most of the patrons were older men, especially foreign businessmen, and concluded that "this was one part of the Swedish cultural heritage not really worth preserving." And so a specialty for which the country was internationally renowned came to an end. In fact, the whole flood of pornography that poured from the presses in the 1960s and 1970s has been, if not stopped, then at least channeled. Debate once focused on sex has been refocused on violence in all its forms, including sexual violence.

The Facets of Privacy

For all the transparency of Swedish society, certain opaque areas remain. Some things are prohibited, and because their number is small they are all the more fiercely protected. Violence, though uniformly condemned and prosecuted everywhere, is still present. Alcoholism is probably the area in which consensus is most tenuous and social control most vigorously challenged. Certain places are jealously guarded and kept strictly private: some exist in geographical space—the home, the boat, the island—while others exist only in poetry or the imagination.

Violence

The passions are soft-pedaled in Sweden. If violence is not significantly more prevalent than in other countries, when it does occur it is much more shocking. Accordingly it is sternly proscribed, even in private, as in the ban on spanking. Sometimes the obsession with preventing violence can seem rather silly. Since 1979, for example, Sweden has prohibited the sale of war toys. In 1978 an exposition on the theme "Violence Breeds Violence" lumped together allegedly violent comic books, estimates of the number of children killed annually in automobile accidents, and statistics on drug use.

The goal is not just to prohibit violence but to prevent

A struggle against violence is a permanent feature of Swedish society: here, a 1978 exposition entitled "Violence Breeds Violence."

it. The government considers open, public violence as the culmination of violence born in private, including at home and on the playing field. At a deeper level, violence, whether internal or external, private or public, constitutes a threat to order and consensus. It remains one of the last areas of Swedish life outside public control.

Alcoholism

Another area yet to be brought under control is alcoholism. To consume alcohol in Sweden is not an innocuous act. Feelings of guilt weigh on those who drink—not just the inveterate drunkards but the average Swedes who line up furtively at the *Systembolaget* (state liquor store) and sneak away with a few bottles carefully hidden away among their other parcels. Regulations governing the sale of alcohol are very strict. Temperance is officially praised, drunkenness publicly condemned. People rarely drink in public, not only because prices are high but even more because the community quietly but firmly disapproves. Drinking is permissible—and even valued—only on specific occasions, at holidays such as Midsummer's Night or the mid-August crayfish festival; at such times one drinks in order to get drunk. According to the official morality, it is just as inappropriate to drink at home in private and for no "social" reason—that is, without a jus-

The *Systembolaget* enjoy an absolute monopoly on the sale of wines and spirits; their windows are filled with posters denouncing the evils of alcohol.

tifying ritual of communication—as it is to drink in public. A daily apéritif or glass of wine can become a reprehensible secret act, something that can produce feelings of guilt.

Swedish laws on alcohol are extremely harsh. There are heavy penalties for drunk driving, which is defined as operating a motor vehicle with a blood level of more than 0.5 grams of alcohol. Alcohol cannot be purchased by anyone under the age of twenty-one, even though the age of legal majority is eighteen. This severity is hard to understand in terms of statistics alone. Alcohol consumption in Sweden in 1979 amounted to 7.1 liters per person, compared with 17 liters for France. Sweden ranks roughly twenty-fifth in the world in per-capita alcohol consumption.

The severity of the law can be understood only in terms of history. The manufacture and sale of alcoholic beverages were regulated long before the turn of the century, but it was around then that the temperance movement, having gained a powerful position in the Swedish Parliament, won adoption of a law unparalleled elsewhere in the world—the so-called Bratt System, under which anyone who wished to purchase alcohol had to present a ration book. Even today, no issue unleashes passions as strong as those connected with the alcohol problem, largely owing to members of temperance societies, whose influence in Parliament is out of proportion to their numbers in the population. Not so very long ago one deputy in three belonged to a temperance organization, and anti-alcohol societies have traditionally been a fertile breeding ground for politicians.

Nevertheless, alcohol seems to be one area in which breakdown of consensus is possible. Swedish unanimity in opposition to alcohol is more apparent than real, for in private Swedes readily violate the ban and boast, like people everywhere, of their ability to "hold their liquor."

Drugs

There is a much more solid consensus in opposition to drugs. Since 1968 laws against narcotics abuse have become stricter. Serious infractions of the narcotics laws incur one of the stiffest penalties in Swedish law: ten years in prison. Furthermore, the law does not distinguish between "soft drugs" and "hard drugs." Compared with alcoholism, however, drug abuse is quantitatively a minor problem.

Violence, alcoholism, drugs: these are the principal forms of deviant behavior in Swedish society, the last areas not entirely controlled by the political sphere, the last transgressions in a society liberated from the taboos of the past.

The Imaginary

In such a highly communitarian society, so tightly controlled by the "public," where can the individual find a private refuge? In his home, his rustic frame *sommarstuga* lost in the forest or tucked away on some lake shore. The individual home is like an island, private space par excellence, cut off and personalized. In "Scandinavian Notes" Emmanuel Mounier remarked that "the most collectivist nations—Russia, Germany, Sweden—are those in which housing is most solitary."[16]

The dream of every Swede is essentially an individualistic one, expressed through the appreciation of primitive solitude, of the vast reaches of unspoiled nature. Often built without running water and with the most rudimentary facilities, the *stuga* enables its owner to return to his rural roots and to commune intimately with nature. Virtually no Swede will travel abroad during that beautiful time in May and June when

Carl Larsson (1855–1919), *Suzanne at the Window with Flowers.*

Tjörnarp, house in the woods.

nature, at last emerged from the interminable sleep of winter, bursts forth with a dazzling and liberating light and Sweden once again becomes the land of 24,000 islands and 96,000 lakes! The small cabin lost in the country or forest thus remains, along with the island, the archipelago, and the sailboat (of which there are more than 70,000 in the Stockholm area alone), the last refuge of individualism in a highly communitarian society.

The themes of isolation, nature, and archipelago are omnipresent in Swedish literature and film. The novel entitled *The People of Hemsö* figures as a moment of illumination in Strindberg's otherwise somber oeuvre. The beautiful film *Summer Paradise* starring Gunnel Lindblom takes place entirely in the enchanting setting of a wonderful lakeside house. Though a genuine refuge, this private space can in certain situations become a tragic trap in which individuals seek desperately to recover some primitive state of communication, some original purity.

In this claustrophobic enclosure, developed to the full in such Ingmar Bergman films as *The Silence* (1963) and *Cries and Whispers* (1972), people wait in vain for a word to be spoken, an exchange to take place. In *After the Rehearsal,* the hero, a director and double for Bergman, expresses the impossibility of communication by repeating the words: "Distance and anguish, distance and ennui." *Scenes from a Marriage,* which enjoyed considerable success in Sweden, recreates the muffled atmosphere and stifled tensions of an intimate relationship in which even violence is held in and damped down. The couples in Bergman's films and Strindberg's plays exhibit a similar harshness, a stifling of the passions.

Crimes of passion are rare in Sweden (when one does occur, it is headline news). People almost never raise their voices and rarely gesticulate; usually they keep silent. Curiously in this society, where all sorts of things are said out loud and with unaccustomed frankness, people have difficulty conversing. Although workplace relations are simple, direct, and devoid of hierarchy and everyone addresses everyone else familiarly, dinner invitations are stiffly formal and prissy, something that constantly surprises foreign visitors. It does not make conversation any easier. In Swedes, Mounier saw "the diffuse mysticism and poetry of lonely men: the Swedish people remains, in a sense, incapable of expression."

This truly private side of a self that manifests itself not so much in action as in imagination is a good starting point for exploring Swedish society and attempting to grasp its paradoxes and contradictions. How else can we understand the coexistence of such highly communitarian and public feeling with such intensely inward individualism? The solitude of that world of silence, the Great North, the intimate communion with nature—therein lies the source of Scandinavian individualism. Primitive solitude compensates for community in all its forms—organization, group study, celebration. Everything, from holidays to laws, is directed toward breaking down solitude, allowing each person a say, maintaining the traditional community intact as a necessary condition of physical survival in the harsh world of the past and of moral survival in the harsh world of the present. What else could account for the incredible popularity of the ancient pagan festivals, generally associated with rural life but now transformed into Christian holidays? Walpurgis Night celebrates spring, Saint Lucy's Night the winter solstice, Saint John's Night the middle of summer (*Midsommar*), to name only a few of the holidays that dot an unchanging calendar. For one night everyone forgets hierarchy, social class, differences, and enmities and, in togetherness and unanimity, recreates the

Midsommar, originally a pagan festival, has become a national holiday in Sweden. At this time people dance around a maypole (*majstrang*), symbol of the Nordic summer that has yet to blossom forth.

perfectly egalitarian, perfectly consensual utopian community. During one unbridled *Midsommar* Miss Julie in Strindberg's play talks, drinks, sleeps, and plans a future with her father's valet. Then morning comes and restores social difference, the impossibility of communication, and rebellion. A night's folly ends in death. How can one possibly understand the Swedish imagination if one sees this as nothing more than an insipid story of impossible love between a countess and a valet?

The Swedish model can be interpreted as a "total" or "totalizing" society. It depends on a perfectly consensual communitarian ethic, which in turn depends on absolute insistence on transparency in social relations (from the old ritual known as *nattfrieri* to the child's right to know the identity of its father today).[17] Private life cannot escape the influence of the dominant ethos. The Swedish model combines yesterday's communitarian morality with the modern social-democratic ethos.

GRANDEUR AND DECLINE OF A MYTH

In the 1930s Marquis Childs referred to "Sweden, the middle way," thus characterizing the country in a manner that would influence first his fellow Americans and, later, others. Sweden's material prosperity, which as early as 1928 included "a telephone in every hotel room, a plentiful supply of electricity, model hospitals, [and] broad, clean streets," along with an almost flawless social organization, lent credence in the 1930s to the notion of a Swedish model. European countries suddenly took a lively interest in the country, hoping to unearth the secret of its astonishing material success.

Spared the ravages of the Second World War, Sweden maintained its productive apparatus intact. To much of postwar Europe it seemed utopia incarnate, and Swedes became "the Americans of Europe." In many respects Sweden was seen as a more attractive model of social organization than the United States because inequality in Sweden was less pronounced. As Queffélec pointed out in 1948, the Swedes "question all this natural prosperity." Also, the country's "moral health" enabled it to "avoid the dreadful consequences of Americanization." Mounier delightedly recounted the comment of one Swedish observer who was quite appreciative of American civilization: "The Swede, however, is actually much more attached to the individual than is the American."

"You are alike not only in dress but also in appearance, with your shining white faces, your hard, friendly features, your fierce blue eyes" (Valéry Larbaud, *Stockholm*).

The Myth of the Swedish Woman

In the 1940s and 1950s some in the West saw the typical Swedish woman as one who was "beautiful, athletic, and healthy." While "the legendary freedom of Scandinavian morals" was taken for granted, "to the traveler these young people seem distant and not very emotional. Couples dance quite properly" (*Action,* September 1946). Louis-Charles Royer wrote in *Lumières du Nord* (*Northern Lights,* 1939): "It is extremely difficult to court women in this country, because they always treat you as a pal." In 1954 François-Régis Bastide in his book *Suède* (Sweden) asked: "What should you say to a young Swedish woman?" His answer: "Whatever you do, it is extremely dangerous to mention the well-known reputation that Swedish women have . . . That is certain to chill things off."[18]

The Swedish woman's reputation was no doubt associated with the campaign to provide sexual information, which since 1933 had done so much to break down sexual taboos. Sweden had provided sex education in the schools since 1942, at a time no other country had gone to such lengths. The West had confused sexual information with sexual freedom, creating an image of Sweden as a sexual paradise.

In 1964 French Prime Minister Georges Pompidou visited "this strange socialist monarchy" and in a famous phrase characterized his social and political ideal as "Sweden with a bit more sun." Thus attention was once again focused on the Swedish ideal, which would attain the peak of its glory in the 1970s. During this period Sweden was in vogue; whenever it was mentioned, it was held up as an example.

Everywhere Sweden was exalted and glorified. Some had dreamed the American dream; others had idealized the Soviet Union or China or Cuba. Now the "Swedish model," the image of a just compromise, seduced Europe. Sweden became a journalistic cliché. The sexual revolution of the 1960s reinforced the myth. A cover story on "Free Love" appeared in 1965, and one French magazine devoted a special issue to Sweden. Seghers inaugurated a new series called Sweden In Question, while Editions Balland issued a book on Scandinavia in its collection Eros International. Sweden was the wave of the future: the press said it, television showed it, books explained it. The "Swedish case" was analyzed and dissected. People also began to ask questions.

By 1975 articles criticizing Sweden had begun to appear. Headlines such as "Women Not Totally Free" and "The Disintegrating Family" were read. Roland Huntford launched a vigorous attack on social-democratic Sweden in his book *The New Totalitarians* (1972). The defeat of the social democrats in 1976, after more than forty-four years in power, raised questions about the political stability of Sweden. From "Dark Spots in the Swedish Model" (*Le Monde,* 1976) to "Delinquents Versus Blackheads" (*La Croix,* 1977), Sweden was portrayed in France as a perverse model, a highly coercive society. This "prodigiously permissive" society was said to have engendered its own destruction. "Sweden: Liberated Lovers in Search of Love," was trumpeted in 1980. That same year one could read: "The Swedish mirror, much admired abroad, is broken. Something is amiss in the world's most unusual system." One headline asked, "Sweden—paradise lost?"

The Swedish model had not lived up to its promise. Racism, xenophobia, suicide, and alcoholism all existed there too. The countermodel was now at its height, even if traces of the old paradise remained. In 1984 *Le Point* asked students at France's leading institutions of higher education what country best corresponded to their idea of the good society. Switzerland led the list, followed by the United States; Sweden came in fifth, behind France.

If the Swedish model had lost its appeal, it was because the country had slipped badly. Claude Sarraute wrote of "incessant investigations by the tax and welfare authorities, unreasonable, Orwellian interventions in people's lives. The government keeps tabs on incomes and individuals. The meddlesome welfare state sticks its nose everywhere, even into the way you bring up your children. It encourages children to turn in 'deviant' parents."[19] Much of the West decided it wanted no part of this "revolution in private life." Though the Swedish model may still exist, the Swedish myth is dead as a doornail.

The Countermyth

A young peasant family of the 1920s poses stiffly, eyes staring fixedly at the camera.

The Italian Family: Paradoxes of Privacy

Chiara Saraceno

Translated by Raymond Rosenthal

"EVERYTHING had happened more quickly than Giacomo thought it would. Now they owned four electrical appliances: the radio, TV, refrigerator, and washing machine . . . For so many years he had been aware that people in other places lived better than they did. Cooking over an open fire as Maria did when they were first married reminded him of the Germanic tribes of Caesar's time that he had read about in the third grade. Little by little they had inched ahead into the modern world; the gas stove he had bought in 1956, the running water he had installed in 1963, and the Vespa were all signs of this. It was a kind of catching up, he thought, catching up with the American way of life that was also becoming the Italian Way of Life. He saw it all on TV. The well-to-do in the big cities like Rome and Milan were way ahead of the likes of him—they would always be—but Giacomo knew that the gap was closing."[1] Such were the reflections of Giacomo Rossi, laborer-handyman of Valmontone, near Latina in central Italy, in autumn 1969, as he returned home on his Vespa after having signed an agreement to purchase on the installment plan a washing machine and a refrigerator.

The history of three generations gathered by the anthropologist Donald D. Pitkin is also the history of transformations in the conditions of daily life of Italian families from the beginning of the century down to the threshold of the 1980s. It traces these conditions as they have been experienced by poor people, forever poised between precarious employment (Giacomo has never held a steady job, although he has always worked) and the longed-for achievement of a permanent position (like those of Salvatore, his wife's brother, and of Giulio and Bruno, his sons). It is a history of technological innovations, of the acquiring of new needs, of transformations in consumption patterns, and the rejection of old duties. (If it is Giacomo who proposes the purchase of a radio, then of a Vespa, it is Maria who requests the gas stove, indoor running water, and the washing machine.) It treats the renegotiations and redefinitions of the balance between familial solidarity and continuity and the recognition or vindication of demands for individual autonomy. The sons request a house for themselves and their families in exchange for the income they have brought to the family for many years; but the younger son knows that he will have to wait until enough money has been saved for his sister's trousseau.

The history is one of the redefinition—with different outcomes—of the boundaries between public and private, between family and society. On the one hand, building a house and using electrical appliances allows greater privacy for fam-

The Vespa and the Lambretta were the first visible signs of the transformation that radically changed Italian customs and standards of living.

ily activities, which no longer must take place in public because of a lack of space and facilities; it also permits a greater individualization of each person's space within the family. On the other hand, school attendance, which has become common for the last generation, exposes the family and its members to models of behavior, norms, and types of judgment that are only partially analogous to the traditional community control. However, school also becomes a right to be demanded. Rosa, Maria's mother, after moving to Valmontone from Calabria, forced the teacher to accept her oldest daughter in first grade, although the child was much beyond the customary age. For her part Maria considers it obvious and normal that her children, especially the boys, should attend school through high school and even further. And when the hard-won degree from a technical secondary school proves insufficient to obtain a decent job, the disappointment is great.

Medical practice is another public intrusion into private life. Maria agreed or asked to be taken to the hospital to deliver her last daughter, defying ancient prejudices about that place "where they neither cure you nor feed you" that were handed down to her by her mother. The memory of the fears and risks of earlier deliveries, the midwife's advice—everything concurred to make her believe that this was now the normal, "modern," and even safe way to behave. Thus, childbirth leaves the family. It no longer takes place in the matrimonial bed, with the husband running for the midwife, the mother and neighbors assisting or crying impotently, the children returning home to find the new baby.

The story of Giacomo and Maria, of their family and of their children's families, is unique, as are all family histories; it also can be classified precisely in terms of social class and geographical situation. Yet, in reading it I have found resemblances—though with a ten- to twenty-year gap where certain matters are concerned—with the generational experience of many families that I know, above all my own (I mean that of my parents), which was shaped in Milan, that big city, that Giacomo believes is similar to America, and within the lower and later the upper middle class. The history of transformations and manifold interactions between familial cultures and social and technological changes is similar. So is the need to chart the change and transmit the elder generations' memory of it to the younger. Maria's adolescent daughters have no intention whatsoever of burdening themselves with the heavy labor of their mother's past, with the clothes she washed in

Tradition regulated the sharp distinction of sexual roles. Here women do the laundry at a public washhouse.

the river, the water she lugged to the house several times a day. My own daughters are astounded by my televisionless childhood and my memories of a home where there was no refrigerator. Similar, above all, is the role not only of the family, but more specifically of women as the mediators of social transformations of everyday life.

Among my earliest memories are the disjointed ones of being awakened suddenly at night to be taken to the cellar because Milan was being bombed, of kindergarten snacks of bread and brown (*rosso,* or unrefined) sugar, of a coal stove heating the room, of smaller brothers whom my mother seemed to wrap endlessly in very long swaddling clothes. I recall, after the war, the iceman's cry, which brought children running downstairs from apartment houses all along the street to buy a few liras' worth for the icebox. The laundryman's cart, pulled by a mule, came every week to pick up dirty laundry and deliver clean. There was our first washing machine: a strange—and probably very dangerous—device, which required much soaping of the laundry beforehand and laborious wringing out afterward. Our family was among the first to own a refrigerator at the end of the 1940s. I remember the first time we bought white bread, and without ration cards. Enormous quantities of bread were consumed by a family as large as ours throughout the 1950s and 1960s—something I recall with astonishment whenever I buy a couple of rolls. Various maids took care of us children during childhood and adolescence, telling terrifying stories to my brothers and me, quarreling with us, washing our clothes and our dishes. As an adolescent in the *liceo*, I wrote their letters to their parents. These letters had to follow a very rigid code of expression so that the senders and the recipients would recognize in them an expression of due respect: "By this letter I wish to tell you that I am well and so I hope are you . . . Your most devoted daughter." They accepted my grammatical superiority, but not the ability to judge how one ought to behave. I found this hard to understand, just as I did not understand why they addressed their parents in so formal a manner. A few years ago, when my daughters discovered a number of letters I had written to my parents as a girl, I in turn found myself in the analogous position of someone "different," a bit comic because of her incomprehensible and unbearable mannerisms. Other random memories concern custom-made clothes, though in a greatly reduced number. The dressmaker arrived with every change of season to turn coats, let out hems, altering and retrimming as needed. (As an adolescent, I badly wanted a readymade dress bought at one of the new big department stores, the kind worn by classmates who were more up-to-date, or poorer, or had mothers who were not adept as mine when it came to sewing.)

Many uncles and cousins live in my memory, but only one grandmother, and only for a few years. My daughters, however, adolescents today, have grown up in a familial world in which the grandparents are a strong affective presence. Through them—at their house—my daughters meet uncles and cousins and see their parents and uncles and aunts in the roles of sons and brothers or sisters; there family rituals are perpetuated, family traditions and cultures compared.

My children have grown up in a world in which washing machine, refrigerator, vacuum cleaner, and television set are taken for granted. The occasional novelties are luxury items

Cluttered messiness and numerous books, newspapers, and magazines characterize the home of a pair of intellectuals.

whose impact on daily life is too slight to affect its rhythms or change the way things are done: color TV, freezer, home computer, VCR. When my children were little they had baby-sitters—a matter of great ambivalence for their grandmother—but we have never had full-time maids. Housework in my home, as in the homes of my contemporaries and even more so of younger people, no longer seems to have that dimension of ritualism undergirding the continuity of daily life that it had in my mother's house. It follows the rhythm established by the presence of the helper hired by the hour, and above all according to any visible and more or less urgent need: floors that are too dirty, an empty refrigerator, enough dirty laundry to load the washing machine.[2] Nevertheless, I can recognize hidden rhythms that reveal a tenacious continuity with the rhythms of my childhood.

My mother recalls the arrival, during her adolescence, of gaslight and of running water—which in Milan's low-income housing, even at the end of the 1950s, only reached certain floors. Those whose homes lacked a bath went to the public baths, which provided a reasonable amount of comfort and the sensation of being waited on.

My parents, who like many of their contemporaries had lost their fathers when very young, remember a world in which child labor was widespread. Even then it revealed sharp differences between otherwise contiguous classes: between those whose children could continue their studies and those others which needed everyone's work and income. Yet both groups shared the ideal model of prolonged schooling and a childhood and adolescence free from economic responsibility. In my mother's world an eleven-year-old girl could look for a job without her mother's knowledge, in order to tell her triumphantly: "Quite soon you no longer will have to work." She thus expressed a culture not only of duty but of familial coresponsibility, which was felt even by the youngest member of a family; it made everyone feel useful, necessary (and not only, perhaps, exploited). Our precious children, burdened though they are with duties as well as rights, are deprived of this dimension.

That same little girl, when older, had to defer to her eldest brother's authority when it came to general behavior, use of leisure time, and male companions. The greater freedom of movement of young female workers during the early years of the twentieth century, when compared to their bourgeois contemporaries, is attested to by Vanessa Maher's study of the young seamstresses of Turin.[3] Families aspiring to middle-class respectability felt the need for controls and rules to defend their daughters both from men and from themselves. The world was one in which the social position of men and women was still strongly differentiated. The family, as the domain of affections, of intimacy and private life, was becoming increasingly identified with a figure of woman-wife-mother protected and removed from exposure to a mixed, extrafamilial sociability and its risks of promiscuity. The ambivalent testimonies gathered by Merli regarding the image that factory workers at the beginning of the 1900s had formed of their female coworkers (and indirectly of themselves) provide a similar impression: women exposed to the desire and violence of men, too "free" and too little protected.[4] It is worth noting that, in a very different cultural and social context, Maria Rossi, when she married, was confronted by the conflict between her family tradition, in which the women had always worked as farm laborers, laundresses, and maids, and the "more advanced" culture of Giacomo's Valmontone. There it was preferable for the women not to work outside the home, although it was acceptable for them to perform heavy labor on the family's land and around the house.

When my mother married, she gave up her job as a seamstress, although she had enjoyed the work very much and had reached almost the top of her field. But she preferred to devote herself full-time to taking care of my father and, later, of us children. Over the years she projected an image that was both victorious and ambivalent about her decision. She presented herself to us and to the world not as submissive and weak but as the strong affective center and pivot of daily life and of familial relations (my father seemed lost without her)—and as someone who could have done other things. There was a strong sense of value and personal autonomy in the women who were aware of being the essential and creative "artisans" of everyday life.

Women like my mother, belonging to the small educated petite bourgeoisie, dedicated to intellectual and social betterment, living in a big city in which the first services were beginning to develop, considered it a social conquest to give birth in a hospital as early as the end of the 1930s. (In the nearby Brianza district this did not become a commonplace until the 1950s.) They sent their children to nursery school, not because they needed to be looked after but as part of an educational project. The "private," intimate, affective-educational family deliberately sought the support of other places, of other institutions. They certainly did not think of delegating to others their educational rights and duties, as mothers often have been accused of doing in the 1970s and 1980s, when attendance at nursery school became the norm for all.

The experiences of the generations who have grown up and created families from the first postwar period until today could be compared at length. Relations between the sexes and between the generations might be considered. Privacy itself, definitions of which are becoming ever more articulated to the point of defending personal private spaces within the very family, could be studied. "Family life is an interference with private life," Karl Kraus has claimed.[5] Other interferences that are not only more articulated but also affected by relations between the family and that form of the public represented by the state, through legislation, social and fiscal policies, and so on would be of interest. The variety of experiences revealed by these comparisons constitutes not only the context of relations between the generations but also the context of the life experience of older generations, those who in the course of their lives experienced different conditions of family life and different definitions of the self-same family relations. The problem of the continuity or discontinuity of experiences, of models and values, concerns not only relations between generations but also individual biographies. Relationships, priorities, and definitions of reality within the latter have changed

not only because of the natural flow of time in which individuals, growing older, have assumed different roles, but because of the historical period in which they have lived. This was a time characterized by great social change and also by ruptures, not least among them that of Fascism and the Second World War. Consider that the cohorts and generations who are the oldest today were born before the First World War, became adult during Fascism, started their families during the Second World War, and have been the protagonists of the advent of the consumer society and of affluence.[6] Women who are more than seventy today have passed in less than twenty years from having to buy milk on the black market for their children to the "consumerism" of meat every day, of refrigerators and automobiles, of summer vacations. They have seen their daughters escape the long summer vacations that bourgeois mothers and children used to take in the 1950s and 1960s; their granddaughters travel by themselves at an ever earlier age.

At the same time, families that had not only very dissim-

Nothing was completely "private" in the age of communication. In 1944 a peasant family in the Roman countryside silently listens to the news.

ilar economic resources but also different cultures and behavioral models at the end of the 1960s at the beginning of the 1980s display very similar modes of behavior, at least with regard to housing and what they consume. In the late 1960s families in Milan's "banister" apartment houses (so called because of the handrails on the tiers of narrow balconies overhanging the central courtyard), and even more in the villages and small towns of the Brianza, lacked indoor toilets and bath tubs, usually had neither washing machine nor refrigerator, knew nothing about the telephone, and adhered to a consumer model that strongly favored savings and sacrifice. By the first half of the 1980s these same families had housing standards and consumption levels not unlike those of the families from which they were far removed twenty years earlier. This phenomenon cannot be explained simply in terms of social mobility, of improved income that permits improved consumption. What is striking is the changing definition and recognition of needs that have occurred in certain families and social groups, greatly accelerated during the last twenty years, that has resulted in an unmistakable cultural leap ahead within a single generation.

Let us try to follow a few strands of this journey of the twentieth-century Italian family. They are interwoven with the socioeconomic history of Italy during a period that has seen the country pass from a prevalently agricultural society to an advanced industrial one, despite the permanence of some social and territorial imbalances, and that has several times seen its structures and political cultures disrupted. These have been many-sided and not linear processes, characterized also by sharp conflicts. The processes include the birth of whatever social state we have in Italy, which, to the extent that it influences social reproduction, also interacts and interferes with the life and organization of the family, helping to mark out new relationships and new borders between public and private.

FAMILY DEMOGRAPHICS, 1920S–1980S

Demographic data are useful indicators of family development during this period and of the dimensions in which changes have taken place, changes whose meaning and direction must be further investigated by other methods. Although problems of interpretation and comparison exist, because the Census Bureau (Central Institute of Statistics, or ISTAT) over

One result of increased population was emigration: here, in 1958, a ship leaves Naples, most of its passengers headed for a new life in a strange country.

the years has changed its definition of family, the family, as it appears from one census to the next, can be synthesized through three interdependent indicators. First, the number of families has increased more rapidly than the population as a whole: in the hundred years from 1881 to 1981 the number of families has tripled, while the population has doubled. This disparity became clear during the period that runs from the special family census of 1936 to the next census, in 1951. Second, the average number of family components, which remained more or less constant for several decades at the value of 4.4–4.5, at the 1951 census declined below 4, a level that continued during the years following. Third, there has been a progressive nuclearization of the family with a reduction of extended families and an increase of nuclear families composed of couples with children, of only two persons, or of persons who live alone (one-person families).

The Effect of a Reduced
Agricultural Population

The process of industrialization and urbanization that started at the beginning of the century did not fully evolve in Italy until after World War II. It resulted in a reduction of the agricultural population and farm families, with a concomitant decline in the number of family production units, with their well-defined division of sexual and generational roles and organization of labor, time, and space. As late as 1931 those employed in the primary sector accounted for over half of the labor force, and 41.5 percent of all families had heads employed in agriculture. In 1951 these percentages had decreased respectively to 42 and 29.7 percent, and in 1981 to 11 and 6 percent.[7]

The decrease in agricultural families has had various consequences. First, it reduced the number of families that were potentially of the extended or multiple type. As Marzio Barbagli remarks, in central northern Italy, given the typical characteristics of agricultural production (sharecropping, tenancy, scattered settlements) the rural family has always been larger and more complex than the urban family.[8] (This was also true when the latter was a productive unit, such as artisan or small merchant households.) The direct consequence of the decrease in complex families was an increase in the number of families. Where once there would have been only a single family, with several conjugal nuclei, now there were two or more, as time passed and sons married, brothers separated. This tendency within the rural family is reinforced by another phenomenon. In 1931 rural families and rural population almost coincided, in the sense that if the head of the family was a peasant, almost all the family members in turn became agriculturists. During the following decade this became less and less true. The diversification of the labor market in the wake of the development of industry and of the traditional and modern tertiary sector meant that many peasant families included members employed in different sectors of the economy. Thus the peasant family ceased to be a productive unit and became an earning unit. As a result it was easier to divide the family home when children married, without destroying the family's solidarity or its emotional and economic interdependence.

Giacomo and Maria Rossi and their children are a good example of such changes. For several years during their married life, economic necessity forced the couple either to live apart from or with his parents; later they took in her widowed, partially invalid mother. When they finally were able to build a house on a three-hectare plot, which they received after a redistribution of the land, they began to lay the foundation of what might be called interdependent nuclearity. In this model each family nucleus headed by a male son lives in a separate but neighboring dwelling, with several services in common— from the furnace and vegetable garden to the care of younger children, and at times to communal meals at Giacomo and Maria's house. Similar models of nearby residences can be found in other areas, especially in family enterprises in which father and sons work together (occasionally in the same building, with the workshop on the ground floor and the various apartments above). Along with the separation of residences goes a separation of income, with each worker receiving his own salary as in a cooperative rather than a family enterprise. Alongside the persistence of old and the formation of strong new interdependencies as well as of flexible boundaries among the families—with children that come and go, everyday cooperation and conflicts—these phenomena signal a desire to create private spaces, to demarcate the boundaries separating the families. Here doors can be closed, rhythms and habits can be diverse, and conjugal relations can be developed privately, away from the constant scrutiny of parents, parents-in-law, brothers, and brothers-in-law. The tenacious survival of intense exchanges within the kinship network, not only affective but also economic and in the area of service, has characterized the contemporary family in Italy and in other countries, although it has received scholarly attention only recently.[9]

A final phenomenon linked to the declining proportion of agricultural families is lower female employment as a labor force expelled from agriculture. Together with the decrease in the female rate of unemployment that began in 1933–1935 (despite the simultaneous decrease in the employment rate), it signals a radical transformation in the experience of a large mass of women, the interruption of the processes of transmission and of traditional models of female behavior and lifestyles in vast strata of the population. Between the 1940s and 1960s, in a sometimes painless, sometimes conflictual manner, a growing proportion of adult married women acceded—or were driven—to the role of full-time housewife that had previously been common in the urban lower and upper middle class. Around this figure—a much more complex one than it first appears, with occasional paid work at home or in domestic service by the hour or day—the model of family as the space of private life developed and spread progressively throughout all classes. The family became the center of affect and of personal services, the organizer as well as the determiner of consumption. Beginning with the second half of the 1950s, this pattern became widespread, a new norm.

The figure of the adult married woman as full-time homemaker, only recently emerged, was short-lived in society and the family—although it lives on tenaciously in the collective imagination. Halfway through the 1960s, female employment again began to increase, and it affected the very women to whom the housewife model applied: married women with children. Now women's participation in the work force takes place within—and must reckon with—an organization of daily life and culture model shaped by a norm of private life that is characterized by a precise division of roles and tasks within the family and specific responsibilities of the wife-mother to satisfy all the needs of family members.

The Growing Popularity of Marriage

Most of the proportionately greater increase in families compared to the population as a whole results from higher rates of marriage than in the past. This is true in all the European countries involved in the industrialization process. In Italy the phenomenon has been less clear. Italian industrialization, late when compared to that of other European countries such as England, France, and Germany, as well as the longer lasting effects of the 1929 Depression in Italy, kept marriage rates constant—about 7 per thousand—in the first decades of this century. The pattern persisted despite various measures taken by the Fascists to promote marriage (with the purpose of increasing births), such as marriage bonuses for war veterans, loans to newlyweds, and a celibacy tax. Temporary increases in the marriage rate between 1921 and 1930, and again in 1937, were the result of marriages postponed by, respectively, the First World War and the war in Ethiopia, rather than by long-term changes.[10] The rate of those who remained permanently unmarried began to drop below 16 percent only in the cohorts of women born after 1920. (In other countries, which historically had higher nonmarriage rates, the phenomenon had begun with the cohorts born in 1910.) In Italy it fell below 10 percent only among those born in the 1930s; it declined more rapidly to 5.4 percent in later cohorts, becoming more like other European countries.[11]

It was not until the 1950s and 1960s that the Italian marriage rate increased appreciably. Not surprisingly, during these years the (nuclear) family model developed, becoming the norm. Then everyone "had to" get married, and the family became the place where one sought and satisfied one's needs for relationship and intimacy. It is paradoxical that the cohorts born during these years and immediately afterward ended the increase in marriages in Italy and, more recently, even reversed the tendency (though to a lesser degree than in other countries).

Italian patterns also differed from those of European countries such as Britain, France, and Sweden where age at marriage is concerned. In other countries, although starting from higher median ages at marriage (over twenty-five), women born in 1910 and later married at a progressively younger age, declining to about twenty-two for women born after 1940. As late as the middle 1930s, however, Italian women married at the age of 25.2, a figure that dropped to 24.2 for those born in 1940 and to 23 for even younger age groups. The age difference between spouses was, and still is, greater in Italy than in other countries (though it fell from approximately four to three years).

The reasons for the persistence of this "delayed" model of matrimony, with a relatively large age gap between the spouses, must be sought in individual and above all family strategies in the face of a difficult economic situation marked by high rates of male and, until the mid-1930s, female unemployment. In this situation families utilized all the labor force available, occasionally sacrificing individual social mobility through advanced schooling. This sacrifice was most often made by daughters, since life-long employment for them was not anticipated. The daughters of less well-to-do families were often sent to work before the sons and were likely to remain in the labor market as long as possible, postponing marriage, which usually required leaving full-time work, as well as loss of income for the family of origin. (This latter factor affected the decision to delay the son's marriages.) From this point of view data on women's participation in the labor market according to age are significant. The census of 1936 showed that 18.5 percent of females between ten and fourteen years of age were employed, 49.8 percent of those between fifteen and twenty, 47 percent of those between twenty-one and twenty-four (and as many as 32.9 percent of those between twenty-five and forty-four). The ratio of females to males in the active population of the same age groups was, respectively, 67.0, 59.0, 50.2 (and 36.2).[12]

The histories of working-class women gathered by Marzio Barbagli and those collected by Guidetti Serra in Turin testify to a very early work experience during the 1920s and 1930s compared to today's standards. This unequal participation of young males and females in the labor force continued during succeeding decades. It did not change until the 1960s, when young women began to attend school longer.

The most interesting change concerning marriage age is not so much the lowering of the average age as the progressive decrease in both marriage at a very young age (under twenty for women), encouraged by legislation in 1975, and late marriages. There is a growing coincidence between the average age of marriage and the age at which the majority of people marry, suggesting the emergence of shared beliefs concerning the most suitable age at which to make certain decisions and to behave in a certain way. In the middle 1980s other tendencies emerged among cohorts, other ways of behaving. The postponing if not the avoidance of marriage might point to increasingly differentiated patterns in this area, although the phenomenon is less clearly identifiable in Italy than in other countries.

Changing Life Cycles

The increase in the number of family households in relation to the population indicates not only that more children set up families on their own but also that more elderly people live apart as couples—or, when widowed, alone. Most couples without children and individuals living alone are elderly. The life cycle of the family is changing, or, rather, family structures are changing. If it is becoming increasingly more likely for a person to be born into a nuclear family, that person is also more likely to spend many years of his or her old age without children and grandchildren in the same house—although they may well live nearby and relations may be close. In certain age groups, persons who were born and grew up in a multiple or extended family may spend their old age in a conjugal family or alone.

There is no reason to believe that this discontinuity of experience and cultural models is always perceived negatively, even though it requires a reorientation of expectations. Large families provided solidarity and relative security; but they also sought to control their members and to limit their privacy and autonomy. To have a house of one's own, a space of one's own, removed from the interference of even the closest relatives, may be an aspiration of the grandmother forced by practical considerations to live with a son or daughter's family. The waning of hierarchies of authority based on age have weakened the traditional modes of assigning rights and duties and of solving (or concealing) conflicts.

Returning to Maria Rossi, she too, during one of her forced returns to cohabitation with parents-in-law and brothers-in-law, set separate kitchens as a condition, even if this meant having to cook in the same room in which she and Giacomo and their two children slept. This request, made possible by the recent acquisition of a gas stove, expressed very well her desire for privacy (considering the room as one's house) as well as independence from the control and demands of her mother-in-law, even in a situation in which both resources and space for privacy were minimal.

The increase in the number of the elderly is the result also of another phenomenon, which occurred during this period: greater life expectancy. More people reach adulthood and can expect to grow old; also old people's own hopes for life expectancy have increased appreciably. In terms of family and generations this phenomenon can be formulated as follows: more children may live to become adults with living parents and grandparents, and more parents may become grandparents and see their grandchildren grow up. The accompanying table shows this graphically. During the many years that have passed since it was prepared, there have been further improvements.

Mortality and family life cycle, 1931–1961

Indicator	Percent change
Median age of married women at time of death	+12.8
Median age of married men at time of death	+ 8.3
Median length of marriage	+19.0
Children without fathers	−22.9
Children without mothers	−61.9
Children without either parent	−70.9

Source: Paolo De Sandre, "Aspetti e problemi di demografia italiana," *Studi di Sociologia* 14 (1964): 180.

These developments, therefore, concern not only family structures and patterns of coresidence but also the possibility of particular generational relationships as earlier patterns and their cultural context change.

*Fewer and "More Planned-
For" Children*

Together with the lengthened life span, which makes a greater number of generational positions within the family and kinship network possible, another phenomenon has been modifying relations between generations: the reduced birthrate. This phenomenon, which affected all European countries, prompted, especially during the 1920s and 1930s, initiatives in demographic policies aimed at encouraging births. During this period we see the beginning of family allowances (in France and Italy, for example), health and support services for maternal and child care (again in Italy, with ONMI—Opera Nazional Maternità e Infanzia—and in Britain, Sweden, and Germany), maternity subsidies, indemnities for working women, and awards to fathers of large families (in Italy). Policies differed from country to country. They might favor the support of individual or family choices, as in Sweden, where alongside a policy of support for large families there existed a policy of liberal access to contraception and voluntary abortion. Or they might support a single model of behavior, like that which occurred in Italy and partially in France, where alongside birth awards and maternity and child-care institutions, abortion was declared a criminal offence and

A prolific peasant family from Alto-Adige (1967).

disseminating birth-control information was prohibited. Obviously such different government attitudes were determined by the various national cultures (countries with a prevalently Catholic culture had more restrictive prescriptions), as well as by the political regime of which they were the expression.

The decline of the birthrate in Italy, as indicated by Massimo Livi Bacci, originally affected the large cities of north and central Italy, magnifying the behavioral differences between urban and rural classes and between populations of the central northern areas and those of the south and the islands.[13] According to the 1931 census, about 89 percent of married women in the south and on the islands had more than four children; for wives of the white-collar class (little more than 10 percent of the women in these areas) median family size was three. In northern and central Italy, by contrast, the blue-collar class which included one-quarter to one-third of all women, had, like the white-collar class, an average of approximately three children; other classes had four or more.

To the extent to which industrialization created a widespread phenomenon of migration from the countryside to the cities and from the south to the north, this discrepancy between the behavior of the rural and southern classes when compared to the central northern urban classes changed considerably within the period of two generations. Urbanized women of peasant origin relinquished their mothers' behavioral patterns to a greater degree, going from 6–10 to 3–4 children. This is evident in many oral histories gathered by Barbagli, for example.[14]

Differences between various classes and geographical areas continue today, although, as public-opinion polls on the ideal number of children show, the continuing reduction of the birthrate involves all classes and all areas.[15] As Santini notes, in the large and medium-sized cities of central northern Italy a third, and more and more often a second, child is becoming increasingly rare. These patterns represent the norm in the great majority of southern families.[16] However, even with the changing importance of procreation in the life cycle of a family (and of a woman), and therefore also of the changed position of the children within the family, different family cultures probably exist regarding both procreation and the place of women. The lower birthrate signals changes not only in behavioral patterns but also in cultures and especially in experiences, although these are not linear and easy to interpret. Such changes have occurred above all in the behavioral pat-

In homes with fewer children, parents can devote more time and energy to them, to each other, and to their own personal happiness.

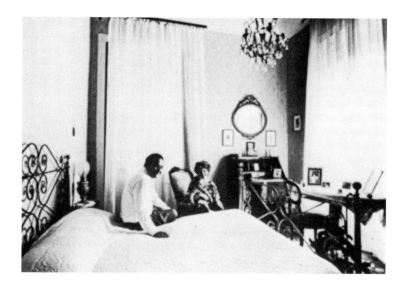

terns and experiences of women, who, faced by increased potential fertility because of improved health (age of menarche has gone down and age of menopause has gone up), reduced the number of children they bore, thus "liberating" a longer nonreproductive period.[17] Moreover, the declining birthrate also signals changes in the parent-children relationship (planned, welcome children in whom investments are made individually, and so on), as well as in relationships between couples (sexuality separate from procreation), based on negotiation or mutual agreement. Finally it signals a change in the experience of growing up in families in which not only cousins, but brothers and sisters, are rare.

Deliberate Severing of the Marital Bond

The most recent demographic indicator of change in the Italian family is the increase in separations and divorces, that is, the increase in deliberate breaks in relationships and forms of family coexistence. If the possibility of being orphaned at an early age or of being widowed in the bloom of life has decreased greatly, and if the long-term migration that in certain regions and classes constituted de facto separation ("white widows," whose husbands had migrated, were still numerous in certain southern inland areas during the 1950s), beginning with the 1960s, the intentional breaking of the conjugal relationship more than tripled in developed Western countries. In Britain the annual divorce rate rose from 11 to 32 percent between 1965 and 1975; in 1981 it reached 40 percent. In

France during the same period it increased from 11 to 25 percent, and in Holland from 1 to 29 percent. It has been estimated that for the younger married cohorts in Sweden it may reach 50 percent, including couples of all ages and marriages of all durations.[18] In Italy the phenomenon was more recent and more contained. Because the relatively late introduction of divorce compared to other countries, separation, legal separation in particular, had been quite limited for a long time. However, from 1965—six years before the introduction of divorce in 1971—to 1985, legal separations increased sixfold, equal to 12 percent of the marriages celebrated each year. This increase, which still indicates a lower rate of dissolution than in other European countries, has only been partially translated into divorce since the law was passed. As Santini notes, the proportion of Italian couples obtaining divorces in 1975 was only one-tenth of the British and Danish and one-eighth of the Austrian or French. The proportion of marital dissolutions in Italy remained quite constant until 1982. At that time their number began to increase; it doubled—from 14,640 in 1982 to 30,876 in 1988.

Even given the later onset of rising divorce rates, the data point to the emergence of new patterns of behavior, new models of couple relationships, reciprocal expectations, and negotiation processes. This is also apparent in the results of a 1983 opinion poll; the majority of respondents favored legal sanctions for the dissolution of marriage and supported current legislation on the subject.[19]

The increase in separations and divorces signals the possible emergence of a new configuration of family group members. It would include men and women who change spouses without being widowed; children and adolescent who, before reaching adulthood, could experience two or three different family structures—a family with both parents, one with a single parent (in most cases, the mother), and one headed by a new couple, with only one biological parent, and other children in varying positions of consanguinity or affinity. Children could belong simultaneously to two families—that of the parent with whom they live and that of the other parent with whom they have a more or less stable relationship. The presence on the social and family scene of the man or woman from whom one has separated distinguishes this experience from the widowhood and orphaned condition of the past. The other person, especially when children are involved, is not only a memory but interferes directly or indirectly in everyday life, contributing to the definition of the household's internal relations and making its boundaries problematic.

The Variety of Family Experiences

The euphoria of a new home and the happiness of a changed condition do not seem to obscure the serious problem of space plaguing this family.

The phenomena summed up in the preceding paragraphs involve men and women, adults and nonadults, and different classes and regions. The family's nuclearization is more visible in central and northern Italy, not only because these regions are more industrialized but also because in the past, at the rural level, they were characterized by more complex family organizations. In the south, given the different type of rural settlement, clustered in villages or agrotowns unlike the large estates or farms of the central and northern parts, peasant families often had a nuclear structure, even when families of

relatives lived close by, or in the same building, or in the same alley. This was true even though traditions and obligations of reciprocity among relatives marked boundaries between public and private, between intimacy and modesty, which were different from those to which we are now accustomed. For example, at the beginning of the century, Rosa, Maria Rossi's mother, "paid homage" to her father-in-law, who lived in another house, by helping him wash himself and cutting his toenails and hair once a week. Her granddaughters would perform such services not out of respect but in case of some disability. Only personal incapacity would be considered sufficient justification for such an intimacy that otherwise would be deemed humiliating and intrusive into the private lives of all concerned.

The increase in the deliberate severing of conjugal relations, like the decline in birthrate, is more visible in cities of central and northern Italy. There too the figure of the full-time housewife as an adult female role model emerged, as did more recently the model of the mother-workingwoman. In other words, the experience of changed generational and sexual roles and relationships continually being redefined between internal and external and between public and private has not followed a linear trend for all classes and for all geographic areas. These changes have altered the complex geography of the Italian family, but it has remained extremely varied. Change cannot be reduced to a single model either in terms of behavior patterns or in terms of values.[20]

DOMESTIC SPACE

Symbol par excellence of private family life in the twentieth century, the home—its ownership, its internal organization, the roles and rights that it delineates—is the scene of often angry interaction and struggle among the various actors involved. Conflicts took place as urban centers were restructured in the 1930s, in the second postwar period, and again in the 1970s. There were negotiations among families, public institutions, and local and central governments concerning the question of how to make sure that this asset would be protected and kept accessible. In addition, the various family members were concerned with family savings and investment strategies and with the allocation of space (who should have a room for him- or herself?).

Technological Development and Domestic Life

Until the end of the 1950s the type of dwelling markedly differentiated not only the countryside and the city but also the various social classes. Urban bourgeois apartments and houses contained, besides bedrooms for the couple and their children, a kitchen, sewing room, formal living room, the study of the husband-father, and sometimes a servant's room. With such commodious arrangements, there was room for the family's communal life, and each individual member enjoyed additional space for his or her private life. But the majority of workers' and farmers' dwellings contained far less space; and what there was had to serve various purposes.

The 1931 census showed that the median number of rooms (any space enclosed by walls that had a window) per dwelling was 3.25; the median number of persons per dwelling was 4.4, with a crowding index inversely proportionate to the number of rooms per dwelling. The same census showed that there was potable water in 66.9 percent of the buildings (not necessarily in each single dwelling), and a toilet in 78.2 percent. The apartments of only 12.2 percent of families had bathrooms. A 1941 inquiry by Fiat's Office of Statistics on a sample of workers and employees indicated that not a single family had a bathroom. Data from the 1951 census were not very different, partly because of destruction caused by the war, especially in large cities.[21] The lack of running water and toilets in rural areas resulted in a great deal of heavy labor, particularly for the women, who had to carry water several times a day. Many women in the south were still doing this in the 1950s and 1960s.[22]

For families living in the "banister" apartment houses of large cities the lack of such services meant difficulty in performing the most elementary domestic tasks. In the absence of rivers and fountains and with domestic space restricted, laundry was a problem, for water had to be carried to the house, heated, poured into tubs, and so on. (Because of this, many families with modest incomes sent their laundry out to be washed as soon as they could afford to.) A certain degree of enforced intimacy with one's neighbors was inevitable; because essential services were shared with them, they were constant witnesses and interlocutors of a family's and individual's most private and intimate behavior. The continuous coming and going through the doors along the common landings to enter other rooms (in houses with an inner ring of balconies above the courtyard, rooms rarely communicated with each

A courtyard in the old quarter of Milan, 1920. This closed-in place is the center of activity and intense socializing that takes place daily.

other, but each had a door opening onto the communal bal-
cony), going to the toilet, getting water, hanging the laundry
out to dry, and so on, provided occasions for sociability–as
well as for disagreements or attempts to control behavior. But
under certain circumstances solidarity too was fostered. Some
of the women interviewed by Guidetti Serra recall how an
entire building would protect people hunted by the Fascist
militia. Others had sympathized with a neighbor who, having
been forced by Fascist toughs to drink castor oil, had to run
all night long—as was heard by everyone—to the common
toilet.[23] All of this constituted an obstacle to the construction
of an authentic private space, not only physically but also in
terms of relationships. Every family quarrel immediately became public property, not even protected by the aloofness that
for the most part governs relations among neighbors in pres-
ent-day condominiums whose thin walls expose the family's
private matters to the curiosity of others.

Limited space also resulted in a certain promiscuity within
the family. Rooms and often even beds were shared by brothers and sisters of the same sex, or by children and adults.
Washing and dressing was done in communal spaces, and the
maintenance of any privacy required careful planning and negotiations concerning schedules. For a long time in lower-
class families the smaller children slept in the parents' room,
if not in the same bed with them. Many of the women interviewed for Barbagli's survey slept in their parents' bedroom—
with a folding screen to mark a labile borderline—until they
married.

In large peasant families, where the family of one or more
sons lived with that of the parents, the matter of space allocation directly impinged on the degree of privacy, of separation (or individualization), granted the couple. The couple was
always given a room to itself in the common home, even at
the expense of space for unmarried brothers or sisters. But
that room represented the entire private space allowed, to be
enjoyed in ways and at times that were established and canonical. In such common dwellings the couple, by itself and
with its own children, had no space in which to carry on a
domestic life of its own; every activity had not only to be
shared but subordinated to the order and division of labor of
the family hierarchy. From the hour of meals to what was to
be eaten, to when fabric should be bought for a dress, and
even more so for a gift, everything had to be negotiated within

the larger family community and subject to its authority. Because the peasant family was a labor unit, life was lived not so much by conjugal units as by sex and age groups. The same was true of activities such as eating, entertainment, and so on, which in other families already had the symbolic quality of the intimacy of family life that spread to the majority of families in the 1950s and 1960s (to the point of provoking resistance to school cafeterias, short lunch breaks, five-day work weeks, and other new developments perceived as destructive of family domestic rituals).

Under such circumstances a different conception, or at least a different experience of privacy existed within the family. Paradoxically, was private life more possible outside the family, in the spaces and relationships of external society, such as the osteria or the bocce games for the men; dances or during the Sunday promenade for the young people; in church, at pilgrimages, or at the washhouse for the women? These places though certainly public, were removed from the control or simply too close a presence of family and neighbors. We might suspect that men and women, adults and youngsters, could enjoy a private life inversely proportionate to the amount of time they spent in the domestic space.

Low-income housing, which had been started in Italy in the 1930s, reflected the distribution of spaces and services between private and communal. The apartments in such housing usually did not have toilets and bathrooms, and often not even running water. This was the result of an image of the working-class family as different from bourgeois and middle-class families in terms of needs and values. The same concept was still present in some of the low-income housing built in rural and semi-rural areas during the 1950s.

The situation in the bourgeois home, as I have pointed out, was different. Space was usually ample, although a large number of children sometimes made it difficult for each to enjoy that "room of one's own," which by custom was set aside at least for the oldest of each sex. Each family activity had its proper place within the bourgeois home, which exhibited spatially the rich articulation of private life, either toward the outside (closed doors, private bathrooms) or toward the inside. The parent's room was inaccessible to the children when the door was closed; the males were separated from the females, the grown-ups from the little ones, the kitchen from the dining room, and the latter from the living room. Servants, and sometimes the smaller children, ate apart from the family; and guests were not to see the kitchen or the bedroom, only the "neutral" space of the living room or dining room.

Lower-middle-class families often approximated this model, providing a small study for the husband, even if he used it only occasionally, furnishing a living room, which often remained closed, its furniture protected by dust covers. The family lived and ate in the *tinello*, or den—this typical space of the lower-middle-class family that separated the place where food was prepared from where it was eaten. This real "family room" was where one listened to the radio (and in a later period watched television), and read the newspapers. Here the children sometimes did their homework and the mother sewed. Sometimes, the room contained, disguised as a sofa, the bed of a son too old to sleep with the others.

All of this began to change quite rapidly at the end of the 1950s. As electrification became widespread and the technology of domestic infrastructures such as plumbing and heating installations and of domestic appliances became more efficient, dwelling standards changed on a mass basis at the very time that families became smaller. Censuses and surveys from 1961 on show that running water, toilets, and bathrooms were becoming normal features in Italian dwellings. After the end of the 1960s—far later than in the United States, or countries of northern Europe, but about the same time as France—the washing machine, refrigerator, radio, television, and automobile become common possessions, radically changing people's habits and modes of domestic work. In all classes the home increasingly became a space that was not only private but also special, a place to be decorated and enriched. Differences between the typologies of the urban and rural house tended to decrease, sometimes to the advantage of the latter, since more building space was available in the countryside.

This process was accompanied by an overall modification in the levels and models of consumption. Whereas in the 1930s families' standards of living had fallen, compared to the decades immediately preceding, and in the 1950s half of the median family's income was still spent on food, by the end of the 1960s this percentage had dropped to 39 percent and by the beginning of the 1980s had leveled off at about 30 percent.[25] This means that even with improved diet, an increasing share of the family income can be spent on other forms of consumption, a greater number of needs recognized and satisfied.

As always there remain vast differences between social

classes and regions in the possibility of owning a house and enjoying a standard of domestic life considered adequate today. A recent survey of poverty in Italy points out the persistent imbalance between the central and northern parts of the country and the south, to which is added the greater risk of poverty for large families (that is, with three or more children) and for the elderly.[26] Technological advances in housing conditions do not seem to have taken place or spread equally in all areas. This has created social—and also, I believe, political—inequalities that are particularly striking because they are so far from the common standards of normality and adequacy. To this day potable running water is not available in houses in many parts of southern Italy, though running water can be pumped from wells (that must be periodically filled). Potable water is available only at specific times at the public fountain, so it must be collected daily. Even in certain large southern cities, such as Naples, Messina, or Palermo, water can be scarce for more or less protracted periods, requiring a different, at the same time more erratic and more planned, organization of housework and personal hygiene. One cannot take a bath according to personal standards of cleanliness, but according to the availability of water. Women who live in certain small towns in Apulia have trained themselves to wake up at two o'clock at night, when the water arrives, to fill the containers in the house and to operate the washing machine, and so on.

An Ambivalent Development

Along with the persistence of marked inequality in the accessibility of "normal" home life goes a discontinuity in the generational experience that has unfolded differently by class. Although many workers' families in the 1960s and 1970s had access to dwellings and consumption patterns that were unthinkable only ten years earlier, the standards of space typical of a middle-class family in the 1950s are not uniformly accessible to its children ten and above all twenty years later. Moreover, in bourgeois families and in many middle-class families throughout the 1950s the heavier domestic tasks were performed by servants. The daughters and sometimes the wives of the more modest classes, especially rural classes, were handed over by their families to the more affluent to guarantee the physical work required for a comfortable domestic life. This practice gradually declined as household appliances were introduced. Women born into the urban bourgeoisie at the beginning of the 1940s perform, as adults (with less effort and perhaps lower standards) tasks that in their childhood and adolescence had been considered servants' work.

Underlying this process are various phenomena, one of which concerns the different cultures of privacy and decorum that have developed in the classes involved. On the one hand, girls who once would have gone into domestic service have increasingly chosen not only the salaries but also the distinction between the public-work sphere and private sphere by taking factory jobs. They are no longer willing to accept the more or less "motherly" supervision of mistresses or the reduction of their private space to a cot in the kitchen or the sewing room, unable to have a room of their own in which to relax and entertain girlfriends. On the other hand, women of the middle and upper classes have found that the presence of strangers, even though subordinate, interfered with their own private life. New forms of social consciousness, new modes of interaction among social classes, render less and less acceptable, in moral terms or simply in terms of good taste, any intimacy in the hierarchy. They find too close relations among different social groups and too visible inequalities (in eating and sleeping, in personal spaces) within the same living unit unacceptable. Only the very rich can afford space enough to safeguard the need for privacy of all those involved in domestic service relations. It is not by chance that, as a result of this two-sided change in values, the number of full-time domestic servants has diminished. Moreover, many of them now come from poorer or less developed parts of the world.

Thus, in the majority of families of all classes, beginning in the late 1950s, domestic privacy was linked not only to greater comforts, such as inside running water, bathrooms, and so on, but also by the internalizing of domestic service, which was being taken over by the woman of the house, the wife-mother. However, although full-time domestic help diminished substantially in Italy much later than, for example, in Britain, Sweden, and the United States, to this day a middle-class Italian family (and woman) enjoys more domestic help than is common in those other countries, even though it usually is in the form of part-time hourly help for a few days per week.

From these transformations an image of private family life emerges that by now has "canonical" spaces and rhythms. Sleeping has become separated from other activities; personal hygiene requires ever more specific and appropriately fur-

The attitude of this Filipino domestic worker reflects a society that is developing new discriminations and a new underclass. At the same time, the mingling of new cultures is a characteristic sign of modernity.

nished space to satisfy not only the need for cleanliness and function but also for aesthetics and comfort (as soon as one can afford it, one insists on two bathrooms). Here cooking is a frequent, complex activity requiring much equipment and so a great deal of space. (Think of the debate on the rational kitchen begun in Germany and the United States in the 1930s, which resulted in the "American-style kitchen.") More and more space is required for consumer goods (domestic appliances, clothing, toys of adults and children) as well as for the equipment necessary to maintain the domestic space (cabinets, closets, and so on). There has emerged a continuous redefinition and renegotiation of both space and family roles.

The history of the kitchen is typical. It varies from a maximum of compression (the kitchenette) that conceals it as a place of work while at the same time allows space (for the den, the living-dining room) for other family activities such as eating and relaxation, and, at the opposite end, provides a maximum of socialization that, with a curious return to the old peasant kitchen, places the kitchen at the center of family life. In this kitchen-den-mini-living room the work of cooking and the person who performs it are not separated from family life. The kitchen furnishings themselves and the pertinent advertising messages oscillate between this twofold meaning, between functionality-efficiency and sociability-warmth. Beginning with the 1960s television often came to define both the center of the family space and the position of the kitchen in respect to this space and its inhabitants.

In these processes classes, and in particular the women of different classes, push in different directions. "A kitchen of my own" is the dream tenaciously pursued by someone who never had one, and the utensils that gradually fill it are symbols of a finally achieved status. For other women who, after marriage, have had a kitchen—and housework—handed to them, following an adolescence of studies, wage work experiences, and fantasies of a life of affection and attachments, "erasing" the kitchen, or the reverse, setting it at the center—can represent practical and symbolic strategies in resuming one's place in space and in family relations. As a contemporary of mine in the 1960s, perplexed and hurt when confronted by the different experience that family responsibility represented for her when compared to that of her mother (who had full-time supervision of a large family, coordinating and watching over the work of the servants with implacable rigor) said: "When

I got married I left my job because I chose to be a mother, not because I chose to be a housewife."

Other spaces are renegotiated and other family protagonists are involved in the process of redefining the standards and goals of family life. If in the majority of cases the parents have achieved the privacy of the nocturnal space, and therefore also of sexuality, they have by contrast, at least in middle-class families, given up many individual spaces that were typical of the father-husband (the den) and of the wife-mother (the sewing room) in the old bourgeois family. At the same time, communal spaces are more accessible to the children. Who would think of telling them to stay away from the living room with its television? They too now have private spaces, rooms where they can receive their friends, arrange their possessions as they please, set apart by their own symbols.

THE COUPLE, CHILDREN, RELATIONAL AND AFFECTIVE STYLES

"My mother," the daughter of a sharecropper born at the turn of the century recalls, "never sat down at the table with us. Not even on Sundays. She stayed in the kitchen, ate in the kitchen, on the chopping board." And another: "We never sat down at the table. Never. Only the men were at the table, the women on chairs in a corner of the kitchen. Not that the table was too crowded. We were really used to this. I remember that in the evening we ate our meal there, sitting on the floor. We ate with our hands. Only the men had forks."[27]

Where once the family table and the ritual of eating together identified the rights of only some within the family, marking divisions of power and authority, in the space of a generation the situation changed. By the 1950s, even in peasant families, family unity was symbolized by sitting around the same table, eating the same food, even though the women continue to serve the men, getting up, changing the dishes, spoon-feeding the children, and serving themselves last. In poorer families the most recent memory is of the mother who, when distributing the food, leaves herself until last and occasionally passes her own food on the sly to her children. In the families of the urban middle class, Segalen too notes an appropriation "by right" on the part of the mother of the leftover, the piece nobody wants.[28] Similarly the custom of

The Growth of the Affectionate Family

favoring the head of the family in the choice of tidbits persists, as Chombart de Lauwe observed with respect to French workers' families of the 1950s.[29]

At the same time, superimposed on the hierarchy of traditional power, which remains very clearly defined in its division of labor as well as, in certain families, its control of the money, a relational style has emerged that leaves room for the expression of affection and suggests some measure of equality in family relations.

According to Barbagli, this process began in the upper urban classes; it reached the agricultural classes last. It is, however, the families of the more modest urban strata—factory workers in particular—that seem most aware of the change, perhaps because in the upper strata it had begun in the previous century and so by now was something to be taken for granted, which at most needed further perfecting.

There is more than one indicator for this change, which, besides identifying ever more specifically the sphere of family relations as a sphere of affection and reciprocity, separates it by that very fact from the spheres of social life in which relations are more distant and formal and the expectation of reciprocity is less. On the basis of his oral sources Barbagli stresses changes in the way that family members address each other: in relations between children and parents, wives and husbands, the formal *voi* has been superseded by the informal *tu*. Such usage has become increasingly symmetrical, in the sense that it is more and more unusual for a husband to address his wife with the informal *tu* while she responds with the formal *voi*. The transition may be long and complicated within a particular family, but the conflicts and repressive reactions bear witness to the fact that the context is changing. The family universe is no longer rigid, so members of one family can try to adopt the habits of another. A woman born at the beginning of the twentieth century, daughter of a tenant farmer, recounts: "A few times I addressed my mother with the informal *tu,* out of curiosity and because certain of my cousins addressed my aunt informally. So sometimes I felt like saying *tu* to my mother, but she scolded me and threatened to beat me, because she did not want us to use the *tu*." On the other hand, another woman remembers that "once the village priest asked my father why we children in speaking to him were using the *tu* and not the *voi*. My father replied that he did not mind. He said: I want children to feel close, affectionate, so I prefer to have them address me informally rather than insisting on the use of the formal *voi*.

This last attitude has become widely accepted by the urban classes, especially the more educated. This group also favors a style of behavior that encourages open demonstrations of affection between spouses and between parents and children, without fear that this might lead to a lack of respect or, in the case of boys, to a weakening of character.[30] To kiss in front of family members is no longer considered unseemly, and children and parents exchange caresses well past infancy.

Physicality, treating the body as an object not only of care but also of tenderness, has assumed an ever more ample place in family relations, paradoxically in inverse relation to the increase in individual private spaces. It is almost as though the decrease in overcrowded conditions has permitted contact between bodies less needful of (self-) control. Tenderness is also expressed in family rituals. Birthdays, wedding anniversaries, Christmas, and other special days have become the focal point of a "domestic religion," of family time in which the precise attribution of values to single relationships finds its own language and symbolism. This process may have cul-

A golden wedding anniversary brings the generations together.

minated in the 1960s, when widespread prosperity allowed many families a chance to give material expression to this ritualism. In later years models of consumption became ever more closely linked to market trends and stimuli. Accordingly, the greater autonomy of individual family members, not only in consumption but also in the use of leisure time and sociability, may have weakened the symbolic importance of many family rituals that spread during the previous decades, at least in respect to certain ages or stages of life.

The Couple: Love, Sexuality, Reciprocity, Autonomy

As family life developed a specific autonomy in the twentieth century, so too did the life of the couple itself. From working companions, partners in the enterprise of survival, spouses have increasingly become mutual confidants, persons who, in theory, share everything with each other. One can expect support and understanding from one's spouse.

This occurred with a different rhythm and intensity in the various classes, paradoxically in a manner inverse to the degree of social difference between the spouses. In working-class and rural families in which the woman had a strong working role, a relationship based on language as well as behavior, on hierarchy and authority between the sexes, prevailed longer. The language of intimacy and affective equality was more apt to be found among middle-class urban couples in which the wife was completely within the domestic space and role. The language of intimacy could coexist with strong imbalances of power in everyday details: from control of the shopping money to control of female sociability. As late as the 1950s, wives in many middle-class families did not know the salaries of their husbands, who controlled the household expenses. And some women could rarely go out alone. Nevertheless, despite the persistence of notable imbalances between the sexes, during the course of the twentieth century the model of intimacy and true partnership became ever more firmly established as the normal model of conjugal relations.

The most striking indication of this transformation is the place attributed in marriage to love and falling in love. At the beginning of the century marriage was still a family matter in the sense that a "well made" marriage began with the consent of the parents, when it was not arranged by them. When single persons made the decision, practical motivations were common ("he/she is a good worker"), as were those of morality ("he/she is a good person," "a reliable person"). During the course of the century affection and physical attraction became more frequent, and above all more legitimate, reasons for marriage. Today simply falling in love may justify the decision to get married.

The 1983 opinion poll I have mentioned found that almost all of those interviewed declared that love is the foundation of marriage. For the generations born at the end of the nineteenth century, mutual respect was what was important in a marriage. Love, understood as tranquil affection, would come later; sexuality, at least for women, was often something to be endured (or at least so it was said). For women born between the two wars, above all for those who belonged to the urban middle and upper middle classes, being in love—or saying that one was—was a precondition for marriage. (It is no surprise that Liala's romances were so successful, for they taught young women what feelings they and their men should experience when they discovered their mutual affection and provided them with a complete and precise vocabulary for those feelings.) The status of sexuality, caught between taboo and its declared aim of procreation, was less clear. The "proper" woman was supposed to submit graciously to the "conjugal debt," letting herself, in the best of cases, be instructed in pleasure by her more experienced husband, or at least not rejecting him. Nevertheless, the decrease in fertility, which began in Italy at the start of the century, suggests that some sort of negotiation, some sort of discussion of sexuality, must have taken place between men and women in the intimacy of their bedrooms, as well as between close friends of the same sex. There definitely must have been much discussion of it in the confessional, as "sexual sins" within marriage increasingly became a matter of contention between women and priests. It was one of the themes most frequently treated in manuals of morality. There the interesting concept of conjugal chastity was elaborated, traces of which are found in the encyclicals *Casti Connubi* of 1930 and *Humanae Vitae* of 1968, as well as the document *Educational Orientation on Human Love* (1983). In the 1950s and into the 1960s married Catholic women shared the name of the priest "who did not ask the question." They sometimes supplied the name of the doctor who performed curettage. This medical procedure disguised many abortions among urban middle-class women, who were much more fortunate than poorer women, forced to turn to midwives or parsley infusions.

This is an interesting paradox of the definition and developing expression of family relations, and more specifically of intimate and private conjugal relations, not subject to the controls and rules of relatives or the community. As the relation between spouses gradually becomes important in itself, conjugal sexuality, released from procreational ends, takes on an autonomous value in the couple's relations. At the same time, there has been increasing direct or indirect interventions by a number of extrafamilial agents, intent on codifying and regulating husband/wife relations in general as well as the practice of conjugal sexuality. From advice in women's magazines to sermons from the pulpit or in the confessional all the way to legislative or welfare-agency interference, conjugal sexuality has become a social and state matter.

Throughout the twentieth century—and not just in recent years as a result of the initiatives of the women's movement—sexuality, the realm of privacy par excellence, has been the subject of continued public discussion and intervention. This obviously is true in the case of repressive intervention, such as the prohibition of abortions or, until 1975, of the advertising and sale of birth-control devices.

The targets of these efforts are almost exclusively women: it is their sexuality that the various agencies wish to regulate. And here the paradox, so to speak, becomes twofold. While they are being held up as the ideal private subjects and the custodians of privacy itself as mothers and as wives, women as never before have become the subject of systematic discussion and close public regulation. They have been the object of a series of prohibition, restriction, and "protection" (above all in the field of work, but for a long time in political and other economic activities as well). The behavior and activities of the "good wife," "good mother," and "good housewife" are delineated clearly in marriage manuals and other normative texts published over the last several decades. The prescriptive claims in these manuals change over time, but they do not become any less important. If in the 1950s a good wife was supposed to be sexually available but passive, in the 1970s she was expected to be active and imaginative. If in the 1930s and 1950s the way to a man's heart was through his stomach, in the 1970s he was captured and kept in bed and in the living room by the woman's intelligence, understanding, and charm (without, however, neglecting dinner and the laundry). If until halfway through the 1960s the agencies that formulated the norms were in agreement, later a lack of homogeneity developed, as did conflict. The results, depending on the particular

The Venetian Lido in the 1950s. Uncertain times shook family unity, undermining the authority of fathers and husbands, permitting the liberation of sons and daughters.

case (that is, on individual resources) were liberating, or, on the contrary, paralyzing, when they did not inspire feelings of guilt.

The discussion of sexuality is but one aspect, even if it is paradoxically the most visible in prescribing comportment that is both "natural" and "private," of the social construction of the family as the space of relationships at once private, intimate and regulated. This conceptualization is particular to the twentieth century, at least to the degree and articulation with which it has taken place. The growing importance attached to love and sexuality within marriage has had a contradictory effect on the relationship of the couple. This is shown clearly by the increase in separations and divorces during recent years, even though in Italy they are less common than elsewhere. If in fact it is love that legitimates the conjugal relationship, when love is no longer there, or when the love object is someone else, it becomes legitimate to terminate the conjugal relationship, since it is no longer possible to maintain intimacy without love, or without reciprocity in love. There is also a tendency to regard as unacceptable a conjugal relationship in which one partner forces his or her sexuality on the other. The legislative changes that, beginning with the 1970s, have taken place or have been proposed indicate the extent of these cultural and behavioral changes.

The culture of love, by implying some sort of parity between two persons who choose each other because they love each other, has the effect of bringing about, together with demands for fusion—the American "togetherness" of the 1950s and 1960s—demands for reciprocity and independence not only on the emotional plane but also in practical life. The complicated renegotiation of conjugal roles, of division of labor, of power, of the respective expectations, responsibilities, and competencies, which attains its greatest visibility in the negotiations surrounding the wife's participation in salaried work and the husband's in the family, is interwoven with partly contradictory expectations: fusion and autonomy, continuity and choice, parity and hierarchy, love and duty.[31]

The manner in which each couple and each social group, on the basis of its resources, cultural traditions, and possible options, defines the point of balance among these different instances produces different marriages, as is evident from the answers to the above mentioned 1983 poll.[32]

The Changed Role and Experience of Children

Affective center of the family, the first members toward whom it is not only legitimate but obligatory to express tenderness, the main reason women are asked to devote themselves to caring for the family and making it a sphere of domesticity and privacy, children have been the object of a twofold and only apparently contradictory process from the beginning of the 1900s to this day. On the one hand, their number per family has progressively diminished by more than half; on the other, the affective space and the amount of care devoted to them by the parents has expanded greatly. In the

1960s what Juliet Mitchell said of Great Britain and the United States was true also of Italy: the same amount of time a woman once had devoted to the procreation of many children was now devoted, with a greater investment of psychic energies and diversified abilities, to the upbringing and education of one or two children.[33] In the same period, though with different rhythms and intensities, paternity has assumed the qualities of increased affect and intimacy, with contemporary fathers becoming ever more involved both in the games and in the physical care of their children, particularly the youngest.

The drop in the birthrate has greatly changed the experience of growing up. Childhood and adolescence are less often shared with others in the family, who are a bit older or a bit younger. Very few peers surround the child in the private space of the home (or within the kinship network), and the relationship with his or her parents is more direct, more individualized, less mediated by other relationships, and therefore more intense and laden with responsibility. A small number of children means more selected, more wanted chil-

Although the father's authority is weaker, its compensation is a new tenderness.

dren, in whom greater expectations are invested; they must "turn out well." Also, as is suggested by the increased recourse to antisterility treatments and artificial insemination, all children desired must be born.[34]

Like falling in love, the concept of choice, or at least of deliberate intent, on the part of a married couple planning to have children in today's world results in strong ambivalence regarding what is desired and what is actually decided upon. It explicitly concerns the value of the individuality of those concerned: mother, father, son or daughter, possibly brothers and sisters. Choice or a deliberate action to ensure that procreation takes place reveals the precariousness of the child's existence, making it dependent on the subjectivity and autonomy of its parents (and on their processes of negotiation). At the same time it affirms the child's value as an individual, somehow distinct, irreducible, and therefore potentially autonomous.

Children today grow up in this ambivalence between dependence on deliberate intent (which, even as it may choose not to give life, may choose not to give love, or find itself incapable of giving it) and a message of autonomy. This ambivalence displays a more material aspect in the prolonged economic and material dependency of contemporary life. Compared to only two generations ago, childhood is prolonged by law and by affection. Yet the specific rights of minors—as minors and as children—are recognized and sanctioned by the law as well as by cultural models. The very fact that the advertising industry has acknowledge that children have become consumers in their own right, besides determining a great part of the family's spending, indicates a growing subjectivity of children, and even more so of adolescents, that is not merely a consequence induced by the media.

Minors are now socially recognized as individuals who have certain rights, for which the family and society are responsible, and are capable of acting as both individual and family consumers. This is not a linear casual process, but an interactive process, whose effects are unforeseen and often undesired, one with strong differences among social groups, family cultures, and geographical localities.

In this complicated process, which has gone through various stages, I am particularly concerned to reemphasize the paradox of a social construction of relationships defined as private. The prolonged dependency of the children, which has changed their place in both the material and symbolic economy of the family and in particular of the parents, does not depend exclusively on choices made by the latter. It is the consequence of measures taken at the legislative level; of changes in the labor market; in the influence of the culture of experts, doctors above all, as well as teachers, psychologists, and so on. In other words, it results from more or less explicit and more or less binding interventions on the part of agencies outside the family, primarily the state. The parent-child relationship, the images that these various individuals have of themselves and of each other, in large measure are the result of public discussions and conditions that have developed in these external spheres.

Two examples are particularly apt. The first is health. The development of hygiene and medicine are the cause of that decrease in infant mortality that, even though later and slower in Italy than in other countries, favored a reduced birthrate and a greater investment in children. The first attempt in Italy at organized intervention, as both welfare and education, was the creation of ONMI (the Opera Nazionale Maternità e Infanzia, National Maternity and Infant Care) in 1936. It was conceived for purposes of encouraging population growth, with strong normative and social-control dimensions (only mothers who obeyed the rules were entitled to assistance). Its services were unevenly distributed between city and countryside and between north and south. It was, nevertheless, the first assumption of public responsibility with regard to procreation and rearing. ONMI addressed the lower classes; in middle-class families it was the family physician, or pediatrician, who instructed mothers about how to perform their duties.

The second example is the school. Rules that deal with obligatory school attendance, which in the twentieth century have progressively raised the age at which a child may legally stop attending school, and those that regulate the curriculum have also codified the responsibilities of the parents and the position of minors within the family. The matter has not been without ambiguity on the part of the state or without conflict on the part of the family. The diversity of the schools available to the various social classes, which until the middle 1960s concerned basic schooling itself, the differences that exist to this day among schools in various geographical regions, the exemptions that for a long period, especially under Fascism, were granted to families regarding scholastic obligations—all of these clearly indicate how defining the duties and rights of minors remained and to some degree still remains very socially differentiated.[35] In this sense the "privacy" of family participation was not affected by public intervention.

Families, especially those with a tradition of a family economy to which all contributed with their work depending on age and sex, often have resisted the state's intrusion into family plans. Traces of this can be found even today in the renewed incidence of child labor, which some families are forced to accept because of economic necessity. There is ambivalence too for the many families that cannot afford to allow their children extended school attendance because it results in the child's continuing economic dependence on the family. Although they may share this educational value, they lack the resources to achieve it. Such an attitude can be seen in the oral histories of many working-class women who had children between the two World Wars or during the early 1950s.

The experience of an education extended beyond childhood, and begun well before the age of obligatory schooling with the growth of kindergartens (and in certain areas, though to a lesser extent, of nursery schools), allows children and adolescents an experience of identification among peers that to some extent influences the way they exist in the family and behave as children. In other words, if being children is only to a limited degree an experience shared with a group of brothers and sisters, it is increasingly becoming an experience partially developed outside the home. At the same time, the

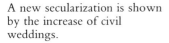

A new secularization is shown by the increase of civil weddings.

prolonged coresidence in the family of adolescents and young-sters who are both economically dependent and the recipients of rights functions in such a way that for long periods family life takes on the features of a community of adults, with rights and duties marked by differing generational positions. This requires constant adjustment of expectations as well as of everyday habits. The inherited culture of proper generational and family relationships was unprepared for these negotiations on rights and duties, on solidarity and autonomy, about what is communal and what personal. The result is that the imag-ination and patience of families and their members are tested every day.

HOW PRIVATE IS THE PRIVATE FAMILY?

During the previous century, but with special intensity and visibility in the twentieth, the family in Italy has been involved in two parallel and apparently contradictory phe-nomena. The first is a growing specification, legitimation, and articulation of its space, relationships, and activities, as pri-vate—if not indeed the private dimension par excellence. The second is the increasing intrusion of other agents, institutions, and in particular state organizations into family activities and relations. This latter phenomenon is itself twofold. There is first direct legislative intervention with regard to the regula-tion of the so-called legitimate family, of relations between spouses, of the rights and duties of the generations, of criteria for the formation (age at marriage) and dissolution of the family, of patrimonial relationships, and so on. There is also indirect intervention through social policies in the material conditions of everyday family life.

Family relations have been subjected to intense legislative regulation in the twentieth century. Profound changes oc-curred when the Rocco code of 1942 was superseded by the new family laws of 1975, including the introduction of di-vorce, modification of legislation on adoption and foster care, the legalization of contraception and abortion, the elimination of the legal defense known as the "crime of honor" in murder cases, and so on. No single aspect of family relations escaped juridical scrutiny; all aspects have been legally redefined during the last fifty years, with marked effects on so-called private relationships. Exemplary from this point of view is the legal

Regulating Family Relations

transformation of the status of the minor or child in the family. He or she has become less and less the object of authority and the subject of duties and more and more the subject of rights. The state has assumed the protection of these rights; it can enter the family's private confines for this purpose, going so far as to intervene to modify generational relations, taking a child away from natural parents deemed inadequate and giving it to others.

Not all families' everyday affairs are equally open to state control and intervention, however; poorer and less socially integrated families are the usual objects of such intrusion and interference. This only demonstrates the many meanings and intentions of state intervention, not only to protect the weak but also to defend them against behavior that is "outside the norm"; as support but also as social control; as social construction through specific legislative definition of what is "normal" in life and in private relations. This mixture of ambiguity and contradiction in the message by which the state socially prescribes (and controls) a sphere defined as private is apparent in many cases. These might include cases when suspicion of child abuse requires intervention, inquiry, and verification (by neighbors, relatives, and so on), which are repugnant to the principle of the inviolability of privacy; or when the need to protect family members from each other collides with the parents' rights to supervise and educate their children. At various times legislation and its juridical application have favored one or the other horn of this dilemma. And if until the 1960s the solidarity and internal privacy of the family seemed protected, privileged, at the expense of individual rights, today the latter seem to have been given precedence.[36]

Social Policies and the Contemporary Family

The second element of the state's intervention, which is accompanied by that of private agencies and institutions, from the Church to volunteer organizations, services, and so on, is that of social policies.

The welfare state was developed specifically to intervene in the area of reproduction, an area formerly entrusted, for better or worse, to family resources alone. Today a good part of the package of resources available to a family, of the material conditions in which its daily life can be organized and its future as well as that of its individual members can be planned, is constituted by resources, conditions, and restrictions produced by redistributive mechanisms: via monetary transfers (pensions, various indemnities, subsidies) and social services. This means that the family organizes its own private life and defines its own strategy in tight interaction with not only the labor market (with its schedules, educational requirements and performance, career stages, and so on) and the market of consumer goods, but also with the definition of needs, the standards of normality, and the resources that originate from social policies.

We have seen how educational policies have played a large role in defining the reciprocal statuses of children and parents. Retirement policies socially define age roles, while forcing a reorganization of the rhythms of everyday life. And regulations regarding working mothers constitute a partial assumption of the costs connected with the procreation and rearing of children, recognizing the legitimacy of a woman's being simultaneously a mother and a worker. This is certainly an ambivalent recognition, since there is no analogous recognition of paternal responsibilities regarding the care and rearing of these same children. Nevertheless, the model of maternity and family that emerges differs from one in which no recognition of dual participation of mothers is considered and procreation either brings about immediate job termination (which still took place in Italy during the 1950s with the support of the law) or is considered a totally private matter over which no public responsibility whatsoever exists.

Social policies display the same dual dimension of support and regulation of the private sphere mentioned earlier. Just as the existence or nonexistence of a hospital, after-school programs, or a nursery school is a crucial factor in family life because they can satisfy specific needs, the manner in which these services operate, the criteria on which they are based, and the needs they address, while they designate areas of rights, also designate family duties, if not actual family and individual schedules. The analyses of family strategies, and in particular of female family work, made in Italy at the beginning of the 1970s showed clearly that, as in other countries, a strong interdependence exists between family organization, the division of labor between the sexes, the labor market, and the functioning of the welfare state.[37]

On the one hand, a great many needs—from the care of small children to the care of the elderly, and in great part care of the sick—are actually still entrusted to the families in a situation of needs that have become more diversified and more expensive because of increased standards and expectations. On the other hand, the very resources offered by social policies are based upon and require family integration. In the case of many pensions and small subsidies, this means direct economic integration; in the case of many other services, it is integration through family work. No service can ever be a true substitute for the family, not even the hospital, which insists that the family aid the patient not only affectively but also materially. And many services explicitly require the presence of the family: in administration and in service activities (washing the laundry of children in crèches and nursery schools, supplementing scholastic endeavors, and so on). One might say that an efficient service is backed up by an efficient family, that is, a family that knows how to interact intelligently and flexibly with its formal and informal regulations, one that knows how to choose as well as how to adapt. Such a family functions as an independent service unit in accordance with standards that are partially defined elsewhere; it works to complement external services in accordance with the rules and programs of the latter.

The Private Family and the Family Woman

A family? More correctly a woman: a wife, a mother, a daughter. Next to the child, the private-family figure most redefined by and intertwined with enterprises outside the family, in particular with social policies, is the adult woman, wife and mother. In the space of a few decades the model of female normality as well as specific female experiences have changed greatly.

As recently as the 1930s and 1940s, the most common adult female family experience—both working-class and peasant—was that of a multifaceted figure, a family-mother-sometime worker, always in and out of the labor market or the family enterprise, depending on the family's needs, torn between the demands of domestic life (and therefore of family work) and the need for income to satisfy them (and therefore of remunerated work). A different experience typified the urban middle and bourgeois classes, where hired help freed the mistress of the house from all or part of the domestic work. During this period state intervention began to be more explicit, directed in particular at women and their behavior patterns and trying to draw the model of a normal family, with a precise division of labor and allocation of power between the sexes. Beyond the more specifically demographic aims of the regime, this intervention had lasting effects. On the legislative level, female labor was regulated. On the level of social policies, ONMI and family subsidies for heads of families were instituted. At the level of propaganda and education, the state's interest in the family and the family's responsibility toward the state can be noted. The family—a "social and political institution" according to an expressive definition in the Rocco code of 1942—was based largely on a precise social and family status for the woman. She was a marginal worker lacking legal guarantees, secondary on the labor market and in the family, and guarantor, by her family work, not only of procreation but also of domestic well-being.[38]

Economic and technological development during the 1950s and 1960s, while favoring the emergence of full-time housewives among the working classes, no longer torn between family work and precarious jobs, extended these conditions to middle-class women.[39] Many observers have noted that the prosperity of the 1960s was owed at least equally to the increase in real wages and to family work, in the increasingly sophisticated though lighter burdens of the housewife. Throughout this period state intervention in reproduction was somewhat restricted in terms of the resources and services offered, but it was high in normative terms. The very organization of existing services—scarcity of preschool child care, short school days, lack of services for the elderly, and so on—posited a careful family organization based on the mother's full-time presence. It is true that discussion of services for the working mother had begun in the 1950s and 1960s. These were understood as surrogate services and assistance in cases where economic necessity did not permit the accepted and codified model of normality to exist. Nevertheless, this legislation concerning working women, with its restrictions and the sex wage differentials it permitted, suggested what the model of normality was, or what the wife-mother model should be.

Moreover, in the 1960s, alongside the state and the traditional agencies (the Church foremost among them) elaborating the norms and models of private life, others were created to address women directly in their role as consumers and family workers. The figure of the housewife of the 1960s was formed by the interweaving of labor market conditions, social and legislative policies, and development of consumption and media models. The last two factors rendered this figure palatable, "modern," and somehow or other emanci-

The feminist explosion of the 1970s found expression in demands for rights and equality in an Italian society in which men wielded virtually all power. Features of this revolution included the acceptance of a woman's individualism; closer communications among women, characterized by tenderness and solidarity; and, ultimately, an end to traditional gender roles that had relegated women to a feminine underclass.

pated.[40] Paradoxically, this partial emancipation through professionalization and general acceptance of the figure of the housewife, which has interacted with changes in reproductive behavioral patterns (a reduced birthrate), and with growing expectations of prosperity, has encouraged the emergence of a third model of the family woman: the wife of the "dual presence" of the 1970s and 1980s. This new woman handles a salaried job and family work at the same time, in a balancing act that changes throughout the family cycle. She has been assisted in this transformation not only by changes in private behavioral patterns but also by changes in public policies. Increased school attendance has affected women to an ever-increasing extent, offering new experiences as they grow up and resources to plan their future differently; state and local care services, while modifying family work, has offered paid employment to women; and so on.

This last development does not lack ambivalence. Although it increasingly identifies the responsibility of the group, of the state, for the conditions of everyday life and for reproduction, it stresses the interdependence of family and state as well as the crucial importance of the position of women in this interdependency. During recent years many social policies have in fact favored the entry of adult women with family dependents into the labor market, by helping them fulfill the demands of both employment and family. At the same time women have become the interlocutors of social policies, which reemphasizes their primary responsibility vis-à-vis managing family life and caring for family members. The most recent trend, in Italy as in other countries, in reexamining the balance between the family and the collectivity in providing services and protection for individuals, reemphasizes the responsibilities of women. The argument about a return to family—women's—work and responsibility, of the services that provide care and nursing for infants, the elderly, and the sick and invalid is the source of greatest controversy.

The last phase of family construction as a private space, at least in terms of time, sees women with dependents as the persons principally responsible for the relation and interface between family and society, between the public and the private. They are the indefatigable translators of the family's needs to the services and of the norms of these services to the family, the integrators of the missing pieces, of the voids. Women are the weavers of the social network in which private life, with its dense and mutable interdependencies, is built.

A nontraditional engagement announcement, 1972.

The German Family between Private Life and Politics

Ingeborg Weber-Kellermann

Translated and edited by Mary Jo Maynes
and Michelle Mouton

A NEW concept of family relations is emerging today in Central Europe. For the first time in the history of the family the authoritarian order is being replaced by a family that might be called democratic. Gradually some families, particularly of the younger generation, are dismantling strictly hierarchical relations and creating new ones based more on the idea of "partnership." At the same time, in contrast with earlier eras, the individuality and search for self-fulfillment of family members is regarded as a given, as is the right of the individual to his or her own life from early childhood on— not in opposition to the family but rather with its support. Still, democratization at all levels of social life is a process that is difficult to bring about. Authoritarian responses often come more readily, especially when "the good of the family," however defined, is held to be the highest priority. Moreover, the emphasis on individuality entails a certain psychic cost as well. The evolution of the German family in the twentieth century has been marked by highly contentious political debates over the nature of the family as well as by persistence and change in everyday practices.[1]

The Historical Background

The model of the German Christian family gradually evolved under the legally established authority of the *Hausvater*, the patriarch. A product of early modern middle-class and peasant family economies, the *Haushaltsfamilie,* or household, included all those living together under one roof who operated a common economic enterprise such as a farm, an artisanal shop, or a commercial business. The group comprised not only blood relations; servants, apprentices, and journeymen also belonged to such household residential and economic communities. This was the predominant familial form of the late Middle Ages and early modern times until the early nineteenth century.

This type of household was often referred to as *das ganze Haus* (the whole house) in the sense of Luther's biblical phrase "I will serve the Lord with all my house." This old usage is still preserved in expressions like "greetings from our house to your house," "household," and "it's on the house." In linguistic usage it was not until the sixteenth century that the Latin term *familia* referring to the household community began to be used. The *Hausvater* exercised legal, economic, and guardianship rights over the entire household personnel; he represented his house, its family, and its residents in communal affairs; he possessed disciplinary powers over all members of his household.[2] Authoritarian and patriarchal principles of rule permeated social thought and practice, and such principles also served as the model for the political order. The prince as *Landesvater* ruled over the *Landeskinder*; at the universities the *Doktorvater* watched over his students. Bound up with religious conceptions of a gracious and vindictive God the Father, political authorities were thus also integrated into the same system of order that governed the household. The institution of marriage, after centuries of influence by religious and political authority, reflected these notions as well.

The Emergence of the Bourgeois Family

Beginning in the late eighteenth century, the Industrial Revolution, a multifaceted and long-term process of technical and economic change, altered productive techniques and the organization of workplaces. The techniques used to administer manual and service workers (if we can apply such recent notions to those times) also changed, and there ensued a separation of workplace and residence.[3] This can be seen as the most decisive change of the modern period, and it brought with it the dissolution of "the whole house." The bourgeois *nuclear family,* which ideally included only parents and children, evolved in its place as the dominant family form. The French Revolution of 1789 also contributed to this development, since it elevated individualism to a new place in political theory and practice. Significantly, in the same era marriage became a matter of secular civic law as a legal contract between two individuals. It required, in theory, only the consent of the two partners.

With the separation of workplace and residence, a new

course of development for middle-class and petty bourgeois families began.[4] The Biedermeier era of the early 1800s witnessed the emergence of a distinctive style of home furnishing. For the first time bourgeois families developed their own autonomous taste in furniture, simple and charming, comfortable and solidly built, which exuded an air of homeyness. The care of this domestic space became the responsibility of the mother and housewife, who sought and found a compensation here for her relegation to the sphere of *Kirche-Küche-Kinder* (church-kitchen-children). Still, in terms of the power structure of the bourgeois family, not much had changed. Family life continued according to the conservative rule of an altered form of patriarchy; the mother was restricted to the home and left unemancipated and the children brought up under traditional authority relations.

The restriction of the family to the realm of interpersonal relations did bring with it an expansion of sentimental life, and in particular a new attention to the world of children.

Heinrich Ahrens (1805–1863), *The Hanusch Family.* The German nuclear family, which evolved in the nineteenth century, remained a patriarchy. (Staatliche Kunstsammlungen Kassel.)

Living room of the Biedermeier era, with its conventional middle-class furniture. (Detmold, Lippisches Landesmuseum.)

Now there were special rooms—nurseries—and a great wealth of toys, especially at Christmas, which developed into a gift fest for children.[5] The separate spaces embodied new concepts of family dynamics. Increasingly in these bourgeois families spatial separations grew out of and reinforced an understanding of children as vulnerable beings who needed to be protected from physical or psychological intimacy with adults.

Because women were presumed to be destined by nature for their domestic role, education seemed less important for daughters than for sons. Relative educational deprivation was the fate of most of the daughters of the upper bourgeoisie, and increasingly so in the nineteenth century.[6] With the founding of the *Kaiserreich* in 1871, increased speculation promoted by a new class of entrepreneurs willing to take risks, the founding of banks and joint-stock companies, and much real estate speculation, a milieu of nouveaux riches developed.

An upper-middle-class salon in Berlin from the era of the *Kaiserreich*.

Their wealth imprinted itself on the fashions of the *Kaiserreich,* and their wives, as ladies of leisure, were important as symbols of status and arbiters of taste. Neo-Gothic and old-German furniture groupings and plush draperies formed suitable settings for bourgeois family gatherings and social occasions. The relatively poor professional middle class and the modest petty bourgeoisie men who had wives and children to support fell behind in the battle to keep up external appearances. Their wives were often consumed by the demands of "conspicuous consumption."[7]

In middle-class circles there was a consensus that women could play a role in society only as wives and mothers. They were considered innocent and vulnerable creatures who needed to marry for their own protection. Norms had certainly shifted from the open discussion of gender roles stimulated by the French Revolution and the Revolutions of 1848.

Slowly, toward the century's end, a countermovement emerged.[8] If society remained permeated with signs of paternal authority, new women's organizations energetically took up struggles for women's right to employment, a better education for girls, and the entrance of women into the universities. By 1900 Baden, the German state closest to the border of liberal Switzerland, opened its universities to women; Prussia followed suit by 1908. The General German Women's Association, under the leadership of Helene Lange (1848–1930), agitated throughout the latter decades of the nineteenth century for better schooling for girls and for the possibility for professional education.

Nevertheless, this movement stopped halfway. The posed alternatives—career *or* marriage and motherhood—demoted women's professional aspirations to the status of fallback measures for the unmarriageable. With such a limited vision the middle-class women's movement could not break through the dominant social order. The bourgeois family model, with the husband as breadwinner and the wife as keeper of the hearth, continued to be widely accepted and even was considered by many working-class women as an ideal to pursue. A partnership between the sexes, which some women saw in the ideals of the French Revolution, and attempted to put into practice in the Berlin salons of the late eighteenth and early nineteenth centuries, remained unfulfilled at the dawn of the twentieth.

Capitalist society had thus brought with it an altered but still patriarchal model of the nuclear family, which was to last for many generations and predominate in social, pedagogical, psychological, and cultural realms. This development was mirrored in many aspects of child socialization. Children were taught conformity through exhortations to good behavior. Good behavior was induced through a system of rewards that culminated in the mythical gift-giving of the *Weinachtsmann* and the *Christkind* who filled to overflowing houses richly decorated for Christmas. These boys and girls, with their tin soldiers, construction sets, and dolls, learned nothing of the larger world nor of the countless children whom no *Weinachtsmann* visited. Everything "filthy" and unpleasant was kept from their tender minds. They learned nothing of money or poverty. The stork brought babies, they were told, and so sexual reality was hidden from them. In family photos, they stand in their Sunday best, in white sailor suits and lace dresses, living images of innocence itself.

These developments applied to bourgeois milieux, whereas working-class families of the nineteenth century lived a very impoverished life and continued to be dependent on the earnings of all their members. These included the women, and children from the age of ten or so. Factory owners would even calculate a sort of family wage that included all the various members' contributions. Excessively long workdays of twelve to fourteen hours barely permitted free time in the evening, and the poor living conditions in the new tenements permitted no space for children's play. Chances for education and upward mobility were scarcely available to the proletarian child.

Working-Class and Rural Families

The life of the working-class woman was especially harsh; for her the class character of society was more than apparent. Her extensive paid work along with housework in a poorly appointed dwelling, combined with a continually growing number of children, brought nearly insoluble problems. Husbands were neither taught nor inclined to help with the housework, and often fled from the discomfort and misery at home to the neighborhood tavern. The working-class woman suffered the most under the conditions of nineteenth-century family life; her new life conditions were without precedent. Certainly the proletarian women's movement of the turn of the century strove for a way out of this vicious circle of childbearing and impoverishment. A number of working-class women sought solutions in political engagement.[9] However, overburdening, repression, and the generations-long lessons of subservience under a patriarchal authority were strong constraints. Inexperienced in resistance and acutely aware of the needs of their families, most working women spent less time on political activities than men did.

As far as that large group of women working—namely, household servants—was concerned, the growing demand brought employment under deteriorating conditions of labor. The increasing economic dependency of the bourgeois "mistress," and her increased need to appear as leisured, led to her contempt for housework. The real work of housework was thus disguised and its burden shifted insofar as possible onto servants. The other side of the practiced idleness of bourgeois daughters was the complete relegation of manual labor to working-class women. These new attitudes produced increased arrogance toward servants and growing snobbishness in the ranks of the new middle classes.

This working–class kitchen in Hanover, 1933, makes clear the difficulties faced by the housewife.

The lives of farming families centered around subsistence and the sale of goods produced on the farm. The agrarian economy structured peasant economic conduct and with it the logic of family organization. In this sector more than others, the household remained directly attuned to the needs of the family business. Work was delegated by sex. The man took care of the fieldwork and held power over his farm in the old manner as household head. The wife presided over the interior of the house and the dairy barns (care of the horses was deemed men's work). The gendered character of the division of labor affected the structure of the farm family; it also helped to perpetuate the patriarchal character of marriage and intergenerational relations. The father was the highest authority. He held the land, organized the work, and guaranteed the obedience and the conduct of his wife, children, and servants both on and off the farm. All family members were dependent on one another, and were aware from early on that the farm defined their life.

Within the peasant family the position of father and director of the enterprise was combined. Masculinity appeared to be a biological, a social, and an economic attribute. The peasant wife, no matter how competent, followed her husband's leadership as a matter of course. Marriage was a work partnership, and the manner of raising children also turned mainly on the roles that youngsters would eventually play on the farm. A separate period of childhood was barely apparent in the countryside. Children merely wore smaller versions of adult clothing and worked with smaller tools. They were not educated theoretically; instead, their training consisted of observation and learning by doing. This was true for all rural classes, even though otherwise there were clear distincions between rich and poor which the hierarchy of landownership demarcated.

The Family of the Weimar Era

Despite the many changes in family form and practices that accompanied the vast socioeconomic transformations of the nineteenth century, the family continued to be seen as a model of "natural" relations and as a basis of continuities in the social order in the twentieth century. The illusion of an unchanging "traditional" family was called into question during the First World War and the revolution which followed. The disasters of the battlefront and the home front and the disruption of family life which the war had brought challenged the usual practices of family life and the larger social order as well.[10]

Timidly the Weimar Republic—the new parliamentary German state established in 1918 after the collapse of the war effort and subsequently the *Reich*—attempted to break down class privileges, and the privileges of aristocratic and bourgeois families. Nevertheless, much of the old society, and the old accustomed patterns of patriarchalism, remained in force.

The economic disruptions literally hit home. The debt incurred in the war and the disastrous inflation it produced eroded the material basis of middle-class family life. The old middle classes, who had lost their savings, suffered the greatest economic losses in the aftermath of the war. In 1918 the value of a mark had sunken to 50 pfennig; by November 1923 one U.S. dollar was worth 4.2 billion paper marks. Many middle-class families still clung to their expectations of a bourgeois standard of living, but their resources no longer could support it. Memoirs of this era tell of strategies for keeping up appearances in the face of new deprivations. For example, according to Walter Kempowski, who recounted the work involved in keeping up the family linen closet, a sign of middle-class pride: "the shelves had to be lined with paper, white with small blue stars, and the inventory made of what one had. Bed sheets, quilt covers with their rows of matching buttons. Once again, check everything and mend it. What did Aunt Basta actually do? From a prominent family, somehow become impoverished, she always was such a help. The good old woman. She sewed the whole dowry then."

For the working classes, fluctuating and often high levels of unemployment were the worst problem. Workers who were employed, armed as they were with the newly acquired right to collective bargaining, managed to keep apace of inflation better than the middle classes. Moreover, the national and local systems of social support, ranging from government-subsidized housing to health services and recreation, expanded greatly under the Weimar regime. Government money was made available for rent subsidies and for the construction of low-income housing. The impact of these programs was especially noticeable in cities like Berlin and Frankfurt, where the new housing projects relocated as much as 10 percent of the city's population in the second half of the 1920s.[11]

In addition to the economic and policy changes that affected family life the ideological basis of the patriarchal nuclear family shifted. Even before the war the emergence of psy-

A Sunday outing in 1930 reflects the changing role of the German father.

The "Frankfurt Kitchen" of the 1920s designed by the architect Grete Schütte-Lihotzky.

chology as a discipline, as well as more popular expressions of psychological insights, had called the patriarchal model into question. But the increasing popularity of psychological interpretations in middle-class circles in the 1920s cast doubt on many older family practices. Through the work of Sigmund Freud (1856–1939) the veil of taboos surrounding sexuality was lifted. Discussion of sexual urges and sexual repression and their social consequences became commonplace and were seen as having a new significance for the development of culture in general. Freud had argued that the subliminal sex drive had an especially important influence on cultural development, that it made possible "higher" psychic activities such as science, art, and philosophy.

Wilhelm Reich (1897–1957) went a step further, arguing that while sexual repression indeed provided a psychological basis for a *specific*—namely, patriarchal—culture in all its forms, it was not necessary as the basis of culture in general. Reich attempted to combine psychoanalysis and dialectical materialism and clearly recognized the historical interaction between family and social structure. His work launched a somewhat different kind of social-psychological tradition, which was particularly important for the psychological critique of authoritarianism that would emerge later.

Carlo Mense (1886–1965). Family portrait. Family size diminished in the 1920s.

But it was not only the *theory* of sexuality that was changing. Prewar changes in sexual behavior, fertility, and relations between married couples accelerated in the twenties and became apparent to social observers. Demographic evidence shows that, although the trend toward smaller families began later in Germany than in many other western European countries, the transition to small families occurred more rapidly once it began. In the 1920s crude birthrates declined faster than at any other point in German history. The large family of German mythology very rapidly shrank to a couple of children. Now not only were proper middle-class women restricting the number of children they bore, but so too, demonstrably, were women of the lower classes. Battles over birth-control clinics and the legality of abortion brought sexual politics to the center of the political stage.[12] Popular culture, especially films, cabarets, and songs, brought awareness of the various messages of sexual revolt into the mainstream, even if the term "New Women" could in fact be applied only to a minority of the younger urban female population.[13]

Some of these changes related to new family strategies in the working classes. Since the turn of the century fewer families had been relying on the labor of young children to make ends meet. In addition, many more women were working outside of the home. As in other countries, the employment of women had accelerated sharply during the war, but high rates of female wage labor persisted afterward. In Germany, 35 percent of the work force was female in the mid-twenties, a figure that was higher than any other European country except for France. Women had long worked on farms, in the textile industry, and as servants. Now many also took jobs in the expanding service and clerical sectors.

Although these changes meant that the old material bases of the patriarchal family eroded somewhat, conditions were far from ideal for these New Women. Those who worked now worked a double day, since they continued to be responsible for household maintenance. The new appliances and more efficient kitchens built in the modern housing projects of the Weimar era helped somewhat, but the overall burden on working women was still great, as the following excerpt from a textileworker's account of her daily life attests: "At six o'clock my alarm clock wakes me up and thus begins my workday. Washing and dressing are my first jobs; as for grooming, there's not much to do in that regard because I have short hair. Then I put on water for coffee and get some bread and butter ready for my husband and me. With that I'm ready and it's also time to wake my husband because he has a half hour bike ride to his workplace. *While he's getting dressed, I get his bicycle ready.* I pump air in the tires and fasten on his lunchbox. He drinks his coffee and soon he's on his way. I go to the front window and wave him goodbye. Now it's 7:45 and I must quickly bring a little order to the place. I have only a small apartment, but it nonetheless takes some doing in order to make it look right. At 8:15 I also have to leave. I work in the colored-pattern weaving section from 8:30 to 12:30 without stop. I eat my breakfast about 9. *But I don't let my looms stop; they continue working, for when one works by contract, one has to keep going in order to earn something.* At 12:30 it's time for lunch and I return home quickly. After eating, I clean the hall and stairs, and meanwhile it's 1:45 and time to go. Work then goes from 2 to 5 without stop. But when it's five, I go back to my little place with a happy heart. Then my husband soon returns, and I have always taken great pains to have his dinner ready on time. Then I wash the dishes and my husband reads me the newspaper."[14]

As this one woman's experience suggests, relations between couples were also changing, though perhaps not as much as the popular culture around sexuality would suggest. On the one hand, emerging sexual norms recognized women's sexual needs as legitimate and countered taboos around discussion of sexual matters. But part and parcel of the "rationalization" of sexuality in the 1920s was the emphasis on heterosexual intercourse and closeness between spouses as the center of a successful marriage. This served to raise expectations on the part of both spouses entering marriage, and also to channel wives' sexuality toward the kinds of pleasure approved by the growing number of experts on marriage. Non-heterosexual forms of physical intimacy, as well as close relationships between women whether or not they included a sexual dimension, became suspect.[15] Networks of association, friendship, and support among women were certainly weakened as a result.

If change was apparent in many German families in the Weimar era, there remained preserves of traditional family life: rural farm families where women still worked as "family helpers" under the direction of their husbands and rarely owned or operated farms in their own right, as well as the more conservative sectors of the middle classes like civil servants, academics, and professionals. Changes that occurred, and those only feared, generated a conservative backlash. Conservative critics saw in the new family patterns grave dangers for German social order. The city of Berlin, with its emancipated sexual mores, its communities of openly practicing homosexuals, its high abortion rate and low fertility, was anathema to those who feared social breakdown and "race suicide."[16]

The racial thinking that was so central to Nazi ideology was based in part in this conservative backlash against the loosening of patriarchy and the changes in sexuality and family life that seemed to typify the Weimar era. The goal of increasing the birthrate among Aryans led the Nazis, once they came to power in 1933, to inaugurate family policies intended to reinvigorate patriarchal models of the family and society and to reestablish older patterns of more prolific childbearing among the racially pure.[17] Nevertheless, Nazi policy with respect to the family was as contradictory as many other aspects of Nazi policy. In the name of restoring tradition, the Nazi state did more than any other regime to break down parental autonomy and to make the family simply a vehicle of state policy.

Intimations of Nazi ideology for the family were already apparent in *Mein Kampf*. For example, Hitler noted that the main emphasis of girls' education would rest upon "physical training, only afterward on the spiritual, and lastly intellectual values. The *aim* of female education is inalterably the future mother." If Hitler's writings formed the inspiration for family policy, a highly politicized science provided a more careful set of guideposts. The writings of Horst Becker (b. 1906), who drew upon the work of the conservative nineteenth-century sociologist of the family Wilhelm Heinrich Riehl, reflected the spirit of the Nazi movement. Becker took from Riehl his static picture of the family. He argued that the family is part of "the

Family Policy under National Socialism

natural order of things" and that it serves as "the protector of blood, the keeper of bloodlines." Becker was also in agreement with Riehl about the origins of the family: the inequality of man and woman within the family are God-willed and "ordained by nature."

The irrationality of his views tie them to the blood-and-soil mysticism that originated in earlier eras. From his starting point it was just a small step to the glorification of the peasant class per se and of its family form, which "seems to have sprung from the depths of unmediated nature like a plant."[18] The glorification of the peasant family, or rather of the *image* that had been constructed of it as an ideology—as emerging victoriously from the Germanic tribes, preserved pure and unaltered in its present form—was the general theme of Becker's book.

The bourgeois family, whose origins Becker documents with a series of interpretations of classic family paintings, aroused his suspicion: "The bourgeois family contains within it the source of its own demise. It is removed from the work of everyday life and from the public world, and it shows a growing tendency toward independence. It has profited from this isolation in that love, the personal side of family relations, has become the basis and center of the family. The farm family exists in a wider world. As a working community led by the father, the farm family is an active member of the economic order of the people. Represented by the farm head, the family exists politically in the village as well. It is much more than a private bond and anything but a site of relaxation and retreat."

This analysis, it is worth noting, makes ahistorical presumptions to serve particular ideological ends. It argues as a constant of history an image of the family that was in fact a continually changing reality. Becker used this imagery to argue for a particular kind of family useful for political purposes. According to this vision, marriage is regarded not, as in the bourgeois family, as "just a matter of love anymore, but rather as a political responsibility and the basis of requirements of racial hygiene and racial politics. To conceive and bear children is a national duty, a necessity for population policy."

At the same time that this kind of thinking put new emphasis on the family as a biological breeding grounds, it also established the state's claims upon the young. Family love, according to Becker, is merely personal. This loving attitude needed to be expanded to include "the whole community of the Volk. In order for this to happen, family socialization must

be supplemented by teams for young people, youth organizations, the army, and the schools."

In particular, the education of boys along the lines of heroic male-bonded models could not, according to National Socialist political ideas, remain a family matter. It had to be placed in the hands of the party. "My pedagogy is hard," said Hitler in his speeches, "the weak must be hammered away. In my new order there will grow a youth before which the world will shrink in fear . . . I don't want an intellectual education . . . rather [boys] must learn to dominate. They must learn in the face of the most difficult trials to conquer the fear of death for my sake. This is the test of a heroic youth."[19]

The Nazi claim that "the family [is] the nucleus of the state" was thus no more than a slogan to allay fears. It was true only from a biological point of view, since as a site of socialization, the family had virtually no role to play as far as the Nazi Führer was concerned. Its function was reduced as never before in its entire social history since the time of the

Drum corps of the Hitler Youth.

The Nazi Mother's Cross—
gold, if she had eight or more
children.

Germanic tribes. This policy affected women in particular. Political activity was the preserve of men; motherhood defined women. An article in the Nazi newspaper *Völkischer Beobachter* in 1934 made this clear: "We must set this as an attainable goal: the mother should be able to dedicate herself entirely to her children, the wife to her husband; the unmarried girl should be trained only for those jobs that are compatible with her female character. Beyond this, employment should be left to the man."[20] The aim then was to take back the rights that women of previous generations had fought for.

Policy measures followed these ideals as well. As one of its earliest acts, the Nazi state forbade public employment to married women whose husbands were employed. Low-interest loans were given to young couples in order to help them marry, again on condition that the bride quit her job. Payments at the birth of each child, loan reductions, tax reductions, even full exemption from taxes for families with five or more children all were to serve to populate the "people's state" with a racially pure new generation.

In the center of this policy stood the newly defined housewife, the bearer of young, who from 1936 on was honored with the Mother's Cross in different degrees, depending on the number of children she had: bronze for a mother of four or five, silver for six or seven, and gold for mothers with eight or more children. The aims of these policies were transparent: awards for getting married, provided that the wife agreed not to work, reduced her function and her interest to the household and the raising of children, who (the boys at least) would be turned over to the guardianship of the state immediately upon reaching maturity. The mother was also cut off from her role as intellectual partner, as independent, thinking citizen. The idealized role division placed the father as the politically active and working authority within the family and the mother as housekeeper and childbearer. Children born and raised under such a regime would absorb a concept of authority that permeated the entire political system.

The pronatalist policy was not the total cultural success its authors had hoped for. According to a January 6, 1937, article in the *Frankfurter Zeitung*: "The Art Council of the Reich has announced that, according to the Office of Racial Policy of the NSDAP, there are many images appearing today in the public eye that still show the German family pictured with one or two children. National Socialism is vigorously combatting the two-child system, because it is leading to the irremediable downfall of the German people. It supports the call for at least four children per family in order to maintain current population levels. Whenever artistic considerations allow it—and this should be possible in most cases—artists, especially painters and commercial artists, should set themselves the goal of depicting within the framework of artistic potential at least four German children whenever a 'family' is portrayed."

Whatever the cause, by the late 1930s the crude birthrate did show an upward turn in Germany, in contrast with all other Western societies of the Depression decade. Just why some women responded favorably to pronatalism is not entirely clear. Certainly Nazi policy addressed the contradictions felt by many women who attempted to combine paid work and childbearing. If most of what the Party offered was symbolic, and demographers argue that the upturn in births was more a result of an increased number of marriages rather than increased family size, it is nevertheless likely that the Party did succeed in using the state to alter family strategies and using its appeal to traditional family values to recruit support for the state.[21]

By the late thirties the extremes to which the state was willing to go in pursuit of its racial policy were becoming clear. The other side of the encouragment of high fertility for racially acceptable couples was the suppression of the sexual and reproductive freedoms of categories of people deemed "undesirable," or "racially alien," as well as the suppression of the rights of Aryan women to limit fertility. Abortion was punished rigorously. Homosexuals were arrested and often interred in concentration camps along with Jews and Gypsies—groups targeted as racial inferiors. Although debate continues about precedents for sterilization policies prior to the Nazi era, that they were in force under the fascist regime is clear. After January 1, 1934, laws forcing sterilizations and the limitation of reproduction along racial and also class lines became standard practice. By creating an ideal standard for "proper" reproduction—a father who earned the sole income and a healthy Aryan mother who ran the household as a dependent of her husband—Nazi policy "barred unwelcome poor and deviant women from procreation and marriage."[22] Because, as Gisela Bock has pointed out, selection of candidates for sterilization was carried out by hospital, school, prison, concentration camp, and welfare authorities, most of whom had greater contact with the poor, lower-class women were overrepresented among the victims of sterilization. In addition, forced sterilization was the brutal fate of those deemed racially inferior and of sex offenders. The horrors perpetrated in the name of racial policy pushed to an extreme its perverted consistencies. The promotion of "healthy" family values for the racially pure, the suppression of women's reproductive rights, and the symbolic elevation of the patriarchal family with many children were one side of a policy whose other side was genocidal brutality.

This racial policy spilled over into, and sometimes collided with other aspects of the Nazi program; the real contradictions inherent in Nazi family policy became clear only with the war. As in other countries, the German war effort placed new demands on its citizens. Among these was the need for additional labor power. In Great Britain, and later in the United States, new labor power was supplied by an increasing number of women who entered, or in the case of Britain, were even conscripted into the labor force. The Nazi leadership was reluctant to recruit or coerce women to join the war effort because of their ideological opposition to women in the workplace and because of the extent to which their popularity no doubt rested on the social benefits they provided, including the system of family supports. The war brought all this into question, as families were separated and male breadwinners

German and foreign labor in the war economy, 1939–1944[a] (in millions).

Year	German labor			Industrial labor		Foreign labor	Overall workforce
	Men	Women	Total	Women	Total		
1939	24.5	14.6	39.1	2.6	10.4	0.3	39.4
1940	20.4	14.4	34.8	2.5	9.4	1.2	36.0
1941	19.0	14.1	33.1	2.6	9.0	3.0	36.1
1942	16.9	14.4	31.3	2.5	8.3	4.2	35.5
1943	15.5	14.8	30.3	2.8	8.0	6.3	36.6
1944	14.2	14.8	29.0	2.7	7.7	7.1	36.1
1944[b]	13.5	14.9	28.4	2.6	7.5	7.5	35.9

Source: Eva Kolinsky, *Women in West Germany: Life, Work and Politics* (Oxford and New York: Berg, 1989), p. 22.

a. Within the borders of the German Reich, September 1, 1939.

b. Data for September 1944 and July 1944 for the labor force and women in industry adapted from R. Wagenführ, *Die deutsche Industrie im Kriege, 1939–1945* (Berlin: Colloquium, 1963), p. 139, and Alan Milward, *The German Economy at War* (London: Athlone, 1965), p. 47.

were conscripted into the army and thus off the farms and out of the factories. But although women were forced to head households under trying circumstances, in the early years of the war at least their numbers in the workforce actually diminished. Their labor, which was significant but not adequate, was supplemented by increasing numbers of slaves, concentration-camp inmates, and prisoners of war.

The eventual defeat in the war, and the destruction that accompanied it, destroyed both the material base for and the ideological justification of the Nazi model family. The postwar states and the occupying powers saw a need for immediate reconstruction—not only of Germany's devastated cities but also of the family in ruins.

Nazi policymakers were not the only ones concerned with connections between family life and political agendas in the 1930s. It is also important to note how critics of the Nazi state, especially a prominent group of émigré social psychologists, regarded these developments. Many analysts of the Nazi regime, during the thirties and later, even felt that they had found the key to the success of Hitler's system in the traditional family arrangements of the German people.

The Authoritarian Family

Max Horkheimer, Erich Fromm, and Herbert Marcuse published many of their studies on authority relations in the family after their emigration in the mid-1930s. Their work, centered on new accounts of individual psychological development, raised important questions about relations between familial and political authorities. Fromm argued that during the phase of superego development the individual internalizes the views of figures who represent external authority. The individual learns to behave according to rules established by these authorities as if they were his or her own. In extremely authoritarian contexts, this act of projection removes from the individual the capacity for autonomous reason and forms the basis of irrational attachments to authority even in adult life. According to this view, "it would be difficult for the adult to hold authorities in the same awe if these authorities did not possess, because of this projection of the superego onto them, the same power that parents once held over the uncritical child."[23] These new views argued that the political system of authoritarian rule had a basis in the early childhood experiences in the family, and particularly in the strict patriarchal family of German tradition. This group of social psychologists succeeded in illustrating the interdependence between authoritarian family socialization and Fascism and in discovering how smoothly the dictators of their time exploited psychological mechanisms.

The Postwar Family

Despite these critiques, the family policy followed by the new West German state in the aftermath of the war reflected conservative family attitudes that were consistent with the Federal Republic's alignment with the West in the early Cold War era. Family policy, and family images, were once again formulated in the light of political necessities. In 1953 the government of the Federal Republic of Germany established a Federal Ministry for Family Concerns (today called the Federal Ministry for Health), formally recognizing the political significance of family life for the first time in history. This move reflected the family's status as a site for regenerating the working population, and also the political plan to use the family as a basis from which to rebuild the old order in the wake of postwar turmoil.

In this political context family sociology too was reestablished on a new footing and new research projects were conducted. Gerhard Wurzbacher, for example, undertook an analysis of the evolution of the nuclear family and its support networks. Hilde Thurnwald interviewed nearly five hundred Berlin families in the late 1940s about their living conditions and perceptions of themselves. The family sociologist Helmut Schelsky argued that the family was the only remnant of stability in the postwar situation. He believed that the restructuring of society could be accomplished only through the family, a view reminiscent of the ideas of Riehl a hundred years earlier. Like Riehl, Schelsky decried the decline of familial authority and attacks on the traditional form of the family, and he turned sharply against the critical ideas of the émigré social psychologists of the 1930s and of the leftist Frankfurt School. He attempted to erect a rigid barrier between the private domain of the family and public laws of society. This lively interest in the subject of family sociology in the period after the Second World War resulted from the belief that at that time the family was often the sole support system that remained after the war and as a result had a great societal relevance.

After this initial phase of West German family sociological research there emerged a second period associated with the *Wirtschaftswunder*—the economic miracle of the late 1950s and 1960s. With economic recovery, severe deprivation disappeared. Some formerly employed wives and mothers returned to their household duties. In many families the husband and father again assumed the breadwinner role. Prestige was attached to the claim that "my wife doesn't need to work." Once again these new arrangements were enshrined as *the* traditional family form. The family's structure was connected with its new political role: "the family" rose from the ashes of ruin for the greater good of the state. This new image was pursued on a variety of fronts, including appropriate family television series. In 1960–1963, for example, there was "Family Hesselbach," developed from a successful radio show of the 1950s. The series portrayed a patriarchal German family, and its influence on the thinking and behavior of the audience was investigated in exemplary communities.

But underneath the image of the restored nuclear family dramatic changes were continuing to occur. Even as new images of female domesticity proliferated in West Germany in the 1950s and early 1960s, women were beginning to move back into the labor force. These changes began once again to lead to questions about sociological thought and government policy in the West. In this context, the work of Elisabeth Pfeil and Helga Pross, for example, is characteristic. Pfeil studied the impact of the move of women from home and kitchen into career. Pross argues that changes in the economic conditions have always been critical for family life and changes in it, and in particular for decisions about the bearing and raising of children.

The Wirtschaftswunder

In East Germany the government that took control after the war approached family law and policy from a very different perspective. The dire need to rebuild the resources and population of the devastated country, in the context of a socialist theoretical commitment to the full participation of women in the workforce, produced very different policies. Women were encouraged to work, and to obtain the training necessary for future jobs. Pressures resulting from the combination of work and family roles for women were eased by official support for child-care services and by the so-called

The Situation in East Germany

"baby year" policy of liberal maternity leave with 70 percent pay. Despite the strong pronatalism behind these measures, the government always supported the right to an abortion for any women who could show physiologial, psychological, or social reasons for wanting one. This law was further liberalized in the early 1970s, removing the need for a woman in the early stages of pregnancy to have her motives examined at all.

The very different consequences of these different policies are apparent from the contrasting postwar histories of women's education and workforce participation, and in the provision of such services as day-care in the two Germanies. First, the proportion of the labor force comprised of women hovered just above a third in West Germany throughout the 1960s and 1970s, whereas in East Germany in the same period it rose to half. (The subsequent rise in the West brought female employment to nearly the same rate, but this is a more recent development.) Second, women represented a far smaller proportion of students in institutions of higher learning in West Germany than in the East, and indeed, lower than in many other Western countries as well. Third, by the late 1970s childcare facilities were available for around two-thirds of pre-kindergarten-aged children, and 90 percent of kindergarten-aged children; the corresponding percentages in the West were 7 and 52 percent respectively. The different abortion policies were reflected in different trends in maternal death rates, with these dropping particularly noticeably in the East after the liberalization of the abortion law there in 1972.[24]

Gender Differences in Contemporary Germany

In both Germanies persistent problems and contradictions confronted families, and from the point-of-view of women facing job and family responsibilities, the end of family history has not arrived. Throughout Germany, as elsewhere in the industrial world, women often face a double burden of paid work and housework. These dilemmas are rooted in old traditions and expectations. "For thousands of years, there has been a widespread belief that there are certain inherent 'male' and 'female' characteristics, but really these should be attributed to different kinds of socialization. These different characteristics are usually the result of unequal treatment. If parental care is differentiated from birth according to the sex of the child—with aggressive behavior, energy and ambition encouraged in one sex and discouraged at every opportunity in the other—how should these children be able to attain equality as adults? Kindergartens and schools, which allegedly practice equality, cannot be very successful so long as boys and girls are trained at home to fill different roles later in life: the one to lead, rule, be self-confident and capable of success; the other to be subordinate and exhibit the so-called 'female' characteristics." This opinion, expressed by a twenty-year-old West German woman in a letter to *Die Zeit* in July 1977, decries attitudes that are still alive. Clichéd sex roles and gender-specific education still exist today. The author of the letter correctly recognized the origins of this apparently insurmountable limitation in the subtle persistence of patriarchal family norms.

How do the traditional relationships between father and mother, son and daughter, brother and sister, older and younger generation, express themselves in contemporary German family patterns, and where can changes be seen? Certainly gender differences in childrearing persist. Boys "learn that it is beneath their dignity to help with housework, and later as spouses they consider it self-evident that the woman does all the housework in addition to her job. Girls usually receive less education than boys; this is justified by the argument that girls will marry. Since girls are socialized from birth to fulfill their future role as wife and mother, they themselves often regard practical training as senseless." This complaint of an eighteen-year-old interviewed in *Die Zeit* in 1977 still hits home, because these roles continue to be taught from a very early age.

Intelligent and well-educated women are often considered to be lacking in erotic appeal and too "difficult" to marry. To this day what really constitutes "female" and "male" behavior remains an issue, but popular slogans suggest that old notions are still alive. Just to mention a few: "Boys don't cry," "You have to learn to hit back," and "Boys don't play with dolls" vis-à-vis "Young ladies don't get dirty," "Girls don't hit," and "As a girl you have to help around the house more." If a girl shows a particular interest in scientific matters, people say "they wasted a boy on you." These clichés, which many children (perhaps somewhat less among intellectuals) internalize from earliest childhood on, lead to conflicts in future life and hinder women as well as men from developing their full potential.

The distance that remains to travel toward egalitarian family and gender attitudes was revealed in the controversy over the reform of family law in the Federal Republic in the

1970s and in surveys taken around that time. "GERMAN FATHER FIGURE UNCHANGED" was the way one headline in *Der Spiegel* reported the situation in the mid-1970s. According to their survey, "in one out of every three 'intact' West German families (husband employed, wife at home, at least two children), fathers found time to spend with his children during the workweek either "never" or "at most twice." Yet half of these fathers belonged to a club, a political party, or some other organization, whose meetings a quarter of the fathers attended once or twice a week or more. Their discussions with wives centered mainly on school assignments and problems with the children. Family decisions reflected his opinions more than hers.

In a questionnaire distributed by the Infas-Institute in 1976 only one citizen in twenty-five thought that wives should have the right to sign contracts in their own name. Women and men disagreed in their responses to such surveys. Women tended to agree that the same general moral concepts should apply for both sexes; they wanted to be treated not like men, but certainly like human beings. Men tended to emphasize the differences between the sexes and their different perspectives.[25] Such findings illustrate that changes in consciousness about the division of family roles does not always follow automatically from changes in women's occupational roles.

The fuller labor force participation of women in the East undermined many of, but by no means eradicated, these attitudes. East German feminists complained about the presumption that it was their responsibility to take on the housework and serve their husbands, even when their workday was just as long. As in the West, the women's movement of the 1970s and 1980s concentrated on the establishment of reproductive rights (the stringent West German abortion law was modified somewhat in the late seventies) and equality in the family and the workplace. But in addition, efforts of East German feminists often turned to the creation of spaces women could call their own, toward the opening of rights of self-expression, and toward examination of the costs they incur as bearers of the double burden.

Rethinking Marriage and the Family

A deep uncertainty about traditional "family" institutions is obvious in contemporary statistical evidence. In West Germany the rate of marriages fell steadily after 1950; in fact it was halved (from 10.7 to 5.4 per 1000). On the other hand, the number of couples living together without marrying rose. This practice is hard to track statistically, but is increasingly accepted.

Parallel to this decline in marriage, the number of births is sinking steadily. In 1900 the crude birthrate was still around 36 births per 1000 population. The rate dropped in the 1920s to half that, rose during the Nazi era to around 20 per 1000, and is now falling again throughout Germany. Whereas before the First World War families of five or six children were common, today the norm is one or two children. Illegitimate births are also on the rise.

Changing patterns of marriage illustrate contemporary family patterns especially clearly. In comparison with a generation or two earlier, the changes in this institution have been symbolically quite dramatic, even if they are diffuse and difficult to document quantitatively. A few decades ago people spoke of illegal cohabitation in whispers. In upper-class circles such marriagelike relationships were called "wild marriage"; among the lower classes they were decried as "illicit." But after the war society began to judge such relationships less harshly. Widely tolerated "uncle marriages," where the couple shunned the marriage bureau so that the war-widow bride would not by remarriage lose her war-widow pension, became common.

It could be that this type of marriage was pioneering. Despite the old norms of sexual virtue, the children of such unions were treated without prejudice. Now marriages "without a license" are quite common, having begun in intellectual and student circles but spread to wider social circles. There are many reasons for this change. Through more effective methods of birth control, above all the Pill, young couples gained a degree of certainty in planning births, which had never before been the case. Another reason for the new form of cohabitation is the clear change in the way the two sexes see themselves and their life plans. Instead of expecting to be taken care of through marriage, of going from dependence on a father to dependence on a husband, young women increasingly look for a partnership between two people with the same rights. In East Germany many young women even used the services and supports made available by the state to bear and raise children on their own.

Even in more conservative West Germany marriage law no longer stipulated that the woman must assume the man's family name. Many combinations are now permitted in Germany, and this change signifies a large step in the direction of emancipation. As a result, the change from Fräulein to Frau, which in previous eras was a change heavily endowed with meaning, no longer means very much, since in official contexts every adult female has the right to the title of Frau. This change in bureaucratic usage banished from official linguistic usage a form of address characteristic of the old patriarchal society that was particularly denigrating to women. The new legal change, at least in theory, means that women will no longer be labeled by marital status—single or married—a distinction which would be unthinkable if applied to men. This linguistic change has begun to catch on only recently and is not recognized by all classes and political groups. It signifies a conscious rejection of the elevation of women who are wives and mothers over unmarried women, and a turn toward a recognition of all women's equality as human beings.

It is another sign of the times that such changes are evolving spontaneously rather than by regulation. Beside the new, creative, or novel ways of doing things, traditional relationships preserve their place. In part this reflects men's fears of skilled and successful career women, who call into question the traditional image of male superiority and strength. This is clear from surveys and studies in both the western and eastern parts of Germany. The submissive housewife is, now as before, more desirable as a marriage partner than is an independent female personality. A number of outward signs reveal this persistence of older conceptions, for example, the continued popularity of bride in white with veil and wreath. The meaning of such customs is rarely the subject of reflection or analysis, but these continued practices indicate the continuance of old marital ideals.

Nevertheless, we should not underestimate even timid steps in the direction of new social forms. That they exist side-by-side with more conservative and even reactionary ways of thinking reflects the pluralism of a democracy. Moreover, these changes affect all social classes; this too is something new. They affect the lives of women most directly in their work and family options, more deeply in their intellectual life and their erotic personalities. Practices considered taboo or ridiculed in the 1950s have become commonplace among young people today, whose individual choices reflect all shades of possibility. Life has become less constrained by custom, freer from hypocrisy.

Not every sign of change is positive. The rate of employment of German women today could indicate their growing emancipation. But as long as attitudes toward marriage and the family and the division of labor in the family do not change fundamentally, a career for women in addition to household and child-rearing often leads not to self-realization but to an unbearable overburden. Tensions between married couples find expression in the growing number of divorces. Divorce rates reflect the extent to which the institution of marriage is being called into question. The old divorce laws, according to which a marriage could be terminated only if one of the spouses was found guilty of destroying the marriage, were superseded in the old Germany by a legal reform in 1977. The state of the marriage, the basis of the decision granting divorce, and the dissolution takes place within a framework of the equal rights of husband and wife.

A new understanding of marriage is reflected in these

Left: A rural bridal couple in Hesse, wearing traditional costumes (1919). Right: A more recent wedding party (1950), with the bride in white, indicates the continuing popularity of formal practices.

A German family scene of the 1970s.

laws. The fragility of relationships built primarily on feelings and dependencies, which bring exaggerated mutual expectations to both partners, is giving way to more independent relationships, in which shared interests and conversations replace the older notion of "eternal love." A general lack of interest in rituals of betrothal is another sign of change. When marriage was seen as the central ceremony of life, the old customs offered a wealth of reminders of the departure from youth, the transition from a free and easy life to a phase of burden and responsibility. For young people today the wedding brings no decisive shift, no surprises. The large number of divorces reflects the impermanence of family relations. Not even the mother-child bond is taken for granted as natural anymore. Role clichés still hold, to be sure, and children have tended to be awarded to the mother in divorce cases decided by West German law. But such stereotyped decisions in custody cases do not always meet today's realities.

A recent ad in the "personals" section of *Die Zeit* gives evidence of new kinds of family arrangements: "Family (31/29/1), tired of the performance principle and of being ruled by others, is seeking partners for an alternative life-style without party line. Details at . . . " As this advertisement suggests, the well-ordered family of the achievement-oriented society, with its traditional roles, is losing ground. Whether this means the demise of marriage and family per se, depends on what these basic forms of social life come to mean. A model of family life dominated by the norms of the upper classes, to which workers were the exception, does not fit today's more open social landscape. Once, in propertied milieux, everything was stipulated and life was regulated from the cradle to the grave by the power of "what will people think." Relations of dependency of different kinds set rules, and deviations were noted. If today many of the younger generation refuse such well-worn patterns of life, it is—we should be clear about this—no less than a rejection of bourgeois values and norms, not necessarily a rejection of all family or familylike living arrangements.

Many seek and discover new kinds of relationships, formalized or spontaneous patterns of everyday personal relationships. Almost anything is allowed; the only condition is freedom from coercion. Still, new patterns of relationships are often pie in the sky, since after more than a thousand years of patriarchal practices and family organization and accustomed patterns of power, it cannot be changed all in one generation. In many circles these initiatives are perceived as dangerous and antifamily. It is therefore problematic to draw a clear outline of "the family" in contemporary German society.

The new trends affect the generations in very different ways. Contemporary life-styles involving less committed relationships are especially difficult for the older generation to accept. The amount of space at hand or the nerves of the young, often both, cannot support intergenerational coresidence. So the nursing home becomes the last refuge for many—a solution synonymous with loveless dependence, isolation, and lack of freedom. Whereas at one time the family had taken over the care of the older generation—though not always in perfect harmony—today public institutions have taken its place. The anonymity of personal relations in this last phase of life, the lack of care, in fact often simply the lack of news from the people they feel closest to, is hard for the grandparent generation to comprehend. The elderly thus have to bear the hardest burden of the new family practices and loosening of social ties, and they suffer the most with increasing emphasis on individuality.

But here too alternative activities are developing. The senior citizens have been discovered by tourism and the entertainment industry as new target groups; they are also beginning to interest themselves in areas that once were not thought of in connection with elderly people. It is becoming clear that family life sometimes means unnecessary passivity and decline for the older generation, habits traditionally associated with growing old. Breaking away from the family, if their health is good, can often mean freedom for older people to enjoy a pleasant phase of life.

For children too the effects have been mixed. There are indications of changing attitudes toward children, for example, the status of the illegitimate. On the one hand, law reforms grant children born out of wedlock better economic and psychological conditions of life and have pulled them out of their previous marginality. More young women today find the strength to have a child without a legal father or to have an abortion. What in the nineteenth century was a theme of melodramatic tragedy—the young girl unmarried and pregnant—is not a comedy today, but it is no longer unspeakable; it is a socially recognized possibility. Also new is the story of the half success of German feminists in the former West Germany in the campaign against Paragraph 218 of the Civil Law Code, a campaign that made abortion more readily available in the Federal Republic and brought into public discussion matters that would have been talked about only behind closed doors a generation earlier.

Sexual matters in general are more subject to discussion; for children new approaches to sex education have brought about the final banishment of the stork. Today's middle-aged and older generations are aware of the stresses and limitations resulting from lack of sex education for adolescents; they therefore tend to appreciate the relative freedom from sexual taboos in which children grow up today.

These developments should by no means be taken as an indication of an eternal upward evolution in family and child-hood conditions. The current upheaval in child-rearing prac-tices also brings many negatives. Besides the fun of learning with "Sesame Street" there are the television shows watched by many children, who, often alone in front of the screen, are confronted with unexplained scenes and fears. Alongside the frank explanations in the biology class, there are the premature sexual discussions and activities with peers, along with the continued taboos of many parents, leaving the child trapped amid many conflicting messages and pressures, indoctrinated in dangerous ways, and hindered in understanding his or her real needs. In the meantime, fables and storybooks, even in this emancipated era, often still convey an ideal of home life centered on a full-time mother, images of stereotyped gender roles, and pictures of a happy world filled with blooming gardens and virtuous craftsmen.

In the arena of violence too the picture is mixed. Certainly corporal punishment is officially frowned upon and forbidden in school. Nevertheless, statistics gathered in West Germany in the 1970s indicated six thousand annual cases of excessive child abuse suspected and approximately two hundred cases resulting in death.[26] World politics revolve around peace and détente, but the toy industry continues to produce war toys, and many parents buy them for their children.

On the social front progress is uncertain. It is apparent that we have not yet arrived at an optimal situation with regard to equality of social openness. The situation of children varies notably by parental social class. Innovations of the last century include such important amenities as playgrounds (in the 1920s public parks and sandboxes for children were a major break-through). Schools are still informally class-structured. From 1970 on the idea of a common comprehensive school predom-inated in the Federal Republic, replacing an earlier system of specific schools for the children of different social classes. The aim has been to equalize opportunities. Still, by 1980 only one in ten working-class children in the former West Germany got an advanced education; children of the lower classes remained as before scholastically disadvantaged, a problem exacerbated by the growing number of the most deprived of all: children of guest workers.[27]

The problems, however, are at least apparent to many and the claims of children and youth of all social groups at least are recognized. The right to attend school without prejudice and fear, and the school as a humane workplace for children—these goals are worth striving for by parents as well.

What Family for a United Germany?

Change is visible on all fronts, but no clear picture of the future emerges. This is probably typical of a democratic era—ambiguity and dissolution of predominant ideological frames. In hierarchical class societies the need for symbolic barriers exists, especially to divide the upper from the lower classes. This need for barriers was true also for the historical family, with its patriarchal authority structure in which children were the subordinate class and had to be trained to conformity and obedience. The era of authoritarian power as the social norm has ended, even if its afterpains are still often perceptible and some long for its return.

As in other historic moments of transformation, the reconstruction of a united Germany that will dominate political development in the 1990s will also bring family matters into the political arena. Some areas of acute conflict have emerged already. Will the new state follow the old West German family law, or will this law be reformed to meet the presumptions of women in the former East Germany about their right to employment, education, and control over their reproductive functions? A woman interviewed in the summer of 1990 commented that in a united Germany the imposition of West Germany's abortion law, "would be a terrible step backward for us." Christa Schmidt, formerly East Germany's minister of health and the family, agreed, noting that "if we recommend copying the West German rule, people will get angry with us."[28] Will the old East German day-care centers, with their largely female workforce, simply shut down? Whose jobs will go first with the projected rise in unemployment? Initial talks between representatives of the two states made it clear that existing inconsistencies are unbridgeable; something has to give, but the future is far from certain. Some discussion of the contradictions between the law and policy in the two regions have already taken place; many more conflicts remain to be addressed in the opening years of the newly unified state.[29]

The transition after so many years of patriarchy to a world of participation and partnership in family life continues slowly and in the face of many difficulties, but it is an unstoppable learning process. Only future generations will understand how radical were the changes that the families of the sixties, seventies, and eighties lived through. From the perspective of 1990 we can say only that these changes promise to be as decisive as those of the years of the French and the Industrial revolutions. There can be for our times no other possible rules and prescriptions than those of open conversation, tolerance, and understanding between the generations and the sexes and the abolition of abuses of power that have marked their interactions in the past.

Fathers take a more active role in caring for their children in today's American family.

Myths and Realities of the American Family

Elaine Tyler May

IN 1920 Lorimer Linganfield, a respectable Los Angeles bar-ber, filed for divorce. Although his wife, Marsha, held him in "high regard and esteem as her husband," there were "ev-idences of indiscretion" in her conduct. Her new bathing suit seemed "designed especially for the purpose of exhibiting to the public the shape and form of her body." To his further humiliation, she was "beset with a desire to sing and dance at cafes and restaurants for the entertainment of the public." When Lorimer complained about her "appetite for beer and whiskey," and her extravagant tastes for luxury, she replied that he was "not the only pebble on the beach, she had a millionaire 'guy' who would buy her all the clothes, auto-mobiles, diamonds and booze that she wanted." But the ul-timate insult was her refusal to have sexual intercourse, claiming that she did not want any "dirty little brats around her." The judge was sympathetic, and Lorimer Linganfield won his suit.[1]

At first glance this case appears to be an example of an unfortunate union between a morally righteous man and a woman whose behavior was something less than proper. But on closer examination, when placed in a broad historical con-text, we see in this personal struggle a larger issue that frames the history of American families in the twentieth century. Over the past hundred years family life in the United States has been powerfully shaped by the expectations brought to it—expectations forged in the context of a family ideology that evolved and changed gradually over time. As the ideology of family life altered to fit the conditions of a rapidly urban-izing and industrializing nation, individual women and men struggled to negotiate the terms of their personal lives to create families that they believed would provide them with personal happiness and fulfillment.

The Linganfields were two such individuals in the early years of the twentieth century who tried to achieve their ideal of marital bliss. They came of age, courted, and wed at a time when time-honored values about domesticity put into place by middle-class white Americans in the nineteenth century were being challenged by young people involved in the emerging urban culture of the twentieth century. Marsha Linganfield was shedding the mores of the Victorian past and eager to enter new areas of work and play previously closed to women. Her husband may well have been attracted to the vivacious young woman he wooed and wed for those very reasons. But like many men of his generation, he expected her to settle into proper wifely decorum after their marriage. When she failed to maintain the modest and frugal demeanor he expected of his wife, he began to lose face with his patrons and customers. Marsha's flamboyant behavior tarnished Lorimer's impeccable reputation. Yet the young wife felt constrained by what she believed to be overly prudish and restrictive behavior on the part of her husband; she flaunted her adventurous spirit in spite of his pleas. In this unhappy situation, ironically, it is quite possible that Lorimer Linganfield divorced his wife for precisely the same reasons he married her. The promise of excitement and sexuality combined with family life and children seemed unattainable, and the marriage collapsed.

The ideal for family life in the United States was not invented by government propagandists, media moguls, or Madison Avenue tycoons; it was a product of middle-class American aspirations. In the late nineteenth century it represented a tranquil haven against a competitive, often corrupt, public arena. In the twentieth century it has become the focus of hopes for the good life—for a secure and stable home providing happiness as well as protection in a rapidly changing world. In the later part of this century, as American public life has become increasingly complicated, organized, and fragmented, as community ties have weakened and work life has become routinized and bureaucratic, individual women and men increasingly have turned to the family for personal satisfaction. This intense preoccupation with the family often rests upon a mythic vision of a golden age in which a timeless, stable domestic haven existed. But the myths need revising. Middle-class family life, which has defined the norm over the centuries, has been rooted in social change and deeply connected to the political world.

The modern domestic ideal that has held sway in the United States is a relatively recent invention. It developed in the early decades of the nineteenth century when the nation began to urbanize. Prior to this time, the home was virtually the same as the workplace. Households were productive units that often included not only parents and children, but other relatives, servants, apprentices, or boarders, all of whom participated in the family's economic endeavors. In the emerging cities, however, those who earned the family income (usually the men) increasingly left the home to work in factories, offices, or businesses removed from the family abode. It was during these years that a distinct domestic ideology began to take shape, one that identified the home as the female sphere and defined the family primarily as the nuclear unit comprised of parents and children. In these urban middle-class families, men left the home to work in the rough-and-tumble public arena, and returned for rest and refuge to a morally uplifting domicile where women took care of the children, the household chores, and the husband's needs.

Victorianism—that set of social and cultural values that characterized the white middle class in England and the United States during most of the nineteenth century—dominated cultural values in America long after the Victorian era came to an end. Several studies locate the seeds of Victorian culture on the East Coast, in the affluent segments of the urban population in the latter decades of the eighteenth century. Economic diversity had begun to give rise to a complex and stratified social order. Men no longer automatically inherited their fathers' land and worked alongside women to maintain family farms. Rather, individuals coming of age often left the parental, rural domain to move into new communities and enter new occupations.

The Victorian Legacy

The growing cities attracted large groups of unattached workingmen, as well as entrepreneurs with families who endeavored to secure lucrative economic positions. At the upper strata emerged a group of well-to-do merchants and professionals. It was this class that began to define the cultural form of Victorianism. Men usually worked in a separate sphere, away from their homes. Their wives comprised America's

A four-generation American family in 1898. Victorian ideals of gentility dominated thinking and behavior.

first leisure class, with the time and money to develop a genteel way of life. These were the women and men whose descendants would fill the ranks of the Protestant churches, engage in various campaigns to reform society, and stand at the forefront of economic development and westward movement. Individuals born into this tradition became leaders of the institutions that set the norms for other classes.

As early as the 1820s and 1830s, what came to be called Victorian values were widely articulated in a profusion of advice books, popular stories, journals, dime novels, sermons, and exhortations of various sorts. Men and women were taught to fulfill separate, but vitally interdependent functions. Young men learned in church, at home, and in the popular literature what was expected of American manhood. The key element was moral autonomy: control over one's instincts and independent pursuit of one's calling. The core of this code was economic self-mastery. Ideally a man would be his own boss, own his own property, and control his own means of production. A striving man was the perfect citizen, for his ambition furthered, rather than hindered, the goal of national progress.

In contrast, women learned that "the domestic fireside is the great guardian of society against the excess of human passion." It was the wife's duty to maintain a home environment free from sensuality, to help protect husbands and sons from dissipation. If men were not properly disciplined, they might lead the country to economic stagnation. In this wider sense the woman's role involved more than mere housekeeping; it was vital to the future of the nation. Accordingly, boys learned from an early age that "nothing is better calculated to preserve a young man from contamination of low pleasures and pursuits than frequent intercourse [that is, social interaction] with the more refined and virtuous of the other sex," which would raise them "above those sordid and sensual considerations which hold such sway over men." The man's duty was to extend the asceticism he learned from women at home into the economy. There he would contribute to building a strong industrial state and, in turn, become personally successful.[2]

This domestic ideal was difficult to achieve. Not all Americans were Victorians. Obviously the code I have outlined was virtually irrelevant for much of the working class and many of the ethnic groups who also inhabited urban centers. Most families with limited resources never experienced the economic autonomy that lay at the center of the Victorian success ethic and domestic ideal. The men were rarely self-made entrepreneurs; usually they were dependent upon whoever owned the company or land where they labored. Their wives rarely had the luxury to be full-time moral guardians of the home; they often worked with their children in menial occupations, pooling their earnings. If they did not have outside employment, they might work in their own homes, taking in boarders, doing laundry, or providing other services to earn additional income. Victorian gentility was unobtainable for most of these women and men. Model gender roles were not only beyond their reach, they were probably not even considered desirable.

Some Americans were deliberately and aggressively excluded from the Victorian ideal. African-Americans were of

The mother's role as guardian of the home and instructor in right thinking is here illustrated in 1905.

course the most systematically excluded. During slavery they were not even allowed to marry legally. Moreover, the foundations of Victorian manhood and womanhood (economic self-sufficiency, chaste leisure) were forcibly denied to slaves, who were required to work for the gain of others, and whose lives were often under the control of white owners who thought nothing of separating spouses from each other and parents from children. The ethic of sexual purity, a cornerstone of Victorian domesticity, was unavailable to slaves, since white owners frequently used the bodies of their female slaves for their own pleasure, while efforts at slave breeding made the sexuality of male and female slaves into a part of the economy of plantation life. The fact that African-American women and men achieved strong family attachments in spite of the brutal conditions of slavery testifies to their ability to resist the system. Nevertheless, during as well as after slavery, African-Americans remained distant from the Victorian domestic ideal because of economic conditions, racist legal practices, and their own preferred sexual and familial values.

Others who stayed apart from Victorianism included immigrant families who came from preindustrial backgrounds. They often had traditions of public and private life that were quite distinct from those of their genteel neighbors. Many preferred dances or camaraderie at the corner saloon to church picnics or temperance meetings. For workers, Sunday was often the only day for frivolous amusement, and their raucous Sabbath behavior was particularly galling to their pious "betters." Tensions between those inside and those outside the Victorian construct often provided the dynamics for public and political activity.

The Modern Family Ideal

As a result of the increasing diversity of the urban centers, the late nineteenth century witnessed a slight straining against the codes of Victorianism emanating from within the white middle class itself. But it was not until the turn of the century that middle-class Americans began a widespread effort to reach beyond the bounds of Victorianism to create a new domestic ideal. Gradually the belief that the family provided the foundation for public life was displaced by a more privatized vision. After 1900 the communal values of sacrifice, voluntarism, and virtuous domesticity were seriously shaken by the rise of urban culture, which brought altered sex roles and post-Victorian expectations of marriage and family life.

The immigrant family—this one is Italian—in 1908 sought to become part of the American dream.

The quest for something new found its most immediate target in the home. But the change that gave rise to a new concept of family life lay in the economy, not in the domestic realm. The corporate order emerged full-blown in the early twentieth century, striking a fatal blow to the entrepreneurial ethos that had given meaning to the gender roles and communal values of America's dominant groups during the previous century. The first evidence of this transformation appeared in the work force. It was here that the carefully defined activities of Victorian men and women were irreversibly altered. For men, the rise of large organizations undercut the possibility for economic autonomy in the open market, long the goal of American middle-class manhood. Beginning in 1870, the proportion of independent businessmen in urban centers declined steadily, and it became more and more difficult for a man to be self-employed. Work changed for the laboring classes as well. The craft tradition had been declining throughout the nineteenth century; but the emphasis on time-clock routine and single-task jobs accelerated during the turn-of-the-century decades. As a result, although men of all classes continued to identify their function in life with their jobs, they began looking for new rewards in leisure. With work becoming more routinized, men began to look to the home not so much for moral uplift, but for fun and pleasure.

The change for women, in terms of both economic activity and public behavior, was even more profound. Between 1880 and 1920 women went to work in unprecedented numbers. While the proportion of men in the work force remained fairly stable, the proportion of women rose 50 percent. This increase was not so dramatic among working-class women, for domestic work and factory labor were not new to them. The most striking increase was among middle-class women. Daughters of Victorians now joined sons of entrepreneurs in the swelling white-collar ranks. Not only did this erode the traditional women's role; it also drastically altered the tenor of the work force. No longer was the business world an all-male arena; now both women and men filed into the ordered and predictable corporate system, to work side by side.[3]

Both men and women, then, became preoccupied with material goods and leisure as the industrial economy generated increasing abundance. Higher wages combined with mass advertising yielded a new consumer ethic. The amount spent nationally for personal consumption nearly tripled between 1909 and 1929, with the most striking increases for clothes, personal care, furniture, appliances, cars, and recreation—primarily activities and goods associated with private life. Mass consumption offered the promise—or the illusion—that the good life was now within everyone's reach. [4]

But the rising standard of living was a mixed blessing for post-Victorian Americans with their tradition of distrust about spending and abundance. The ascetic values of self-control and frugality rested on a belief that too much spending and leisure easily could lead to decadence and corruption, eroding the work ethic. Yet it was much more than material abundance that disturbed them; much of their cultural tradition was undercut by the new organizational life. Most frightening of all, perhaps, was that corporate employees, including their own young women, were being drawn to the sorts of public amusements that were once the domain of despised ethnic minorities.

"Will You Go Home with Your Outfit?" World War I army posters stressed good hygiene and sexual purity.

Go back to them
physically fit and morally clean

Now middle-class individuals, particularly youths, had the time, money, and inclination to indulge in these pursuits.

One way to combat the danger of pleasure zones was to alter home life. If the home was not so much the staid, genteel domicile of the past, which seemed to breed restlessness and make young people vulnerable to the allure of urban amusements, it might be possible to incorporate some of the new leisure ethic into domestic life itself. Social reformers in the early twentieth century, known as Progressives, turned to home life—a reinvigorated, leisure-oriented home—to fulfill the desires of restless urbanites and combat the threat of what they perceived as dangerous public amusements. Reformers believed that if the family could offer wholesome pleasures and still retain its character-building function, the moral community might be preserved. Domestic life would have to be expanded and altered to accommodate this need. In the process, the concept of a new, leisure-oriented domestic life-style gradually evolved.

The twentieth-century family was indeed something new. The socially beneficial family had a new locale: the single-family home in the suburbs. Suburbs first emerged in the nineteenth century, as transportation advances made it possible to live a distance from one's place of work. By the late nineteenth century most American cities were developing suburbs at an accelerating pace. During this time suburbs became more than places to live; they signaled a new life-style.[5]

Suburbs opened up the possibility of a new, more leisure and consumer-oriented life-style for the family. A writer in *Cosmopolitan* in 1903 claimed that the suburb offered a "compromise for those who temper an inherent or cultivated taste for green fields . . . with an unwillingness to entirely forego the delights of urban gaiety." Urban gaiety was a new feature of the domestic ideology that emerged in the early twentieth century. Yet middle-class Americans were equally intent upon protecting their homes and neighborhoods from what they perceived as the unsavory elements of the city. *Cosmopolitan* continued, "The householder can rely upon quite a rigid enforcement of the restrictions designed to ensure the erection in the suburbs of residences of a uniformly creditable character, and he is protected from the encroachments of manufacturing and other interests likely to include uncongenial neighbors. Saloons and shops, also, are excluded from these sacred precincts."[6] Zoning laws were instrumental in defining the restrictions and protecting the residents' private domains, while

Immigrant families like these in the 1920s faced hardship and discrimination. But in later decades their children and grandchildren may well have settled in the suburbs, along with countless other assimilated white ethnic families.

keeping out the "influx of foreigners with low ideals of family life."[7]

In these ways suburbs remained exclusive residential communities, which included white middle-class families along with only those affluent members of the working class and people from foreign backgrounds who conformed to the prevailing community norms. Modern family life found its ideal locale in the suburbs. But place alone would not achieve the desired domestic results. Women and men themselves would need to change their attitudes and shed the repressive moral codes of the past. In case individuals did not know how to do this, there were many messages emanating from the popular culture showing them the way. New sexual roles, styles of courtship, and marriage itself received thorough treatment in the burgeoning film industry.

One of the most popular motifs in the movies of the 1920s and 1930s was modern marriage and how to achieve it. Although there were new elements in the formula for wedded bliss, traditional patterns were not discarded entirely. Americans struggled to come to terms with modern matrimony without fully giving up the values and norms of the past. As couples tried to tread the fine line between the new and the old, the movies began offering ideas on how the two might be merged. The filmmaker who most successfully capitalized on the formula was Cecil B. DeMille, who showed the public how to combine new sexual styles and affluence with traditional virtues. In a series of extravagant films, DeMille portrayed an entirely new type of marriage. One typical example of this genre, *Why Change Your Wife?*, emphasized the need to enhance domesticity with excitement and allure. The husband, bored at work, looks forward to his hours off the job when he can enjoy life with his wife. But she constantly thwarts his eagerness for fun and sensuality. He invites her dancing but she prefers a concert. He buys her revealing lingerie; she rejects

Why Change Your Wife? (1920) was one of the earliest films on the theme of modern marriage.

A 93-83

it as "indecent." The husband is rebuffed one more time when he telephones his wife from his singularly drab and sterile office. Just then, the model from the dress shop enters and agrees to go dancing with the exasperated man. This event leads to a divorce, and the husband goes on to marry the model, Sally.

The ex-wife, overhearing some women remark that she lost her husband because she "dresses like an aunt, not his wife," decides to change her ways and "go the limit." She buys a new wardrobe of seductive clothes and takes on a flirtatious personality. Meanwhile, the husband finds that Sally wants to "play" too much and is only after his money. Finally they divorce, as Sally comments that the "only good thing about marriage is alimony." Soon afterward the husband meets his first wife at a fashionable resort. She is clad in a revealing swimsuit and surrounded by admiring men. He is attracted to her before he realizes who she is. They reunite, and the exciting style is then brought back into the moral home.[8]

The same formula worked in reverse, with numerous movies depicting an old-fashioned man who needs to be transformed before he can make a happy marriage with his fun-loving wife. These films, such as *Don't Change Your Husband,* reflect the Hollywood solution to the dilemma faced by the Linganfields, the young middle-class couple we met earlier. In the movie version, after the divorce it would not be Marsha, the defiant flapper, who would repent. Instead, Lorimer would see the folly of his prudish ways and would adopt the modern life-style himself. Hollywood's happy ending would then have Marsha realize that kids could also be part of the fun, and they would live happily ever after.

But the movies did not endorse a total overthrow of traditional domesticity. The film heroes wanted both excitement and domestic virtues in a wife, who could then revitalize men in the home. The first wife in *Why Change Your Wife?* was initially *too* moral; the second wife was *im*moral. In the end, the two qualities merged into a new style of marriage that promised to combine both elements successfully.

How was this modern marriage to be achieved? The Hollywood ideal found its way into the lives and aspirations of American women and men by shaping their outlook on marriage and family life. Robert Lynd and Helen Merrill Lynd, in their classic sociological study of American life in the 1920s, noted that new expectations surrounding love and marriage were among the most profound changes affecting women and men in Muncie, Indiana, since the 1890s. The Lynds noted that Muncie's young people increasingly underscored the notion of "romantic love as the only valid basis for marriage." The city librarian noticed an increasing interest in "sex adventure" fiction that "centers about the idea of romance underlying the institution of marriage." In Muncie and elsewhere in the country this intensified emphasis on romance and marriage yielded striking results: twentieth-century Americans were marrying younger, and more often, than their predecessors.[9] Although part of the downward trend in the marriage age can be explained by increasing opportunities for young men to earn a living in the city, the new emphasis on romance and excitement in marriage also played a role.

The Rise in Divorce

The increasing emphasis on and participation in marriage reflected the heightened expectations brought to family life. Young couples presumably would establish families in tranquil suburban neighborhoods, where the restlessness generated by twentieth-century life could be safely channeled and indulged. Young urbanites hoped that an expanded and perfected home—complete with youthful adults, exciting leisure activities, and an abundance of consumer goods—might compensate for long and tedious hours at work in routinized jobs. Given the high expectations for personal fulfillment focused on family life, however, marriage might turn out to be disappointing. Indeed, in the early decades of the twentieth century dissatisfied spouses like Lorimer and Marsha Linganfield turned toward the divorce courts more than ever.

During the late nineteenth and early twentieth centuries, at the very time that marital expectations were changing dramatically, American marriages began to collapse at an unprecedented rate. Between 1867 and 1929 the population of the United States grew 300 percent, the number of marriages increased 400 percent, and the divorce rate rose 2000 percent. By the end of the 1920s more than one in every six marriages was terminated in court, and the United States had achieved the dubious distinction of having the highest divorce rate in the world.[10]

Observers at the time claimed that the emancipation of women was responsible for the rising number of broken marriages. One turn-of-the-century social scientist from Columbia University argued that "so far as women's work has become masculine, her ability to make and keep a home happy is diminished." Others were not so quick to condemn either the change in women's roles or the rise in divorce. A University of Pennsylvania sociologist, in 1909, also linked women's emancipation to the rising divorce rate; but he viewed the development positively. A woman "is not forced into marriage as her only means of support," he wrote. "If marriage is a failure, she does not face the alternative of endurance or starvation. The way is open for independent support . . . She is no longer compelled to accept support or yield to the tyranny of a husband whose conduct is a menace to her health and happiness."[11]

The increasing opportunities for women to find paid employment outside the home undoubtedly had an impact on divorce. Women who divorced were more likely to have held jobs than their nondivorcing counterparts.[12] But critics who claimed that women were opting for independence and jobs over home and marriage were simply wrong. A job may have provided some women with the economic security they needed to leave an unhappy marriage. But the income women earned from employment was meager, and many divorcing women complained that it was their husbands' failure to provide for them that forced them to seek employment. Very few rejected the ideal of marriage that rested on a breadwinner and a full-time homemaker.[13]

In fact heightened expectations surrounding the home, more than restless urges to abandon marriage for independence, propelled the divorce rate. In the few decades between 1880, during the peak of Victorianism, and 1920, the beginning of the Jazz Age, not only the numbers but the causes for divorce changed dramatically, revealing the way in which rapidly shifting marital expectations wreaked havoc in many homes. The Linganfields were one couple among thousands who found that both partners did not embrace modern life to the same extent. For others, similar problems emerged as women and men found that marriage did not easily provide the material comforts, sexual delights, or leisure activities they had hoped it would yield.

By the 1920s traditional virtues were not enough to keep marriage alive. Now women and men wanted more fun and excitement out of family life. But there was some confusion surrounding domestic aspirations. Contrary to observers at the time, most divorcing urbanites were not in the vanguard of a moral revolution. Although they displayed desires for new excitement and sensuality, most were caught between traditions of the past and visions of the future.

In general, wives in 1920 still preferred care and protection over jobs and independence. These modern women were still antagonistic to sexual excesses and inclined toward a peaceful domestic life with children, albeit with more opportunities for fun, leisure, and affluence than their Victorian predecessors. Men also demonstrated some ambivalence. They may have been attracted to the youthful and exciting "new women," but they also wanted domestic, frugal, and virtuous wives who would keep house and tend to the children.

Divorce provides a window into the struggles of couples who attempted to blend traditional family values with the new expectations of the twentieth-century home. Problems erupted as couples tried to negotiate new terms of consumerism, sexuality, and leisure. Balancing women's work against new consumer desires caused many strains. Lisa Douglas, for example, told the divorce court that her husband was "insulted to think I would so disgrace his name by going to work, and that was why he left me . . . He considered it incompatible with his dignity to have me work." Harold Atweis also objected to his wife's employment, but for different reasons. He was annoyed, he said, because "she went to business all week and did her housework on Saturday and Sundays and it was not to my satisfaction."

James Howland had yet another objection. He claimed that since taking a job, his wife had become "careless in housekeeping and refused to cook and wash dishes . . . and would refuse to arise in the morning and prepare breakfast or attend to any housework." Yet there is no evidence that these women were thrilled with their work. Many employed divorcing women said they would be more than happy to give up their jobs if their husbands would support them adequately. Elizabeth Treadwell, for example, claimed that she would give up her job as a hotel chambermaid, "whenever he gives me satisfactory assurance that he will treat me in the future as a husband should treat his wife, pay my lawyer fees, advance me $50 as part payment on my expenses since he left . . . and provide for me in the future."[14]

At the same time, new desires for leisure, excitement and sexual fulfillment in marriage created tensions that led to divorce. Although female sexuality was now affirmed as a positive part of marriage (in contrast to Victorian notions of chastity and sexual restraint), many women resisted what they considered to be excessive sexual demands. Typical was the response of Edith Foster, who claimed that her husband "insisted upon intemperate sexual intercourse . . . He practiced depraved and degenerate acts upon her, over her protest, and by main physical force, making her submit, to the great peril of her weakened health and to her inordinate disgust and loathing." Similarly, Helen Mall claimed that her husband was "lewd and unnatural in his sexual desires and habits" and "forced her to have unnatural intercourse with him." Most of these complaints were not specific, but they did reveal the sensibilities of wives such as Mary Pflager, who claimed that her husband committed "acts of sexual depravity and degeneracy so revolting as to be improper of expression or description."[15]

Issues surrounding the youth cult, consumerism, and leisure also found their way into the divorce courts. One former flapper explained why she left her first husband in 1920, fleeing the Idaho farm for the excitement of Hollywood: "He never wanted to go anywhere or do anything. He was a jerk, dear." Men often complained about women who were too fun-loving. Edward Moley said of his wife that "no damn man living could keep her from going to dances or doing as she pleased . . . and that she expected to continue to dance and go to dances as long as she liked." On the other hand, men wanted glamorous wives. One man bluntly told his wife of seven years: "Bert, I am simply tired of you and furthermore you are getting too fat, you are too much of the washerwoman type for me." Another man said to his wife, "You are too old. I'm getting myself a young woman."[16]

One of the most poignant illustrations of the tension between old and new values comes from a young husband whose wife was "tired of living on a farm" after three years of marriage. "She was fond of moving pictures and wanted to go [to her home town] most of her time, where things were more active." The husband's father described his farm-bred son as "a boy of good habits. He never uses liquor or tobacco. He is a church member and a good boy. He has always been industrious and works every day. He has always been a good worker." That apparently was not enough for his wife, who deserted him for the excitement of city life.[17]

By the 1920s the notion of the family as an institution within society had undergone dramatic change. Although the nineteenth-century middle-class home did not function directly as an economic unit as it had in the preindustrial era, the roles of household members were defined vis-à-vis the productive system. The Victorian family was expected to produce producers. The twentieth century brought a shift in this ethos. Now the home became one of the primary places where the fruits of production would be consumed. Family members became not merely producers (or nurturers of producers), but purchasers of the goods they helped to create. In order to keep the system thriving, ascetic discipline was no longer crucial; indulgence served this new economic function more efficiently. Suburban families became consuming units, absorbing abundance and leisure into the home. In this sense, although the home may have lost some of its previous social functions, it evolved into an even more important institution for satisfying personal desires.

The Domestic Ideal in Crisis

The companionate marriage, a term some historians use to describe the modern couple-centered family, developed during the early decades of the twentieth century. It was based on the premise that the strongest family was a nuclear unit with a breadwinner and a homemaker working together to provide for the family's material and emotional needs, while enjoying the fruits of modern life in their leisure hours together. But the events of the 1930s and 1940s would seriously strain that ideal. The economic collapse of the Great Depression and the massive disruptions of World War II created chaos in many families. At the same time, the upheavals of these years opened up new possibilities for domestic life that held the potential for a major redefinition of the ideal family.

The Depression yielded not only misery but also tremendous energy and radicalism. Union-organizing and reform movements of all kinds flourished as the crisis challenged Americans to abandon the constraints of the past and move forward, boldly, into the future. Recovery in the family, as in the economy, would be achieved not simply by returning to ways of the past, but by adapting to new circumstances. The economic crisis opened the way for a new type of family based on shared breadwinning and equality of the sexes.[18]

The Depression thus paved the way for two different family forms: one with two breadwinners who shared household tasks, and the other with spouses whose roles were sharply differentiated. In the latter form the father earned the "family wage" while the mother cared for the children, supplementing her husband's earnings with a job, if necessary.

Young people could have chosen either path. In the words of one young wife, "Our marriage should be rational and controllable. He has two legs and so do I; there is no insuperable burden on either side."[19] Couples entered marriage with open eyes, facing new challenges and possibilities. But by the time the Depression was over and World War II had come and gone, it was clear that millions of middle-class American families would take the path toward polarized gender roles. What caused the overwhelming triumph of "traditional" roles in the "modern" home? The answer can be found in the seeds sown during the Depression, and how those seeds were cultivated in the 1940s.

Efforts to save the family from financial disaster began when the Depression first gripped the nation. Communities and kin networks came together to provide mutual aid and support. Sometimes these informal modes of assistance were sufficient; often they were not. As a result, the state began to intervene in private life to an unprecedented extent. President Franklin D. Roosevelt not only told Americans that they had "nothing to fear but fear itself"; he also taught them not to fear the power of the national government as it encroached on the home to alleviate the extreme hardships. From social security, which provided support for the elderly, to numerous public works programs that gave jobs to unemployed breadwinners, the New Deal brought the government directly into people's lives. Although some people resisted the intrusion, most of the nation backed Roosevelt and his programs so overwhelmingly that the political coalition that came together around the New Deal retained national hegemony for three decades.

The Depression did not affect everyone in the same manner, but it created a general state of crisis that altered expected roles and rewards. One thing that changed was the role of marriage in people's lives. The marriage rate plummeted to an all-time low during the early 1930s, as young women and men postponed marriage or chose to remain single. Men were reluctant to marry if they thought they would not be able to provide for a family. Numerous educators, clergy, and observers from many professions worried that delayed marriage would lead to sexual transgressions. Fearful that calls for restraint would prove ineffectual, they advised parents who could afford to do so to help young lovers with financial assistance to enable them to marry.

According to a 1937 Roper poll, so widespread was the

The Depression created a major economic upheaval and often resulted in widespread geographic dispersal.

concern about delayed marriage that over one-third of Americans favored the extraordinary idea of governmental subsidies to help young couples marry. Early marriage with financial dependence was considered preferable to sexual involvement prior to marriage, with the possibility of illegitimate children. This was the first expression of an idea that would become much more widely advocated during the war and postwar years: early marriage as an antidote to illicit sex. As the well-known marriage counselor Paul Popenoe wrote, "In heaven's name, why wait? If you are sincerely in love, old enough to know what you are doing, understand what marriage means and are free to enter into it, you have no right to let anything, least of all money, bar you from happiness."[20]

In spite of such exhortations, the marriage rate limped along during the 1930s, below the rate of the 1920s. It did not begin to rise significantly until 1940. The birthrate also declined more sharply in the 1930s than previously, and divorces increased as marriages collapsed, mostly under financial strain. At the same time, the Depression created opportunities for a growing number of single women to be self-reliant. These working women were able to support themselves and their families through their own efforts.[21]

The popular culture at the time, particularly movies and fan magazines, glamorized single working women and affirmed their active role in public life. In the 1930s record numbers of young men and women watched the films and read the stories about Hollywood celebrities. The motion picture industry was one of the few economic enterprises that did not suffer serious losses during the Depression. Although few moviegoers lived like the Hollywood stars, they identified with the personal dramas enacted on and off the screen. As both a barometer and a beacon, Hollywood was a focal point for the nation's mass culture.[22]

In on- and off-screen portrayals of stars' lives, Hollywood encouraged the independence of women and the equality of the sexes. The popular culture bolstered the side of the 1930s that challenged traditional gender arrangements. Changing images in the nation's most popular fan magazine, *Photoplay,* provide powerful evidence of the emergence of these themes from the 1930s onward. The 1920s had witnessed a shift away from Victorian models of womanhood, as stars like Clara Bow or Greta Garbo experimented with new moral styles and sexual ethics. By the 1930s, however, a new female image— strong, autonomous, competent, and career-oriented—had gained momentum. Yet for all its affirmation of emancipated women, Hollywood fell short of pointing the way toward a restructured family that would incorporate independent women. These strong and autonomous women of the thirties no longer represented ideal wives, as did their counterparts in the twenties who brought their emancipation into revitalized marriages. Rather, these tough and rugged career women were admired as *women,* not as wives. Hollywood perpetuated the notion, reminiscent of the Victorian era, that if a woman chose to pursue a career, she would have to forego marriage. As one advice writer in *Photoplay* concluded, "There is a pretty big conflict between a career in pictures and our unconscious longing for a domestic life."[23]

Hollywood in the 1930s promoted equality of the sexes, but it did not provide a new model of marriage that incorporated equality. Major films of the decade illustrate this ambivalent stance toward emancipated women who married. Films such as *Blonde Venus,* a 1931 movie starring Marlene Dietrich, warned viewers about the perils of role reversals in homes where men lost their jobs and women became the

breadwinners. Even as late as 1940, films such as *His Girl Friday,* a huge box-office hit, reflected pessimism about the possibility of happiness in marriage for autonomous career women.[24]

These ideas prevailed in the world beyond Hollywood as well. Even the most radical measures of the New Deal, created to alleviate hardship, failed to promote the possibility of a new family structure based on gender equality. Although many families depended on the earnings of both spouses, federal policies supported unemployed male breadwinners but discouraged married women from seeking jobs. Section 213 of the Economy Act of 1932 mandated that whenever personnel reductions took place in the executive branch, married persons were to be the first discharged if married to a government employee. As a result, 1,600 married women were dismissed from their federal jobs. Many state and local governments

Marlene Dietrich, who starred in *Blonde Venus,* plays a wife gone bad when her breadwinning husband loses his job. Such fears were prevalent in the 1930s.

followed suit; three out of four cities excluded married women from teaching, and eight states passed laws excluding them from state jobs. The government provided relief for families in need, but not jobs for married women.[25]

These efforts to curtail women's employment opportunities were directly related to the equally powerful imperative to bolster the employment of men. Although most Americans experienced some form of hardship, it was the nation's male breadwinners—fathers who were responsible for providing economic support for their families—who were threatened or faced with the severest erosion of their identities. Those who lost income or jobs frequently lost status at home, and self-respect as well. Economic hardship placed severe strains on marriage. Going on relief may well have helped the family budget, but it would do little for the breadwinner's feelings of failure.[26]

In *His Girl Friday* Rosalind Russell, in the role of Cary Grant's ex-wife, competes as an equal in the rough-and-tumble world of journalism.

With the breadwinner's role undermined, other family roles shifted dramatically. Frequently wives and mothers who had never been employed took jobs to provide supplemental or even primary support for their families. Their employment often meant facing intense social condemnation as well as miserably low wages. Although women rarely displaced male workers (the vast majority held "women's jobs" that men would not take in any case), they were considered selfish if they were employed when men were out of work. Women also suffered the hardships of low wages and poor working conditions. Despite the needed income these jobs provided, employed wives were not likely to resist pressures to quit if they could be certain of adequate support from their husbands. A 1936 Gallop poll indicated that 82 percent of American women and men surveyed believed that wives of employed husbands should not work outside the home. By 1939 nearly 90 percent of the men who were polled believed that "women should not hold a job after marriage," and most women agreed. Public praise was reserved for self-supporting single women or for frugal and resourceful homemakers whose domestic endeavors helped their families through the crisis.[27]

Given the need for women's earnings, the widespread employment of women might have been one of the most important legacies of the Depression era. But discriminatory policies and public hostility weakened that potential. As women's paid work increased only slightly, their domestic roles expanded considerably. In the home women made significant contributions to their families' resources by spending frugally, reusing previously purchased goods, and devising a variety of other small economies. Because of such efforts, many families with reduced incomes were able to maintain their pre-Depression standard of living.[28]

The Depression thus created a tension between traditional domestic roles and challenges to those roles. The prevailing family ideology was gravely threatened during the 1930s, when women and men adapted to hard times by shifting their household responsibilities. In the long run, however, these alternatives were viewed as temporary measures caused by unfortunate circumstances, rather than as positive outcomes of the crisis. Young people learned, on the one hand, to accept women's employment as necessary for the family budget; on the other hand, they saw that deviations from traditional roles often wreaked havoc in marriages. Children who grew up in economically deprived families during these years watched their parents struggle to succeed as breadwinners and home-makers, and they suffered along with their parents if those expectations proved impossible to meet. The realities of family life combined with institutional barriers to inhibit the potential for sustained radical change among white middle-class American families. The sociologist Glen Elder, in his pioneering study of families during the Depression, found that the more a family's traditional gender roles were disrupted, the more likely the children were to disapprove of the altered balance of power in their homes.[29]

The idea of the companionate marriage gained additional support in the Depression, when men and women had to pull together to keep their households intact. Although men were expected to be the household heads, Depression-bred women envisioned more egalitarian unions than did women in the past: 60 percent of women polled by the *Ladies Home Journal* in 1938 objected to the word "obey" in marriage vows; 75 percent believed in joint decisionmaking; and 80 percent believed that an unemployed husband should keep house for a working wife. Yet 60 percent said they would lose respect for a husband who earned less than his wife, and 90 percent believed a wife should give up her job if her husband wanted her to do so. This vision of modern marriage, then, included a measure of equality within the relationship but distinct roles for breadwinners and homemakers.[30]

Women's acceptance of their domestic roles makes more sense if one keeps in mind the constraints they faced in the work world. The economic crisis legitimated employment for single women, and for married women whose earnings supplemented the male breadwinner's income. But women's jobs remained in the pink-collar sector of the economy, yielding lower pay and status and fewer possibilities for advancement than did men's jobs.[31]

If the paid labor force had been more hospitable, and if public policies had fostered equal opportunities for women, young people in the 1930s might have been less inclined to aspire to prevailing gender roles. Viable long-term job prospects for women might have prompted new ways of structuring family roles. In the face of persistent obstacles, however, that potential withered. Popular culture reflected widespread admiration for independent women, but even the cultural vanguard in Hollywood fell short of affirming an alternative to the traditional family arrangement.

And so the potential for radically altered gender roles in

the family never reached fruition in the 1930s. As the Depression continued, the path toward traditional domestic arrangements appeared to be the one most likely to bring Americans toward the secure homes they desired. The obstacles to gender equality might have lifted with the end of hard times. With full employment, women's jobs would no longer be seen as contributing to men's unemployment and loss of status. When World War II brought a sudden end to the Depression, producing full employment and a booming economy, many of the obstacles to a fundamental restructuring of public as well as private roles were removed. The national response to this new crisis determined which of the two paths created by the Depression Americans would ultimately pursue.

Like the Depression, World War II brought new challenges and new disruptions to families. The war put on hold the hopes of many who looked forward to building stable and secure homes after the Depression. As thousands of men were called to war, their manly responsibilities as soldiers took precedence over their roles as breadwinners. While the men vanished to foreign shores to fend off the enemy, the women were left to fend for themselves.

Wartime Challenges

The war emergency required society to restructure itself and opened the way for the emancipation of women on an unprecedented scale. The potential for gender equality, thwarted during the 1930s, now had a chance to develop. The Depression ended abruptly: the unemployment rate fell from 14 percent to nearly zero. In response to the needs of an expanding wartime economy, public policy shifted dramatically, from barring women from jobs to recruiting them. Married women were encouraged to take "men's jobs" as a patriotic duty to keep the war economy booming, while the men were off fighting. Public opinion followed suit. During the Depression, 82 percent of Americans objected to wives working outside the home; by 1942 only 13 percent still objected.[32]

As a result of the combined incentives of patriotism and good wages, women began streaming into jobs. By 1945 the number of employed women had leapt 60 percent. Three-quarters of these new workers were married, and a third had children under age fourteen.[33] War-production needs might have led to a restructuring of the labor force along gender-neutral lines, ending sex segregation in the workplace and

bringing about a realignment of domestic roles. The disloca-
tion of wartime might have led to the postponement of marriage and child-rearing, continuing the demographic trends of
the 1930s toward later marriage, a lower marriage rate, and
fewer children. But nothing of the kind took place. The potential for significant alterations in gender arrangements was,
once again, thwarted. In spite of the tremendous changes
brought about by the war, the emergency situation ultimately
encouraged women to keep their sights set on the home, and
men to reclaim their status as the primary breadwinners and
household heads.

Instead of deterring Americans from embarking on family
life, the war may have sped up the process. Women entered
war production, but they did not give up on reproduction.
The war brought a dramatic reversal to the declining marriage
rate of the 1930s. Over one million more families were formed
between 1940 and 1943 than would have been expected during
normal times, and as soon as the United States entered the
war, fertility increased. Between 1940 and 1945 the birthrate
climbed from 19.4 to 24.5 per one thousand population. The
marriage age dropped and the marriage rate accelerated,
spurred in part by the possibility of draft deferments for married men in the early war years and by the imminence of
the men's departure for foreign shores. Thus a curious phenomenon marked the war years: a widespread disruption of
domestic life accompanied by a rush into marriage and
parenthood.[34]

Tangible as well as intangible factors spurred this increase
in the formation of families. Economic hardship was no longer
a barrier to marriage, as it had been in the 1930s, and dependents' allowances eased the burdens of families if the breadwinners were drafted. But perhaps more important was the
desire to solidify relationships and establish connections to the
future when war made life so uncertain. Widespread war-
propaganda efforts called on the nation to support the men
who were fighting to protect their families back home. The
popular culture carried many such appeals. Under the sponsorship of the Office of Facts and Figures, in 1942 all the major
radio networks aired a series of programs to mobilize support
for the war. These appeals were aimed not at the need to
defeat fascism in Europe, but at the goal of promoting family
life at home. One highly acclaimed segment, "To The
Young," made it clear to listeners why it was important to
support the war effort:

Young Male Voice: "That's one of the things this war's about."

Young Female Voice: "About us?"

Young Male Voice: "About *all* young people like us. About love and gettin' hitched, and havin' a home and some kids, and breathin' fresh air out in the suburbs . . . about livin' and workin' *decent,* like free people."[35]

Here we see the suburban ideal of the nuclear family promoted as the centerpiece of the war effort. Movies carried similar messages, and their sponsorship by the government did nothing to dampen their popularity. The 1943 war propaganda film *This Is the Army,* starring Ronald Reagan, was the most successful film of the decade. The plot revolves around the efforts of the central character's sweetheart, an army nurse, to persuade her reluctant soldier to marry her. She finally succeeds, and the duo wed just before the hero leaves to fight on foreign shores.[36]

At the climax of *This Is the Army* the hero (Ronald Reagan) weds his sweetheart before leaving for the front during World War II.

The popular culture reflected widespread admiration for the many thousands of female war workers, but affirmed the primacy of domesticity for women. These themes represent a dramatic departure from the advice prevalent in the 1930s, which urged women to follow their own ambitions, even if it put their chances for a happy marriage at risk. Overall, Hollywood's professed advocacy of gender equality evaporated during the 1940s. The dramatic shift in the popular culture raises a fundamental question: Why did the emphasis on domesticity reach such intensity in the era of Rosie the Riveter? Clues to this apparent irony are found in what some historians consider to be the most substantial change of the 1940s: the entry of an unprecedented number of women into the paid labor force. In examining who these women were and what they did—particularly their long-term opportunities—it becomes clear that the possibilities for employed women were much more limited than they seemed.[37]

During the war the proportion of all women who were employed rose from 28 percent to 37 percent, and three-fourths of these new female employees were married. By the end of the war fully 25 percent of all married women were employed—a huge gain from 15 percent at the end of the 1930s. Because most of these workers had spent their early adult years as homemakers, they were unlikely to enter careers that required training and experience and that had significant potential for good pay, advancement, or job security. As a result, their large number contributed to the increasing segregation of women into low-level "female" jobs.[38]

Rosie the Riveter was the notable exception, but the women she represented were a temporary phenomenon. Nearly all the "men's jobs" filled by women went back to men when the war ended, largely as the result of pressure from male-dominated unions. Even during the war, the popular literature and the politicians exhorted married women to return to their domestic duties and urged single women to relinquish their jobs and find husbands when the hostilities ceased.[39]

Women's wartime independence also gave rise to fears of female sexuality as a dangerous force on the loose. Men were urged to avoid single women and Victory girls who frequented the amusement areas near bases, and women were urged to keep their behavior and aspirations focused on the home. Wartime purity crusades and propaganda efforts reflect widespread fears that single women might not be willing to settle down into domesticity once the war ended. These anxieties may have stemmed from the fact that the war years brought so many women out of their homes and traditionally sex-segregated jobs into occupations previously reserved for men. In addition, the war removed men from the home front, demonstrating that women could manage without them. Single women now became targets of government-sponsored campaigns urging women to return to their domestic roles.

There is no evidence to suggest that these anxieties were well-founded. More families were formed than torn asunder during World War II. Nevertheless, many observers continued to fret about the new economic and sexual independence of women and its potential effect on the family. Wartime ushered in a fear of all forms of nonmarital sexuality that had been dormant since the Progressive era and that continued in the postwar years. This preoccupation ranged from a concern about prostitution and "promiscuous" women to fierce campaigns against homosexuals and other "deviants" in military as well as civilian life.[40]

Ultimately, the vast changes in gender arrangements that some feared and others hoped for never fully materialized. Actually the war underscored women's tasks as homemakers, consumers, and mothers just as powerfully as it expanded their paid jobs. For all the publicity surrounding Rosie the Riveter, few women took jobs that were previously held exclusively by men, and those who did earned less than men. Developments in the female labor force foreshadowed a pattern that continued after the war: the numerical expansion of opportunities flowing into an increasingly limited range of occupations. Although women demonstrated their eagerness for nontraditional work and proved themselves competent, few were able to retain those jobs after the war. As a result, wartime ultimately reinforced the sex-segregation of the labor force.

In the wake of World War II the short-lived affirmation of women's independence gave way to a pervasive endorsement of female subordination and domesticity. In addition to the ambivalence surrounding new roles for women, postwar life in general seemed to offer mixed blessings. Americans had postponed their desires to create something new and liberating, but unleashing those desires could lead to chaos as well as security. During the war, savings reached an all-time high as people banked one-fourth of their disposable income.[41] They looked forward to spending their money when the war

World War II was followed by a renewed emphasis on the joys of motherhood.

ended, and to satisfying other pent-up desires for sexually charged relationships, leisure, and the good life. But according to widely expressed fears, too much money, strong women, and too much sex might destroy the dream of the good life unless channeled in appropriate and healthy ways. If things went awry, happiness and security would remain out of reach.

Given the impetus for a return to the familiar, along with the quest for something new and yet secure, the potential for a new model family, with two equal partners who shared breadwinning and homemaking tasks, never gained widespread support. In the long run, in spite of the opportunities opened up by the Depression and the war, neither policymakers nor the creators of the popular culture encouraged that potential. Instead, they pointed to traditional gender roles as the best means for Americans to achieve the happiness and security they desired. Public policies and economic realities during the Depression and the war limited the options of both women and men and reinforced traditional arrangements in the home. Even during the war, Americans were heading homeward toward gender-specific domestic roles. But it was not until after the war that a unique domestic ideology fully emerged.

The Baby Boom

Along with a revitalized ideology of domesticity, children took on a new centrality in American family life in the postwar years. For the nation, the next generation symbolized hope for the future. But for individuals, parenthood was much more than a duty to posterity; the joys of raising children would compensate for the thwarted expectations in other areas of their lives. For men frustrated at work, for women bored at home, children might fill the void.

The postwar consensus was nowhere more evident than in the matter of having children. The baby boom was not the result of the return to peace, or of births to older parents postponed because of the war. The baby boom began *during* the war and continued afterward because younger couples were having babies earlier. Part of the boom can be explained by the drop in the marriage age. But a lower marriage age would not necessarily result in a higher birthrate. In fact during the first few decades of the twentieth century the marriage age and the birthrate both declined steadily. In the 1940s, however, the birthrate skyrocketed, reversing a decline in fertility that had lasted for nearly two centuries. How did this reversal happen? Demographers have shown that the baby boom did not result from women suddenly having huge numbers of children; the number of children per family went up modestly. Women coming of age in the 1930s had an average of 2.4 children; those who reached adulthood in the 1950s gave birth to an average of 3.2 children. What caused the baby boom was that everyone was doing it—and at the same time.[42]

The birthrate rose among all social groups. One demographic study of the sources of the baby boom concluded that all ethnic, racial, and occupational groups participated. In addition, Americans behaved with remarkable conformity during these years. They married young and had an average of at least three children in a few years. Most couples in the 1940s and 1950s completed their families by the time they were in their late twenties.[43]

The baby boom reflected a number of demographic, economic, and ideological shifts that were deeply tied to the historical developments of the era. Efforts to explain away the baby boom as merely the result of a desire for a return to "normal" family life after the war, or as a response to improved economic conditions, fail to understand how dramatic a development it was in terms of long-term trends. There have been other wars and depressions, but none concluded by ushering in a booming birthrate. In fact, earlier in the century rising affluence seemed to coincide with a falling birthrate, perhaps reflecting the lessened need for children as economic assets, or perhaps reflecting greater expectations for providing children with the fruits of abundance, making each child an expensive proposition.[44] There is no doubt that the return of prosperity had something to do with the rising

Mothers and their baby-boom progeny.

birthrate. But the extent of the phenomenon cannot be explained without taking into consideration the rise of a powerful ideology that placed children at the center of family happiness.

Whether or not the 1950s was the golden age of the family is a matter of considerable debate. But there is little doubt that it was the golden age of domestic ideology. The companionate family ideal, which had developed throughout the century with an emphasis on romance, excitement, leisure, consumerism, and sexuality, came to fruition in the postwar years. There can be no doubt that Americans aspired to the ideal. Never before or since have Americans married at such young ages, in such high numbers, and with such conformity to a pattern of early childbearing. The notorious American divorce rate, rising since the late nineteenth century, with only a slight dip in the Depression, took a downturn in the 1950s as marriages remained remarkably stable. Popular culture and political rhetoric centered on family values, as millions spent their evenings at home watching families like those portrayed on popular TV sitcoms such as "Ozzie and Harriet" or "Leave It to Beaver." Even the Cold War centered on family values: Vice President Richard Nixon spent two days arguing with Soviet Premier Nikita Khrushchev over who had better household appliances and more glamorous housewives, turning one of the major skirmishes of the Cold War into the renowned Kitchen Debate.[45]

Along with the new national obsession with family life came an intense and widespread endorsement of pronatalism— the belief in the positive value of having several children. A major study conducted in 1957 found that most Americans believed parenthood was the route to happiness. Childlessness was considered deviant, selfish, and pitiable. Twenty years later these pronatal norms began to break up. But in the 1940s and 1950s nearly everyone believed that family togetherness, focused on children, was the mark of a successful and wholesome personal life. One study of nine hundred wives in the 1950s found that the desire for children was second only to companionship in stated marriage goals. Younger women echoed these sentiments. A study of eighteen- to twenty-one-year-old women in 1955 revealed a strong pronatalist sentiment. These young women were much more likely to express their desire for children than their eagerness for marriage, stating that children—rather than marriage itself—was the most important aspect of married life. These attitudes indicate the strength of the baby-boom ideology, which would keep the birthrate booming for nearly another decade.[46]

By the time of the postwar family boom, the nuclear family ideal that had first taken shape in the nineteenth century had undergone significant changes. White middle-class families were no longer seen as the well-disciplined bulwark of public life, rearing future citizens and providing men with the necessary moral uplift to enable them to withstand the temptations of the rough-and-tumble male world. The family became an end in itself, a reward for hard work, and compensation for the stresses, strains, and frustrations of the highly organized corporate order. New elements in the domestic ideology included consumerism, eroticism, leisure, and fun-oriented child-rearing.

The place of children in the family reflects larger concerns surrounding domesticity. In the Victorian era children were sentimentalized; parents were to protect the innocence of children and set examples for them to grow up to be model citizens. The Progressive era brought in a new emphasis on scientific child-rearing, which called for strict scheduling, minimal physical affection, and discipline in order to fit children for the more scientific, rational needs of modern society. Gradually the rigid child-rearing advice of the early twentieth century softened, as advice to parents in the 1920s and 1930s moved toward an emphasis on personality development. Parents were encouraged to be less rigid, more permissive and affectionate with their children.[47]

By 1946, when Dr. Benjamin Spock wrote his famous *Baby and Child Care,* Americans were already obsessed with children. Spock reinforced popular notions that children were an all-consuming responsibility. Echoing the almost universally held belief that child-rearing was a mother's duty, Spock addressed his book to women. Ironically he urged mothers to trust their own instincts, while at the same time providing his own expert advice. Children became the primary focus of family goals, activities, and values.

According to advice writers as well as popular films and stories at the time, children could prevent American families from unraveling. At a time when fears of an out-of-control postwar world were rampant, children were seen not only as the hope of the future but as the hope for the present as well. Children promised to provide security as well as fulfillment for a generation of young adults desperately seeking both. Family life centered on children would tame the wayward

The 1950s suburban family was expected to be fun-loving and child-centered.

tendencies of postwar youth. The editor of *Better Homes and Gardens* articulated these sentiments: "The young fellow who lives in the little house with the vines . . . used to be quite a 'stepper.' He didn't change his ways much when he married his little redhead. Nor, for that matter, did she. Her bright mop of hair was a danger signal, all right . . . We don't worry about this couple any more. There are three in that family now. The little fellow['s] mother lives every moment for his comfort and welfare. His father is thinking, not about an evening with the 'boys,' but away off in the future—about the kid's schooling, about the sort of country and the sort of world in which the lad will live someday . . . Perhaps there is not

In the post–World War II era the pleasure in caring for their children became known to many American males for the first time. In *Penny Serenade* Cary Grant played a man willing to accept a boring job in order to reap the joys of fatherhood.

much more needed in a recipe for happiness . . . we become complete only thru our children."[48]

These themes filled the nation's movie screens as well. Popular films such as the 1941 box-office hit *Penny Serenade*, focused on the potential of children to tame men and make them willing to submit to the monotony of corporate life. In this film the adventurous father put his family at risk through his insistence on being his own boss. But when faced with the loss of his adopted child, he promised to mend his ways and settle into a routine job to provide security for his family. His reward: becoming a family man.

The postwar era not only glorified motherhood, it also marked the creation of the "dad." Middle-class men had largely lost their role as family patriarch in the early twentieth century when the workplace became more distant from the home and mothers took over control within the home. Although recent research has suggested a brief moment of "masculine domesticity" in the early twentieth century, fathers became fairly remote throughout most of the first half of the century.[49] But by the 1950s fatherhood had changed again. Being a "dad" now became a new badge of masculinity. Men began attending classes on marriage and family in unprecedented numbers. In 1954 *Life* magazine announced "the domestication of the American male." Fatherhood was important not just to give meaning to men's lives, but to counteract what was believed to be a potentially dangerous overabundance of maternal care. Although mothers were of course expected to devote themselves full-time to their children, excessive mothering posed dangers that children would become too dependent upon female attention. The unhappy result would be "sissies." "Being a real father is not 'sissy' business," wrote a male psychiatrist in *Parents Magazine* in 1947, "It is an occupation . . . the most important occupation in the world."[50]

Dads were important as buddies to their children, providing a masculine influence. But they were not in charge of child-rearing. That remained the task of mothers. What is most remarkable about the family ideology after World War II is the polarized gender roles that it contained. In spite of the new empasis on togetherness and companionate marriage, the distinct roles for male breadwinners and female homemakers reflected a separation of the sexes more reminiscent of the Victorian era than anything in the twentieth century.

This polarization remained ideologically intact even in the face of powerful institutional and economic challenges. The very years that witnessed the reinvigoration of the breadwinner-homemaker dichotomy also witnessed the first significant influx of married women into the paid labor force. In increasing numbers of middle-class as well as working-class families, a wife's income became essential to sustain the desired standard of living. This widespread and widely noticed phenomenon did virtually nothing to erode the belief that men should be the providers for their families and women the full-time wives and mothers.

Institutional constraints facing employed women no doubt contributed to the relative invisibility of the massive influx of married women into jobs. Job opportunities for women expanded in numbers, but the range of possible occupations narrowed into largely clerical and service jobs with low pay and little opportunities for advancement. Because

For Better or For Worse

these were "jobs" more than "careers," middle-class women continued to define their "careers" in terms of their home-making and child-rearing responsibilities. In their efforts to elevate their domestic tasks to a level of status and responsibility worthy of a career, women were largely responsible for the heightening of standards and professionalization of homemaking that characterized these years. Given the lack of prestigious and rewarding work for women outside the home, it is no wonder that women downplayed their employment, claiming it was merely a means of supplementing the family income as well as diverting women during the hours when their children were in school. Homemaking provided women with the real rewards of status and meaning.[51]

Women understood the choices they faced. Many deliberately gave up jobs or decided not to pursue professional careers because it would be virtually impossible to combine those kinds of occupations with their work at home. As one middle-class woman explained in the 1950s, "I always hoped to be just what I am—a wife and a mother." Many women in the 1950s gave up occupational ambitions to become career homemakers. They described their choice by using the word "career," something for which they sacrificed and worked hard. Often the pursuit of that goal required tolerating a less-than-ideal marriage, scaling down expectations, and resigning oneself to a great deal of unhappiness. Maria Kimball was one woman whose marital saga includes many of the difficulties facing women in the postwar era who were forced to make difficult choices, and whose only route to respect and appreciation was the apparent achievement of a successful family life. Like many of her peers surveyed in a 1955 study of married life, she was determined to make the best of her situation. The advantages of suburban family life, combined with the extreme personal, emotional, and financial costs of divorce at the time, kept her in an unhappy marriage for more than three decades.

Maria Kimball's marriage was poisoned from the very beginning. Her husband, eager to enjoy premarital sexual relations, at the same time believed in a double standard of sexual morality. According to Maria, "The freedom of our relations before marriage saved us many stresses and strains we might otherwise have had. On the whole, however, I would say it was unfortunate. Despite his failure to recognize it then—or now, for that matter—I have concluded that my husband has deep emotional conventionality such that the attitudes our 'free

In the 1940s even the spunky female stars of the 1930s, like Joan Crawford, became domesticated. (Here she is shown in a publicity photograph.)

love' experience fostered undermined his respect and admiration for me. This is pure guesswork—but I think we established a set of 'mistress patterns' that had far-reaching unhealthy effects for our marital adjustment. Also it was stupid of me not to anticipate that his oft-expressed philosophy of the desirability of sexual freedom indicated that he would be prone to infidelity. I didn't expect it, and it came as a severe blow. An even worse blow was his amazement at this, and his statement that faith in a partner's constancy is sheer stupidity. I have been faithful, but doubt if he believes this."

Maria admitted that she quickly lost her "complete faith in the continuation of that romantic relationship," and that she no longer had "the hope of being loved—the security of living with someone I was sure was fond of me." Yet she stayed with the marriage for the "selfish satisfaction of physical nearness to someone whose nearness alone provides a thrill and a pleasure, two lovely children, an economic position stable enough so I can work at an ill-paid job I enjoy and have leisure time for friends I care about." She expressed the "purely female pleasure of having a husband whose behavior is never an embarrassment, who never lets one down in public, never vents malicious humor, and whose ideas and attitudes rarely jar one's own beliefs. In outside contacts, we work like a well-oiled team. It may be wryly amusing at times, but there's some satisfaction in having acquaintances envy one's apparent compatibility." She described what she called her "working marriage" saying, "So long as we maintain a breakdown in communication, we get along fine." Nevertheless, she continued, "He gives me no approval or affection and very rare support. Sex, which is completely without affection, gives me no lasting satisfaction, and it is the only kind I get. Our marriage works very well, yet I am frequently dreadfully *lonely.*" Years later, in the 1970s, when their children were grown and divorce became more acceptable, the Kimballs divorced.[52]

The Kimballs' case was not unique. The idealized family of the 1950s was nearly impossible to achieve. Yet successful family life was the badge of status, respectability, and good citizenship. Couples like the Kimballs went to great lengths to hide their difficulties and present themselves to the world as a happy family. Although divorce was relatively rare, many couples lowered their expectations and resigned themselves to living in unsatisfying unions. It was a choice that made sense at the time. The costs of deviating from the norm in the age of consensus was extremely high. Unmarried women and men were suspected of being selfish and immature at best, perverted at worst. Divorce left women with few opportunities to earn a decent living and a heavy stigma of having failed in life's main task. For men, the inability to succeed as a "family man" was tantamount to being un-American. As difficult as it was to live up to the domestic ideal, abandoning the effort posed even greater problems.

The domestic ideal, as it evolved during the twentieth century, had even more destructive effects on those who were outside its scope. Black families, for example, suffered from the combined effects of racism and poverty. White America excluded black families from suburban areas by redlining policies based on race. Thus even black families who could afford to live in suburbs were unable to move into them and had to remain in expensive, substandard inner-city apartments. Forced to rent when whites of modest means could buy, they lost the chance to build up equity in homes, which became a major means for white upward mobility after the war. The resulting abandonment of the inner cities by whites left blacks with a historical legacy of poverty.

At the same time, the kinship networks and extended household patterns of black families differed dramatically from the nuclear family ideal. Gender roles in black families rarely conformed to the homemaker-breadwinner dichotomy, since African-American women have usually worked to help sustain their families. Black families have been remarkably strong throughout American history in the face of powerful forces that worked against them (from slavery to an ill-designed welfare system). But African-American culture never included much of the Victorian domestic ideal, such as sexual repression and female domesticity, that came to define American "mainstream" values.

Immigrants and poor families who lacked the resources to achieve the "normative" affluent life-style suffered a stigma when compared to their middle-class contemporaries. For people who choose a different path altogether—gay men and lesbians, individuals who preferred to remain single, "career women" or men in nontraditional roles—the social ostracism could be nearly intolerable. Many homosexual men and women at the time married to protect themselves from becoming total social outcasts. Single women and men faced constant suspicion that there was something abnormal or dangerous about them. Meanwhile, the vast majority of white middle-class and working-class Americans conformed as best they could to the prevailing ideology, marrying young, having several children, and defining themselves first and foremost as homemakers or breadwinners.

The powerful domestic ideology that defined the successful family as an affluent, child-centered suburban household with a male breadwinner and female homemaker came under sustained attack. It failed to reflect reality accurately, even for those prosperous white families who presumably lived according to its precepts. In the early 1960s an increasing number of white middle-class Americans began to question

The 1960s: A New Watershed

the powerful domestic ideology that had prevailed since World War II. Among the first critics were postwar parents themselves. In 1963 Betty Friedan published her exposé of domesticity, *The Feminine Mystique*. Friedan gave a name to the "problem that has no name" for career homemakers. A postwar wife and mother herself, she spoke directly to women who had tried to conform to the homemaker role, urging them to break away from their domestic confines, go back to school, pursue careers, and revive the vision of female independence that had been alive before World War II. *The Feminine Mystique* became an immediate best-seller and created a national sensation. Hundreds of women, and many men as well, wrote to Friedan expressing their gratitude to her for voicing their feelings. The common thread linking those who responded to Friedan's book was their hope for their children. These postwar parents wanted to leave a different legacy to their children than that provided by the model of their own lives.[53]

By the end of the 1960s the new feminist movement had pushed beyond Friedan's call for self-realization into a full-fledged assault on sexism in all its forms, organized by younger women who emerged from their activism in the civil rights movement and the New Left with newly discovered skills and strengths. The new feminists demanded access to professional occupations and skilled jobs, protested low wages, and worked for pay equity. They formed consciousness-raising groups throughout the United States, challenged the gender division of labor in the home, and railed against the sexual double standard. Young middle-class men also began to rebel. They reacted against the rigidity of male gender expectations by letting their hair grow long, rejecting the "gray flannel suit" for flowered shirts and beads, and resisting the ethos of masculinity that defined the path of their breadwinner fathers.[54]

In spite of these challenges, attitudes changed only gradually. In 1965, 80 percent of those polled believed that schools should prohibit boys from wearing their hair long. A 1966 poll to determine the "ideal" family size yielded results that matched surveys taken in 1945 and 1957: the most common response was four or more children, given by 35 percent of those polled. It was not until 1971 that the figure dropped markedly, to 23 percent. In 1968 three out of four of those polled believed that the nation's morals were getting worse, and as late as 1969, more than two-thirds believed that premarital sex was wrong.[55]

Yet 1960 signified a demographic watershed that ultimately challenged normative behavior. After decades of decline, the age at marriage began to rise. The birthrate began
to dwindle as the first baby boomers reached child-rearing
age; within a decade, it was at an all-time low and still plum-
meting. The marriage rate also declined, as more people remained single or lived together as couples, families, and
households without marriage. The divorce rate, after more
than a decade of stability, began to rise gradually in the early
1960s and then dramatically in the late sixties, skyrocketing
to unprecedented heights in the early 1970s.

Critics of the youths of the 1960s complained that the
family-centered ethic of "togetherness" gave way to the hedonistic celebration of "doing your own thing." They failed
to perceive that the baby boomers pursued the quest for meaning through intimacy and private life that had been at the heart
of the domestic ideology, merely using different routes to
achieve it. Many abandoned the traditional family, home-
centered consumerism, marriage-centered sex, polarized gender roles, and the quest for meaning through children. The
youth culture, as well as the booming economy, encouraged
them to be risk-takers in fashioning their identities in ways
that their security-oriented parents found unthinkable.

Marriage became much less "normative." In the late 1970s
only 62 percent of all households included a married couple
and only one-third contained two parents and children under
age eighteen. Nearly one out of every four households consisted of an individual living alone. Compared to their parents,
baby boomers were less inclined to scale down their expectations to sustain unsatisfying unions. As divorce became more
common—50 percent of all new unions ended in divorce—the
stigma surrounding it began to lift. Divorce did not mean a
rejection of marriage, however; four out of every five divorced
persons remarried, half within three years. Divorced individuals at every age in fact were more likely to marry than those
who had never been married.[56]

Marriage remained a popular institution, but it began to
take on a different look. The birthrate declined and voluntary
childlessness was on the rise. Women had their children later
and held jobs outside the home to a greater extent than their
mothers had, even when their children were small. In the early
1980s half the married women with school-age children held
jobs, as did one-third of those with children under age six. A
solid majority of wives aged twenty to twenty-four were

In recent years, increasing numbers of women have been unwilling to choose between the joys of motherhood and the satisfactions of a career. While it remains difficult to do both, it is not impossible, especially for those who have ample resources.

employed, compared to only 26 percent in 1950. The vast number of married women in the paid labor force called into question the assumption that they should be responsible for all household chores when they, like their husbands, came home after a hard day at work. According to polls taken in the late 1970s, a majority of young single men, as well as women, believed that after they married both spouses would be employed and would share child care and housework equally. What did not change much was that domestic gender roles remained similar. The evidence suggests that although men began to "help out" more with domestic chores, women still suffered from double duty and remained responsible for the lion's share of child care and housework.[57] In America's private lives, resistance to some changes was glacial.

In spite of all the challenges to the status quo, institutions were slow to change. As the baby boomers matured, many found that their aspirations had moved far beyond their opportunities. Young women still faced enormous difficulties if they hoped to combine a career with marriage. Equal opportunity in the workplace was hindered by continued discrimination, sexual harassment, and low wages. Problems surrounding child care, parental leaves, and the burdens of housework continued to bedevil employed mothers. These persistent obstacles became so well known so quickly that female college students had high levels of anxiety and ambivalence toward the future. Political activism had done a great deal to improve opportunities for women and minorities, but only the tip of the institutional iceberg had begun to melt. Sex segregation still prevailed in the work force, and deeply entrenched attitudes about male and female roles still affected domestic arrangements at home. Although more women entered male-dominated professions, most working women still faced what their mothers had tried to avoid: overwork, inadequate pay, and extra burdens at home.[58]

Women who took the risk of divorce may have escaped oppressive or even brutal marriages, but they also encountered what their security-oriented mothers had feared: poverty, loneliness, difficulties in caring for their children, and the exhausting life of a single parent. Divorced women often experienced an immediate and sharp decline in their standard of living. Since they usually gained custody of children and received less-than-adequate child support, the meagerness of their incomes made their lives even more difficult. Divorced women and their children were much more likely than men to fall into poverty; men generally experienced a higher standard of living after divorce.[59] Even the legal triumphs that were hailed as harbingers of a more humane future often backfired, such as the no-fault divorce statutes. Because these new laws treated men and women "equally," they ignored the inequalities that marriage created and the lower earning power that left women with even more disadvantages after the dissolution of their marriages.[60]

Married or divorced, professional as well as nonprofessional wage-earning women continued to face inequalities at work and at home. Nevertheless, women finally achieved the opportunity to make choices that had been unavailable to their mothers. Women of the 1950s, constrained by tremendous cultural and economic pressures to conform to the ideology of domesticity, gave up their independence and personal ambitions. Once they made the choice to embrace domesticity, they did their best to thrive within it and claimed that their sacrifices were ultimately worthwhile. Many of their daughters abandoned security and material comfort to follow a more autonomous path that brought them face to face with economic hardship and pervasive discrimination. Yet, like their mothers, many would say that the struggles were worth it. Their mothers paid a price for security and dependence; the daughters paid a price for autonomy and independence. In both cases the lack of equal opportunity for women and the persistent beliefs about women's proper roles limited their options. Yet the daughters unquestionably had more opportunities than their mothers as a result of the hard-won political achievements of the 1960s and 1970s.

Political goals were only partially achieved, however. Even before the end of the 1960s, the "silent majority" rose up against the noisy, youthful minority to reassert what they believed to be traditional and timeless family values. The ideology of domesticity, once the centerpiece of the national consensus, now became the political rallying cry of the conservative right. After the Supreme Court in 1973 affirmed women's right to choose abortion, powerful forces of reaction mounted a crusade to recriminalize abortion in an effort to regain control over women's lives. It is no accident that in the wake of feminism and the sexual revolution of the 1960s and 1970s, the New Right emerged as a powerful political force with the dual aims of promoting a conservative political agenda and reasserting the ideology of domesticity.

Within four decades following World War II the American family had undergone such a massive transformation that it would have been almost unrecognizable to a 1950s Rip Van Winkle who awoke in the 1980s. The family that television situation comedies defined as typical during the peak of the baby boom—breadwinning father, homemaking mother, and dependent children—represented fewer than 15 percent of all families in the United States by the mid-eighties. The stigma attached to what were once called "broken homes" eased as divorce became increasingly common. Nearly half of all children born in the 1980s would spend some of their early years in a single-parent household. The baby boom turned into a baby bust, from a high of 3.8 children per family down to fewer than 2 in the late eighties. The number of unmarried couples cohabiting quadrupled during the same years, while the proportion of women waiting until marriage before engaging in sexual intercourse dropped from half in 1960 to one-fifth three decades later. Out-of-wedlock births increased fourfold.

Employment patterns for women changed as dramatically as sexual, marriage, and childbearing norms. In 1950, 25 percent of wives were employed. By 1988 the proportion had reached 60 percent. The most striking change within this pattern was among women with children. Only 12 percent of mothers of preschoolers were employed in 1950; by 1980 the number had grown to 45 percent. By the late 1980s over two-thirds of all three- and four-year-olds were in day care or nursery schools.[61]

These statistics point to a dramatic transformation in American family life that has had profound ramifications. On the positive side, there is a much greater tolerance for a wide range of family arrangements than existed before. Since no "typical" family represents normative behavior, even the popular culture has begun to reflect the variety of family forms that exist today. At the same time, as the harsh reality of domestic violence and child abuse has gained national attention, some of the mythic haze that once surrounded the image of the nuclear family has lifted. On the negative side, however, public institutions of work and civic life operate as though the mythic nuclear family of the Victorian era exists today. Because women's wages often continue to reflect the fiction that men earn the family wage, single mothers rarely earn enough to support themselves and their children adequately. And be-

The 1980s: Recasting the Family

The tremendous increase in working mothers has resulted in a proliferation of day-care centers for young children.

cause work is still organized around the assumption that mothers stay home with children, even though few mothers can afford to do so, child-care facilities in the United States remain woefully inadequate.

Changes in the family have occurred more rapidly than American political or economic institutions could adjust to them. As a result a backlash has developed in which politicians calling themselves "profamily" have tried to institute policies that will force families to function together in ways that they allegedly did in the past. These policymakers favor legislation requiring parental consent for teenagers to get abortions and oppose measures that would provide increased child-care facilities for working mothers.

At a time when American teenagers have the highest pregnancy rate of any industrialized nation, it is not likely that such measures will force American women and men into the sort of family arrangements favored by these politicians. It is much more likely that the policies will create increased difficulties for young mothers and their children. Since 1960 the number of babies born to unwed women has quadrupled. Among sexually active teenage girls in the late 1970s, nearly one-third of whites and nearly half of blacks had become pregnant by the age of eighteen. Today more than half of all black babies are born to unmarried women, and half of all black children grow up in poverty.[62] Punitive laws will not improve the lives of these children. Eventually institutions will be forced to change to meet the reality of the nation's families. Without such changes the future might look bleak, with most of the nation's parents forced to work long hours for low wages, while their children receive inadequate care. The "typical" family under such circumstances would be marked by poverty and neglect, rather than the comfort and solace that characterized the domestic ideal of the past.

Unfortunately the old mythic vision still holds sway in the American imagination. Observers and moralists continue to bemoan the collapse of the American family. But it is not the first time, nor is it likely to be the last. The demise of the family was proclaimed in the seventeenth century, as the earliest European settlers arrived on American shores. The family has evolved continuously since then. The rapid changes that have occurred in the past few decades have been dramatic, and they pose challenges that the nation has never faced before. But American women and men continue to carve out their lives as best they can, inside or outside society's norms.

Summary: The Family and
American Political Culture

The American family is an institution that has changed slowly, shaped by an ideology only recently in flux, influenced by major historical events, and constrained by deeply held and remarkably persistant attitudes about the proper roles of women and men. The twentieth-century family ideal has its roots in the nineteenth century, when Victorian Americans defined the family in new ways that differed radically from those of the past. The Victorian family, though culturally situated in a realm separate from public life, remained deeply tied to civic values and the goals of the larger political culture.

As the twentieth century progressed, the public functions of the home receded as the ideal of family life became more leisure-centered and more privatized. But the polarized gender roles that provided the philosophical underpinnings of the Victorian family continued to permeate public and private life. The tenacity of these attitudes and their institutionalization in political and economic institutions is all the more remarkable given the enormous challenges to them throughout the century.

In spite of the persistence of many of its features the American family continues to evolve. The wide diversity of family structures that exist today has profoundly challenged beliefs about the "ideal" or "normative" family. Divorce has become so common that today's families are frequently arranged around relationships between ex-spouses and stepparents, stepsiblings and quasi-in-laws. Marriage is no longer the determining factor in family life, as couples live together, and as single-parent families become increasingly common. Even parenthood is being defined in new ways. With recent developments in such areas as open adoption and new reproductive technologies, children can have up to five "natural" parents: genetic mother, birth mother, nurturing mother, genetic father (or sperm donor), and nurturing father. At the same time, the full-time homemaker as well as the male breadwinner who earns the "family wage" exist in fewer than 10 percent of American homes, as most families rely on the income of virtually all the adults within it. As life expectancy increases, families are faced with the care of additional dependents, not only the children and stepchildren of the household, but elderly parents as well.

Gradually, and ironically, the "normative" American family is coming to resemble family patterns that have historically been typical of "marginalized" Americans: black families or-

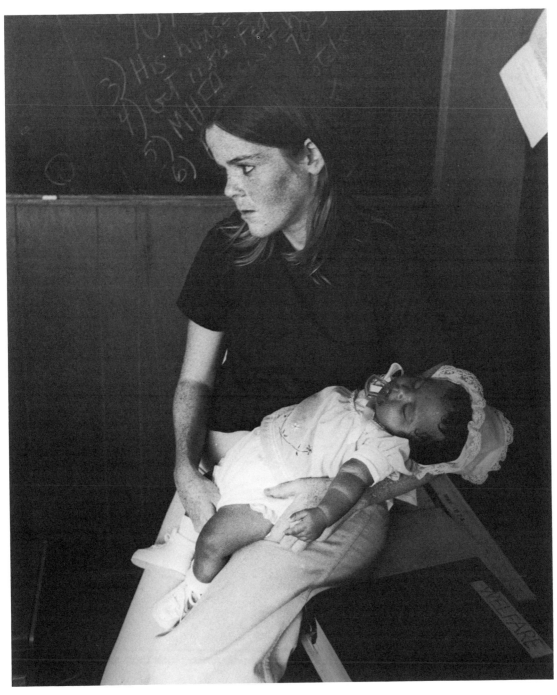

Teenage mothers of today frequently choose to keep their children, rather than put them up for adoption. Many high schools have responded with special programs for student parents.

ganized around kinship and fictive kin, and households organized around divorce rather than marriage. The white middle class may be losing its place as the trend-setting group in American domestic arrangements. Working-class and African-American family patterns may be replacing those of the white middle-class and taking the lead in new definitions of family life. The middle class seems to be adopting patterns first established by "outsiders" to the nuclear family ideal, as single-parent, double-earner, and extended kinship patterns become increasingly common.[63]

Eventually American institutions will have to adjust to the new realities of family life. If families are to be healthy and stable units, the home as well as the economic realm must be more flexible to allow for greater sharing of responsibilities and more available options to men as well as women. Until that time individual women and men will need to negotiate the terms of their private lives in the face of public or institutional constraints and archaic beliefs about what it means to be a man or a woman in American society, and what a stable, happy, and healthy family requires.

Notes

Bibliography

Credits

Index

Notes

1. Public and Private Spheres in France

Introduction (Antoine Prost)

1. Baroness Staffe, *Usages du monde. Règles du savoir-vivre dans la société moderne* (Paris: Victor-Harvard, 1893), pp. 342, 317, 320.

2. Guy Thuillier, *Pour une histoire du quotidien en Nivernais au XIXe siècle* (Paris: Mouton, 1977), p. 178.

3. Jean-Paul Sartre, *Lettres au Castor et à quelques autres* (Paris: Gallimard, 1983), I, 79.

Changing Workers and Workplaces (Antoine Prost)

1. This hierarchy is clearly evident in studies of the situation of young women at marriage. See Antoine Prost, "Mariage, jeunesse et société à Orléans en 1911," *Annales E.S.C*, July–August 1981, pp. 672–701.

2. Serge Grafteaux, *Mémé Santerre, une vie* (Paris: Editions du Jour, 1975).

3. Léon Frapié, *La Maternelle* (1905; Paris: Albin Michel, 1953). Frapié worked in an office in Paris's city hall and was an adept of the Belleville section of the city, which is described in his novel.

4. Jean Guéhenno, *Journal d'un homme de quarante ans* (Paris: Grasset, 1934), pp. 67–73.

5. For a long time scholars endorsed Le Play's view that in traditional families one or more married children remained under parental authority even after having children of their own. When Peter Laslett's work on seventeenth- and eighteenth-century England made it necessary to reexamine the question, it was discovered that the average family in many villages consisted of no more than three to four individuals. At Chardonneret (Oise), for example, in 1836, only 15 percent of all households contained extended families. See the special issue of *Ethnologie française*, nos. 1–2, 1974.

6. Ephraïm Grenadou and Alain Prévost, *Grenadou, paysan français* (Paris: Seuil, 1966).

7. Patrick Fridenson, *Histoire des usines Renault* (Paris: Seuil, 1972), I, 332, includes plans for these factories as of 1898, 1914, 1919, and 1926.

8. Gérard Noiriel, *Longwy. Immigrés et prolétaires, 1880–1980* (Paris: Presses Universitaires de France, 1984), p. 42. The differentiation of factory space at the immense Le Creusot plant began in the mid-nineteenth century. Compare Christian Devillers and Bernard Huet, *Le Creusot, naissance et développement d'une ville industrielle, 1782–1914* (Seyssel: Champ Vallon, 1981).

9. Ibid., p. 91, based on a report of the Conseil d'Etat following an investigation carried out in cooperation with the Comité des Forges. The observations concerned the Nord département.

10. Georges Lamirand, *Le rôle social de l'ingénieur. Scènes de la vie d'usine* (Paris: Revue des jeunes, 1932, 1937), pp. 164–166.

11. Yves Lequin, *Les Ouvriers de la région lyonnaise (1848–1914)*, 2 vols. (Lyons: Presses Universitaires de Lyon, 1977), II, 115–116, stresses the importance of factory dormitories in the Lyons region at the turn of the century.

12. Yvonne Knibiehler, ed., *Cornettes et blouses blanches. Les Infirmières dans la société française, 1880–1980* (Paris: Hachette, 1984), p. 50.

13. Nicolas Dubost, *Fins sans fin* (Paris: Maspero, 1979).

14. Pierre-Jakez Hélias, *Le Cheval d'orgueil. Mémoires d'un Breton du pays bigouden* (Paris: Plon, 1975).

15. Jules Payot, *La Morale à l'école (cours moyen et supérieur)* (Paris: Armand Colin, 1907), p. 193.

16. These examples are based on studies of documents pertaining to the 1911 census in Orléans.

17. Noiriel, *Longwy, immigrés et prolétaires,* p. 211.

18. Jean-Paul Depretto and Sylvie V. Schweitzer, *Le Communisme à l'usine: Vie ouvrière et mouvement ouvrier chez Renault, 1920–1939* (Roubaix: Edires, 1984), p. 61.

19. The phrase is that of the general secretary of the CGT, quoted in *Action directe*, April 23, 1908. See Jacques Julliard, *Clemenceau, briseur de grèves* (Paris: Julliard, 1965), p. 31.

20. The expression is that of M. Jacquet, a smelter from Clermont-Ferrand. See Edwin Shorter and Charles Tilly, *Strikes in France (1830–1968)*

(Cambridge: Cambridge University Press, 1974), p. 35.

21. Letter published in *Le Peuple*, August 21, 1936. This particular industrialist owned factories in Brazey, Genlis, and Trouhans.

22. Georges Ribeill has thoroughly analyzed the negotiations leading up to the 1937 compromise. See Ribeill "Y a-t-il eu des nationalisations avant la guerre?" in Claire Andrieu, Lucette Le Van, and Antoine Prost, *Les Nationalisations de la Libération* (Paris: Presses de la FNSP, 1989), pp. 40–52.

23. Olivier Kourchid, *Production industrielle et travail sous l'Occupation* (Paris: Groupe de sociologie du travail, 1985), vol. 3, mimeographed, describes the organization of the social committee of the Lens Mines. CEGOS recommended that worker members of the social committees be chosen by election. A memo circulated by the Paris regional subcommittee of the UIMM, the business group representing firms in the mining and metals industries, recommended that workers who engaged in political or union activity not be excluded from election unless they were Communists.

THE FAMILY AND THE INDIVIDUAL (ANTOINE PROST)

1. Roger-Henri Guerrand, *Les Origines du logement social en France* (Paris: Editions Ouvrières, 1966).

2. Jean Guéhenno, *Journal d'un homme de quarante ans* (Paris: Grasset, 1934), pp. 57–58.

3. Guerrand, *Les Origines*, based on Dr. J. Bertillon, *Revue d'hygiène et de police sanitaire* (May 1908): 377–399.

4. Odette Hardy-Hemery, *De la croissance à la désindustrialisation. Un siècle dans le Valenciennois* (Paris: Presses de la Fondation Nationale de Sciences Politiques, 1984), p. 39.

5. Michel Quoist, *La Ville et l'homme* (Paris: Editions Ouvrières, 1952).

6. Paul-Henri Chombart de Lauwe, *La Vie quotidienne des familles ouvrières* (Paris: CNRS, 1956).

7. Quoist, *La Ville et l'homme*, pp. 64–65.

8. Lucien Bernot and René Blancard, *Neuville, un village français* (Paris: Institut d'Ethnologie, 1953).

9. A. de Foville, *Les Maisons types*, 1894, cited by Guerrand, *Les Origines*, p. 218.

10. Léon Frapié, *La Maternelle* (1905; Paris: Albin Michel, 1953).

11. Susan Carol Rogers, "Female Forms of Power and the Myth of Male Dominance: A Model of Female-Male Interaction in Peasant Society," *American Ethnologist* 2 (1975): 727–756.

12. Martine Segalen, *Mari et femme dans la société paysanne* (Paris: Flammarion, 1980), translated as *Love and Power in the Peasant Family* (London: Blackwell, 1983).

13. Martha Wolfenstein, "French Parents Take Their Children to the Park," in Margaret Mead and Martha Wolfenstein, eds., *Childhood in Contemporary Cultures* (Chicago: University of Chicago Press, 1955), pp. 99–117.

14. Henri Mendras, *Etudes de sociologie rurale, Novis et Virgin* (Paris: Armand Colin, 1953).

15. "Comment élever les enfants" (How to Raise Children), poll conducted by *Confidences*, 29 July 1938 (results published 14 October 1938).

16. The magazine repeated the same poll in 1977. In answer to the same question, the noes (89 percent) far outweighed the yeses (4.4 percent).

17. Marc Martin, "Images du mari et de la femme au XXe siècle. Les annonces de mariage du *Chasseur français*," *Revue d'histoire moderne et contemporaine* 2 (1980): 195–311. For 50 percent of the men and 67 percent of the women, the 1930 announcements indicated the existence of a dowry or "expectations"; and for 90 percent of the men and 38 percent of the women they indicated the profession or social position.

18. Anne-Marie Sohn, "Les Rôles féminins dans la vie privée, approche méthodologique et bilan de recherches," *Revue d'histoire moderne et contemporaine* 4 (1981): 597–623.

19. "Comment concevez-vous le bonheur conjugal?" (What Is Your Idea of Marital Happiness?), poll conducted by *Confidences*, 17 June 1938 (results published 26 August 1938).

20. Philippe Ariès, "Familles du demi-siècle," in Robert Prigent, ed., *Renouveau des idées sur la famille* (Paris: Presses Universitaires de France, 1953), pp. 162–170.

21. See the texts of lectures by André Le Gall, Serge Lebovici, Michel Cenac, André Berge, Juliette Boutonier-Favez, and Clément Launay in *L'Ecole des parents*, November 1953.

22. Caption of a photo published in *La Croix*, 5 May 1954, showing a young couple with the father carrying the child.

23. "La Femme de marbre," *Confidences*, 17 March 1950.

24. *Femmes françaises*, 12 August 1950.

25. Louis Roussel, "La Cohabitation juvénile en France," *Population* 1 (1978): 15–41. The preceding

analyses of marriage owe a great deal to Roussel's work, especially *Le Mariage dans la société française contemporaine. Faits de population, données d'opinion* (Paris: Presses Universitaires de France, 1975) and, in collaboration with Odile Bourguignon, *La Famille après le mariage des enfants, étude des relations entre générations* (Paris: Presses Universitaires de France, 1976) and *Générations nouvelles et mariage traditionnel, enquête auprès des jeunes de dix-huit/trente ans* (Paris: Presses Universitaires de France, 1979).

26. François de Singly, "Le mariage informel. Sur la cohabitation," *Recherches sociologiques* 1 (1981): 61–90.

27. Guy Thuillier, *Pour une histoire du quotidien en Nivernais au XIXe siècle* (Paris: Mouton, 1977); Eugen Weber, *Peasants into Frenchmen: The Modernization of Rural France, 1870–1914* (Stanford: Stanford University Press, 1976), and *France: Fin de Siècle* (Cambridge, Mass.: Harvard University Press, 1986).

28. I am indebted for this anecdote to my colleague Michel Vovelle, whose mother was the school principal.

29. Octave Mirbeau, *Journal d'une femme de chambre*, cited by Georges Vigarello, *Le Propre et le sale. L'Hygiène du corps depuis le Moyen Age* (Paris: Seuil, 1985), p. 231.

30. See the letters column of *Marie-Claire*, 7 May 1937. Editor Marcelle Auclair writes: "A grandmother from Neuilly-sur-Seine criticizes me for encouraging selfishness in men when I recommend that women make an effort to stay beautiful in order to please their husbands as long as they can."

31. Gilles Lipovetsky, *L'Ere du vide. Essai sur l'individualisme contemporain* (Paris: Gallimard, 1983), p. 191; Pascal Ory, *L'Entre-deux-Mai. Histoire culturelle de la France, mai 1968–mai 1981* (Paris: Seuil, 1983), p. 129.

32. Paul Yonnet, "Des modes et des looks," *Le Débat* 34 (1985): 113–129.

33. The five included: one Parisian killed during a demonstration; a policeman in Lyons on the Pont de la Guillotière; the student Gilles Tautin, drowned in the Seine near Flins; and two workers in Sochaux. The student demonstrations of December 1986, in which the death of a student sparked a tremendous outcry, offer striking confirmation of the views expressed here prior to the events.

34. Lipovetsky, *L'Ere du vide*, p. 223.

35. Henri Hatzfeld, *Le Grand tournant de la médecine libérale* (Paris: Ouvrières, 1963), points out that the payment schedule specified in the law of 1930 was not binding on doctors; it simply determined the amount of reimbursement under national health insurance. After the law was passed, doctors, reassured that they would not be imposing an undue burden on their poorest patients, did not hesitate to insist on payment.

THE TRANSITION FROM NEIGHBORHOOD TO METROPOLIS (ANTOINE PROST)

1. Luce Giard and Pierre Mayol, *Habiter, Cuisiner* (Paris: Union Générale d'Editions, 1980). The first part of this book is a monograph on the life of a working-class family in Croix-Rousse, to which I am greatly indebted.

2. Daniel Bertaux and Isabelle Bertaux-Wiame, "Artisanal Bakery in France: How It Lives and Why It Survives," in Frank Bechofer and Bryan Elliott, eds., *The Petite Bourgeoisie: Comparative Studies of the Uneasy Stratum* (London: Macmillan, 1981), pp. 155–181.

3. Giard and Mayol, *Habiter, Cuisiner*, p. 97. I wish there were room to quote this dialogue in its entirety.

4. Laurent Marty, *Chanter pour survivre. Culture ouvrière, travail et technique dans le textile: Roubaix, 1850–1914* (Liévin: Fédération Léo-Lagrange, 1982), pp. 123 ff.

5. Colette Pétonnet, *Espaces habités. Ethnologie des banlieues* (Paris: Galilée, 1982).

6. Richard Hoggart, *The Uses of Literacy: Changing Patterns in English Mass Culture* (Oxford: Oxford University Press, 1957). This remarkably perspicacious book argued that, at the time of its publication in 1957, working-class culture in England had survived the onslaughts of the media, advertising, and consumer society.

7. *La Population française de A à Z* (Paris: La Documentation Française), *Les Cahiers français*, no. 219, January–February 1985, p. 9.

8. Centre d'étude des groupes sociaux. Centre de sociologie urbaine. *Logement et vie familiale. Etude sociologique de quartiers nouveaux* (Paris: CSU, 1965).

9. Nicole Haumont, *Les Pavillonnaires* (Paris: Centre de recherches d'urbanisme, 1975).

10. Jean Rousselet, *L'Allergie au travail* (Paris: Seuil, 1974).

11. Felix S. Dossou, "L'insertion des jeunes dans la vie professionnelle, conditions et mécanismes de l'insertion," *L'Entrée dans la vie active* (Paris:

Presses Universitaires de France, 1977), pp. 181–332 (Cahiers du Centre d'études de l'emploi, no. 15).

12. Bernard Galambaud, *Les Jeunes Travailleurs d'aujourd'hui* (Toulouse: Privat, 1977).

13. Georges Lamirand, *Le Rôle social de l'ingénieur. Scènes de la vie d'usine* (Paris: Editions de la Revue des Jeunes, 1932).

14. Jean-Pierre Barou, *Gilda je t'aime, pas le travail* (Paris: Les Presses d'aujourd'hui, 1975), p. 67.

15. Nicolas Dubost, *Flins sans fin* (Paris: Maspero, 1979), p. 172.

16. Daniel Mothé, *Militant chez Renault* (Paris: Seuil, 1965), pp. 32, 40.

17. Charles Piaget, *Lip* (Paris: Stock, 1973), pp. 43, 54, 95, 97. The Lip Company, which manufactured watches, faced stiff competition from low-priced imports and the new digital watch technology.

18. Alain Ehrenberg, "C'est au Club et nulle part ailleurs," *Le Débat* 34 (March 1985): 130–145. The phrase "relaxed society" is borrowed from this article.

19. Edgar Morin, *L'Esprit du temps* (Paris: Grasset, 1962), p. 97. This book, written almost thirty years ago, proposed a diagnosis confirmed by subsequent events.

20. The argument in this section owes much to Gilles Lipovetsky, *L'Ere du vide. Essai sur l'individualisme contemporain* (Paris: Gallimard, 1983).

21. Roland Barthes, *Système de la mode* (Paris: Seuil, 1967).

22. André-Jean Tudesq, "L'évolution de la presse quotidienne en France au XXe siècle," *Revue d'histoire moderne et contemporaine* 3 (1982): 500–507.

23. Jean-Pierre Rioux, "Les trente-six chandelles de la télé," *L'Histoire* 86 (February 1986): 38–53, and Pierre Albert and André-Jean Tudesq, *Histoire de la radio-télévision* (Paris: Presses Universitaires de France, 1981).

24. Pascal Ory, *L'Entre-deux-Mai. Histoire culturelle de la France, mai 1968–1981* (Paris: Seuil, 1983), p. 47.

25. See the surveys conducted by Jacques Valdour in the early 1920s; for example, *Ateliers et taudis de la banlieue de Paris: Observations vécues.* (Paris: SPES, 1923).

26. Evelyne Sullerot, *La Presse féminine* (Paris: Armand Colin, 1966), p. 58.

27. Henry Raymond, "Hommes et dieux à Palinero," *Esprit* 6 (1959): 1030–1040, refers to celebrities as "Olympians."

28. Significantly, this analysis was given long ago by Morin, *L'Esprit du temps,* esp. p. 142.

2. A History of Secrets?

THE SECRETS OF HISTORY AND THE RIDDLE OF IDENTITY (GÉRARD VINCENT)

1. J.-D. Bredin, "Le droit, le juge et l'historien," *Le Débat* 32 (1984): 93–111.

2. See *Legislation sociale,* no. 5285, 31 January 1983, D 344.

3. See Arnaud Lévy, "Evaluation étymologique et sémantique du mot 'secret,'" *Nouvelle revue de psychanalyse* 14 (1976): 117–130.

4. Serge Leclaire, "Fragments de langue d'avant Babel," *Nouvelle revue de psychanalyse* 14 (1976): 207–216.

5. E. Pleynel, *Le Monde,* 5 May 1984.

6. Sigmund Freud, *Civilization and Its Discontents,* trans. Joan Riviere (London: Hogarth, 1951), pp. 63–64, 121, 136.

7. Charles David, "Le Cauchemar d'un curieux," *Nouvelle revue de psychanalyse* 14 (1976): 261–274.

FAMILY SECRETS (GÉRARD VINCENT)

1. G. Calot, "Forces et faiblesses de la population française. La population française de A à Z," *Les Cahiers français* 219 (1985): 69–72.

2. The account given here is modeled on that of Pierre Simon in *De la vie avant toute chose* (Paris: Mazarine, 1979).

3. This information is taken from Dr. Pierre Coutant et al., "Les Mères de substitution," Institut d'Etudes Politiques internal document, mimeographed, 1985.

4. Yvonne Verdier, *Façons de dire, façons de faire. La Laveuse, la couturière, la cuisinière* (Paris: Gallimard, 1979).

5. André Béjin, "Le Mariage extraconjugal aujourd'hui," *Communications* 35 (1982): 138–146.

6. Sabine Chalvon-Demersay, "L'Union libre," *Encyclopedia Universalis,* 1985, pp. 408–411.

7. Evelyne Sullerot, Report on "Marital Status and Its Legal Consequences" presented to the Economic and Social Council on January 24 and 25, 1984.

8. See Marc Martin, "Images du mari et de la femme au XXe siècle: les annonces de mariage du *Chasseur français,*" *Revue d'histoire moderne et contemporaine* (April–June 1980): 295–311; Sarah Roberts and Olivier Robin-Mariéton, "Les Petites Annonces de mariage du Chasseur français," Institut d'Etudes Politiques internal document, mimeographed, 1972.

9. Philippe Ariès, "Le Mariage indissoluble" and "L'Amour dans le mariage," *Communications* 35 (1982): 123–137, 116–122.

10. Alain Girard and Jean Stoetzel, *Les Valeurs du temps, une enquête européenne* (Paris: Presses Universitaires de France, 1983).

11. See François de Singly, "La Lutte conjugale pour le pouvoir domestique," *Revue française de sociologie* (January–March 1976): 81–100; and François de Singly, "Sociologie de la famille: La Porte et le pont," *Encyclopaedia Universalis, Les Enjeux* (1985), pp. 670–679.

12. Elena Gianini Belotti, *Du Côté des petites filles* (Paris: Edition des Femmes, 1974).

The Body and the Enigma of Sex (Gérard Vincent)

1. Philippe Perrot, *Le Travail des apparences* (Paris: Seuil, 1984).

2. Véronique Nahoum, "La belle femme ou le stade du miroir en histoire," *Communications* 31 (1979): 22–32.

3. Pierre Bourdieu, "Remarques provisoires sur la perception sociale du corps," *Actes de la recherche en sciences sociales* 14 (April 1977).

4. Mary Douglas, "Les structures de culinaire," *Communications* 31 (1979): 145–170.

5. Yvonne Verdier, *Façons de dire, façons de faire. La Laveuse, la couturière, la cuisinière* (Paris: Gallimard, 1980), p. 322.

6. C. Fischler, "Gastro-nomie et gastro-anomie. Sagesse du corps et crise bioculturelle de l'alimentation moderne," *Communications* 31 (1979): 189–210.

7. Claude and Christiane Grignon, "Styles d'alimentation et goûts populaires," special issue of *Revue française de sociologie* (October–December 1980): 531–569.

8. Francine Muel-Dreyfus, "Le Fantôme du médecin de famille," *Actes de la recherche en sciences sociales* 54 (September 1984): 70–71.

9. M. Bariety and C. Coury, *Histoire de la médecine* (Paris: Fayard, 1963).

10. Gérard Vincent, *Les Jeux français. Essai sur la société moderne* (Paris: Fayard, 1978), pp. 82–100.

11. Paul Paillat, "La Vieillesse," *Encyclopaedia Universalis*, 1985, pp. 32–36.

12. E. Andréani, *Indicateurs sociaux pour la population âgée. Documents d'information et de gestion. Gérontologie*, September–November 1974.

13. Paillat, "La Vieillesse," p. 33.

14. For the Ariès quotations in this section and the next, see Philippe Ariès, *Essais sur l'histoire de la mort en Occident du Moyen Age à nos jours* (Paris: Seuil, 1975); and "La Mort inversée, le changement des attitudes devant la mort dans les sociétés occidentales," *Archives européennes de sociologie* 8 (1967): 169–195.

15. The most recent statistics can be found in *Données sociales* (1984) published by INSEE in 1985, pp. 348–383. See also G. Desplanques, "L'inégalité sociale devant la mort," *Economie et statistique* 162 (January 1984): 29–50.

16. Jean-Claude Chamboredon, "La restauration de la mort, objets scientifiques et fantasmes sociaux," *Actes de la recherche en sciences sociales* 2/3 (June 1976).

17. Claudie Herzlich, "Le Travail de la mort," *Annales ESC*, January–February 1976, pp. 197–217.

18. Denys Pouillard, "Le Droit de vivre sa mort," *Encyclopaedia Universalis*, 1979, pp. 162–164.

19. Louis-Vincent Thomas, *Anthropologie de la mort* (Paris: Payot, 1975).

20. Pierre Guiraud, *Dictionnaire historique, stylistique, rhétorique, étymologique de la littérature érotique* (Paris: Payot, 1978).

21. Karima Dekhli, "Civilité du sexe moderne," *La Chose sexuelle, Nouvelle Revue de psychanalyse* 29 (1983). Although there is much discussion of sexuality, little of it is serious. There are countless surveys, but most are conducted casually. One exception, already out of date, is the *Rapport sur le comportement sexuel des Français*, known as the "Simon Report," edited by René Julliard and Pierre Charron in 1972. Between June 20 and September 25, 1970, 2,625 persons were interviewed and asked to fill out written questionnaires. The survey was conducted by 173 specially trained investigators, each of whom attached notes to each questionnaire and prepared an overall summary at the end of the survey.

22. See Jean-Louis Flandrin, "La Vie sexuelle des gens mariés dans l'ancienne société: de la doctrine de l'Eglise à la réalité des comportements," *Communications* 35 (1982): 102–113.

23. André Béjin, "Crépuscule des psychanalystes et matin des sexologues," and "Le Pouvoir des sexologues et la démocratie sexuelle," *Communications* 35 (1982): 159–171, 178–191.

24. Michel Pollak, "L'Homosexualité masculine ou le bonheur dans le ghetto?" *Communications* 35 (1982): 37–53.

25. The figures in this section are taken from two important studies of homosexuals: Martin Dan-

necker and R. Reiche, *Der gewöhnliche Homosexuelle* (Frankfurt: Fischer, 1974), and A. P. Bell and M. S. Weinberg, *Homosexualities: A Study of Diversity among Men and Women* (New York: Simon and Schuster, 1978).

26. Philippe Ariès, "Reflexions sur l'histoire de l'homosexualité," *Communications* 35 (1982): 57.

27. Ibid., p. 63.

3. Cultural Diversity in France

CATHOLICS: IMAGINATION AND SIN (GÉRARD VINCENT)

1. Results of this study are given in G. Bessière et al., *Les Volets du presbytère sont ouverts*, summarized in J.-C. Petit, "Les Volets du presbytère sont ouverts," *La Vie* 2091 (September 26–October 2, 1985).

2. Alain Girard and Jean Stoetzel, *Les Valeurs du temps: une enquête européenne* (Paris: Presses Universitaires de France, 1983). A summary of the findings for France can be found in "Les Français et les valeurs du temps présent," *Revue française de sociologie* (January–March 1985): 3–31.

3. Roger Mehl, *Rapport présenté au Conseil de la fédération protestante de France le 30 mai 1981.* Mehl used the results of the IFOP survey of March 1980, administered to a representative sample of 9,871 persons fifteen years of age or older; 414 of these said they were "close to Protestantism."

4. André Dumas, "Les Protestants français," *Encyclopaedia Universalis*, 1984, p. 336.

5. James Joyce, *A Portrait of the Artist as a Young Man* (New York: Penguin, 1960), pp. 132, 130, 131, 129.

6. Yves Lambert, "Crise de la confession, crise de l'économie du salut: le cas d'une paroisse de 1900 à 1902," *Pratiques de la confession. Les Pères du Désert de Vatican II* (Paris: Cerf, 1983).

7. Philippe Boutry, "Réflexions sur la confession au XIXe siècle: autour d'une lettre de soeur Marie-Zoé au curé d'Ars (1858)," *Pratiques de la confession.*

8. Lambert, "Crise de la confession," pp. 257, 259.

9. Some of this information comes from Boutry, "Réflexions."

10. Michel de Certeau, "L'Eglise catholique: La Fin de la période postconciliaire," *Encyclopaedia Universalis*, 1977, pp. 141–144.

11. Ibid.

COMMUNISM AS A WAY OF LIFE (GÉRARD VINCENT)

1. André Harris and Alain de Sédouy, *Voyage à l'intérieur du parti communiste* (Paris: Seuil, 1974), p. 34.

2. Dominique Desanti, *Les Staliniens, une expérience politique, 1944–1956* (Paris: Fayard/Marabout, 1975), pp. 513, 520.

3. Cited by Marc Lazard, "Le Mineur du fond. Un exemple de l'identité du PCF," *Revue française de science politique* (April 1985): 190–205.

4. Laurent Casanova, *Le PCF, les Intellectuels et la Nation* (Paris: Editions Sociales, 1949), pp. 67–68.

5. Desanti, *Les Staliniens*, pp. 205, 206, 36.

6. Herbert Marcuse, *One-Dimensional Man.* The analysis here is virtually identical with that given in Gérard Vincent, *Les Jeux français* (Paris: Fayard, 1978), pp. 256, 257, 272, 273.

7. Desanti, *Les Staliniens*, p. 33.

8. Harris and de Sedouy, *Voyage*, p. 35.

9. Annie Kriegel, *Les Communistes français (1920–1970)* (Paris: Seuil, 1985).

10. Philippe Robrieux, *Maurice Thorez, vie secrète et vie privée* (Paris: Fayard, 1975).

11. Georges Sorel, *Réflexions sur la violence* (Paris, 1908), p. 55.

12. Martin E. Malia, *Comprendre la révolution russe* (Paris: Seuil, 1980).

13. Henri Lefebvre, *La Somme et le reste* (Paris: NEF, 1959), I, 73.

14. On this question, see Henri Chambre, *Le Marxisme en Union soviétique* (Paris: Seuil, 1955), pp. 468 ff., and Hélène Carrère d'Encausse and Stuart Schram, *Le Marxisme et l'Asie, 1853–1954* (Paris: Armand Colin, 1965), which considers the shift in the center of communism from Europe to Asia.

15. Desanti, *Les Staliniens*, p. 510.

16. *Le Monde*, July 7, 1977.

17. James Joyce, *Ulysses* (Paris, 1922); quotation from the 1971 Penguin reprint, p. 31.

JUDAISM IN FRANCE (PERRINE SIMON-NAHUM)

1. Dominique Schnapper, "Une Mémoire de l'enracinement: les juifs français avant 1940," *Revue des sciences humaines de Lille-III* 191 (July–September 1983).

2. Edmond Jabès, *Judaïsme et écriture* (Paris: Gallimard.)

3. Schnapper, "Mémoire de l'enracinement," p. 91.

4. Information in private archives of the Rein-

ach family. A photograph shows Barrès visiting one of the Reinach brothers on the battlefield.

5. Jacques Tchernoff, *Dans le creuset des civilisations*, 4 vols. Vol. 4: *Des Prodromes du bolchévisme à la société des nations* (Paris: Rieder, 1938), p. 246.

6. Annie Benveniste, "Les Structures de la communauté judéo-espagnole du quartier de la Roquette entre les deux guerres," *Traces* (special edition on Jews and Judaism) 9–10 (1984): 34–37, p. 36.

7. Georges Wellers, *De Drancy à Auschwitz* (Paris: Edition du Centre, 1946), p. 117.

8. André Harris and Alain de Sédouy, *Juifs et français* (Paris: Poche, 1980), p. 44.

9. Lucien Lazare, "L'Aliyah de Strasbourg," *Dispersion et Unité* 11 (1971): 63.

10. Doris Bensimon-Donath, *L'Intégration des juifs nord-africains en France* (Paris and La Haye: Mouton, 1971), p. 117.

11. Claude Tappia, "Les Enfants de Belleville," *L'Arche* 155 (February 1970): 43–49.

12. Alain Finkielkraut, *Le Juif imaginaire* (Paris: Seuil, 1980).

THE ROLE OF IMMIGRANTS (RÉMI LEVEAU AND DOMINIQUE SCHNAPPER)

1. Rémi Leveau and Catherine Wihtol de Wenden, "L'évolution des attitudes politiques des immigrés maghrébins," *Vingtième Siècle* 7 (July–September 1985).

2. The Arabic terms are *roumi* and *ntourmi*, equivalent to Christian and renegade.

3. Stephane Vlocevski, *L'Installation des Italiens en France* (Paris: Alcan, 1934), p. 84.

4. Georges Mauco, *Les Etrangers en France, leur rôle dans l'activité économique* (Paris: Armand Colin, 1932), p. 558.

5. Ibid., p. 315.

6. Abdelmalek Sayad, "Les Trois âges de l'émigration algérienne en France," *Actes de la recherche en sciences sociales* 15 (June 1977): 59–79.

7. Serge Bonnet, *L'Homme de fer (1930–1959)* (Nancy: Centre lorrain d'Etudes Sociologiques, 1979), II, 147.

8. Dominique Schnapper, "Identités et acculturation: à propos des travailleurs émigrés," *Communications* 43 (1986): 141–168.

9. Louis Köll, *Auboué en Lorraine du fer* (Paris: Karthala, 1981), p. 201.

10. Mauco, *Les Etrangers*, p. 332.

11. A.-M. Blanc, *Marie Romaine* (Metz: Serpenoise, 1978), pp. 146–147.

12. Mauco, *Les Etrangers*, p. 333.

13. Köll, *Auboué*, p. 109.

14. Quoted in Gérard Noiriel, *Longwy, immigrés et prolétaires, 1880–1980* (Paris: Presses Universitaires de France, 1984), p. 183.

15. Blanc, *Marie Romaine*, p. 125.

16. Mauco, *Les Etrangers*, p. 337.

17. Blanc, *Marie Romaine*, pp. 150, 151.

18. Quoted in Noiriel, *Longwy*, p. 225.

19. Vlocevski, *L'Installation*, p. 83.

20. Bonnet, *L'Homme der fer*, pp. 146, 20.

21. Muslims do not understand why the French are revolted by the idea of keeping and sacrificing a sheep in an apartment. On the other hand, since they rarely have pets, they are shocked by French attitudes toward dogs and by the number of them in France. To them the dog has a doubly negative connotation, not only because of its place in their cultural tradition but also because many dog-owners use their pets in a manner demonstrating hostility toward immigrants.

4. Nations of Families

THE RISE AND FALL OF THE SWEDISH MODEL (KRISTINA ORFALI)

1. *Le Monde*, March 18, 1976; Yves de Saint Agnès in *Paris Match*, August 3, 1979; Robert Sarner in *Le Monde*, 1980; Marie Müller in *Le Nouvel Observateur*, May 26, 1980.

2. Emmanuel Mounier, "Notes scandinaves," *Esprit*, February 1950.

3. Switzerland has its secret bank accounts, Germany its lugubrious past. Even American values are suspect of concealing "imperialism, neocolonialism, and violations of the rights of man." Swedish values seem to derive from Kant's categorical imperative: anyone may will that they become universal laws.

4. Most of the French probably would agree with General de Gaulle, who considered discussions of money "improper." Pollsters find that direct questions about income and wealth at best elicit a response that underestimates the true value and at worse provoke a defensive reaction.

5. Denunciation of tax fraud plays an important role in France also, but French fiscal authorities have never gone so far as to announce publicly the amount of money recovered by such means. According to an article in *Sydsvenska dagbladet*, the city of Malmö collected 150,000 kroner in local taxes in this way in 1984.

6. In the words of Jan Freese, inspector general of computing machinery.

7. André Gide, October 1950, letter to Lucien Maury.

8. Although the law distinguishes between the biological father and the legal father and stipulates that all responsibility falls on the legal father (and that in no case can the biological father be forced to assume any responsibility whatsoever), the first consequence of the measure was a spectacular decline in the number of donors.

9. *Barn och vuxna* (Children and Adults), SOU (1980): 27.

10. According to Kajsa Sundström-Feigenberg, the gynecologist in charge of the parents education program under the National Public Health and Social Insurance Agency.

11. Government study on *Homosexuella och Samhället* (Homosexuals and Society), SOU (1984): 63. A majority of those questioned (54 percent) opposed marriage between homosexuals, but 46 percent agreed that homosexuals living together should be able to obtain a mortgage (25 percent were opposed).

12. A third of the RFSU budget consists of subsidies from the government and public health councils. The organization has a staff of about a hundred, not counting part-time physicians and other auxiliaries.

13. See *Sexuella Overgrepp* (a public study of sex crimes), SOU 1976.

14. *Prostitution in Sweden*, SOU 1981: 71. Streetwalking is virtually unknown in Sweden.

15. Retraining, tried most extensively in Malmö, yielded successful results 50 percent of the time. In 1980 the number of "massage parlors" and other such places in the Stockholm area had dropped to twenty-five.

16. Mounier, "Notes scandinaves."

17. Various authors such as Vilhelm Moberg and Alva Myrdal discuss liberal sexual customs in rural Sweden. In some provinces engaged couples were allowed to spend the night together in the same bed but without consummating the sexual act. *Natt-frieri* was the word for this custom.

18. François-Régis Bastide, *Suède* (Paris: Seuil, 1954).

19. Claude Sarraute in *F Magazine* (1984), p. 109.

THE ITALIAN FAMILY: PARADOXES OF PRIVACY (CHIARA SARACENO)

1. Donald D. Pitkin, *The House that Giacomo Built. History of an Italian Family, 1898–1979* (Cambridge: Cambridge University Press, 1985), p. 154.

2. See the observations of Helene Strohl on the use of electrical appliances by women who have incorporated them into domestic routines established before their appearance, as well as by women of later generations, for whom the use of electrical appliances is as normal as running water and electric light. See Helene Strohl, "Inside and Outside the Home: How Our Lives Have Changed through Domestic Automation," in Ann Showstack Sassoon, ed., *Women and the State* (London: Hutchinson, 1987).

3. See Vanessa Maher, "Un mestiere da raccontare. Sarte e sartine torinesi fra le due guerre," *Memoria* 8 (1983): 52–71.

4. See Stefano Merli, *Proletariato di fabbrica a sviluppo industriale. I caso italiano: 1800–1900* (Florence: La Nuova Italia, 1972).

5. Karl Kraus, *Detti e contradetti* (Milan: Adelphi, 1972), p. 102.

6. The concept of "generation" refers to family relations (grandparents, parents, children), that of "cohort" to persons born during a certain time period. Persons of the same generation can belong to very different groups on the basis of age, the life-cycle phase, and so on. For a review of these problems, see Chiara Saraceno, ed., *Età e corso della vita* (Bologna: Il Mulino, 1987). See also G. H. Elder, Jr., "Age Differentiation and the Life Course," *Annual Review of Sociology* 1 (1945): 165–190; David Kertzer, "Generation as a Sociological Problem," *Annual Review of Sociology* 9 (1983): 125–149.

7. See Antonio Cortese, "Le modificazione della famiglia attraverso i censimenti," in *Atti di Convegno La Famiglia* in a special edition of *Annali di Statistica*, year 115, series IX, vol. 6, (Rome: ISTAT, 1986), pp. 145–166.

8. See Marzio Barbagli, *Sotto lo stesso tetto. Mutamenti della famiglia italiana dal XV al XX secolo* (Bologna: Il Mulino, 1984), chap. 3.

9. See, for example, the results of Inquiry into Family structures and behaviors carried out by IS-TAT (Central Institute of Statistics) in 1983, analyzed by Giovanni Sgritta, "La struttura delle relazioni interfamiliari," in *Atti del Convegno La Famiglia in Italia*, pp. 167–200. Agnes Pitrou has reached analogous observations regarding France; see *Vivre sans Famille* (Toulouse: Privat, 1978). When in the 1960s

scholars began to realize the importance of the kinship network in family strategies there was coined the fortunate, though conceptually ambiguous, term of "modified extended family." See Eugene Litwack, "Occupational Mobility and Extended Family Cohesion," *American Sociological Review* 25 (1960): 9–21, and "Geographic Mobility and Extended Family Cohesion," *American Sociological Review* 25 (1960): 385–394.

10. I examine this period more systematically in "La famiglia operaia sotto il fascismo," in *Annali* of the Fondazione Giangiacomo Feltrinelli, 1979/80, pp. 189–230; see also the bibliography there.

11. See Antonio Santini, "Recenti trasformazioni della famiglia e della discendenza in Italia e in Europa," in *Atti del Convegno La Famiglia in Italia,* pp. 121–144, also for the data on the age of marriage discussed later.

12. See Patrizia Sabbatucci Severini and Angelo Trento, "Alcuni cenni sul mercato del lavoro durante il fascismo," in *Quaderni storici* 10 vols. II–III, 1975; Luisa Fornaciari, "Osservazioni sull'andamento del lavoro femminile in Italia," *Rivista internazionale di scienze sociali* 27, 4 (1956); Nora Federici, "Caratteristiche e problemi della occupazione e disoccupazione femminile," in *Inchiesta parlamentare sulla disoccupazione,* bk. IV, vol. 5.

13. See Massimo Livi Bacci, *A History of Italian Fertility During the Last Two Centuries.* Office of Population Research Series (Princeton, N.J.: Princeton University Press, 1976).

14. In his research into the changing Italian family, reported in *Sotto lo stesso tetto* (see Note 8), Barbagli surveyed a sample of 801 women born between 1890 and 1910, from all social strata and various regions of north central Italy. The quotations used from here on are from the last two chapters of his book. Other oral sources quoted to develop my discussion of the changes in family relations come from about fifty interviews carried out, using the same questions Barbagli used, by Giovanni Vianello for a Ph.D. thesis at the Faculty of Sociology of Trento in 1979. Vianello's subjects were working-class and upper-class Venetian women, born at the turn of the century. I have also used testimonies gathered by Bianca Guidetti Serra in *Compagne,* 2 vols. (Turin: Einaudi, 1977); by Nuto Revelli, *Il Mondo dei vinti* (Turin: Einaudi, 1977); and *L'anello forte* (Turin: Einaudi, 1985); and by Luisa Passerini, *Torino operaio e Fascismo: una storia orale,* (Rome and Bari: Laterza, 1983).

15. Rossella Palomba, ed. *Vita di coppia e figli.*

Le opinioni degli Italiani degli anni Ottanta (Florence: La Nuova Italia, 1987).

16. See Santini, "Recenti trasformazioni."

17. See Antonia Pinnelli, "La longevitá femminile. Cifre dimensioni, valori," in *Memoria* 16 (1986): 38–60.

18. See Santini, "Recenti trasformazioni."

19. See Palomba, *Vita di coppia e figli.*

20. I once tried to trace a "geography" of the Italian family, relating forms of family organization, local labor markets, and forms of redistribution through public policies of transfers and services to it. See Chiara Saraceno, "Modelli di famiglia," in Sabino Acquaviva et al., *Ritratto di famiglia degli anni Ottanta* (Rome and Bari: Laterza, 1981). See also Chiara Saraceno, "Between State Intervention, the Social Sphere and Private Life: Changes in the Family Role," in Adalbert Evers, Helga Nowotny, and Helmut Wintersberger, eds., *The Changing Face of Welfare* (Brookfield, Vt.: Gower, 1987), pp. 60–78.

22. See also Giancarlo Consonni and Gresielle Tonon, "Casa e lavoro nell'area milanese. Dalla fine dell'Ottocento all'avvento del fascismo," in *Classe* 9, 14 (October 1977); Chamber of Deputies, *Atti della Commissione Parlamentare di Inchiesta sulla Miseria in Italia 1903–1958* (Rome, 1959), vol. III.

22. See, for example, Fortunata Piselli, *La donna che lavora* (Bari: De Donato, 1975); Maria Rosa Cutrufelli, *Disoccupata con onore* (Milan: Mazzotta, 1975).

23. See Guidetti Serra, *Compagne.*

24. See the research done in the 1950s by Paul Chombart de Lauwe, *La vie quotidienne des familles ouvrières* (Paris: CNRS, 1856).

25. See Mario Saibante, *Il tenore di vita del popolo italiano prima dell'ultima guerra in confronto con quello degli altri popoli,* in Rapporto al ministro dell'industria e del commercio, edited by the Commission for Reconversion (Rome: Poligrafico dello Stato, 1947); C. D'Apice, *L'arcipelago dei consumi* (Bari: De Donato, 1981).

26. See Commission on Poverty, *La Povertà in Italia* (Rome: Poligrafico dello Stato, 1985).

27. These and the preceding statements come from Barbagli, *Sotto lo stesso tetto.*

28. See Martine Segalen, *Sociologie de la famille* (Paris: A. Colin, 1981), p. 249; trans. by J. C. Whitehouse and Sarah Matthews as *Historical Anthropology of the Family* (Cambridge: Cambridge University Press, 1986).

29. See Chombart de Lauwe, *La vie quotidienne.*

30. Traces of such an attitude remain in the

fear of "spoiling" children, of raising them with "vices." In her analysis of the correspondence between parents (mothers in particular) and children in the Moncalieri boarding school at the turn of the century, Simonetta Tabboni shows how families of the ruling class of that time—which, according to Barbagli, was the first to elaborate and legitimatize affective manifestations—still clung to an educational model that feared intimacy, tenderness, as a "fault" of love. See Simonetta Tabboni, *Il real collegio Carlo Alberto di Moncalieri* (Milan: F. Angeli, 1984).

31. There are few studies in Italy of couple relationships or of how men experience married life, paternity, and domestic existence. Though confined to the division of labor in family work, one of the few studies that have interviewed husbands is Chiara Saraceno, ed., *Il lavoro mal diviso* (Bari: De Donato, 1980). Testimonies of couples are in Marisa Rusconi, *Amati amanti* (Milan: Feltrinelli, 1981). On paternity, see also Giovanni Starace, *La paternità*, (Milan: F. Angeli, 1983).

32. Palomba, *Vita di coppia e figli.*

33. Juliet Mitchell, *Woman's Estate* (New York: Random House, 1973).

34. This in turn points to unsuspected developments not only in family relations but also in the relation between public and private that I cannot discuss here for lack of space. For the first reflection of this theme, see a collection of essays with the very suggestive title: *La famiglia moltiplicata* (The Multiple Family), ed. Carmine Ventimiglia (Milan: F. Angeli, 1987); see also Marina Sbisá, *I figlia della scienza* (Milan: Emme, 1985).

35. See Dina Bertoni Jovine, *L'alienazione dell'infanzia* (Rome: Editori Riuniti, 1963); see also *La scuola italiana dal 1870 ai giorni nostri* (Rome: Editori Riuniti, 1969).

36. For an analysis of legislative transformations in the family sphere, see Carla Rodota and Stefano Rodota, "Il diritto di famiglia,' in Acquaviva et al., *Ritratto di famiglia.*

37. See, for example, Laura Balbo and Renate Siebert Zahar, eds., *Interferenze* (Milan: Feltrinelli, 1979); Marina Bianchi, *I servizi sociali* (Bari: De Donato, 1981); Laura Balbo and Marina Bianchi, eds., *Ricomposizioni* (Milan: F. Angeli, 1982); Paolo De Sandre, "Linee di analisi della divisione del lavoro per la riproduzione sociale quotidiana," in *Sociologia e ricerca sociale* 1 (1980), nn. 2–3; Marco Ingrosso, *Strategie familiari e servizi sociali* (Milan: F. Angeli, 1984); Franca Bimbi and Flavia Prestinger, *Profili sovrapposti* (Milan: F. Angeli, 1985). See also Massimo Paci, "Pubblico e privato nel sistema italiano

di welfare," in Peter Lange and Marino Regini, eds., *Stato e regolazione sociale* (Bologna: Il Mulino, 1987).

38. I have developed this discussion in greater length in "La famiglia operaia sotto il fascismo"; see also "Percorsi di vita femminile nella classe operaia. Tra famiglia e lavoro durante il fascismo," in *Memoria* 2 (1981).

39. Lorenza Zanuso reveals that until the very end of the 1960s the female status or profession that has increased most rapidly was that of housewife, an increase that constituted one of the reasons for the prosperity of those years. See L. Zanuso, "La segregazione occupazionale: i dati di lungo periodo (1901–71)," in G. Barile, ed., *Lavoro femminile, sviluppo tecnologico e segregazione* (Milan: F. Angeli, 1984), pp. 24–90.

40. See the analysis by Achille Ardigó in *Emancipazione femminile e urbanesimo* (Brescia: Morcelliana, 1969); Alessandro Pizzorno, "Appunti su lavoro femminile organizzazione domestica," in *Passato e Presente* (January 1958): 75–77. For a more recent and clear discussion on the relation of women to the development of consumption, see Bimbi, "La doppia presenza: diffusione di un modello e trasformazioni dell'identità," in Bimbi and Prestinger, *Profili sovrapposti.*

The German Family between Private Life and Politics (Ingeborg Weber-Kellermann)

1. For an overview of Central European family history that discusses alternative forms of family organization, see Michael Mitterauer and Reinhard Sieder, *The European Family: Patriarchy and Partnership from the Middle Ages to the Present*, trans. Karla Oosterveen and Manfred Hörzinger (Chicago: University of Chicago Press, 1982). This chapter is based on three books and essays by Professor Ingeborg Weber-Kellermann: *Die deutsche Familie* (Frankfurt-am-Main: Suhrkamp, 1974), and the afterword to the 6th edition, published in 1980; *Die Familie* (Frankfurt-am-Main: Insel, 1976), and "Die Sozialgeschichte der Familie in Deutschland—besonders in Hinblick auf die Stellung der Frau," in B. Paetzold and L. Fried, eds., *Einführung in die Familienpädagogik* (Weinheim and Basel: Beltz, 1989), pp. 21–33. Additional material on the Weimar era and on the family in Eastern Germany, as well as notes to guide the American reader, have been added.

2. For a discussion of the notion of *Hausvater*, see Julius Hoffmann, *Die "Hausvaterliteratur" und die "Predigten über den christlichen Hausstand." Ein Beitrag zur Geschichte der Lehre vom Haus und der Bildung für*

das häuslichen Leben (Göttingen, 1954). See also Marion Gray, "Prescriptions for Productive Female Domesticity in a Transition Era: Germany's *Hausmutterliteratur, 1780–1840,*" *History of European Ideas* 8 (1987): 413–426, and Michael Mitterauer and Reinhard Sieder, *The European Family.*

3. Early theoretical studies of the transformation of the Central European family during the era of the Industrial Revolution include Heidi Rosenbaum, ed., *Familie und Gesellschaftsstruktur. Materialen zu den sozioökonomischen Bedingungen von Familienformen* (Frankfurt, 1974), and Hans Medick, "The proto-industrial family economy: the structural function of household and family during the transition from peasant society to industrial capitalism," *Social History* 1 (1976). Historical works on specific aspects of this transformation include Edward Shorter, *The Making of the Modern Family* (New York: Basic Books, 1975), and R. J. Evans and W. R. Lee, eds., *The German Family* (London: Croom Helm, 1981).

4. A key article examining the ideological polarization between male and female spheres in Karin Hausen, "Family and Role Division: The Polarisation of Sexual Stereotypes in the Nineteenth Century—An Aspect of the Dissociation of Work and Family Life," in Evans and Lee, eds., *The German Family.*

5. There is a full analysis of the evolution of middle- and upper-class childhood in Ingeborg Weber-Kellerman, *Die Kindheit. Kleidung und Wohnung, Arbeit und Spiel* (Frankfurt, 1979). See also Jürgen Schlumbohm, *Kinderstuben. Wie Kinder zu Bauern, Bürgern, Aristokraten wurden* (Munich: DTV, 1983), and Donata Elschenbroich, *Kinder werden nicht geboren* (Frankfurt, 1977).

6. See Ingeborg Weber-Kellermann, *Frauenleben im 19. Jahrhundert* (Munich: Beck, 1983). For a good recent historical study of women's education in nineteenth-century Germany, see James Albisetti, *Schooling German Girls and Women. Secondary and Higher Education in the Nineteenth Century* (Princeton: Princeton University Press, 1989).

7. For a very interesting analysis of some of the tactics employed by poorer middle-class women struggling to keep up appearances, see Sibylle Meyer, "The Tiresome Work of Conspicuous Leisure. On the Domestic Duties of the Wives of Civil Servants in the German Empire (1871–1918)," in Marilyn Boxer and Jean Quataert, eds., *Connecting Spheres. Women in the Western World, 1500 to the present* (New York: Oxford University Press, 1987).

8. There are a growing number of studies of the turn-of-the-century middle-class women's movement in Germany, as well as more general histories of women's conditions in the nineteenth century. See, for example, Ute Gerhard, *Verhältnisse und Verhinderungen: Frauenarbeit, Familie und Rechte der Frauen im 19, Jahrhundert* (Frankfurt, 1978); Ute Frevert, *Women in German History. From Bourgeois Emancipation to Sexual Liberation* (Oxford and Hamburg: Berg, 1988); R. J. Evans, *The Feminist Movement in Germany, 1894–1933* (London, 1976); Marion Kaplan, *The Jewish Feminist Movement in Gemany* (Westport, Conn.: Greenwood, 1979); John Fout, ed., *German Women in the Nineteenth Century* (New York: Holmes and Meier, 1984); and Ruth-Ellen B. Joeres and M. J. Maynes, eds., *German Women in the Eighteenth and Nineteenth Centuries* (Bloomington: Indiana University Press, 1986).

9. For analyses of the working-class women's movement, see Jean Quataert, *Reluctant Feminists in German Social Democracy, 1885–1917* (Princeton: Princeton University Press, 1979); Werner Thonnessen, *The Emancipation of Women: The Rise and Decline of the Women's Movement in German Social Democracy, 1863–1933* (London, 1970); and Heinz Niggemann, *Emanzipation zwischen Sozialismus und Feminismus* (Wuppertal: Peter Hammer, 1981).

10. Elizabeth Domansky presented a part of her research on the gender dynamics of the First World War in "World War I as Gender Conflict in Germany," at a conference on "The *Kaiserreich* in the 1990s" in Philadelphia, February 1990.

11. Christiane C. Collins, "Concerned Planning and Urban Design: the Urban Experiment of Germany in the 1920s," in F. D. Hirschbach et al., eds., *Germany in the Twenties. The Artist as Social Critic* (Minneapolis: University of Minnesota Press, 1980).

12. See Atina Grossmann, "Abortion and Economic Crisis: The 1931 Campaign against Paragraph 218," in Renate Bridenthal, Atina Grossmann, and Marion Kaplan, eds., *When Biology Became Destiny. Women in Weimar and Nazi Germany* (New York: Monthly Review Press, 1984).

13. For analysis of the situation of women during the Weimar era, see Renate Bridenthal and Claudia Koonz, "Beyond Kinder, Küche, Kirche: Weimar Women in Politics and Work," in Bridenthal, Grossmann, and Kaplan, eds., *Biology*; Timothy Mason, "Women in Germany 1925–1940: Family, Welfare and Work," *History Workshop* 1 (1976): 74–113, and 2 (1976): 5–32; and Atina Grossmann, "The New Woman and the Rationalization of Sexuality in Weimar Germany," in Ann Snitow

et al., eds., *Powers of Desire: The Politics of Sexuality* (New York: Monthly Review Press, 1983).

14. Quoted in Bonnie Smith, *Changing Lives. Women in European History since 1700* (Lexington, Mass.: D. C. Heath, 1989), p. 424.

15. Grossmann, "The New Woman."

16. See Mason, "Woman in Germany."

17. For an analysis of the family and reproductive policy of the Nazis, see Rita Thalmann, *Frausein im Dritten Reich* (Frankfurt: Ullstein, 1987); Gisela Bock, "Racism and Sexism in Nazi Germany: Motherhood, Compulsory Sterilization and the State," in Bridenthal, Grossmann, and Kaplan, *Biology*; and Claudia Koonz, *Mothers in the Fatherland. Women, the Family and Nazi Politics* (New York: St. Martin's, 1987).

18. Horst Becker, *Die Familie* (1935), p. 14; further quotations are from pp. 103, 146, and 139.

19. *Der Nationalsozialismus. Dokumente 1933–1945* (Frankfurt-am-Main: Fischer Bucherei, 1957), p. 88.

20. Rudolf Frick in *Völkischer Beobachter*, June 12, 1934.

21. For a full discussion of these issues, see Koonz, *Mothers in the Fatherland*.

22. Bock, "Racism," p. 287.

23. Erich Fromm in Max Horkheimer, ed., *Studien uber Authorität und Familie* (1936), p. 84.

24. For these and other pointed comparisons, see Harry G. Shaffer, *Women in the Two Germanies* (New York: Pergamon, 1981).

25. Barbara Zahlmann-Willenbacher, *Kritik des funktionalistischen Konzepts geschlechtstypischer Arbeitsteilung*, in Roland Eckert, ed., *Geschlectsrollen und Arbeitsteilung* (Munich: Beck, 1979), p. 69.

26. Arbeitsgruppe Kinderschutz, *Gewalt gegen Kinder* (Reinbeck bei Hamburg: Rowohlt, 1975).

27. Wolfgang Klafki, "Gesamtschule," *Worterbuch der Erziehung* (Munich, 1974).

28. Quoted in Marlise Simons, "Abortion issue divisive as East, West Germany move toward unification," *The St. Paul Pioneer Press*, July 20, 1990, p. 4.

29. A comparison of East and West German policies with respect to family and women's issues was made in a conference paper by Dorothy Rosenberg, "Social Policy measures GDR/FRG," presented at the annual meeting of Women in German, meeting near Minneapolis, Minnesota, October 1990.

MYTHS AND REALITIES OF THE AMERICAN FAMILY (ELAINE TYLER MAY)

1. Case D492, 1920, Los Angeles County Archives. All names used in cases cited in this chapter have been modified to protect the privacy of the individuals and their families.

2. Quotes are from Ebenezer Baily, *The Young Ladies' Class Book* (Boston, 1831), p. 168; and William Alcott, *The Young Man's Guide* (Boston, 1833), pp. 299, 231.

3. Bureau of the Census, *Population 2* (Washington, D.C.: United States Government Printing Office, 1920): 22, 33; William Henry Chafe, *The American Woman* (New York: Oxford University Press, 1972), p. 56.

4. Department of Commerce, *Historical Statistics of the United States* (Washington, D.C.: United States Government Printing Office, 1960), pp. 139, 179.

5. See, for example, Sam Bass Warner, Jr., *Streetcar Suburbs* (Cambridge, Mass.: Harvard University Press, 1962); Kenneth Jackson, *Crabgrass Frontier: The Suburbanization of the United States* (New York: Oxford University Press, 1985); Margaret Marsh, *Suburban Lives* (New Brunswick, N.J.: Rutgers University Press, 1990).

6. Waldon Fawcett, "Suburban Life in America," *Cosmopolitan* (July 1903): 309–316.

7. Bartlett, *Better City*, p. 84.

8. Cecil B. DeMille, *Why Change Your Wife*, 1919.

9. Robert S. Lynd and Helen M. Lynd, *Middletown* (New York, 1956 edition), pp. 117, 241; U.S. Bureau of the Census, *Historical Statistics of the United States* (Washington, D.C.: Government Printing Office, 1960), p. 15; Paul H. Jacobson, *American Marriage and Divorce* (New York: Rinehart, 1959), p. 21. See also Elaine Tyler May, *Great Expectations: Marriage and Divorce in Post-Victorian America* (Chicago: University of Chicago Press, 1980), p. 167.

10. Alfred Cahen, *Statistical Analysis of American Divorce* (New York: Columbia University Press, 1932), pp. 15, 21.

11. Walter F. Willcox, *The Divorce Problem* (New York, 1987), pp. 66–67; James P. Lichtenberger, *Divorce, A Study in Social Causation* (New York, 1909), pp. 169–170.

12. See Elaine Tyler May, *Great Expectations: Marriage and Divorce in Post-Victorian America* (Chicago: University of Chicago Press, 1980), p. 170.

13. See May, *Great Expectations*, esp. chap. 7.

14. Cases are from the Los Angeles County Archives and the New Jersey State Archives: X-59-628 (New Jersey), G-60-226 (New Jersey), D322 (Los Angeles), 1920.

15. Cases X-59-623 (New Jersey), D40 (Los Angeles), 1920.

16. Interview with the author's grandmother-in-law, Mrs. June Glassmeyer, 12 July 1974; Cases D486 (Los Angeles), H-60-199 (New Jersey), D452 (Los Angeles), 1920.

17. Case H-60-1206 (New Jersey), 1920.

18. Susan M. Hartmann, *The Home Front and Beyond: American Women in the 1940s* (Boston: Twayne, 1987), pp. 16–19; Sherna Berger Gluck, *Rosie the Riveter Revisited: Women, the War, and Social Change* (Boston: Twayne, 1987), pp. 13–14.

19. Case 147, Kelly Longitudinal Study, Henry Murray Research Center, Radcliffe College, Cambridge, Mass.; hereafter referred to as KLS.

20. Paul Popenoe, as quoted in John Modell, "Institutional Consequences of Hard Times: Engagement in the 1930s," in Joan Aldous and David M. Klein, eds., *Social Stress and Family Development* (New York: Guilford, 1988).

21. U.S. Bureau of the Census, *Historical Statistics of the United States, Colonial Times to 1970* (Washington, D.C.: U.S. Government Printing Office, 1975), pt. 1, pp. 20–21, 64; Ruth Milkman, "Women's Work and the Economic Crisis: Some Lessons from the Great Depression," *The Review of Radical Political Economics* 8 (Spring 1976): 73–91, 95–97; Peter Filene, *Him/Her/Self: Sex Roles in Modern America*, 2nd ed. (Baltimore, Md.: Johns Hopkins University Press, 1986), p. 158.

22. Lary May, "Making the American Way: Moderne Theatres, Audiences, and the Film Industry, 1929–1945," *Prospects: Journal of American Culture* 12 (1987): 89–124.

23. David Seabury (psychologist), "Why Can't the Stars Stay Married?" *Photoplay* 51 (June 1937): 12.

24. *Blonde Venus*, 1931, directed by Erich Von Sternberg; *His Girl Friday*, 1940, directed by Howard Hawks.

25. See Lois Scharf, *To Work and To Wed: Female Employment, Feminism, and the Great Depression* (Westport, Conn.: Greenwood, 1980), pp. 46, 111.

26. See Winifred D. Wandersee, *Women's Work and Family Values, 1920–1940* (Cambridge, Mass.: Harvard University Press, 1981); Susan Ware, *Beyond Suffrage: Women in the New Deal* (Cambridge, Mass.: Harvard University Press, 1981); Scharf, *To Work and To Wed*, chap. 5; Filene, *Him/Her/Self*, pp. 155–157; Mirra Komarovsky, *The Unemployed Man and His Family* (New York: Dryden, 1940), pp. 23–47.

27. Glen Elder, Jr., *Children of the Great Depression: Social Change in Life Experience* (Chicago: University of Chicago Press, 1974), cites polls on pp. 50 and 202. See also Judith Smith, *Family Connections: A History of Italian and Jewish Immigrant Lives in Providence, Rhode Island, 1900–1940* (Albany: State University Press of New York, 1985), p. 115.

28. Milkman, "Women's Work," pp. 73–91; Susan Ware, *Holding Their Own: American Women in the 1930s* (Boston: Twayne, 1982), p. 6.

29. See Elder, *Children of the Great Depression*.

30. Cited in Filene, *Him/Her/Self*, pp. 150, 160–161.

31. Elder, *Children of the Great Depression*, p. 233.

32. Polls cited in Filene, *Him/Her/Self*, pp. 161–162.

33. Filene, *Him/Her/Self*, p. 163.

34. Hartmann, *The Home Front and Beyond*, pp. 7, 164.

35. Quoted in John Morton Blum, *V Was for Victory: Politics and American Culture During World War II* (New York: Harcourt Brace Jovanovich, 1976), p. 28.

36. *This Is the Army*, Warner Brothers, 1943.

37. See William H. Chafe, *The American Woman: Her Changing Social, Economic and Political Roles, 1920–1970* (New York: Oxford University Press, 1986), pp. 15–16.

38. Karen Anderson, *Wartime Women: Sex Roles, Family Relations, and the Status of Women During World War II* (Westport, Conn.: Greenwood, 1981); and Hartmann, *The Home Front and Beyond*, pp. 19–21.

39. Hartmann, *The Home Front and Beyond*, chap. 5; Leila Rupp, *Mobilizing Women for War: German and American Propaganda, 1939–1945* (Princeton: Princeton University Press, 1978), esp. chaps. 4–6.

40. See Allan M. Brandt, *No Magic Bullet: A Social History of Venereal Disease in the United States Since 1880* (New York: Oxford University Press, 1985), chap. 5; John Costello, *Virtue Under Fire: How World War II Changed Our Social and Sexual Attitudes* (Boston: Little, Brown, 1985); U.S. Bureau of the Census, *Historical Statistics of the United States, Colonial Times to 1970* (Washington, D.C.: U.S. Government Printing Office, 1975), pt. 1, p. 49; John D'Emilio, *Sexual Politics, Sexual Communities: The*

Making of a Homosexual Minority in the United States, 1940–1970 (Chicago: University of Chicago Press, 1983), chaps. 2 and 3; Allan Berube, *Coming Out Under Fire: The History of Gay Men and Women in World War Two* (New York: Free Press, 1990).

41. *Economic Report of the President* (Washington, D.C.: U.S. Government Printing Office, 1987), p. 274.

42. Andrew Cherlin, *Marriage, Divorce, Remarriage* (Cambridge, Mass.: Harvard University Press, 1976), pp. 19–21.

43. Ronald Rindfuss and James A. Sweet, *Postwar Fertility Trends and Differentials in the United States* (New York: Academic, 1977), p. 191; Ira S. Steinberg, *The New Lost Generation: The Population Boom and Public Policy* (New York: St. Martin's, 1982), p. 3. The conformity to patterns is described in John Modell, Frank Furstenberg, Jr., and Douglass Strong, "The Timing of Marriage in the Transition to Adulthood: Continuity and Change, 1860–1975," in John Demos and Sarane Spence Boocock, eds., *Turning Points: Historical and Sociological Essays on the Family*, supplement to the *American Journal of Sociology* 84 (1978): s120–s150.

44. See Viviana A. Zelizer, *Pricing the Priceless Child: The Changing Social Value of Children* (New York: Basic Books, 1985).

45. For an analysis of the Kitchen Debate and the centrality of the family ideology to the Cold War, see Elaine Tyler May, *Homeward Bound: American Families in the Cold War Era* (New York: Basic Books, 1988), esp. chap. 1.

46. Joseph Veroff, Richard A. Kulka, and Elizabeth Douvan, *Mental Health in America: Patterns of Help-Seeking from 1957 to 1976* (New York: Basic Books, 1981), pp. 6, 31; Joseph Veroff, Elizabeth Douvan, and Richard A. Kulka, *The Inner American: A Self-Portrait from 1957 to 1976* (New York: Basic Books, 1981), p. 200; Robert O. Blood, Jr., and Donald M. Wolfe, *Husbands and Wives: The Dynamics of Married Living* (Glencoe, Ill.: Free Press, 1960), p. 117; John Campbell and John Modell, "Family Ideology and Family Values in the Baby Boom: A Secondary Analysis of the 1955 Growth of American Families Survey of Single Women," Technical Report No. 5 (Minneapolis: Family Study Center, University of Minnesota, 1984).

47. Steven Mintz and Susan Kellogg, *Domestic Revolutions: A Social History of American Family Life* (New York: Free Press, 1988), pp. 117–123.

48. Frank McDonough, "Are Children Necessary?" *Better Homes and Gardens* (October 1944): 7.

49. Mintz and Kellogg, *Domestic Revolutions*, pp. 117–123; Margaret Marsh, *Suburban Lives*, chap. 3.

50. "The New American Domesticated Male," *Life* 36 (4 January 1954): 42–45; *Parents Magazine*, quoted in Filene, *Him/Her/Self*, pp. 172–173.

51. See May, *Homeward Bound*, esp. chap. 8.

52. Case 244, KLS.

53. Betty Friedan, *The Feminine Mystique* (New York: Dell, 1963); collection of letters to Betty Friedan, in Friedan Manuscript Collection, Schlesinger Library Manuscript Collections, Radcliffe College, Cambridge, Mass.

54. See Sara Evans, *Personal Politics: The Roots of Women's Liberation in the Civil Rights Movement and the New Left* (New York: Alfred A. Knopf, 1979), pp. 3–23.

55. Polls and trends are gathered from George H. Gallup, *The Gallup Poll: Public Opinion 1935–1971* (New York: Random House, 1972), vols. 1, 2, 3.

56. Graham B. Spanier and Frank F. Furstenberg, "Remarriage and Reconstituted Families," paper prepared for an Ad Hoc Meeting on Separation, Divorce and Family Reconstitution organized by the Committee on Child Development Research and Public Policy of the National Academy of Sciences, Stanford, California, April 15–16, 1982.

57. Ellen Rothman, *Hands and Hearts: A History of Courtship in America* (New York: Basic Books, 1984), pp. 306–311; U.S. Bureau of the Census, *Historical Statistics of the United States*, pp. 133, 134; Valerie Kincaid Oppenheimer, "Structural Sources of Economic Pressure for Wives to Work: An Analytical Framework," *Journal of Family History* (Summer 1979): 195; and "U.S. Expecting Smaller Families, Waiting Longer to Have Children," *Family Planning Perspectives* 13 (July–August 1981): 191. On the family patterns of the baby boomers, see, for example, Landon Y. Jones, *Great Expectations: America and the Baby Boom Generation* (New York: Ballantine, 1981); and Sar A. Levitan and Richard S. Belous, *What's Happening to the American Family?* (Baltimore, Md.: Johns Hopkins University Press, 1981), p. 43; A. Regula Herzog, Jerald G. Bachman, and Lloyd D. Johnston, "Paid Work, Child Care, and Housework: A National Survey of High School Seniors' Preferences for Sharing Responsibilities Between Husband and Wife," *Sex Roles* 9 (January 1983): 109–135; and Andrew Cherlin and Pamela Barnhouse Walters, "Trends in United States Men's and Women's Sex-Role Attitudes, 1972–78," *American Sociological Review* 46 (1981): 453–460.

58. Andrew Cherlin, "Postponing Marriage:

The Influence of Young Women's Work Expectations," *Journal of Marriage and the Family* 42 (May 1980): 355–365; Stephany Stone Joy and Paula Sachs Wise, "Maternal Unemployment, Anxiety, and Sex Differences in College Students' Self-Descriptions," *Sex Roles* 9 (April 1983): 519–525.

59. Thomas J. Espenshade, "Economic Consequences of Changing Family Structures for Children, Families, and Society," Ad Hoc Meeting at Stanford, 1982; Thomas J. Espenshade, "The Economic Consequences of Divorce," *Journal of Marriage and the Family* 41 (August 1979): 615–625; Mary Corcoran, "The Economic Consequences of Marital Dissolution for Women in the Middle Years," *Sex Roles* 5 (March 1979): 343–353; and Ruth A. Brandwein, Carol A. Brown, and Elizabeth Maury Fox, "Women and Children Last: The Social Situation of Divorced Mothers and Their Families," *Journal of Marriage and the Family* 36 (August 1974): 498–514.

60. For an excellent study of this problem, see Lenore J. Weitzman, *The Divorce Revolution: The Unexpected Social and Economic Consequences for Women and Children in America* (New York: Free Press, 1985), esp. pp. ix–xxiv.

61. Stephen Mintz and Susan Kellogg, *Domestic Revolutions: A Social History of American Family Life* (New York: Free Press, 1988), pp. 203–237.

62. Ibid., pp. 204–219; John D'Emilio and Estelle B. Freedman, *Intimate Matters: A History of Sexuality in America* (New York: Harper and Row, 1988), p. 342.

63. See, for example, Judith Stacey, *Brave New Families* (New York: Basic Books, 1990).

Bibliography

Albisetti, James. *Schooling German Girls and Women: Secondary and Higher Education in the Nineteenth Century.* Princeton: Princeton University Press, 1989.

Anglade, J. *La Vie quotidienne des immigrés en France de 1919 à nos jours.* Paris: Hachette, 1976.

Ariès, Philippe. "L'Amour dans le mariage," and "Le Mariage indissoluble," *Communications.* Paris: Seuil, 1982, pp. 116–137.

Bagnasco, Arnaldo. *Le Tre Italie.* Bologna: Il Mulino, 1977.

Bahloul, J. *Le Culte de la table dressée.* Paris: A.-M. Métaillé, 1983.

Bailey, Beth. *From Front Porch to Back Seat: Courtship in Twentieth-Century America.* Baltimore: Johns Hopkins University Press, 1988.

Balbo, Laura. *Stato di famiglia.* Milan: Etas, 1976.

Banfield, Edward C. *The Moral Basis of a Backward Society.* Glencoe, Ill.: Free Press, 1956.

Barbagli, Marzio. *Provando e riprovando: Matrimonio, famiglia, divorzio, in Italia e in altri paesi occidentali.* Bologna: Il Mulino, 1990.

Barbagli, Marzio, and David Kertzer, eds. "Italian Family History, 1750–1950," special issue of *The Journal of Family History* 15 (1990).

Barile, Giuseppe, and Lorenzo Zanuso. *Lavoro femminile e condizione familiare.* Milan: F. Angeli, 1980.

Bell, Richard M. *Fate and Honor, Family and Village: Demographic and Cultural Change in Rural Italy since 1800.* Chicago: University of Chicago Press, 1979.

Bellah, Robert N., et al. *Habits of the Heart: Individualism and Commitment in American Life.* Berkeley: University of California Press, 1985.

Bensaïd, Norbert. *La Consultation.* Paris: Mercure de France, 1974.

Bensimon-Donath, Doris. *L'Intégration des juifs nord-africains en France.* Paris and The Hague: Mouton, 1971.

Berger, Brigitte, and Peter L. Berger. *The War over the Family: Capturing the Middle Ground.* Garden City, N.J.: Anchor/Doubleday, 1983.

Bergström-Walan, M. B. *Den svenska Kvinnorapporten.* Stockholm: Trevi AB, 1981.

Bernot, Lucien, and René Blancard. *Neuville, un village français.* Paris: Institut d'Ethnologie, 1953.

Bettelheim, Bruno. *The Informed Heart: Autonomy in a Mass Age.* Glencoe, Ill.: Free Press, 1960.

Billy, A., and M. Twerdsky. *Comme Dieu en France: L'Épopée de Muraché Foigel.* Paris: Plon, 1927.

Blasquez, A. *Gaston Lucas, serrurier.* Paris: Plon, 1976.

Boltanski, Luc. *Prime éducation et morale de classe.* Paris and The Hague: Mouton, 1969.

Bonnet, Serge. *L'Homme de fer, mineurs de fer et ouvriers sidérurgistes lorrains.* 4 vols. Nancy: Centre Lorrain d'Études Sociologiques, 1976–1985.

Boyer, R. *Les Religions de l'Europe du Nord.* Paris: Fayard, 1974.

Bridenthal, Renata, Atina Grossman, and Marion Kaplan, eds. *When Biology Became Destiny.* New York: Monthly Review, 1984.

Bruch, Hilde. *The Golden Cage: The Enigma of Anorexia Nervosa.* Cambridge, Mass.: Harvard University Press, 1978.

Bruhat, J. *Il n'est jamais trop tard.* Paris: Albin Michel, 1983.

Buchanan, William, and Hadley Cantril. *How Nations See Each Other.* Urbana: University of Illinois Press, 1953.

Burguière, André. *Bretons de Plozévet.* Paris: Flammarion, 1975.

Carles, E. *Une soupe aux herbes sauvages.* Paris: Simoën, 1978.

Caute, David. *Le Communisme et les intellectuels français, 1914–1966.* Paris: Gallimard, 1967.

Chabot, M. *L'Escarbille: Histoire d'Eugène Saulnier, ouvrier-verrier.* Paris: Les Presses de la Renaissance, 1978.

Chafe, William H. *The Paradox of Change: American Women in the Twentieth Century.* New York: Oxford University Press, 1991.

Childs, Marquis W. *Sweden: The Middle Way on Trial.* New Haven: Yale University Press, 1980.

Chombart de Lauwe, Paul-Henri. *La Vie quotidienne des familles ouvrières.* Paris: CNRS, 1956.

Couetouy, M., et al. *Figures du secret.* Grenoble: Presses Universitaires de Grenoble, 1981.

CRESM. *Maghrébins en France: Émigrés ou immigrés?* Paris: CNRS, 1983.

Davis, Kingsley, ed. *Contemporary Marriage: Comparative Perspectives on a Changing Institution.* New York: Russell Sage, 1985.

de Certeau, Michel. *L'Invention du quotidien,* vol. I. Paris: Union Générale d'Editions, 1980.

de Faramond, G., and C. Glayman. *Suède, la réforme permanente.* Paris: Stock, 1977.

Del Boca, Daniela, and Margherita Turvani. *Famiglia e mercato del lavoro.* Bologna: Il Mulino, 1979.

D'Emilio, John, and Estelle B. Freedman. *Intimate Matters: A History of Sexuality in America.* New York: Harper and Row, 1988.

Depretto, Jean-Paul, and Sylvie Schweitzer. *Le Communisme à l'usine: Vie ouvrière et mouvement ouvrier chez Renault, 1920–1939.* Roubaix: Edires, 1984.

Desanti, Dominique. *Les Staliniens: Une expérience politique, 1944–1956.* Paris: Fayard-Marabout, 1975.

Desplanques, G. "L'Inégalité sociale devant la mort," *Economie et statistique* 162 (January 1984): 29–50.

Douglass, William A. *Emigration in a South Italian Town: An Anthropological History.* New Brunswick, N.J.: Rutgers University Press, 1984.

——— "The South Italian Family: A Critique," *Journal of Family History* 5 (1980): 338–359.

DuBois, Ellen Carol, and Vicki L. Ruiz, eds. *Unequal Sisters: A Multi-Cultural Reader in U.S. Women's History.* New York: Routledge, 1990.

Dumont, Louis. *Essais sur l'individualisme: Une perspective anthropologique sur l'idéologie moderne.* Paris: Seuil, 1983.

Durand, F. *Les Littératures scandinaves.* Paris: Presses Universitaires de France, 1974.

Duras, Marguerite. *La Douleur.* Paris: Pol, 1985.

Elmer, A. *Svenks Social Politik.* Lund: Liber Läromedel, 1981.

Ertel, R. *Le Shtetl, la bourgade juive de Pologne de la tradition à la modernité.* Paris: Payot, 1982.

"Etrangers, immigrés, Français," special issue of *Vingtième siècle* (July–September 1985).

Evans, Richard J. *The Feminist Movement in Germany, 1894–1933.* London and Beverly Hills: Sage, 1976.

Evans, Richard J., and W. R. Lee, eds. *The German Family.* London: Croom Helm, 1981.

Evans, Sara. *Born for Liberty: A History of Women in America.* New York: Free Press, 1989.

Fout, John, ed. *German Women in the Nineteenth Century.* New York: Holmes and Meier, 1984.

"Français-Immigrés," special issue of *Esprit* (May 1985).

Frapié, Léon. *La Maternelle.* Paris: Librairie Universelle, 1904.

Freeman, Gary P. *Immigrant Labor and Racial Conflict in Industrial Societies: The French and British Experience, 1945–1975.* Princeton: Princeton University Press, 1979.

Frevert, Ute. *Women in German History: From Bourgeois Emancipation to Sexual Liberation.* Oxford and Hamburg: Berg, 1988.

Fridenson, Patrick. *Histoire des usines Renault,* vol I. Paris: Seuil, 1982.

Gaillard, A.-M. *Couples suédois: Vers un autre idéal sexuel.* Paris: Editions Universitaires, 1983.

Garson, J.-P., and G. Tapinos, eds. *L'Argent des immigrés: Revenus, épargne et transferts de fonds de huit nationalités en France.* Paris: INED, Cahier no. 94, 1981.

Giard, Luce, and Pierre Mayol. *Habiter, Cuisiner.* Paris: Union Générale d'Editions, 1980.

——— *L'Invention du quotidien,* vol. 2. Paris: Union Générale d'Editions, 1980.

Ginsborg, Paul. *Storia d'Italia dal dopoguerra ad oggi.* Turin: Einaudi, 1989.

Gordon, Linda. *Heroes of Their Own Lives: The Politics and History of Family Violence.* New York: Viking, 1988.

——— *Woman's Body, Woman's Right: A Social History of Birth Control in America.* New York: Grossman, 1976.

Grafteaux, Serge. *Mémé Santerre, Une Vie.* Paris: Editions du Jour, 1975.

Gras, A., and R. Sotto. *La Suède et ses populations.* Brussels: Complexe, 1981.

Green, Nancy L. *Jewish Immigrant Workers of the Belle Epoque.* New York: Holmes & Meier, 1985.

Grenadou, Ephräim, and Alain Prévost. *Grenadou, paysan français.* Paris: Seuil, 1966.

Grossmann, Vassily. *Life and Fate,* trans. Robert Chandler. London: Collins Harvill, 1985.

Guéhenno, Jean. *Journal d'un homme de quarante ans.* Paris: Grasset, 1934.

Guerrand, Roger-Henri. *Les Origines du logement social en France.* Paris: Ouvrières, 1967.

Gutman, Herbert G. *The Black Family in Slavery and Freedom.* New York: Pantheon, 1976.

Hatzfeld, Henri. *Du paupérisme à la Sécurité sociale.* Paris: Armand Colin, 1971.

——— *Le Grand tournant de la médecine libérale.* Paris: Ouvrières, 1963.

Haumont, Nicole. *Les Pavillonnaires.* Paris: Centre de Recherches d'Urbanisme, 1975.

Hélias, Pierre-Jakez. *Le Cheval d'orgueil.* Paris: Plon, 1975.

Hélys, M. *A travers le féminisme suédois.* Paris: Plon, 1906.

Hill, Reuben, and René König, eds. *Families in East and West.* Paris: Mouton, 1970.

Huntford, Roland. *The New Totalitarians.* New York: Stein & Day, 1972.

Hyman, P. *De Dreyfus à Vichy.* Paris: Fayard, 1985.

"L'Immigration maghrébine en France: Les faits et les mythes," special issue of *Les Temps modernes* 452–454 (March–May 1984): 1556–2192.

Jackson, Kenneth. *Crabgrass Frontier: The Suburbanization of the United States.* New York: Oxford University Press, 1985.

Joeres, Ruth-Ellen B., and Mary Jo Maynes, eds. *German Women in the Eighteenth and Nineteenth Centuries.* Bloomington: Indiana University Press, 1986.

Kaes, R. *Vivre dans les grands ensembles.* Paris: Ouvrières, 1963.

Kayser, P. *La Protection de la vie privée: Protection du secret de la vie privée.* Aix: Presses Universitaires d'Aix-Marseille, 1984.

Kertzer, David. *Family Life in Central Italy, 1880–1910: Sharecropping, Wage Labor and Coresidence* (New Brunswick, N.J.: Rutgers University Press, 1984).

Knibiehler, Yvonne. *Cornettes et blouses blanches: Les Infirmières dans la société française, 1880–1980.* Paris: Hachette, 1984.

Kohn, Melvin L. *Class and Conformity: A Study in Values.* Homewood, Ill.: Dorsey, 1969.

Koonz, Claudia. *Mothers in the Fatherland: Women, the Family, and Nazi Politics.* New York: St. Martin's, 1987.

Korkaz, S. *Les Juifs en France et l'Etat d'Israel.* Paris: Denoël, 1969.

Kriegel, Annie. *Aux origines du communisme français.* Paris: Flammarion, 1969.

——— *Les Communistes français dans leur premier demi-siècle, 1920–1970.* Paris: Seuil, 1985.

Labrousse, C. *Le Droit de la famille.* Vol. 1, *Les Personnes.* Paris: Masson, 1984.

Lazard, M. "Le Mineur de fond: Un exemple de l'identité du PCF," *Revue française de science politique* (April 1985): 190–205.

Leijon, A. G., and M. Karre. *La Condition familiale en mutation.* Paris: Seghers, 1972.

Lengrand, L., and M. Crapeau. *Louis Lengrand, mineur du Nord.* Paris: Seuil, 1974.

Lequin, Yves. *Histoire des Français.* 3 vols. Paris: Armand Colin, 1983–1984.

Levinas, Emmanuel. *Difficile liberté.* Paris: Le Livre de Poche, 1984.

Linner, B. *Sexualité et vie sociale en Suède.* Paris: Gonthier, 1968.

Lipovetsky, Gilles. *L'Ere du vide: Essai sur l'individualisme contemporain.* Paris: Gallimard, 1983.

Martin-Fugier, Anne. *La Place des bonnes.* Paris: Grasset, 1979.

Marty, Laurent. *Chanter pour survivre: Culture ouvrière, travail et technique dans le textile: Roubaix, 1850–1914.* Liévin: Fédération Léo-Lagrange, 1982.

Mauco, Georges. *Les Etrangers en France: Leur rôle dans l'activité économique.* Paris: Armand Colin, 1932.

May, Elaine Tyler. *Great Expectations: Marriage and Divorce in Post-Victorian America.* Chicago: University of Chicago Press, 1980.

——— *Homeward Bound: American Families in the Cold War Era.* New York: Basic Books, 1988.

Mayeur, J.-M. *Histoire religieuse de la France XIXe-XXe siècle: Problèmes et méthodes.* Paris: Beauchesne, 1975.

Maynes, Mary Jo, and Tom Taylor. "Children in German History," in N. Ray Hiner and Joseph Hawes, eds., *Children in Comparative and Historical Perspective: An International Handbook.* Westport, Conn.: Greenwood, 1991.

Michelat, G., and M. Simon. *Classe, religion et comportement politique.* Paris: Presses de la Fondation Nationale des Sciences Politiques—Editions Sociales, 1977.

Mintz, Steven, and Susan Kellogg. *Domestic Revolutions: A Social History of American Family Life.* New York: Free Press, 1988.

Miquel, P. *Histoire de la radio et de la télévision.* Paris: Richelieu, 1973.

Mitterauer, Michael, and Reinhard Sieder. *The European Family: Patriarchy and Partnership from the Middle Ages to the Present,* trans. Karla Oosterveen and Manfred Hörzinger. Chicago: University of Chicago Press, 1982.

Moberg, V. *Min svenska historia berättad för folket.* Stockholm: Norstedt & Jöners, 1970.

Modell, John. *Into One's Own: From Youth to Adulthood in the United States, 1920–1975.* Berkeley: University of California Press, 1989.

Morin, Edgar. *L'Esprit du temps.* Paris: Grasset, 1962.

Musset, Lucien. *Les Peuples scandinaves au Moyen Age.* Paris: Presses Universitaires de France, 1951.

Myrdal, A. *Folk och familj.* 1944.

Noiriel, Gérard. *Longwy, immigrés et prolétaires, 1880–1980.* Paris: Armand Colin, 1984.

Ory, Pascal. *L'Entre-Deux-Mai: Histoire culturelle de la France, mai 1968–mai 1981.* Paris: Seuil, 1983.

Paci, Massimo, ed. *Famiglia e mercato del lavoro in un'economia periferica.* Milan: F. Angeli, 1980.

Parent, J. *Le Modèle suédois.* Paris: Calmann-Lévy, 1970.

Perrot, Michelle. *Le Mode de vie des familles bourgeoises, 1873–1953.* Paris: Armand Colin, 1961.

Petit, J.-C. "Les Volets du presbytère sont ouverts," *La Vie* 2091 (September 26–October 2, 1985).

Petonnet, Colette. *On est tous dans le brouillard: Ethnologie des banlieues.* Paris: Galilée, 1979.

Piselli, Fortunata. *Parentela e emigrazione: Mutamenti e continuita in una comunità calabrese.* Turin: Einaudi, 1981.

Ponty, J. "Une intégration difficile: Les Polonais en France dans le premier XXe siècle," *Vingtième Siècle* 7 (July–September 1985).

"La Population française de A à Z," *Les Cahiers français* 219 (January–February 1985).

Pratiques de la confession, quinze études d'histoire, colloquium of the Bussière group. Paris: Le Cerf, 1983.

Prigent, Rorbert, ed. *Renouveau des idées sur la famille.* Paris: Presses Universitaires de France, 1954.

Prost, Antoine. *L'Ecole et la famille dans une société en mutation (1930–1980).* Vol. 4, *Histoire générale de l'enseignement et de l'éducation en France.* Paris: Nouvelle Librairie de France, 1982.

Queffélec, H. *Portrait de la Suède.* Paris: Hachette, 1948.

Quillardet, M. *Suédois et Norvégiens chez eux.* Paris: Armand Colin, 1900.

Quoist, Michel. *La Ville et l'homme.* Paris: Ouvrières, 1952.

Ravault, R.-J. "L'Impérialisme boomerang," *RFEA* 24–25 (May 1985): 291–311.

Redclift, Nanneke, and Enzo Mingione, eds. *Beyond Employment: Household, Gender, and Subsistence.* London: Basil Blackwell, 1985.

Régis-Bastide, F., and G. de Faramond. *Suède.* Paris: Seuil, 1976.

Rémy, J., and R. Woog. *La Française et l'amour.* Paris: Robert Laffont, 1960.

Roblin, M. *Les Juifs de Paris: Démographie, économie, culture.* Paris: A. and J. Picard, 1952.

Robrieux, Philippe. *Histoire intérieure du parti communist.* 4 vols. Paris: Fayard, 1980–1984.

——— *Maurice Thorez, vie secrète et vie publique.* Paris: Fayard, 1975.

Roland, C. *Du Ghetto à l'Occident: Deux générations yiddish en France.* Paris: Minuit, 1962.

Rothman, Ellen. *Hands and Hearts: A History of Courtship in America.* New York: Basic Books, 1984.

Roudinesco, Elisabeth. *La Bataille de cent ans: Histoire de la psychanalyse en France.* 2 vols. Paris: Seuil, 1986.

Roussel, Louis. *Le Mariage dans la société française contemporaine: Faits de population, données d'opinion.* Paris: Presses Universitaires de France, 1975.

Roussel, Louis, and Odile Bourguignon. *La Famille après le mariage des enfants, étude des relations entre generations.* Paris: Presses Universitaires de France, 1976.

——— *Générations nouvelles et mariage traditionnel, ênquete auprès des jeunes de dix-huit/trente ans.* Paris: Presses Universitaires de France, 1979.

Roussel, Louis, and Paul Festy. *Recent Trends in Attitudes and Behaviors Affecting the Family in Council of Europe Member States.* Council of Europe. Strasbourg, 1979.

Royer, L.-C. *Lumières du Nord.* Paris: Editions de France, 1939.

Saint-Agnès, Y. de, *Eros international-Scandinavie.* Paris: Balland, 1971.

——— "Les Suédois," *Le Crapouillot* 70 (1966).

Saraceno, Chiara. "Family Strategies and Patterns of Work," *Marriage and Family Review* (1990).

——— "Shifts in Public and Private Boundaries: Women as Mothers and Service Workers in Italian Daycare," *Feminist Studies* 10 (Spring 1984): 7–30.

——— "The Social Construction of Childhood: Childcare and Education Policies in Italy and the United States," *Social Problems* 31 (February 1984): 351–363.

——— *Sociologia della famiglia.* Bologna: Il Mulino, 1988.

Sayad, A. "Les Trois âges de l'émigration algérienne en France," *Actes de la recherche en sciences sociales* 15 (June 1977): 59–79.

Schnapper, Dominique. *Juifs et Israélites.* Paris: Gallimard, 1980. Trans. Arthur Goldhammer as *Jewish Identities in France.* Chicago: University of Chicago Press, 1983.

——— "Modernité et acculturations: A propos des

travailleurs émigrés," *Communications* 43 (1986): 141–168.

Schneider, Jane, and Peter Schneider. *Culture and Political Economy in Western Sicily.* New York: Academic Press, 1976.

Segalen, Martine. *Mari et femme dans la société paysanne.* Paris: Flammarion, 1980. Trans. as *Love and Power in the Peasant Family.* London: Blackwell, 1983.

Shaffer, Harry G. *Women in the Two Germanies.* New York: Pergamon, 1981.

Shorter, Edward. *The Making of the Modern Family.* New York: Basic Books, 1975.

Silverman, S. "Agricultural Organization, Social Structure and Values in Italy: Amoral Familism Reconsidered," *American Anthropologist* (1970): 1–20.

Simon, Pierre. *De la vie avant toute chose.* Paris: Mazarine, 1979.

——— et al. *Rapport sur le comportement sexuel des Français.* Paris: Julliard-Charron, 1972.

Smith, Judith. *Family Connections: A History of Italian and Jewish Immigrant Lives in Providence, Rhode Island, 1900–1940.* Albany: State University Press of New York, 1985.

Stacey, Judith. *Brave New Families: Stories of Domestic Upheaval in Late Twentieth-Century America.* New York: Basic Books, 1990.

Statut matrimonial et ses conséquences juridiques, fiscales et sociales, Le; known as the *Sullerot Report.* Conseil Economique et Social, January 1984.

Sutter, J. *La Vie religieuse des Français à travers les sondages d'opinion, 1944–1976.* Paris: CNRS, 194.

Swedish Institute. *Actualités suédoises.*

Talha, L. "L'Evolution du mouvement migratoire entre le Maghreb et la France," *Maghreb-Machrek.* Paris: La Documentation Française, no. 61, 1974, pp. 17–34.

Tchernoff, Jacques. *Dans le creuset des civilisations.* 4 vols. Paris: Rieder, 1936–1938.

Thuillier, Guy. *Pour une histoire du quotidien en Nivernais au XIX siècle.* Paris: Mouton, 1977.

Ullerstam, L. *Les Minorités érotiques.* Paris: J.-J. Pauvert, 1965.

Valdour, Jacques. *Ateliers et taudis de la banlieue de Paris: Observations vécues.* Paris: Spes, 1923.

Verdès-Leroux, J. *Au service du Parti: Le PC, les intellectuels et la culture, 1944–1956.* Paris: Fayard-Minuit, 1983.

Verdier, Yvonne. *Façons de dire, façons de faire: La Laveuse, la couturière, la cuisinière.* Paris: Gallimard, 1980.

Vigarello, Georges. *Le Propre et le sale: L'Hygiène du corps depuis le Moyen Age.* Paris: Seuil, 1985.

Vlocevski, Stephane. *L'Installation des Italiens en France.* Paris: Alcan, 1934.

Weber, Eugen. *France: Fin de Siècle.* Cambridge, Mass.: Harvard University Press, 1986.

——— *Peasants into Frenchmen: The Modernization of Rural France, 1870–1914.* Stanford, Calif.: Stanford University Press, 1976.

Weber-Kellermann, Ingeborg. *Die deutsche Familie.* Frankfurt am Main: Suhrkamp, 1974.

——— *Die Familie.* Frankfurt am Main: Insel, 1976.

——— "Die Sozialgeschichte der Familie in Deutschland, besonders in Hinblick auf die Stellung der Frau," in B. Paetzold and L. Fried, eds., *Einführung in die Familienpädagogik.* Weinheim and Basel: Beltz, 1989.

Weil, Simone. *La Condition ouvrière.* Paris: Gallimard, 1964.

Winick, Charles. "Prostitutes' Clients' Perception of the Prostitutes and of Themselves," *International Journal of Social Psychiatry* (1982): 289–297.

Wistrand, B., "Le Mythe de l'égalité des sexes en Suède: La Lutte continue," *Cultures* 8 (1982).

Wylie, Laurence. *Village in the Vaucluse.* Cambridge, Mass.: Harvard University Press, 1974.

Zehraoui. *Les Travailleurs algériens en France: Etude sociologique de quelques aspects de la vie familiale.* Paris: Maspero, 1976.

Zeldin, Theodore. *France, 1848–1945.* 2 vols. Oxford: Clarendon, 1973–1977.

Zelizer, Viviana A. *Pricing the Priceless Child: The Changing Social Value of Children.* New York: Basic Books, 1985.

Ziegler, Edward F., ed. *Children, Families and Government: Perspectives on American Social Policy.* Cambridge: Cambridge University Press, 1983.

Zonabend, F. *La Mémoire longue.* Paris: Presses Universitaires de France, 1980.

Credits

The objects illustrated in this book (on the pages noted) are found in various locations, as follows: Alte Pinakothek, Munich, 174; Borghese Gallery, Rome, 276; Boymans-Van Beuningen Museum, Rotterdam, 176; Christie's, London, 184; Galerie de France, 291 (© ADAGP, 1987); Joachim Jean Aberbach Collection, Sands Point, N.Y., 144; Lippisches Landesmuseum, Detmold, 506; Louvre, Paris, 232; Musée de l'Affiche et de la Publicité, Paris, 90, 130, 139; Musée des Beaux Arts, Quimper, 149; Musée Picasso, Paris, 326 (© SPADEM, 1987); Museum für Deutsche Geschichte, Berlin, 316; Museum of Fine Arts, Boston, 182–183; Museum of Fine Arts, Bucharest, 324; Museum of Fine Arts, Ghent, 248; Museum of Fine Arts, Lyons, 249; Museum of Modern Art, New York, 230 (photo by Soichi Sunami); National Gallery, London, 280a; National Museum, Rome, 212; Nierendorf Gallery, Berlin, 154; Prado, Madrid, 172; Private Collection, 152 (© ADAGP, 1987), 153, 244, 256; Schlemmer Family Collection, Badenweiler, Germany, 146; Staatliche Kuntsammlungen Kassel, 505; Stadtische Galerie im Lenbachhaus, Munich, 259; Sterling and Francine Clark Institute, Williamstown, 274, 275.

Photographs were supplied by the following institutions, agencies, and individuals: ADM, Varsovie, 390; APEP, Villerupt, 393, 396; American Heritage Center, University of Wyoming, 575; American Social Health Association, 570; Anderson-Viollet, 276; Archiv Weber-Kellermann für Familien-und Kindheitsforschung, Marburg, 502, 510, 514, 519, 520, 531a, 531b, 532; Archives Centre Culturel Suédois, 428, 443; Archives R. Damiani, 397; Archives Dazy, 384a; Archives Gesgon, 342 (© SPADEM, 1987); Archives Mémoires Juives, 366, 367, 370, 373; Archives K. Orfali, 441b, 444; Archives Seuil, 151, 153, 172; Archives G. Silvain, 365; Archives Sirot-Angel, 356; B. Barbey, 433; Bernard, 181; D. Berretty, 100b; Bibliothèque Nationale, Paris, 307, 331 (© SPADEM, 1987); Bildarchiv Foto Marburg, 507, 515; Bildarchiv Preussischer Kulturbesitz, Berlin, 513; Bildhuset: B. Arvidsson, 492; Boyer-Viollet, 8b, 22; F. Brenner, 237; M. Brucker, 123; Bulloz, 182–183, 232, 248, 249; R. Burri, 61b; CIRIC, 294,

303, 304, 305, 308, 309; CNAC, Paris, 144 (photo B. Hatala); Cahiers du Cinéma, 175, 179; H. Cartier-Bresson, 74, 124, 187; J.-Ph. Charbonnier, 17, 26, 57, 59, 62, 108; J.-M. Charles, 242; J.-L. Charmet, 76, 200; D. Chayito, 131, 227; R. Chenchabi, 282, 399; Chevojon, 72; J. Choisnel, 135, 159, 320 (© SPADEM, 1987), 321 (© SPADEM, 1987); Ciccione, 78; Cinémathèque Française, 178; Collectif: L. Perenom, 99; Collectif: E. Prouvost, 88; J.-L. Courtina, 260; G. Dagli Orti, 154, 156, 244, 259; J. H. Dahlstrom, 216, 441a; R. Dazy, 42; Y. Dejardin, 82; R. Delpit, 180, 346, 352, 375; Deluc, 239; Departmental Archives, Blois, 21; M. Desjardins, 12a; C. Despoisse, 34, 55; Ecomusée de la Communauté Urbaine, Le Creusot-Montceau, 27, 28; Ph. Faure, 113, 226; Feinstein, 384b; Fotogram: Chapman, 359; Franck Daniel, 351, 354, 358, 374; M. Franck, 169, 314; R. Frieman, 207, 209; A. Gamet, 6; J. Gaumy, 267; Gery, 93; Giraudon, 149, 170a, 170b, 174, 319 (© SPADEM, 1987); Giraudon-Anderson, 212; Giraudon-Bridgeman, 176 (© SPADEM, 1987), 184; H. Gissinger, Zurich, 234 (© SPADEM, 1987); Harlingue-Viollet, 11, 12b, 164, 203; E. Hartmann, 167; J. Houzel, 310; Hubert, 23; Im'media: O. Leshaf, 404b; L. Ionesco, 52, 133; J. K., 138; Andrea Jemolo, 452, 454, 456, 459, 468, 470, 472, 475, 481, 485, 489, 491, 494, 500; K. Johansson, 447; R. Kalvar, 102, 112; Keystone, 134a, 190, 204b, 208, 306, 318, 337, 338; W. Klein, Düsseldorf, 166; La Vie Catholique: C. Boisseaux, 298, 313; M. Langrognet, 339; Lapi-Viollet, 32, 58, 86; J.-P. Le Bihan, 157; Le Diascorn, 241; G. Le Querrec, 30, 266; L'Humanité, 323, 329, 332, 334, 340; Library of Congress, Washington, D.C., 559; M. Lounes, 97; Y. Machatschek, 118; Maeght-Lelong Gallery, facing 1; J. Marando, 404a, 405, 407, 410a, 410b; G. Marineau, 141, 168; P. Michaud, 73, 110, 257, 311; Midas, 435, 436; Minnesota Historical Society, 542 (Olof A. Holm), 544, 546, 550, 572; Musée d'Art et d'Industrie, Saint-Etienne, 157; Museum of Modern Art/Film Stills Archive, 551, 561, 562, 567, 576, 579; Niepce, 15, 29, 50, 60b, 61a, 96, 134b, 160, 167, 201, 215, 225, 252; Notre Temps: M. Clément, 254; B. O. Olsson, 427; S. Oredson, 76; Parente, 378; Paris Match, 189; O. Pawel, 412; R. Phelps,

Index